S0-CBH-028

Technical Services in Libraries

NUMBER SEVEN
COLUMBIA UNIVERSITY STUDIES
IN LIBRARY SERVICE

Technical Services in Libraries

ACQUISITIONS, CATALOGING, CLASSIFICATION, BINDING, PHOTOGRAPHIC REPRODUCTION, AND CIRCULATION OPERATIONS

By MAURICE F. TAUBER and ASSOCIATES

Columbia University Press, New York and London

First printing 1954
Ninth printing 1971

ISBN 0-231-02054-6

LIBRARY OF CONGRESS CATALOG CARD NUMBER: 54-10328

PRINTED IN THE UNITED STATES OF AMERICA

15 14 13 12 11 10

ASSOCIATES

RALPH U. BLASINGAME, JR.

C. DONALD COOK

CARLYLE J. FRAREY

BERTHA M. FRICK

JANE H. HALL

RICHARD O. PAUTZSCH

IRVING VERSCHOOR

COLUMBIA UNIVERSITY STUDIES IN LIBRARY SERVICE

Preface

A preliminary draft of *Technical Services in Libraries* was prepared in 1952 in mimeographed form. This experimental edition was used by six classes of students in the School of Library Service, Columbia University. The present edition contains most of the material in the earlier draft. However, certain chapters have been reorganized and rewritten, new material has been added, and charts are now included.

The volume purposes to survey the various "technical services" and to orient the student to the range of operations and techniques associated with the procurement, recording, preservation, and handling of library materials. The specific aims are: (1) to familiarize the student with problems in the technical services and with current thought concerning the best solutions of them; (2) to familiarize him with sources of published and other information concerning the practice and administration of the technical services; (3) to indicate methods that have been used in studying the technical operations; (4) to point out those areas in which research or special study is needed or likely to prove fruitful; and (5) to furnish a background of information that may be useful in performing the technical services in libraries.

The student will find that the material for certain areas varies somewhat in the specific directions for procedure. Although the chapters on acquisitions deal with many of the problems which arise in procurement, there is no effort to describe in minute detail every possible step in the process of obtaining books, pamphlets, serials, and other materials. These steps vary from library to library, and adjustments are usually made on the basis of the quantity and complexity of the acquisitions and according to the special needs that have to be met. The solution to the problem of handling serials, for example, will be different for a small public library, which may receive several score titles, as compared to a large research library, which may receive thousands of titles. Special manuals, such as *Technical Libraries: Their Organization and Management,* edited by Lucille Jackson (Special Libraries Association, 1951), David Grenfell's *Periodicals and Serials: Their Treatment in Special Libraries* (Aslib, 1953), R. L. Collison's *The Cataloguing, Arrangement, and Filing of Special Material in Special Libraries* (Aslib, 1950), and similar works, are available for consultation by students. Neither has it been deemed necessary to describe actual cataloging problems with illustrative entries since they are available in such guides and sources as the ALA *Cataloging Rules for Author and Title Entries* (2d ed., 1949), the Library of Congress *Rules for Descriptive Cataloging in the Library of Congress* (1949; *Supplement,* 1949–1951, 1952) and other Library of Congress compilations of rules, Susan G. Akers' *Simple Library Cataloging* (revised, 1954), Margaret Mann's *Introduction to Cataloging and the Classification of Books* (1943), and the Columbia University School of Library Service's *Sample Catalog Cards* (1950). Chapter VIII, which is concerned with the functions and scope of cataloging, provides historical information on the development of card records and discusses some current problems facing the profession. A useful volume for background material is *The Acquisition and Cataloging of Books,* edited by William M. Randall (1940). The October, 1953, issue of *Library Trends,* published by the University of Illinois Library School, is a useful source of information on current trends in cataloging and classification and also contains extensive bibliographies. The article by Evelyn Hensel on "Treatment of Nonbook Materials," for example, considers the status of current cataloging of archives, manuscripts, and audio-visual materials including films, phonorecords, maps, and picture collections. The *Journal of Cataloging and Classification,* issued by the Division of Cataloging and Classification of the American Library Association, is a current source of information for articles on projects and experiments, reports, and other relevant material. Other periodical publications of interest to technical services personnel are *Serial Slants*, *American Documentation*, and the *Journal of Documentation* (London). *Library Trends*, the *Library Quarterly*, the *Library Journal*, the *Harvard Library Bulletin*, the Library of Congress Processing Division's *Cataloging Service*, the Library of Congress *Information Bulletin*, and the *Wilson Library Bulletin* include pertinent articles, reviews, and memoranda. Annual and special reports and surveys of libraries contain material not otherwise available in the journal literature.

A study in progress which should be useful to administrators is concerned with "Technical Services: Policy, Organization, and Coordination"; this report is being prepared by the Committee on Administration of the ALA Division of Cataloging and Classification.

While it is hoped that the volume will be of interest to librarians in various types of libraries, many of the problems discussed in it are related principally to the research library. Moreover, certain types of libraries—law libraries, medical libraries, and other kinds of special libraries—have special technical problems or problems involving control of materials which are not treated in detail in this volume. School libraries, many public libraries which are not particularly concerned with research, and some college libraries are likely to simplify some of the operations described.

In connection with some subjects discussed in this volume, the student will find that he will need other sources to supplement the material presented. While some terms are explained in the body of the work, use of glossaries and dictionaries should be made whenever necessary. Students who are unfamiliar with terms used in this text or in readings and bookdealers' catalogs, should early become acquainted with such sources as Frank K. Walter's *Abbreviations and Terms Used in Book Catalogs and Bibliographies* (Boston Book Company, 1912), Axel Moth's *Glossary of Library Terms* (Boston Book Company, 1915), L. M. Harrod's *The Librarian's Glossary* (Grafton, 1938), A.L.A. *Glossary of Library Terms* (American Library Association, 1943), Jerrold Orne's *The Language of the For-*

eign Book Trade (American Library Association, 1949), John Carter's *ABC for Book Collectors* (Knopf, 1951), and a work of Henri Lemaître (completed by Anthony Thompson), *Vocabularium bibliothecarii* (UNESCO, 1953). It may be profitable for beginning students to become familiar with the backgrounds of individuals cited in the literature. The various "Who's Who" volumes, *Who's Who in Library Service* (now being revised), and other biographical sources are useful for this purpose.

The volume has been in preparation for a number of years. The general outline and various chapters were originally prepared by the author for use in lectures to beginning students. The author, in his position as professor in the School of Library Service, has encouraged students to work on problems which need solution. As editor of *College and Research Libraries,* he has sought articles and reports on projects in libraries and has encouraged practitioners to write on experimental programs. Ralph U. Blasingame, Jr. (now assistant librarian, California State Library), C. Donald Cook (formerly of the United Nations Library in Geneva and now an associate in Library Service, Columbia University), and Carlyle J. Frarey (now assistant librarian, Duke University Libraries), as research assistants and teaching fellows in the School of Library Service, have contributed to the volume by checking bibliographical material, abstracting, and preparing preliminary drafts of several of the chapters. Mr. Frarey made many pertinent criticisms of the first draft and helped with the proofreading. Special mention should be made of Mr. Cook, who has worked closely with the final version as a whole. Irving Verschoor, also a former research assistant of the School of Library Service and now Public Library Consultant, Library Extension Division, the New York State Library, assembled much of the material for the chapters on circulation service. Miss Bertha M. Frick, associate professor in the School of Library Service, helped to develop the general framework of the volume and gave pointed criticism to the text as she used it with her classes. She also assisted in the proofreading. Mrs. Jane H. Hall, who has taught in the School of Library Service and is now on the faculty for library courses at Queens College, prepared the first draft of Chapter IX, which deals with catalog entries and descriptive cataloging. Richard O. Pautzsch, of the Brooklyn Public Library staff, developed the major portion of the original draft of Chapter XI, Classification. Alfred H. Lane, head of the Gifts and Exchanges Division of the Columbia University Libraries, read the manuscript and offered many helpful suggestions, especially for the chapters on acquisitions. Hubbard Ballou, head of the Photographic Service of the Columbia University Libraries, helped with the chapter on photography and prepared the table on reading machines. Miss Darthula Wilcox, librarian of the School of Library Service, was extremely helpful in the search for bibliographical sources useful in the preparation of the volume. A debt of gratitude is owed to Miss Dorothy Charles, Miss Dorothy E. Cole, Byron C. Hopkins, and John Jamieson, for reading the manuscript in whole or in part and making many suggestions, and to Miss Elizabeth E. Adams, of the Columbia University Press, for her invaluable help in preparing the manuscript for the printer.

For various services we are indebted to many librarians, particularly staff members of the Brooklyn Public Library, the University of California Libraries, the University of Chicago Library, the Columbia University Libraries, the Enoch Pratt Free Library in Baltimore, the University of Illinois Library, the Library of Congress, and the New York Public Library.

Thanks are especially due Dr. Lowell Martin, Dean of the Graduate School of Library Service, Rutgers University, and formerly Associate Dean and Melvil Dewey Professor in the Columbia University School of Library Service, for his encouragement and support of the project. Acknowledgments are also made to Dr. Carl M. White, Dean of the School of Library Service, and to members of the Editorial Committee of the Columbia University Studies in Library Service for examining the manuscript and for offering suggestions.

A number of students in the classes at Columbia University made suggestions which were considered in the revision. Three students, Henry Birnbaum, James C. Dance, and Miss Lois Harder, assisted in bibliographical checking. Miss Virginia Bradley and Richard G. Rogers, of the School of Library Service office, aided in the preparation of the mimeographed edition of the work.

In a volume of such broad scope as this one there are likely to be some errors of omission and commission. We hope that we have kept them to a minimum. We trust that students and practicing librarians who use this volume will make suggestions for the improvement of future editions.

MAURICE F. TAUBER

New York, April, 1954

Contents

Technical Services in Libraries

I. Introduction

THE layman who uses the public library, the student who uses the college or university library, and the specialist and technologist who use a scientific, governmental, business, or association library generally are not much concerned with the library's pattern of procedure for acquiring materials and for recording and preserving them. It may be suggested that many people using libraries have a mental picture of a librarian who simply sits behind a desk and dispenses books on the presentation of call slips. This is especially true unless these readers have had the experience of not obtaining a needed item because of slowness in acquisition, delay in cataloging, faulty classification, loss in the stacks, or unavailability owing to poor physical condition or lack of binding. Those who use reference departments of libraries have a further idea of a librarian—a person who can either answer questions or show inquirers how to get materials which will answer their queries.

In most modern libraries, however, many of the library personnel are not known to the clientele. These are the order or acquisition librarians, the catalogers and classifiers, the binding librarians, the photographic assistants, and certain members of the circulation staff. These are not all the personnel who work behind the scenes, away from the service desks, but, primarily, they are the ones who perform the technical work of acquiring, recording, preserving, and circulating materials for the use of patrons.

It will be useful at the outset to define certain terms which are used in connection with the work of a library. The literature of librarianship contains references to such words as *work, routines, treatments, procedures, actions, activities, operations, methods, services, tech-*

niques, and *processes.* Sometimes the words have been used interchangeably, but for several of them there are distinct shades of meaning. For this discussion, attention may be directed to three of these terms—*services, operations,* and *techniques*—as applied to librarianship. A *service* includes all the work connected with some activity; such as acquisitions, cataloging, binding, photography, or circulation. The steps involved in performing the service may be described as a series of *operations.* The *techniques* are the methods of executing the operations involved in a service. The recording of serials by the cataloging service is an example of an operation. One of the techniques is the use of punched cards to perform this operation.

The use of the term *technical services,* or any one of its variants (*technical operations, technical activities,* or *technical processes*), is comparatively recent in library terminology. This does not mean that the services are of recent origin. In fact, the services involving the operations and techniques for acquiring, recording, and preserving materials are among the oldest aspects of librarianship. In the past few years, however, there has been a growing realization that the "technical services" are only a part of the total profession of librarianship and for effective service need to be placed in proper relationships to the other parts. This does not mean that key functions in the technical group are any less professional than those in the public service departments of libraries. The use of the term *technical,* however, does denote that certain operations which are usually carried on away from the public desks are likely to be more susceptible to codification than those of the readers' departments. Some of the operations of the circulation and reference departments are also "technical" in this sense and are therefore considered in this volume.

In recent years considerable attention has been directed, for several important reasons, toward technical services in libraries. Libraries, like other institutions, have had to re-examine their policies during a period when funds for noncommercial organizations have become scarcer. The decrease in library budgets, when costs and inflation are taken into account, has led a number of boards of trustees and administrative officers in educational institutions to review expenditures for the technical services, which ordinarily comprise a large part of the budget. Moreover, the tendency of librarians in recent times has been to direct their attention to readers and books. Extension of services and purchase of materials require funds, and with a shortage of funds it is a normal reaction to inquire into the costs of operations which have come to be considered secondary in importance.[1]

The criticisms that have been made of various technical services, particularly cataloging and classification, are not entirely new. Librarians of the past, such as Melvil Dewey, John Cotton Dana, Charles Martel, and Herbert Putnam, came to grips with the problems, and some later suggestions are primarily variations of their proposals. New approaches to difficulties, however, are being made at the present time.

The development of cooperative measures among librarians has been another reason for revived attention to technical problems.[2] The realization that libraries cannot continue to acquire everything issued from the presses of the world has brought into play new plans for specialization in collecting. Such matters as the possession of large quantities of uncataloged materials, duplication of cataloging among libraries, the growth of union catalogs and bibliographical centers, and consolidations of collections have made it necessary to formulate principles and aims in acquisition, cataloging, and preserving of materials. Finally, the development of microfilm, microcards, Microprint, and other techniques of reproduction has shed new light on the problems involved.

It should be apparent that the great increase in the number of books and in the extension of knowledge has added to the responsibilities of librarians who have assumed that in addition to collecting and preserving books and other graphic materials they have the obligation of making their contents available as easily and quickly as possible. The assumption of this responsibility carries with it the duty to undertake every available means for its fulfillment; to seek out better means than those already known; to work constantly at their improvement; and to employ these means as effectively as possible. This involves discarding operations and techniques which are found to be outmoded, inadequate, or inefficient. The problem exists in the small as well as the large library.[3]

In the following chapters, attention is called to the problem of personnel in the technical services. Particularly important are the aspects of recruitment and training. The demand for heads of technical services, acquisition librarians, head catalogers, supervisors of catalog sections, subject specialists in cataloging departments, binding librarians, heads of library photographic departments, and circulation librarians has not abated in recent years. Governmental, special, academic, and school libraries or library systems require a constant supply of qualified individuals who are trained in the operations and techniques involved in these services. The librarian who is interested in these important parts of a library's service might well explore the possibilities for specialized careers in them.

The beginner in technical services should be aware of the various groups which are concerned with the professional development of the several areas. Prominent among these is the American Library Association, which has a number of special boards, divisions, and committees directly involved in the study of technical problems. The Board on Acquisition of Library Materials, the Archives and Libraries Committee, the Bibliography Committee, the Audio-Visual Board, the Book Acquisitions Committee, the Bookbinding Committee, the Friends of Libraries Committee, the Library Equipment and Appliances Committee, the Public Documents Committee, the Relations with Publishers Committee, the Relations with Subscription Books Publishers Committee, the Board on Resources of American Libraries, the Statistics Committee, the Serials Round Table, and the Joint Committee on Microcards are among the particular groups of interest to those working in the technical services. The Division of Cataloging and Classification of the American Library Association is the major body concerned with cataloging and classification. It has many committees and a Board on Cataloging Policy and Research which have continuous programs for study and evaluation of rules, operations, personnel, and other matters. An Executive Secretary at American Library Association headquarters in Chicago is available for counsel on cataloging and classification questions. Other divisions of the American Library Association, such as the Association of College and Reference Libraries and the American Association of School Librarians, have committees working on various aspects of the technical services. The Special Libraries Association also has been active in the study of technical problems of all kinds. It, too, has an organization which includes special committees and groups which investigate problems of direct interest to technical services personnel. The Medical Library Association, the Association of American Law Libraries, the Music Library Association, the Catholic Library Association, the American Archivist Society, the Bibliographical Society of America, the Theatre Library Association, the American Theological Library Association, the Association of Research Libraries, the American Documentation Institute, and the Chemical Literature Section of the American Chemical Society are other groups which retain committees devoting time to special study of such matters as cataloging, classification, acquisitions, binding, and photography. Regular examination of the periodical and other publications of these groups should keep the practitioner informed of developments and proposals for future study.

It should also be pointed out that personnel in the technical services can obtain considerable assistance in the way of either suggestion or direct application by keeping in touch with the literature of organizations in related fields, such as the American Standards Association and the American Association for the Advancement of Science. The American Library Association is represented in these and other groups.

Librarians should join organizations whose varied programs are related to their work. They should attend meetings, participate in discussions, take part in committee work, write papers on subjects with which they are familiar, and thus contribute to the profession. As will be noted in the chapters which follow, there are many problems, including a large number of national scope, that await study by specialists in the technical services.

II. The Technical Services in the Library Program

MOST practicing librarians recognize that an effective organization of technical services is essential if the library is to provide its users with high quality service. These technical services take their place along with direct work with readers as necessary parts of a library's organization. Together, these two groups of services, well organized and properly balanced, constitute the basis of a total library program. It has been well demonstrated that an effective technical program is woven deeply into the fabric of efficient library service, and an impotent and expensive library program tends to accompany unorganized and inadequate operations and techniques.[1]

It has been pointed out that so far as university libraries are concerned, there is no standard pattern in the grouping of the various departments into functional units.[2] Such factors as tradition, personnel, physical quarters, financial support, types and distribution of collections, and the personalities, qualifications, and attitudes of administrative officers and staff have accounted for variations in organization. Most large libraries today, however, approximate a functional organization, with separate departments for acquisitions, cataloging, binding, photography, reference, circulation, and other units.

Despite this general pattern, there exists an administrative organization which groups the various services into two major units —the technical services and the readers' services. In a recent study, Cohen [3] located forty-seven institutions with technical services divisions. Since his study was made, many more libraries of various types have been organized on this basis. In the group that Cohen investigated were eighteen public libraries, nineteen university libraries, six college libraries, and four governmental libraries. The Berkeley (California) Public Library, the Chicago Public Library, the Brooklyn College Library, the University of Chicago Library, and the New York State Library are among those which have established such divisions. These libraries vary in size, as well as in the number of patrons served and variety of services offered.

Integration of related operations and techniques is designed to afford an organization which is more efficient than the traditional pattern based on strict function. Joeckel and Carnovsky, when recommending a technical services division for the Chicago Public Library, observed: "The intent of putting all technical processes under the direction of an assistant director is to emphasize the essential *unity* of the whole process of acquisitions and preparation of library materials. The processing of 200,000 volumes annually, together with pamphlets, serials, and much other material, is a task of great magnitude. Every effort and every device should be used to simplify routines and records and to expedite the flow of books through the various stages of preparation for use." [4]

Among the specific reasons advanced for the merging of functional units into a technical services division are the following: to decrease the span of control of the head librarian; to accelerate the flow of processed materials; to reduce the cost of preparing materials for use; and to develop among the various departments a spirit of cooperation. There has not been unanimous agreement that this type of organization accomplishes all this. Swank,[5] for example, has taken the position that combining the catalog and acquisition departments, while offering certain advantages, tends to narrow the conception of both cataloging and acquisition, because technical similarities, rather than distinctive professional functions, are emphasized. His plea for a broader view of the function of cataloging in the whole area of bibliographical organization is sound, but it does not necessarily follow that the administrative affinity of acquisition and cataloging should be discounted. The two ideas are not mutually exclusive. Both Swank and Metcalf[6] call attention to the expense of this type of organization, as well as to the difficulty of employing individuals who are at the same time top-rank administrators, bookmen, and technicians. It might be better, it is argued, to invest in first-class department heads.

These are cautions which are not to be taken lightly in the individual library situation. It is possible to build up a top-heavy administration which does not result in more efficient service or increased production in the technical services. The development of technical services divisions does not in itself mean that setting up these divisions is the only method of solving the complex problems of incorporation of materials into a library.

But librarians have seen values in this type of organization. While it may not be easy to demonstrate the various economic advantages that were implied by Joeckel and Carnovsky, observations by individuals who have been working with divisional organization suggest gains which indicate the desirability of examining further both its character and its accomplishments.[7]

THE TECHNICAL SERVICES DIVISION

Although the technical services division varies in different libraries, the general basic pattern is to combine the acquisition department with the cataloging department. In some libraries, the technical services also include the binding and photography departments. At the University of Chicago Library, acquisition, cataloging, and binding are parts of the "Preparation Division," another name for a technical services division. In the Brookline (Massachusetts) Public Library, "Technical Processes" include "adult cataloging," "children and school cataloging," ordering, marking, and binding. The "Processing Service" in the Detroit Public Library includes book selection (in part), acquisition, cataloging and classification, and physical maintenance of the collection. In this library, the assistant director has advisory, though not supervisory control of all processing activities carried on in all branches of the system. Figure 1, which illustrates the organization of the University of Illinois Library, shows a

FIGURE 1. ORGANIZATION CHART OF THE UNIVERSITY OF ILLINOIS LIBRARY AND LIBRARY SCHOOL (1954)

Supplied by Robert B. Downs

- Board of Trustees elected by people of the state
  - President of the University
    - Director of the Library and Library School
      - Associate Director of Library School
      - Assistant University Librarian for Personnel
      - Library Administrative Assistant
      - Medical Sciences, Chicago
      - Undergraduate Division, Chicago
      - Associate Director for Technical Departments
        - Acquisition Department
          - Purchase Division
          - Gift and Exchange Division
          - Periodical Division
          - Photographic
        - Binding Department
          - Binding Preparation Division
          - Book Repair and Pamphlet Binding Division
        - Catalog Department
          - General Cataloging Division
          - Serials Cataloging Division
          - General Clerical Division
          - Card Division
      - Associate Director for Public Service Departments
        - Reference Department
          - Information Desk
        - Circulation Department
          - Undergraduate Library
        - 23 Departmental Libraries
        - 5 Special Reading Rooms

OF THE ENOCH PRATT FREE LIBRARY, BALTIMORE, MARYLAND (FEBRUARY, 1954)

Prepared by Esther J. Piercy

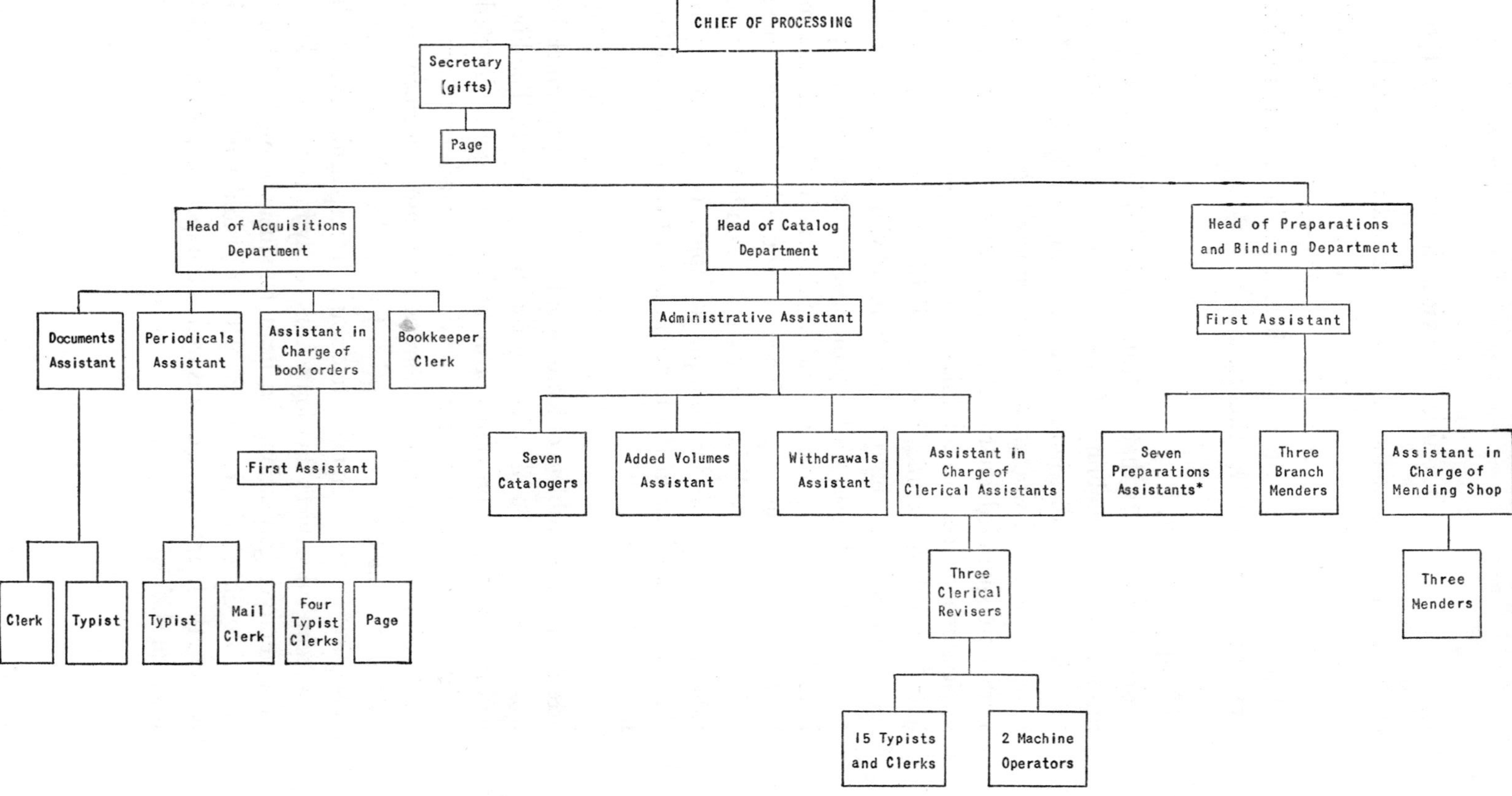

*Letterers, pasters, machine operators, clerks, pages.

complete, or what might be called a standard, technical services division, and its relation to the public services departments. Figure 2 illustrates the organization of a technical services division in more detail and represents the approach of a public library, the Enoch Pratt Free Library of Baltimore.

PERSONNEL

Despite the difficulty that Metcalf prophesied in his 1940 paper in respect to the availability of suitable personnel for headships of technical services divisions, the data assembled by Cohen [8] reveal that the men and women who were supervising such divisions in 1948 were qualified on the basis of academic training, technical services experience, and administrative ability. Some libraries which have established technical services divisions have not always been successful in their attempts to obtain individuals who meet all the requirements set forth for the positions. While most of the persons have had cataloging and general administrative experience, many have not had extensive experience in acquisitional operations and techniques. Fewer still have been really familiar with the complicated problems of binding and photography. This is not surprising, since such positions in the larger libraries have developed for the most part into specialties.

Undoubtedly, if these positions continue to increase in the future, attention to the problem of recruitment of suitable personnel should come from both the libraries and the library schools. The libraries will need to set up programs of in-service training and directed experience. The library schools, particularly in advanced programs, must seek to strengthen their courses which are concerned not only with cataloging but with the other technical services as well.

Some effort has been made to outline the responsibilities of a head of a technical services division.[9] Admittedly in charge of a key spot in a library organization, the head (frequently an "assistant" or "associate director" or a "chief of the division") has duties which concern the library as a whole as well as the specific units to which he is assigned.

GENERAL RESPONSIBILITIES OF THE HEAD. In his relation to the general program of the library, the officer in charge of technical services is generally concerned with the development of plans and policies and their implementation, as well as with the direction and supervision of operations. These high-level administrative assignments require an individual who has a capacity for leadership and whose experience has shown that he has good judgment, initiative, intellectual curiosity, and resourcefulness. He should have the ability to select, train, direct, and supervise people who are experts in their work. His knowledge of acquisitional and other operations should be sufficient to enable him to evaluate programs and make suggestions for improvements.

As a top-line officer, he represents the director of libraries in all areas listed under technical services; he works closely with the director in the fulfillment of the plans, aims, and programs of the libraries; he cooperates with other administrative officers in coordinating the work of his units with other units; and he offers suggestions for the improvement of the library service as a whole.

SPECIFIC DUTIES. The head of the technical services may be involved with problems dealing with book selection, acquisitions, cataloging and classification, binding, and photographic reproduction. On a broad administrative basis, he is concerned with organization and supervision of his areas of responsibility, including personnel management, budget preparation and supervision of book purchases, and reporting.

Although book selection is generally a responsibility of the head of the readers' services and of departmental librarians, to whom may be delegated the task of building up the collections, the head of the technical services is involved usually in two ways. In the first place, he normally cooperates in the selection of materials for the entire library system, and, in the absence of the head of the readers' services, may make the decisions for purchases, gifts, or exchanges. In the second place, he has the responsibility of assisting in the building up of the reference collections which are useful in acquisitions, cataloging and classification, or other technical services.

In acquisitions, he is responsible for the organization and functioning of procurement after selection has been made. In all matters relating to the acquisition of material, he sets the pattern, working with the head of the acquisition department; he selects agents, establishes relations with bookdealers and publishers, arranges for acquisition through exchange, either attends or sends representatives to book auctions, assists in decisions concerning duplicates, assists in making decisions on discarding and organizes such work, effects transfers of gifts to the library, acknowledges gifts, confers with the director on matters relating to gifts, conducts arrangements to obtain gifts, and signs order cards in the absence of the head of the readers' services.

In cataloging and classification, the head of the technical services is constantly concerned with the study of operations and techniques. This requires attention to developments in changes of rules of cataloging as well as to the flow of work. He must be concerned with minute details, as these are directly related to the prompt handling of large quantities of material.

Conservation of materials of a library also requires continuous attention. The head sets a program of conservation of books and other materials, draws up periodically the specifications for library binding, and studies methods, equipment, materials, and costs.

Similarly, in photographic reproduction he is concerned with methods, equipment, and costs. This is a changing field in which new developments call for constant scrutiny for possible library applications. The head of the technical services is also responsible for familiarizing library users with the services of the photographic unit and for studying new ways of utilizing this medium to the fullest extent.

On the level of organization and supervision, he examines the various relationships among the technical services and revises these in the interest of improved operations. Major changes are usually made after consultation with the director of libraries, and in meetings often attended by other administrative officers. Making a change in binding specifications, for example, without consulting the staff members who are concerned would result in ill feeling and lack of cooperation in executing the program.

With the approval of other administrative officers, the head of the technical services establishes the minimum number of positions needed to perform the work of his units and he develops and approves specifications for these positions. In addition to placing each individual in the position where he will be most effective, he provides for the proper supervision of all work and personnel, delegating to supervisory officers such duties as are consistent with sound administration.

In addition to these duties concerning personnel, he is also responsible for assisting in recruiting and interviewing prospective members for the technical services, conducting exit interviews, assigning duties, approving schedules of work, taking up with the proper administrative officers matters relating to individual staff members, and providing for the filling of impending vacancies.

One of the chief responsibilities of the head is budget preparation. From the heads of the services he receives budget recommendations which, after review, he submits to the proper officer; he analyzes expenditures for library acquisitions, cataloging, and binding, informs the library office of exhausted book funds, acts on decisions regarding transfer of funds, and places requests for supplies and equipment for technical services. To him may also be delegated the responsibility of signing for such requisitions in the absence of other officers. He also signs (or he may delegate the responsibility to the head of acquisitions) invoices for book purchases and book sales and requests for cancellations of orders.

Through annual and special reports the director of libraries is kept informed of the progress of the technical services. The head of the technical services analyzes, through statistical and other records and with the help of the supervisors and other staff members, the work of the services. In this way, intelligent planning is possible.

Thus, the head of the technical services, because of his position in the hierarchy of library organization, needs a sound grounding in the theory of administration. He should be familiar with the best administrative practices in planning, organizing, staffing, directing, budgeting, and reporting. He should have a clear comprehension of such principles as division of labor, authority and responsibility, discipline, unity of command, unity of management, subordination of individual interests to the common good, centralization, span of control, and departmentalization, as well as such matters as equity of treatment, initiative, stability, and morale of the staff.

ACCOMPLISHMENTS OF TECHNICAL SERVICES

In a discussion of the accomplishments of technical services divisions, it may be well to recapitulate the possible areas of achievement singled out by Coney.[10] These are: (1) transfer of information assembled in one process to another; (2) use of essential tools and records by two or more services; (3) use of a sufficiently coarse, rather than a fine, division of work so that certain activities will not be repeated; (4) use of machinery which eliminates or reduces the amount of work in an operation; and (5) use of by-products of one operation for another. Libraries do not need technical services divisions in order to accomplish these results. Information can be transferred even if a library is organized on a strictly departmental basis. Records and tools can be made available to several services. Coordination of machinery and the use of forms for several purposes are possible under functional organization. Job analysis and proper supervision should reduce or eliminate repetitive operations within the departments.

Coordination under the departmental organization, however, may not be as productive as under a centralized authority. This may seem to imply that department heads do not work as effectively when they pursue their tasks without over-all supervision from an officer below the librarian or director. The truth is that they frequently do not. Pressure of work, a tradition of a hard-and-fast distinction of provinces of authority, difficult personalities, factors relating to physical arrangements, or a combination of two or more or all of these possibilities, may account for the lack of coordination among the several technical services in some libraries. It is not unusual to find situations where there is little or no relationship between the acquisitions personnel and the catalogers and where neither group works closely with the binding staff. The numerous small problems which cut across departmental lines are sometimes the very ones which interfere with the efficient service of the library if they are not solved promptly and effectively. In a library system with branches or departments it is easy for the heads of the separate units to become department-minded rather than library-minded. The inclusion in such a system of an assistant director to relieve the librarian or director of the many minor but important problems and to coordinate the operations of the related departments appears to be, therefore, a plan of organization that should become increasingly fruitful in improving these services of the library. Not all libraries require such organization, nor do they need to establish it as a permanent arrangement if the aggravating factors are eliminated. In large libraries, the importance of the factor of span of control may be a decisive one in organizing a technical services division.

Consideration of specific library situations may help to clarify the question of achievement. Ladenson,[11] for example, has enumerated the various ways in which a technical services division at the Chicago Public Library has been organized for productive service. Among these are a clear recognition of the essential unity of the technical services; the organization of the technical units so that materials move along in fixed sequences; the setting up of techniques designed to handle materials on a mass-assimilation basis; the avoidance of duplication, such as in records, catalogs, files, and statistical compilations; the introduction of fluidity in personnel, so that staff members can be shifted to points where congestion or pressure of work develops; and the discontinuance of any operation or technique when it does not serve a current need. The director of technical services is in a position to insist on adoption of new procedures and the discarding of obsolete methods. Although this may appear to be a forced cooperation, rather than a spontaneous one, it has the effect of eliminating the condition where "each department is a law unto itself, with little or no reference to the work of the other departments." [12] Ladenson cited, with illustration, how under independent departmental organization the acquisition department in filling a large order for a branch library may not take into consideration the load that would later be placed upon the cataloging and binding services. In one case that he described, it was possible to do adequate advance planning by having the assistant librarian in charge of preparations call together all the department heads involved.

The head of the processing unit at the Detroit Public Library reports coordination between the catalog and the book-selection departments, between the catalog department and the bindery, and between each of the processing departments and the several public services. Custer [13] cites a situation where the book-selection department transferred to the catalog department responsibility for receiving and certifying book orders. Although the change was made in the interest of sound accounting practice, Custer calls attention to the fact that it resulted in a smoother flow of materials and in speedier checking of invoices. Moreover, the placing of the destination symbols in volumes was combined to some extent with the cataloging procedure, as well as with the marking of call numbers and other cataloging symbols. In addition to hastening attention to missing volumes, incorrectly filled orders, overdue invoices, and other such snags, the step cut the time between the receipt of the branch books to their placement on the shelves in the branch libraries from two or three weeks to less than a week for nonfiction, and to one or two days for fiction.

Coordination of records, transfer of information in searches, development of binding schedules in relation to cataloging production, and establishment of closer relations with the service agencies and branches have also been accomplished at Detroit. Although there were other factors, such as quality of personnel and new equipment, which had to be taken into consideration, greater coordination and changes in procedure by the assistant librarian in charge of processing have brought about increased production. Cataloging increased nearly thirteen percent per cataloger; new catalogs were completed; coverage of new titles by the book selection department increased forty percent and coverage of dealers' catalogs increased by several hundred percent; the binding production increased about ten percent. Detroit officials, as well as those of several other libraries, are convinced that the coordination of technical services may be a highly important factor in modern library adminstration.

Similar accounts have been given of the work in the State University of Iowa Libraries, the Brooklyn College Library, the Brookline Public Library, Northwestern University Library,[14] and the Cornell University Library. That much of the initial success of technical service divisions has depended on able administrators is apparent. Constant and continued success, however, depends on the further training of prospective technical services heads, able staffs, ample support, and close cooperation of the services. Brown,[15] writing of the reorganization of the Brookline Public Library, wisely observes that the program depends on the understanding and cooperation of every member of the staff. Not only routines and techniques but also the habits and thinking of the staff members require reorganization. Librarians, no less than other professional groups, change only slowly their habits and modes of thinking. Moreover, as Barnard [16] has pointed out, the persistence of cooperation depends upon its effectiveness. It is no easy task to satisfy designs, which is the test of effectiveness, and to get individuals to cooperate, which is the test of efficiency. The extent to which a type of organization demonstrates its value should determine whether or not it should be retained.[17]

III. Acquisitions: Functions and Organization

ROBERT B. DOWNS concluded a discussion of problems involved in the acquisition of research materials by saying that "future generations will probably blame us or praise us, not for our fine catalogs, classification schemes, circulation systems, and reference techniques but for what we manage to save and pass on to them." [1] The acquisition of materials is of primary importance for any type of library and except in the smallest, which may have only one or two staff members who perform all duties, there generally exists a separate acquisition or order department for this purpose.

FUNCTIONS

The functions of the acquisition department stem from the acquisitional policy of the library of which it is a part. Too frequently, however, this policy has not been clearly defined. This lack of clarification has often resulted in haphazard collection of materials which do not meet the purposes of the library and in neglect of areas necessary to the institution or community which the library serves. While it may be presumptuous to attempt to set down what an acquisitional policy should be without dealing with a specific institution, it may be useful to inquire into the general objectives of acquisition. Such objectives, paraphrased from those of the Library of Congress,[2] may be given first in terms of a university library.

On this basis, four general objectives or obligations might be proposed: (1) the library should own and make available such books, periodicals, and other library materials as are required by the students and the faculties of the university in the performance of their individual research work; (2) the library should own and make available such books and other materials as are related to the instructional and research programs of the university; (3) the library should own and make available those parts of the past and present graphic records of those cultures and peoples whose experience is related in any way to the educational and research program of the university; and (4) the library should own all materials relating to the history, development, and character of the university. In many cases, the materials may be acquired in suitable copy, if originals are not obtainable.

An illustration of a projected acquisitional program for a specific institution is taken from the Wilson and Swank survey of the Stanford University Library.[3]

Acquisitional Program. The most significant part of acquisitional work—that which involves the planned selection of materials, both new and old, best calculated to strengthen the University's resources for instruction and research—takes place before the books are actually ordered. The Faculty, of course, is in large part responsible for the selection of materials in their special fields, while the Library takes responsibility for special subject fields neglected by the Faculty, for pulling the whole thing together into a coordinated all-university program, and for offering specialized, bibliographical assistance to the Faculty in the form of desiderata lists based on studies of the Library's holdings. A well-developed acquisitional program, as it relates to the activities of the Order Division, may be said to include the following elements:

1. The program itself—a statement, developed in cooperation with the Faculty and known to both Faculty and Library staff, describing the fields in which materials are sought and, in as much detail as possible, the types of materials sought. Such a program should be clearly based upon and designed to support specific instructional and research projects and should anticipate to whatever extent is possible the development of future projects.

2. The continuous systematic analysis of weak spots in the book collections through the checking of bibliographies against the Library's holdings, the submission to the Faculty of lists of materials not owned, the rating by the Faculty and library staff of these titles, and finally, the

preparation of want or desiderata lists. These lists should be transcribed to cards and interfiled in the Order Division.

3. The routine and prompt checking of secondhand and auction catalogs, exchange lists, etc., against the general desiderata list, as well as the library catalog, process file, etc., and the immediate ordering, by telegram or cable, if necessary, of needed items.

4. Distribution of publishers' announcements, catalogs, and other information relative to the availability of materials to the book-selection representatives of the instructional departments and to the appropriate members of the library staff.

Keyes D. Metcalf, in considering the essentials of an acquisitions program, has stated that the library attempting to collect research materials should have a guiding policy on such matters as whether to concentrate on new or old materials, the fields to be covered and the extent of coverage, whether to collect manuscripts and rare books, and how it plans to integrate its collection with others in the same region.[4]

In contrast, the public library's collecting policy, though directed at the needs of its clientele, generally does not cover such a wide range as that of the university library. While demands of the users are taken into consideration, the policy of collecting is influenced by other factors, such as the age of the library, its income, and its location in relation to other community agencies for the distribution of print. In the *Post-War Standards for Public Libraries,*[5] five general principles for book collecting were promulgated:

1. The book stock of the public library must reflect the five basic objectives of the public library—education, information, aesthetic appreciation, recreation, and research—and the important areas of concentration of library effort in post-war America.
2. Book selection for the public library should aim at meeting reading needs common to all communities as well as the specific needs of each community.
3. The book collection should be conceived as a living and changing organism, subject to the inevitable processes of obsolescence, wear and tear, and loss.
4. Procedures of book selection should be carefully planned and organized in every public library. Book selection should be an objective task, based on a wide acquaintance with literature and affairs, accurate

knowledge of community needs, the existing book stock, and available books in print.
5. Evaluation of the book stock of a public library cannot be dissociated from the effectiveness of its services, the qualifications and energy of its staff, the aggressiveness of the public relations program, and the location and physical aspects of library buildings and service outlets.

The standards also take into account such matters as the size of the collection, which, generally, should "be sufficient to insure at all times an adequate collection for consultation and home use." Further, "enough books should be added . . . annually to reflect important contemporary literature, to provide currently useful information, to represent important literature of civilization, and to replace worthwhile but worn out volumes." In discussing standards of quality for the book collection, reference is made to the additional need of acquiring "imaginative literature and books dealing with a wide variety of matters of general concern as well as the essentially local or regional interests, and with issues of contemporary national and international concern." Finally, enough books of good quality should be made available to the younger clientele to assist in the development of good reading taste and to satisfy its reading interests.

If the general policies of collecting for other types of libraries were stipulated, a similar pattern would be found. Research libraries and special libraries of various kinds generally do more intensive collecting in narrow fields.[6] Such ventures as the Library of Congress Cooperative Acquisitions Project [7] and the Farmington Plan [8] suggest that perhaps the future will bring a greater degree of specialization in collecting among the libraries of America. Special libraries usually have rather carefully developed programs of collecting, based on the needs of their special clienteles, and are more concerned than are some research libraries (and even many public libraries) with up-to-date materials. Both school and special libraries frequently have highly developed systems for the careful selection and regular discarding of materials.

Many proposals concerning cooperative acquisitions programs have been offered, and a few concrete plans are in operation. Downs [9] has suggested several methods which might be employed to insure the acquisition of research materials for the country at large. His suggestions are threefold: (1) discovering library resources—here the individual library must investigate its own collection thoroughly, and resources of the region must be examined (the use of the union catalog will be helpful in the regional aspect); (2) library surveys—such as Potter's survey of the Harvard Library [10] and Downs' *Resources of Southern Libraries* [11]; and (3) acquisition agreements among libraries, the logical consequence of (1) and (2). The new Midwest Inter-Library Center [12] is an outstanding example of cooperation in acquisition on a regional basis.

However, the "division of fields" basis for cooperative acquisitions has been subjected to rather severe and significant criticism. For example, Fremont Rider, after pointing out the difficulties involved in dividing subject fields and at the same time insuring complete coverage, states:

> . . . it still remains, a stark and devastatingly clear fact, that, if division of fields is to have any really effective result it must—if it be that and nothing more—deprive all our research scholars of the one thing that they rate at present above everything else in importance in the daily doing of their work—*their libraries!*
>
> Nor will it do any good to explain to them that—once division of fields is in full flower—although there may be in their own library only a smattering of research materials on—shall we say metabolism? there is a collection of books on metabolism in New York that is the ultimate word in comprehensiveness, bibliographical perfection of cataloging, and expertly classified accessibility. It will do no good to explain to them that, poor as their own library may be in materials on Chinese history, there is out at Berkeley a collection that is likewise the scholar's dream of research perfection in that particular field. It will not even do much good to explain to them, finally, that, through a wonderfully complete, printed, national union catalog of which you have a copy, they can find out *exactly* what books are in these two almost perfect collections, and that, if they want any of these books, you can get them for them.[13]

Any program of cooperative acquisitions in which a library participates has direct effects upon the technical services. For example, if a library is a member of the group obtaining materials through the Farmington Plan, it may not need to set up individual orders for the items which would come automatically through the project. This is an essential part of the Plan, although routines in earlier cooperative projects, such as those of the Advisory Group on College Libraries and the Advisory Group for Junior College Libraries of the Carnegie Corporation,[14] involved preparation of requests. In these projects, routines were set up whereby the libraries prepared their requests on uniform order blanks and sent them to a central agent for purchase. The use of the central agency, however, made it possible to undertake work for 92 junior college libraries and 29 teachers college libraries. "Since purchases on the junior college grants began in the fall of 1937," wrote Barcus, "we have bought books from eighty different firms, but the majority of the orders have gone to four or five big dealers in New York and Chicago." [15]

Cooperative acquisitions projects on such a large scale have not been common. Colorado libraries, through the Rocky Mountain Bibliographical Center in Denver, were able to carry on a project in which there were successful results. The Library of Congress during World War II took the initiative in developing what was known as the Library of Congress Cooperative Acquisitions Project. The plan had its inception in a letter from the Librarian of Congress to the Department of State, July 17, 1945, in which it was proposed that the Library of Congress make use of the State Department's facilities to secure books and other library materials from foreign countries to supply American research libraries. After the State Department agreed in principle, the plan was worked out through a committee headed by Robert B. Downs. A list was prepared which assigned some 8,000 priorities to 115 libraries in 254 subject fields. In assigning priorities the following factors were considered: (1) strength of existing holdings, (2) location of highest priorities among geographical areas, (3) rotation of high priorities among different institutions in the same region so as to prevent undue concentration in a few libraries, (4) current research and publications of institutions as well as current appropriations for new books, (5) bibliographical centers with well-developed plans for cooperative buying. Libraries assuming responsibility for an entire field would be favored against those assuming responsibility for a subdivision thereof.

Boyd [16] called attention to certain weaknesses in the program, despite its over-all soundness. These were (1) the failure to exact continuing commitments, (2) the lack of participation by the constituency in setting up the criteria, the work having been done by a committee, and (3) the too few classifications of material and failure to define subject fields narrowly enough. Adjustments were made in the later stages of the project, although many of the smaller libraries were not satisfied with the types of material they received.[17]

Actually preceding the Library of Congress project was the discussion proposing a similar plan of obtaining foreign materials for American research libraries. This has become known as the Farmington Plan.

> Its objective is to make sure that at least one copy of each new foreign book and pamphlet that might reasonably be expected to interest a research worker in the United States will be acquired by an American library, promptly listed in the Union Catalog at the Library of Congress, and made available by interlibrary loan or photographic reproduction.[18]

In the current program certain categories of materials, such as school texts, music scores, translations, reprints, juvenilia, elementary popular works, newspapers, maps, and even periodicals are excluded.

Early reactions to the Plan included the objection that cooperation is too difficult to achieve and that the project ignored the fact that selection is paramount in the philosophy of librarianship. The first objection was discounted, and it was pointed out that by insuring the placing of one copy of each book in a United States library the plan gives most librarians a greater opportunity to exercise selection without having misgivings that they were overlooking certain items. However, Metcalf has noted that:

> Coverage will always be a basic problem; some libraries have complained that they are not receiving as many publications as ought to come to them, while others object to the quantity of worthless material they receive. The original proposal simply stated that the plan would include everything that might reasonably be expected to interest a research worker in America; it is not surprising that the librarian who thinks only good

books worth keeping should interpret this very differently from one of his colleagues who would like to see almost everything preserved somewhere. European libraries have generally been more selective than American; European agents and advisers have tended to supply fewer publications than most American research libraries would prefer to have.[19]

In 1952, the library which received the largest number of volumes through the Farmington Plan was that of the University of Illinois, with 2,414, of a total of the 17,508 acquired by all cooperating libraries.[20]

The Farmington Plan's effects upon the importations of a particular group of libraries have been noted by David and Hirsch,[21] who show how many titles from a sample were acquired by libraries through the Farmington machinery. Moreover, they show which libraries obtained certain titles. Although they found a number of shortcomings (for example, several important titles were overlooked and not obtained by any library), the investigators conclude, "We still retain our confidence that shortcomings will be overcome, indeed that they are already in process of being overcome, and that we shall before long arrive at a complete coverage of significant publications in United States libraries." [22]

There have been other cooperative plans in acquisitions. The Documents Expediting Project is one of the more important. Through a central office at the Library of Congress, a group of about seventy-five libraries subscribe to a service which provides them with documents over and above what they may receive as depository libraries. For a certain sum, based on a sliding scale ranging up to $500, depending on the size of the library, the Documents Expediter performs a number of services. These include the revision of mailing lists of a number of government agencies, the distribution of the publications of certain other units, establishment of basic procedures to facilitate the release of classified publications after security restrictions have been removed, securing processed material for the Superintendent of Documents for listing in the *Monthly Catalog*, collection of Congressional committee prints for microfilming, collection of Voice of America scripts for the Library of Congress (which are subsequently available through the Photoduplication Service of LC), and publication of the *Classified Checklist of United States Government Processed Publications*. The Project also distributed military documents procured by the Library of Congress Mission in Europe. During the first four years of the Project, it distributed to cooperating libraries a total of two million pieces.[23]

Other types of cooperative acquisition programs involve smaller groups, such as the libraries of Chicago. John Crerar Library, for example, works closely with Newberry, Chicago Natural History Museum, Chicago Public Library, Northwestern University, and the University of Chicago in its acquisition policy. There are examples of cooperation in collecting in the Philadelphia, Denver, Seattle, New York, and Chapel Hill–Durham areas. Much of this cooperation, however, has been informal and only partially effective, but every step in the direction of group action will result in spreading the responsibility of collecting, recording, preserving, and servicing.

These types of specialized collections have a definite bearing on the acquisitional program of libraries. If a library collects old and rare materials, many periodicals and other serials, maps, photographs, pictures, music, manuscripts, and films, it will need to set up records and operations that may differ some from those of libraries which obtain mainly current books. The quantity and variety of materials in foreign languages bears a relation to the type of personnel required. The type of clientele affects directly the operations and techniques of the acquisition department. In a public library, where emphasis is placed on getting materials quickly to the user, operations are put into effect which make it possible to provide new titles on publication date or very soon thereafter. In a research library, which collects older materials, there may be more leisurely purchasing operations, although speed will at times be an important factor if the library is to be successful in obtaining items which appear on the secondhand market.

Out of these major programs of book collecting certain essential functions of the acquisition department may be formulated. These are in general terms: (1) assisting in book selection, (2) coordinating purchase, gift, exchange, and depository activities, and (3) serving as a clearing house for information regarding publications, publishers, dealers, prices, and book markets.

ASSISTING IN BOOK SELECTION. The energetic acquisition department will be more than a checking and verifying agency. Although in some libraries, the department serves merely as a center for placing orders, it is frequently in a particularly good position to participate in the program of building up the collections of the institution.[24] In the public library, some responsibility for book selection is usually assigned to the acquisition department, although the actual amount of selecting done by acquisition personnel may be limited and is but a small part of their work.[25] This responsibility may or may not be shared with others, such as the librarian, branch librarians, and subject specialists on the staff, depending to some extent on the size and complexity of the library. There is obviously a close relationship between book selection and order work, and that relationship is more likely to serve in the public library as a basis for assigning responsibility than it is in the college or university library.

Although the usual assumption is that in academic libraries the faculty, either individually or working through committees, will handle the bulk of book selection, the findings of certain studies [26] indicate that unless the library staff or special bibliographers participate, book selection will probably be uneven and sporadic. Metcalf, in outlining the acquisition program,[27] has indicated that the acquisition department, while not the principal selection agency, has the responsibility of seeing that the fields in which the library has decided to collect are covered.

Participation can be obtained in several ways. In the first place, the acquisition personnel should have a thorough knowledge of the collecting policy of the institution. If it is a university library, the staff should have a clear idea of the educational and research program; they should know what special fields are being collected and what programs are being planned; and they should understand the strengths and weaknesses of the collections through seeing the requests which come to the library from the faculty and other departments and staff members of the library. In order to obtain this knowledge the members of the staff, especially the supervisors of the sections, must be alert to opportunities for getting needed items as they appear on the current and secondhand book market.

The book selection responsibility of the general library staff has been described by McCarthy in his survey of the New Hampshire University Library:

It is understood that the chief responsibility for selecting materials to be purchased on the general funds of the Library rests with the Order Librarian. While there is no criticism to be made of such an arrangement, it is suggested that greater effort be made to encourage other members of the professional staff to recommend titles for purchase. Highly desirable results have been obtained in some libraries by asking interested members of the staff to take the responsibility for recommending titles for addition to the collection. This has the advantage not only of bringing a broader group of interests and backgrounds to bear on the task of book selection, but it may also help to give the staff a greater sense of participating in a joint effort. It is believed that little can be achieved in this respect without taking some very definite steps to put the plan into operation. To do so requires a clear understanding as to the subject or type of books for which the staff member is taking responsibility, information as to the approximate amount of money that can be spent for this purpose, and some indication of the scope of coverage which the Library has attempted to achieve, or wishes to achieve in the future. If such a plan is set up, staff members should be given reports on their recommendations in the same way as are members of the faculty. Nothing is more effective in destroying staff interest than to have recommendations disregarded without explanation. If staff members suggest purchases which the Order Librarian or the Librarian decide should not be made, the staff member is entitled to a brief indication of the reasons for the decision.[28]

Another particularly apt statement of the coordination necessary to the building up of the library's collections was made by Robert W. Orr:

Yesterday a young man from Costa Rica stopped in at the Library to find out how Iowa State managed to build up fairly adequate collections of books and periodicals in the subject fields which are stressed here.

I explained to him that the "magic" formula he sought was one known and employed with varying degrees of success by most colleges and universities.

The "secret" is one of support by the administration and cooperation between the library staff and the faculty. The library staff cannot by itself do the job. It is doubtful if any group of non-specialists could do something in numerous subject fields which specialists find difficult to accomplish in their respective areas, namely, know their literature well in its broadest aspects.

In some instances the history of building up a collection of books and periodicals in a subject field is a dramatic one inasmuch as a single faculty member, plugging away over the years, deserves the major share of credit for the results obtained. More often, however, the best results are achieved through careful planning and sustained teamwork.[29]

Finally, the personnel of the acquisition department can further the selection process through their knowledge of the habits and practices of various agencies (commercial and otherwise), by making the best use of such knowledge to make funds go as far as possible, and by careful attention to desiderata lists.

COORDINATING ACQUISITIONS. It has been found through experience that the most effective results are obtained when the acquisition department of a library is the coordinating unit for purchases, gifts, and exchanges, even though the library may have several branches or several departmental or school libraries. In some instances, it may also control the acquisition and records of depository collections. This simply follows the principle of centralization of a functional activity. Where such coordination is lacking, it has not been unusual to find waste in manpower, equipment, records, and duplication of materials. If all the branches of a public library system bought their own materials, it is apparent how serious this waste might become. Similarly, if all the departments of a university library system purchased their own books, periodicals, and other library materials, there would be waste of staff time, multiplication of records, loss of discounts resulting from disparate rather than coordinated buying, and a potentially chaotic condition in the relationships between the technical and the readers' services.[30]

However, despite the advantages of centralization in acquisition, in some unusual cases it may be desirable to permit departmental units to do their own purchasing. For example, in an academic library system, some libraries which are located off-campus (as is frequently the case with law and medical school libraries) may more effectively do their own purchasing. The importance of separate acquisition units for departmental libraries has not been studied intensively. In some cases apparent success in prompt receipt is outweighed by extra expenditures. Decentralized receipt of materials is another matter, and in some libraries may be desirable. Records, of course, should be coordinated.

SERVING AS A CLEARING HOUSE ON MATTERS RELATING TO ACQUISITION. The acquisition department's part in channeling information to those individuals interested in the development of the library's collection has already been noted. A centralized acquisition department can be an effective clearing house for information about publication, publishers, dealers, prices, and book markets. By assembling appropriate trade and national bibliographies, publishers' announcements, dealers' catalogs, auction catalogs, and other aids, it is in a position to answer certain kinds of inquiries regarding publications. Within its own sphere of operation, the department has certain obligations to disseminate information about books and other materials. This may be done through systematically checking book lists and by working closely with those individuals who have supervision of budgetary allotments for the purchase of materials. The acquisition department personnel should be aware of potential sources of gifts and exchanges and should make such knowledge available to the proper officials.

ORGANIZATION

Although the physical arrangement of an acquisition department may influence its type of organization, the accommodations for staff should provide for the following functions:

1. Maintenance and use of bibliographic aids peculiar to acquisitions work (e.g., dealers' catalogs, trade lists, etc.).

2. Maintenance of order files, "in process" files, desiderata lists, and other records essential to acquisitions work.
3. Making up, dispatching, and filing of orders for books, Library of Congress cards, and other materials ordered through the department.
4. Receipt, handling, and inspection of incoming shipments.
5. Packing and shipment of returns and exchange materials.
6. Any preparation of materials ordinarily done by the department (e.g., stamping, perforating, and plating of books).
7. Preparation of bills for payment, bookkeeping, and other financial activities assigned to the department.
8. Preparation of accession lists.
9. Informing individuals recommending the purchase of the status of such recommendations.
10. Ordering and checking in of periodicals and continuations.
11. Following up on items not promptly received.

These functions need to be translated into terms of space and equipment necessary to carry them out. Card cabinets are needed which will take care of and provide for further expansion of outstanding order files, "in process" files, desiderata lists, and similar records. Vertical files are needed for the extensive departmental correspondence as well as for holding copies of outstanding orders. Shelving needs will be determined by the volume of ordering and by the library's policy on holding books in the department until invoices arrive. Desk space for the professional and clerical members of the staff must be available, and some arrangement should be made so that the order librarian may have some privacy when interviewing library clientele and publishers' agents. Typewriters must be replaced periodically and other items of mechanical equipment must be kept in good repair. Adding machines, visible files, and other business aids should be purchased as needed.

Effective acquisitional organization requires not only that the physical surroundings be planned to speed the flow of work, but also that the principles of administration relating to the centralization of homogeneous activities, direction, supervision, and control be applied to its functioning. Moreover, the administrator of the acquisition department, whether he reports to a director of technical services or to the librarian or director of libraries, should clearly comprehend the sphere of his activity, its relations to the other technical services and to the readers' services, and the personnel necessary to carry out the functions of the department.

TYPES OF ORGANIZATION. The procedures, apart from book selection, involved in obtaining materials have had some effect upon the type of organization. A department may be arranged by sections, each responsible for acquiring certain kinds of materials: books and pamphlets, serials, documents, and archives. It may be arranged by the method of acquisition: purchases, gifts, and exchanges. In the smaller libraries, there is usually no reason to set up sections based on either types of materials or methods of acquisition. At Illinois, the acquisition department consists of a purchase division, a combined gift and exchange division (a common combination), a periodical division, and a photographic reproduction laboratory (Fig. 1). At Columbia University, the acquisition department is made up of an order division, a combined documents and serials section, and a combined gift and exchange section. The book selection department at the Detroit Public Library has a selection unit and an order unit.

Centralization and coordination are the major ideas in these organizations. Although there are variations as to what units or sections are included, the organizational goal may be described as functionalism. This means coordinating the function of acquisition in one unit of the library organization, rather than dispersing the acquisition effort among various units. Where the acquisition function is scattered—in what has been termed a divisional organization—there might be an all-purpose serials division which would do not only its own acquisition work but also its cataloging and reference service. Some libraries have set up document and map divisions on the same basis. To the objection that such arrangements are excessively costly, proponents of the plan reply that the personnel working under such an arrangement gain a specialized knowledge of materials and sources of materials which cannot be the case in a general acquisition department; that the personnel can be shifted from one function to another as the need demands; and that all records essential to the acquisition, cataloging, and use of the materials are kept in one place.

RELATION TO THE OTHER TECHNICAL UNITS. The close relationship between the acquisition and the catalog department has already been suggested. A merging of units into a technical services division usually involves these two departments. In the well-appointed library building, in which careful consideration has been given to the relationships of the two departments, the maximum results will be obtained in such spheres as the use of common records and bibliographical tools, the transfer of information so as to avoid duplication of work, and the smooth flow of materials. The catalog department expects the order or acquisition department, since it uses the card catalog extensively, to send along information regarding entries, to indicate copies and editions, to point out errors in cataloging which may be found during searching, to indicate sources of materials, and to mark items needing rapid attention. On the other hand, the acquisition department expects the catalog department to catalog materials quickly, to provide sufficient information on the catalog cards so that unintentional duplication will not result, to assist in difficult checking, to file cards quickly, to make sufficient cross references so that entries will be easily located, to place temporary cards in the catalog when cards are removed for additions or corrections, and to remove temporary cards as soon as possible, to correct mistakes after they have been pointed out, and to provide aids such as guide and information cards which will facilitate the searching operation.

Relations with the bindery depend upon the organizational as well as upon the physical arrangements. In some libraries, the acquisition department is responsible for preparing unbound books for the bindery before they are cataloged, and its serial section may be concerned with the binding of serials. The acquisition department can aid the bindery by not accepting unbound materials (if bound copies are available), by watching for incomplete or damaged volumes, and by making certain that staff members who receive and handle materials do not damage them.

The acquisition department in some libraries also has a direct relation to the photography unit in that it orders materials to be reproduced by other libraries, and purchases photographic supplies (although this might well be the responsibility of the administrative office of the library through the service of a supply clerk).

RELATION TO READERS' SERVICES. Both the circulation department and the reference department are closely related to the acquisition department, since they could not function effectively if materials were not obtained promptly. This is also true of branch or departmental libraries in the larger systems. The acquisition department in its book selection operations keeps a constant watch on the book market and, when appropriate, informs the service staffs of available materials. The circulation department frequently assumes the responsibility for making decisions concerning the replacement of books which are lost, missing, or worn. In the large library, the reference department may sometimes assist the acquisition department in the checking of book lists and dealers' catalogs. It is not unusual for the reference department to do some acquisition work, in that it may be delegated to make direct requests for free and inexpensive materials. When the volume of such work interferes with the primary function of the service department, this burden should be transferred to the acquisition department.

PERSONNEL. It has been pointed out by recent writers, including R. W. Christ [31] that most of the work of the acquisition department is clerical in nature. Christ has indicated that of a staff of four, one person should be professional. He also observed that if a staff consists of three persons, the head librarian with clerical assistance will usually spend part of his time in acquisitions. Also, the conditions of the library may alter the ratio of professional to clerical staff, although Christ's formula is essentially that which most libraries follow. In larger libraries, with acquisition subsections, such as gifts and exchanges, the heads of these sections are usually professional librarians. The evidence indicates that unless the heads are trained personnel, the library will lose certain advantages inherent in its program.

The chief acquisition librarian has the responsibility of developing procedures, handling difficult problems relating to the ordering of materials, making recommendations concerning book selection, examining catalogs of book auctions and out-of-print works, obtaining reproductions of materials when originals are unavailable, interviewing publishers' representatives, and supervising the receipt of gifts and exchanges. Such a person needs a good knowledge of administrative theory and practice, some training in business methods, knowledge of book markets, ability to recognize able bookdealers, knowledge of the objectives of the library, and the ability to meet cordially patrons and staff members who are seeking information about books. Acquisition work requires a superior memory, accuracy, resourcefulness, good judgment, initiative, tact, a keen sense of orderliness, and ability to get things done quickly. All other professional members of the staff should have a flair for books, a capacity for detail, and a sound knowledge of bibliographical practice.

The nonprofessional employees, such as checkers, filers, sorters, typists, shipping clerks, and accession clerks are usually young people out of high school and business schools. In most libraries, there is rapid turnover in this part of the staff. Hence, it is essential for the acquisition head to have the procedures and operations of the department definitely outlined, so that training periods may be reduced to a minimum. Close to the professional work is searching, which requires a type of knowledge peculiar to the library profession; yet searching has not been recognized as a professional task in many places. The searcher must have competence in foreign languages and a knowledge of the details of bibliographical entry; in the large library he must also have stability and physical endurance, since the work involves a great deal of walking and standing. Fleming and Moriarty [32] recognized the professional character of some aspects of the searching process, and went on to state that "the alert searcher will also strengthen the collection by suggesting the purchase of essential bibliographies." [33] Ability of the searchers to report accurately on their checking is essential to an economical acquisition program.

In order to expedite the training of all personnel of the department, whether clerical, subprofessional, or professional, manuals of procedure should be developed. Recording these operations and procedures in detail will not only assist in training but it may also lead to modifying some phases of the work by enabling them to be reviewed in proper perspective in relation to the activities of the whole department. Manuals, however, should never be permitted to solidify departmental organization and procedure, since changes in acquisition policy, personnel, and subject areas to be covered, as well as the mere passage of time, may render advisable some changes in organization and practice.

In the ten college libraries studied by Christ[34] the acquisition department staffs range in size from one to five. In a library such as that of Columbia University, there was in 1948 an acquisitions staff of 22, of whom 2 were professional; in 1954 there was a staff of 30, of whom 5 were professional. In the Library of Congress in 1947 there were 33 in the Order Division, and of these 17 were professional; in 1953 there were 40, of whom 24 were professional. In the Exchange and Gift Division in 1947 there were 46 staff members; of these, 10 were professional; in 1953 there were 33, of whom 16 were professional.[35] Although there has not been a complete study made of the demand in libraries for acquisition personnel, available evidence indicates that more and more opportunity is being provided for promising young librarians to work with problems which are both challenging and engrossing in their ramifications and complexities.

IV. Types of Materials and Their Sources: Purchases

THE acquisitional policy of the library should determine the quality and quantity of materials to be obtained for the use of a particular clientele. The funds available have a direct bearing on what may be procured. While the Albany (New York) Public Library was spending $24,743 for books and periodicals in 1952, the Chicago Public Library allotted $468,889 for this purpose; [1] while the University of Arizona spent $50,181 for books, periodicals, and binding in 1952–53, the University of California at Berkeley had a budget of $422,805 to purchase these types of materials.[2] The Columbia University Libraries have resources from the Bancroft Fund of about $40,000 annually to purchase materials in just one field—American history, broadly defined. Harvard, Yale, Princeton, Chicago, the New York Public Library, the Cleveland Public Library, and many other institutions, large and small, have similar special or endowment funds on which to draw for buying current or older materials. Sometimes the funds are restricted to fields much narrower than American history. Harvard, for example, has 23 unrestricted funds, 137 restricted funds, and 9 funds belonging to other administrative units but with income transferred in whole or part to the Library in accordance with the terms of the original gift.[3]

This concern with funds is important, since the complexity of acquisition work in a library may derive somewhat from the amount of funds available for the purchase of materials. Members of the general public often think in terms of current fiction and nonfiction, especially best-sellers, when a library's collecting policy is brought to attention. Some of the smaller public or school libraries restrict their buying to relatively few titles, and these are primarily books and popular magazines, but the research or special library, in addition to current and older books and pamphlets, may obtain many other kinds of materials: serials (scholarly periodicals, annuals, reports, catalogs, yearbooks, memoirs, journals and transactions of societies, and proceedings—in all languages); documents (federal, state, county, municipal, and foreign); dissertations of domestic and foreign academic institutions; newspapers (domestic and foreign); maps; music; manuscripts; brochures, leaflets, and travel folders; recordings of various kinds; charts; clippings; playbills; posters; tracts; broadsides; archives (including letters, tax books, receipt books, telegraphic dispatches, plantation records, family histories, business and industrial records, medical records, weather observations, personal diaries and travelogues); such graphic materials as data sheets, tabulation sheets, filled-in questionnaires, original work sheets or cards, graphs, and drawings; such visual materials as photographs, pictures, lantern slides, prints, microfilms, microprints, microcards, motion pictures, and newsreels; and museum pieces (paintings, statuary, cuneiform tablets, models, coins, designs, stamps, views, and postal cards). Acquiring and preserving these materials—to say nothing of organizing and recording them—is obviously a large order.

What does a year's program for acquisition by purchase look like? While it would not be practical to list every item which a library acquires by purchase during a twelve-month period, the following excerpt from the report of the director of libraries of a large university is worth examining:

> Much important material was acquired by purchase during the year. The income from the Bancroft Foundation was spent in acquiring: (1) the New York Historical Society collection of pamphlets and books on the slavery question in the United States; (2) the John Brown collection of Oswald Garrison Villard, representing one of the three greatest collections relevant to John Brown; (3) the regimental and company histories of World War I, from Louis C. Haggerty; (4) microfilms of manuscript collections in the Library of Congress, Pennsylvania Historical Society, and other libraries; (5) collections of American state laws for the Law

Library; and (6) numerous books, pamphlets, periodicals, and other materials relating to American history appearing in dealers' catalogs.

In April, 1947, a collection of early books on accounting and bookkeeping was purchased from the firm of Van Tobel and Carr of Denver. The earliest item in this collection is a parchment roll relating to the Manor of Wilburton in Isle of Ely, reign of Henry IV, 1400–1402. Many sixteenth- and seventeenth-century items are included in the collection. This purchase was made from the Colonel H. Montgomery Fund. . . .

Among other purchases were the following: (1) Azariah Cutting Flagg papers, containing some twenty-five letters written by Martin Van Buren; (2) the Russian collection of Alexandre Popoff; (3) the Ernest Boyd collection of German dramatic criticism; (4) 570 titles in 604 volumes and 939 *ts'e* (fascicules) for the Chinese collection; (5) 124 letters from Tolstoi and members of his family to Aylmer Maude, an outstanding translator of his works; (6) Mehul's opera *Stratonice*; (7) the collection of chamber music purchased from Otto Hass of London; (8) a collection of microfilms of materials in the Bibliothèque Nationale and the Bibliothèque du Conservatoire National de Musique et de Déclamation, Paris (primarily Beethoven manuscripts and fifteenth-century secular material); (9) *Chefs d'oeuvre classiques de l'opéra français* (25 vols.); (10) the Hartshorne copy of Fra Colonna's *Hypnerotomachia Poliphili*, Aldus Press, 1499; (11) two important editions of Vitruvius (Nuremberg, 1548, and Paris, 1547); (12) Bosboom's *De vyf colom-orden met derzelver deuren en poorten* (Amsterdam, 1654); (13) *Fréart de Chambray's Parallèle de l'architecture antique et de la moderne*; (14) Wilheim's *Architectura civilis* (Frankfurt a. M., 1649); (15) materials issued by the United Nations and affiliated and related organizations and agencies.[4]

A mere reading of this paragraph reveals the interest in almost every type of material needed by a large research institution. Books, periodicals, pamphlets, manuscripts, incunabula, and music are evident. Old and modern items are included, and the works of presses in many different countries are represented. Examination of the list does not reveal the considerable correspondence, the many personal interviews, cablegrams, and visits abroad by representatives of the libraries which were necessary in order to close many of the transactions. The art of acquisition work indeed involves a combination of the talents of the detective, the diplomat, and the businessman.

While many of the above categories of material are acquired

through gift and exchange, a number of American libraries have positive buying policies in regard to them. Acquisitional problems related to the more important groups will be discussed in this chapter.

BOOKS

The book collections of libraries range from incunabula to the most recently published items, domestic and foreign. Although it is sometimes difficult to tell *exactly* how many books a library has, since counting procedures differ,[5] a large number of American libraries report holding a million volumes or more.[6] The larger university and research libraries are likely to purchase, or otherwise procure, practically every new scholarly publication, domestic and foreign, that is available. That there is a wide gap between the published output of the presses of the world and acquisition by American libraries, however, has been demonstrated by Merritt.[7]

DOMESTIC BOOKS. The procurement of domestic books for general use—the so-called regular trade books—usually presents little difficulty. The library's policy in regard to collecting determines how the appropriation will be apportioned so that each part of the collection—adult, juvenile, reference or other special units—will receive a proper share of new acquisitions.

Information concerning new books is obtained from various sources—publishers' announcements, book reviews and listings in newspapers and periodicals, and listings provided by agencies. Once the library has determined what books it will acquire, the predominant practice is to employ various agents. Among the most important of these is the local bookdealer, who is used as a rule if he provides satisfactory service. Public libraries which purchase many copies of individual titles frequently use jobbers. In some instances, libraries purchase directly from publishers. This is especially true of some publications of certain organizations or societies.

The responsibility imposed upon the librarian for the wise expenditure of funds makes it necessary for him to obtain materials at the least cost. Economy comes from wise selections based on experience and judgment, a knowledge of the collections, and the needs of the patrons; and choice of a bookdealer in whom the librarian has confidence. The latter's knowledge can supplement the librarian's knowledge but should not be a substitute for it.

The effectiveness of a bookdealer depends on his experience, his stock, his contacts with publishers, and his competence in providing reliable information promptly.

Since the book business is one involving considerable detail, the active bookdealer gradually builds up a background of experience. Thousands of titles are printed annually, many old titles go out of print, publication privileges are sold, prices change, and new editions appear. With serials, changes are likely to be even more complex. Not only must the bookdealer have knowledge of usual bibliographical data, but he must use his experience and daily contacts to keep informed of changes of all kinds.

It is also important to know about a dealer's efforts to keep materials in stock. Some of the larger dealers retain widely diversified stocks, reaching 100,000 titles or more. These dealers, through experience, have been able to judge the demand of particular titles and make regular provision to fill the needs of libraries quickly.

Dealers also have contacts with publishers. They know of publications in advance and of new editions of standard works. In New York especially, dealers are in a position to keep up with developments in the publishing world. These contacts increase the ability of the dealer to render special service to librarians.

The acquisition librarian is always concerned about the immediate filling of an order, or, if the order cannot be filled, why the material is unavailable. The reliable dealer, large or small, will equip himself to gain information concerning newly published items, to maintain records of changes in publication dates and prices, and to assist in the searching for older materials. The experienced dealer will not only provide prompt service in the handling of orders, he will also render accurate bills and answer inquiries willingly.

Many of the larger libraries have found it advisable to concentrate their orders in the hands of one dealer in order to build up a relationship of good will as well as to take advantage of the discount that comes with a large account. Moreover, it is obvious that spreading current business among a large number of dealers or ordering directly from publishers will increase the expense of acquisition work in correspondence, records, maintaining separate accounts, checking separate bills, writing more orders and checks, and handling a larger number of packages. One of the real drains on the work of the acquisition personnel is the detail involved in orders; experience has demonstrated that scattering of orders adds to the clerical routines without saving in discount or in other ways. This does not mean that an acquisition department will not use other dealers when the occasion requires it. A university library, for example, may order the bulk of its current book material through the university bookstore, but will find it necessary to purchase its older materials from a number of dealers or agents.

OLDER BOOKS. Most librarians will at some time need to acquire books which the publisher is no longer able to supply. The books have gone out of print, and the librarian usually seeks the help of secondhand bookdealers in obtaining these. What is the nature of the secondhand book market? How does it function?

The market consists of private bookdealers, usually small entrepreneurs, engaged in acquiring books from various sources and offering them for sale through the catalogs mentioned above. Generally, it has no relation to the new book market except in the case of "remainder" dealers, or in a few instances with dealers who also handle new titles.

In the United States approximately 2,000 dealers [8] are grouped into seven types: (1) general with miscellaneous stock, (2) subject specialists, (3) out-of-print specialists, (4) search specialists, or "book hunters," (5) the remainder trade, (6) textbook and schoolbook specialists, and (7) dealers combining old and new stock. These dealers carry materials in every subject field of interest to librarians and are found throughout the country, although the major concentration is in the East. The market, which is highly competitive, employs a number of individuals who are experts in the field of books, and who are highly conscious of their ability to know books and their contents.

Although the market is loosely organized, there are close relationships among dealers. This is evident in their routine for supplying books to each other in order to fill customers' requests. Their chief sources of supply appear to be auction buying and purchase of private libraries. Van Patten has described how difficult, if not impossible, it would be for a new or emerging library to build up its collections without obtaining the volumes from the book collectors. "The greater number [of out-of-print volumes] come directly from the last [book collector] in a sequence of private owners or from the stocks of dealers who have acquired them from a previous private owner."[9] In recent years, members of the trade have endeavored to organize. With headquarters in Philadelphia, the American Antiquarian Booksellers represent many of the prominent dealers of the country.

Among the services to libraries furnished by these dealers is the searching for scarce and rare books. Many dealers provide this service, but some specialize in searching, with far-flung channels of supply in this country and abroad. Their most important medium for locating books is through advertising in trade and library journals. Examples of these are the *Antiquarian Bookman*, *TAAB* [The American Antiquarian Booksellers], *Want List*, and *Thumin's List*. There is a weekly bulletin just for dealers called *The Book Trade Wants* which gives extensive listings of titles desired by various firms. *The Clique*, a publication of British antiquarian booksellers, also includes want lists of American dealers.

The individual book dealer frequently has an elaborate pattern of searching for materials. The procedure for searching and obtaining out-of-print books has been outlined by one dealer as follows:

> The diligent search for out-of-print books is one of the most interesting and stimulating tasks of the bookseller, for constant alertness and keen memories are required if the bookseller's staff is to ferret out needed titles, especially to find scholarly and other rare books. Mr. Joseph C. Borden, associate librarian of the University of Arkansas, in an article entitled

"Tapping the O.P. Market" stresses the advantages of the library that concentrates out-of-print orders with a dealer "who can give the orders more active attention than the library can give. If the librarian has a knowing and trustworthy agent he need not worry." Surveying our Out-of-Print Department, we believe we fulfill Mr. Borden's qualifications; for in addition to a well-trained staff experienced in covering the market thoroughly, we maintain a large and varied stock of several hundred thousand volumes from which many requests are filled immediately.

The hunt for an out-of-print book starts as soon as the request reaches us. It is checked against our stock and available titles are sent at once. Personal visits to bookstores bring in other books, and typewritten lists mailed to dealers in other cities locate more of them. Books not found by this time are listed in the *Antiquarian Bookman* or in *Thumin's List*, and are later included in our own want lists mailed to several hundred booksellers in the United States and abroad. Those still not located are listed in a permanent file and, after an interval of several months, are sought again in the same way.

Every possible source is sifted continually, including auction sales, the catalogs of other dealers, and trade journals listing new editions, reissues and reprints. Those books that are most rare and difficult to get (for which a number of orders usually accumulate) are often found only in a general collection or a complete library we have bought. These purchases make it possible to supply many books on old orders and to cull unusual items which otherwise might never have been found. All out-of-print books coming into the department are systematically checked against the order file, and those in demand are either supplied at once or, if the order is more than two years old, offered to the library whose order has been on file longest. If that library no longer needs the book, the next in line is notified.

Our foreign offices have similar procedures for locating foreign language out-of-prints. Like the New York staff, they are specialists in procuring out-of-print publications and assure our customers that they will cover the market completely and get a copy of any book if it is available at all.[10]

The above statement has been quoted in full because it describes many of the difficulties that are encountered in the searching for out-of-print items. In college and university libraries, which frequently are called upon by faculty members and research workers to provide older materials, the constant search for titles is part of the regular routine of the acquisition department.

Discounts on current books are generally allowed in the library book trade. There have been some observers, such as Van Patten,[11] who have suggested that libraries have not been fair with the book trade and that they should pay more rather than less for books. This point of view is not generally shared by librarians or by dealers. The usual competition among the dealers leads to discounts to libraries. This discount, of course, varies on the basis of quantity buying and the service rendered to the libraries. A library which is always buying on approval and then sending the items back will not be in a favored position with dealers; a library which constantly asks a number of dealers to obtain an item is likely to create ill feeling as well as to increase the cost of the item; the library which regularly makes errors in its orders and then requests adjustment will also make a poor impression on dealers. As the representative of the library, the acquisition librarian who frequently commits such mistakes will gradually become *persona non grata* among the personnel of the secondhand and current book trade. Librarians also may be placed in an awkward relationship if their comptroller or others who have charge of payment of bills delay consistently in clearing invoices.[12]

It would not be correct to imply that only librarians are open to criticism. Dealers come in for their share as well. Many of the complaints of librarians stem from the dealers' catalogs and practices concerning them. By far the most important contact of libraries with the secondhand market is through catalogs. These catalogs, which are distributed to libraries, vary in format and in bibliographic content. Some are excellent in both of these features, while others are obviously prepared with no consideration for library searching methods. Since dealers send their catalogs to prospective buyers other than libraries, it is perhaps unjust to criticize them for taking all sorts of liberties with entries. But librarians have long complained about the difficulties in their use. J. A. Hulbert, after studying a group of sixty catalogs, reached the following conclusions: (1) dealers should give more attention to uniformity in physical format, paper, and typography; (2) tables of contents should be supplied when straight alphabeting is not used; (3) an author index should be supplied when the catalog is a miscellany or contains numerous breaks in the alphabeting; (4) only authorized abbreviations and symbols should be used; (5) information concerning ordering, terms, discounts, and postage should be specified; and (6) simplified arrangements should be used.[13] In addition to arranging catalogs unsystematically and including insufficient data in them, dealers also have been guilty of allowing many errors to creep into the catalogs, in permitting favoritism to play an important part in the distribution of catalogs to certain institutions, of using the "prices-on-request" technique, and in including items marked "sold" in a catalog. These practices have been eliminated from the catalogs of reputable dealers, and acquisition librarians have been able to recognize them.

Checking catalogs, even in a pattern of random searching, is likely to be a laborious and time-consuming task. This is generally intensified by the large number of catalogs which reach libraries. It is a difficult job under any circumstances. In order to reduce the amount of checking, libraries frequently compile want lists and send them to one or several dealers specializing in searching. As McCarthy noted in the survey of the University of New Hampshire Library, in academic libraries this procedure may be a fruitful method for obtaining needed materials. He made the following observation:

> There is complaint from some members of the faculty that the Library's efforts to obtain out-of-print titles are not as persistent or successful as they should be. In order to improve this aspect of the library's operations it is recommended that more vigorous attention be given to it. Many libraries have found it advantageous to advertise their wants in various book-trade journals, to compile at intervals mimeographed want lists which are distributed to second hand dealers with a request for quotations, and to maintain an active desiderata file which is checked against the catalogs of second hand dealers. This type of work is far more time-consuming and difficult than purchasing new books; it is, therefore, naturally the first thing to be neglected when the staff is short and the pressure of work heavy. However, it is work which must be done, if a library is to acquire this type of material. It is the experience of most college and university libraries that they cannot serve their faculty members and students

satisfactorily without a certain amount of retrospective buying and the volume of this type of material which must be acquired increases as there is greater emphasis on graduate study and research work.[14]

The Cornell University Library follows a program for prompt checking of catalogs in order to minimize the number of failures in filling orders which are put through for out-of-print items.[15] Catalogs are dated when received by the library, and faculty members and departmental heads are given twenty-four hours to indicate items which they want the library to obtain. Quick checking and virtually complete cooperation by the faculty has resulted in raising the success in obtaining items from about fifty to ninety percent. It should be obvious, of course, that if all libraries were as efficient, the intense competition for titles would still exist. It is the resourceful library that is able to acquire materials at the present time.

FOREIGN BOOKS. The use of bookdealers in foreign countries is similar to that in the United States. However, in the procurement of foreign materials many college and university libraries also use faculty members or other representatives who are traveling or staying in European or other countries. In his annual report for the year 1948–49, Lawrence C. Powell, librarian of the University of California at Los Angeles, calls attention to the work of a faculty member in this connection:

> The most spectacular book buying of the year took place in China where Professor Richard C. Rudolph travelled on a Fulbright Fellowship. With $10,000 provided him by the Regents and the Library Committee, he has made strenuous efforts to get books out of the war-harassed country. He was among the last American citizens to leave Peking early in the fall, and as he left Canton late the next spring, the Communist armies were approaching that coastal city. Despite the difficulties of locating and buying books, of documenting his expenditures in the midst of a madly fluctuating currency, and of arranging for the safe shipment or storage of his finds, and in the face of harsh personal difficulties—Professor Rudolph managed to secure enough books to put our Chinese program on a sound footing. He was indeed of real service to the University.[16]

While other faculty members may not have had the adventure which is apparent in the book searching of Professor Rudolph, they have had varying degrees of excitement in their work for libraries. In the same report, the librarian refers to the book buying of California professors in Italy, the Philippine Islands, Spain, South America, eastern Canada, Bermuda, and Czechoslovakia. An examination of reports of other institutions reveals similar use of academic and official staff for the procurement of library materials in foreign lands.

Libraries that import ordinary books from foreign countries usually have their agents stamp the packages with the information needed for prompt customs clearance. When shipments are held up, a customs broker is sometimes used to obtain clearance. A collection of books, in contrast to a single or several volumes, generally has to go through customs before being released to the library. The Customs Simplification Act of 1953 was intended to remove the necessity for formal entry of shipments (whether by mail, freight, or express) of any value whatsoever. Purchase of books from foreign countries may be facilitated through the use of UNESCO book coupons. Some of the details of foreign acquisition have been comprehensively treated by Fall.[17]

Before leaving the question of purchasing books, some mention should be made of the practice of using standard book lists as acquisition guides. Gosnell [18] has studied this problem from the point of view of college libraries, but his findings are applicable to other libraries interested in obtaining materials as they relate to a library program.

SERIALS

A large number of dealers who handle books also stock or acquire periodicals and other serials. These materials represent important resources of libraries, particularly research libraries, and a great deal of care is usually taken in their selection, acquisition, and preservation. Some of the larger libraries have as many as 50,000 different titles represented in their serials files, while the *Union List of Serials* contains between 115,000 and 120,000 entries.

PERIODICALS. The term *periodical* refers to a publication, with a distinctive title, usually appearing unbound in successive numbers or parts at stated or regular intervals. Periodicals may be divided into general and special types. *Life*, *Time*, *Newsweek*, and *The Atlantic* are examples of the general types acquired by even the smallest libraries, while such titles as *Archiv für physikalische Chemie*, *Journal of Engineering*, and the *American Journal of Sociology* illustrate special journals which are subscribed to by the larger libraries and those institutions with research workers.

The earlier discussion concerning the policy of the library in acquiring materials is directly related to the problem of selecting periodicals. Since there are so many of these available, the librarian must exercise careful selection in building up the periodical collection. The research library will differ from the general public library or the school library in the type of periodicals to which it subscribes or which it acquires through gift and exchange. It should be remembered that acquisition always carries with it expenditures for cataloging, housing, and binding. The maintenance costs are continuous.

Selection of periodicals has been given serious attention by librarians. In *The University Library*, a summary was made of the various studies on the evaluation of periodicals.[19] These studies, based on the Gross and Gross method of checking references in journals, provide useful suggestions for procedure in the building up of periodical collections. However, as has been pointed out, this method has certain limitations in that the results depend upon the choice of the periodical or periodicals selected for checking. Librarians have used other methods to select periodicals: choosing those which have the most articles in periodical indexes and abstract journals, making selections from lists of holdings of a group of libraries, basing decisions on the opinions of subject specialists and others, and estimating value on the basis of observed use of titles.

Whatever the method of choice, it should be pointed out that periodicals change.[20] In the academic library, changes in emphasis in curricula may warrant the discontinuance of certain subscriptions and the addition of new ones. But extreme caution must be used in canceling a subscription.[21] In the public library, the changing interests of readers may make it desirable to acquire new periodical titles at the expense of others. The school library, the special library, the research library, and other types of libraries may, on the basis of developments in the publication of periodicals, revise the list of periodicals received at regular intervals.

Whatever periodical titles are selected for purchase, the librarian is faced with the responsibility of deciding how to subscribe to them. The generally accepted practice is to assign the responsibility to an agent or dealer who has had considerable experience in the handling of periodical subscriptions. The agent assumes responsibility for: (1) placing the order, (2) proper addressing of issues, (3) claiming of missing issues, and (4) notifying the library when subscriptions cease or if changes are made in the publication. Agents have instituted the procedure of ordering "until forbid," which places the library on a subscription list for a particular title until the library requests that it be removed. This automatically reduces correspondence and the cost of regularly renewing subscriptions.

Foreign periodicals are obtained in much the same way. Dealers who have contacts with publishers of foreign periodicals make arrangements for the continuous flow of issues to libraries. In some cases, the agents may be more effective than libraries in acquiring subscriptions to foreign titles. In other cases, the libraries may have to make their own contacts. The acquisition staff will have to know a number of important characteristics of foreign publications, such as the frequent method of issuance in parts and the tendency to make changes in prices.[22]

OTHER SERIALS. In addition to the task of securing scholarly periodicals, the library is confronted with the problem of obtaining other serial publications such as annuals, reports, catalogs, yearbooks, memoirs, journals and transactions of societies, and proceedings. Frequently, some of these publications are obtainable only by membership of the library in the society or organization. This is generally an approved method for the library. Other types of publications, such as yearbooks, are generally acquired through subscription on a basis similar to that for periodicals. Reports and catalogs are for the most part distributed free. Because many organizations do not maintain up-to-date mailing lists, the acquisition personnel must watch carefully for gaps which may appear in serial receipts.

DOCUMENTS

The question of policy in regard to the acquisition of documents is a highly important one. Many libraries have received documents of all kinds which are not suitable to the purposes or needs of the users.[23] Federal, state, county, municipal, and foreign documents are usually obtained through deposit or exchange relations. Libraries which have been designated as full depositories for federal documents receive publications automatically, although many titles, especially those in processed form, are not distributed. Other libraries are able to obtain documents on a selective basis. It is not as easy to acquire documents issued by the states, counties, and municipalities. All the ingenuity of acquisition personnel is required to obtain many of these items which are listed in various sources. State publications, for example, are in the *Monthly Checklist of State Publications* (issued by the Library of Congress). While there is no single place for locating county and municipal publications, the *Bulletin of the Public Affairs Information Service* (known as *PAIS*) does contain some titles. Publications of some of these agencies are also included in special lists, such as those of the Municipal Reference Library of New York, and the Municipal Reference Library of Los Angeles. United Nations documents are issued in the United States through the Columbia University Press.

Current documents cause librarians enough trouble. Locating older titles that are out of print is even more difficult. A number of dealers in Washington and New York specialize in obtaining federal documents. Other dealers may be able to locate other types of documents. The possibility of using exchanges to obtain documents should not be overlooked. It is important for the acquisition personnel to watch the serial records of their libraries and to claim promptly; otherwise, documents are unavailable. This is especially true of many processed documents which are issued in limited editions.

The acquisition of nondepository documents which are printed is a relatively simple task for libraries. Purchase of materials from the Superintendent of Documents or from an agency (such as the Library of Congress) is much the same as buying materials from other publishers or through agents. However, in the area of processed materials or unpublished research reports, it is a different matter. Jackson,[24] for example, indicates that an organization such as the National Advisory Committee for Aeronautics may get unpublished materials from as many as 2,000 different sources each year. These items include materials which may be classified as restricted, confidential, secret, top secret, or AEC (Atomic Energy Commission) restricted data. The sources include the researchers themselves or "research factories" located at colleges, universities, industrial concerns, organizations, governmental units, and similar agencies. If a library has no clearance for security publications, it can obtain the items as they are declassified or can find information about them as it appears in the *Bibliography of Technical Reports* prepared by the Office of Technical Services, Department of Commerce. Documents from OTS are available by purchase only.

DISSERTATIONS

Generally, domestic dissertations, unless they are published in book form, are unavailable to libraries except through exchange or purchase from the issuing institutions or the authors. Dealers sometimes handle these publications, but not as a rule. Dissertations on microfilm or microcard are ordinarily available for purchase. Foreign dissertations are usually offered for exchange, but a few institutions distribute them through dealers.

NEWSPAPERS

Subscriptions to newspapers are usually direct, but arrangements can be made for dealers to handle them like other serials. The question of selection is important in newspapers, not only from the point of view of use but because of the great amount of space necessary to house them and the relatively high cost of binding. It is in the area of newspapers that cooperative acquisitions programs make an impression upon librarians and administrative officials.

Large libraries, such as the New York Public Library, receive a large number of newspapers regularly. Others, like the Texas A. and M. Library, receive representative titles. Orr and Carlson write of newspapers at Texas A. and M. as follows:

> The Library now receives 45 newspapers, including representative metropolitan and regional newspapers, such as the *New York Times*, the *Washington Star*, the *Christian Science Monitor*, the *Houston Post*, the *New Orleans Times–Picayune*, the *San Francisco Examiner*, the *Atlanta Constitution*, and others. This excellent list, which includes the Argentinian paper *La Prensa*, should be maintained. The Library might well give consideration to adding to it a representative paper from the New England area (the *Christian Science Monitor* not being a regional paper), from the Rocky Mountain region and from the Pacific Northwest. The defunct *Chicago Sun* should also be replaced by a strong Chicago newspaper, perhaps the *Chicago Daily News*. An outstanding midwestern newspaper such as the *Kansas City Star* or the *Des Moines Register* might also well be added to the list.[25]

Older newspapers, of course, comprise important collections in historical society, state university, public, and research libraries. Wilson and Swank, writing of the holdings of the Stanford University Library, make the following observation:

> The Library has recently acquired all the duplicate colonial and early American newspapers belonging to the American Antiquarian Society, Worcester, Massachusetts. The collection consists of 104 long files and in excess of 10,000 scattered issues of other papers.[26]

Among the more important files are runs of the *Boston News-Letter*, *Independent Chronicle*, *Pennsylvania Packet*, *Boston Daily Advertiser*, and *Liberator*.

Within the last few years, more and more newspapers have become available on microfilm.[27] The use of microfilm results in considerable savings in stack space and binding costs, and the handling of perishable pulp newspapers can be avoided.

MAPS

While the Division of Maps of the Library of Congress has about 2,000,000 maps and atlases, the University of Chicago Library approximately 140,000 maps, and the American Geographical Society Library over 200,000 maps, most general libraries and college libraries will not collect maps on such a grand scale. Many of the larger libraries, such as the New York Public Library, the libraries of Columbia University, Cornell University, Harvard University, and Yale University have developed relatively large map collections. The accent on map use during World War II added to the importance of these resources, and because of the demands libraries have become interested in collecting and preserving not only geographical and physical maps, but military, meteorological, industrial, petroleum, agricultural, and other types of maps as well.

Espenshade [28] has recently described some of the problems of acquiring maps:

> Unfortunately, the acquisition of maps poses certain special problems to librarians, making them more difficult to obtain than books. In the first place, we lack established bibliographic aids, corresponding to cumulative book lists and lists of current book publications. There is no single guide to maps already issued or to new maps being published. Most maps are published outside the United States. Information about material published in foreign countries is always more difficult to obtain. Purchase of such materials accordingly presents further difficulties.[29]

Espenshade, after pointing out that language does not provide a particular barrier to the use of maps, indicates that two other problems relating to acquisition of maps are the greater number of sources, as compared to books, and their "fugitive" character. In the first instance, the sources are complicated by the peculiar relationships of printers, publishers, and issuing agencies; in the latter case, the governmental aspect of map making and the serial nature of maps add to the confusion.

Yonge [30] has pointed out the need to maintain an effective program of map acquisition; otherwise, the value of the map collection declines quickly. She lists the various sources for the selection of maps and atlases as follows: (1) publishers' catalogs, including those of three major federal map-making agencies (topographic, geologic, and hydrographic), and those of foreign and domestic commercial map publishers, (2) foreign and domestic periodicals issued by geographical, geological, historical, and archeological societies, (3) the *Catalog of Copyright Entries* listing maps, published by the Copyright Office, Library of Congress, and (4) miscellaneous sources, such as parts of books and periodicals, reports of proceedings of professional groups, exhibits, bibliographical compilations of other map libraries, and maps issued by various commercial, industrial, and technical services (oil and gas companies, airlines, etc.). De Wald [31] has further suggestions for procurement of maps by government agencies. These include official and civilian mapping agencies as well as other sources indicated by Yonge.

MUSIC

Until recent years few libraries had music collections of any real importance. Recently, however, both public and academic libraries have been concerned about the collecting of musical and other recordings (tape, wire, and disc). The so-called "audio-visual" programs of libraries have been somewhat hampered by the lack of a clear definition of policy. Typical of this situation is the one at Stanford as described by the surveyors:

> Audio-visual materials . . . have been acquired less extensively [than micro-films]. A faculty committee on audio-visual materials has recently been appointed to study the best methods of handling these materials, but no report had been made when the surveyors were at Stanford. The opinion previously held by the departments, however, was that such materials should be serviced entirely apart from the library. In this respect, the opinion is quite different from that of some universities that have centralized the production, housing and servicing of both types of materials in a special library department or in different departments within a library.[32]

Lyle [33] has called attention to a similar problem in college libraries. Public libraries, which have been collecting music and records for longer periods of time, have not been faced with the same problems of organization.

The need for a definite policy in collecting music and related materials should be apparent. They are relatively expensive items and require considerable attention in both organization and preservation. The Music Library Association *Notes*, published quarterly, is a mine of information on music, new publications about music, recordings, and other topics of interest to librarians maintaining music collections. Any library collecting music and recordings, of course, will need to provide adequate quarters and apparatus for listening.

PHOTOGRAPHIC MATERIALS

Reference has already been made to newspapers which are on microfilm. Other materials are also available in this form. The *Union List of Microfilms* contains about 25,000 entries, all of which have been checked against some authoritative bibliographical tool. Entries have been supplied by 197 libraries, and the information includes location of both positive and negative films, as well as originals, when available. Thus, the order librarian is in a position to obtain copies in many instances.

Microcards are becoming more and more common in libraries. The Microcard Foundation, in Middletown, Connecticut, issues the *Microcard Bulletin*, which contains listings of titles available on microcards.

Filmstrips, microprint, motion pictures, newsreels, and stills are other photographic materials which libraries may at times acquire. Filmstrips are being issued by various concerns, including publishers of periodicals, and are useful as teaching aids in schools and colleges particularly. The libraries may be responsible for acquiring and preserving such items. Microprint has been developing gradually and it is likely that this method of reproduction may expand in the future.

v. Operations in Order Work

THE various types of library materials and the sources from which they are acquired have been discussed, and the place of the bookdealer in the acquisition program has been described in some detail. However, knowledge of materials and of potential dealers alone will not insure the proper and effective operation of an order unit of an acquisition department. It is necessary, in addition, to deal with the technical operations for order work and with the records, forms, and tools which facilitate these operations.

MAJOR OPERATIONS

The operations involved in the ordering of a book have been fairly well standardized in the efficient library. These may be broken down into six categories: (a) preliminary activities concerned with the order card, (b) checking and searching, (c) bibliographical preparation, (d) placement of orders, (e) receiving, billing, and distribution, and (f) claiming and canceling. Shipping problems are also involved in the return of materials and in exchange programs.

PRELIMINARY ACTIVITIES. In the public library or in the academic library, the usual procedure in ordering a title is to work with a request card submitted by a staff member or by some other interested individual. For this purpose most libraries use standard order forms obtained from commercial library supply houses or printed by the libraries. If subsequent operations are to proceed efficiently, it is important that these request cards be made up completely and in proper form.

The cards usually provide for the following information: author, title, edition, volume (if serial), publisher, date of publication, price, account or fund being used for payment, code number (if a code is used), and the name of the person recommending the book. Most acquisition departments insist, although they may not always obtain complete cooperation in this respect, that individuals filling in these cards provide all information available. This procedure not only may eliminate rechecking details, but also makes it possible for the acquisition personnel to search more easily and reach a decision more quickly concerning the request. As pointed out earlier, the acquisition department works closely with the cataloging staff, and in so far as the acquisition personnel can provide any of this preliminary information which may later be useful to the catalogers, they should do so. Those who need to search booksellers' catalogs and lists, trade and special bibliographies, and the many and various special sources in order to prepare order cards properly for the acquisition department know that a uniform procedure is necessary if the work is to be done advantageously and inexpensively. The quality and speed of the searchers' work is affected by factors such as the physical layout of the building, the nature and number of records that have to be searched, the extent of the bibliographical collection, the ability of the catalogers to keep up with current accessions, the availability of in-process files, and the general competence of the searchers.

Searching involves working from dealers' or other lists, as well as from title pages themselves. In working from lists, each library will try to standardize the searching technique so that the operations will be efficient. It is not always possible to rely upon the checking done by professors, their secretaries or assistants, or students who are interested in having a college or university library order certain materials. Although in many cases the entry for an item will be immediately clear, at other times the searcher must check any and all possible forms in order to establish what may be the correct entry before reporting to the acquisition department that the library owns or lacks the item. When an item is identified according to a reliable authority, that entry should be given in full in the proper place on the card, and to save time later, the symbol or symbols which stand for the name of the authority also should appear in readable form on the request card. If the checking is done directly from the dealer's catalog or list, this symbol and related notes should appear so that the assistant who types the cards from the list will be able properly to present the essential data on the order card. A title may be unnecessarily shortened, or it may be garbled or misspelled, and the searcher will clarify this for the typist.

To illustrate how a searcher might mark the request card which has been presented satisfactorily, reference may be made to some of the notations which may be used to indicate the checking operation. Libraries will vary in their abbreviations of reference sources checked in search of entries, but those included in the *Cooperative Cataloging Manual* [1] of the Descriptive Cataloging Division of the Library of Congress would serve the acquisition personnel as effectively as they serve the catalogers. Thus, "Medina" may represent J. T. Medina's *Biblioteca-Hispano-Americanica* (1493–1810), 1898–1907, or "BM" the *Catalogue of Printed Books* of the British Museum. There are a number of trade bibliographies, such as the *Publishers' Trade List Annual* (*PTLA*) which will be used more frequently than the reference sources searched by catalogers.

The acquisition searchers have a notational system which is similar in some respects to the records made by the catalogers in their establishing of authority cards. A check (√) after a source means that the item was identified there; any additional information should appear if it is necessary to the handling of the book. A zero (o) after a source indicates that the item was not verified in the work cited. The record of such searches will eliminate unnecessary rechecking.

In some of the larger libraries, where checking is done in catalogs and lists, the time consumed in arranging the material is likely to be considerable. The U.S. Department of Agriculture Library has sought to solve this problem by photostating citations on 3″ x 5″ slips and alphabetizing them to facilitate searching, culling of duplicate citations, and addition of notes for order typing.

BIBLIOGRAPHICAL PREPARATION. After the searcher has found the necessary information for ordering the item requested, the card or marked dealer's catalog is sent to the staff member of the acquisition department who has the authority to approve orders. Once the approval is given, the material is turned over to the typist for preparation for the bookdealer or agent.

In recent years, many libraries have been using multiple or correlated order forms. These vary according to the library, but almost all include an original dealer's slip, an outstanding order record, a Library of Congress card order slip, and usually a comptroller's copy or fund record. Although more complicated than those used in smaller libraries, the forms and operations involved in the Columbia University Libraries' system will be described:

> The instructions below were developed for the handling of the eight correlated order forms which are now being used in the Acquisition Department for purchasing materials from bookdealers. Departmental librarians can cooperate in making the new procedures work effectively by filling out order cards completely. This requires that departmental librarians examine all order cards for correct form of entry, full title, imprint, edition, price, number of volumes or separate volumes wanted, etc. It is more important than ever that the entry be correct and full, since the forms are to be used in cataloging procedures.
>
> Form 1: Record Copy
>
> 1. The Record Copy is designed to replace the present sheet which goes into the Order Book retained in the Acquisition Department. This form comes in strips of four. The plan is to include 500 of these strips of four in a volume consisting of 2,000 orders. Note that each item has a separate order number.
> 2. The last line of this form contains space for insertion of "Date received," "Cost," and "Date of Bill." These are entered when the material and bill arrive; see also forms 4, 5, and 7.
> 3. CCA refers to "Checked Catalog Annotation" (dealers' catalog). If checked, it indicates there is information in the secondhand dealer's catalog useful to the cataloger.
>
> Form 2: Controller's Copy
>
> 1. These are also issued in strips of four items. They are to be sent to the Controller in the same way that we now send the Controller's copy.

2. The Controller will place the information on the punched cards, and will file the sheets numerically.

Form 3: Original Purchase Order

1. The Original Purchase Order goes to the dealer; directions for filling the order are on the back of each slip. It is advisable for the typist to keep together all slips going to a particular dealer. It is further suggested that mimeographed envelopes be available for dealers which are used constantly.
2. Although forms 1 and 2 cannot be detached until four items are typed, it is possible to remove the slips from 3–8 without difficulty if done in sequence. While it is probably convenient to rip off four at a time, it is not necessary to withhold ordering a single item until four are typed.
3. Form 8, a dealer's report form, is sent with the original order to the dealer.

Form 4: Outstanding Order Record

1. This buff-colored form follows the Original Purchase Order form. It is to be kept in the order processing file, together with form 6 (rider and information slip) and form 7 (claim). See explanations under each of these forms for related directions.
2. Date of receipt stamped.
3. After item is received, a card is replaced in order processing file.
4. Order card for items received have corner note removed to allow for punched card sorting for an entire year's receipts.

Form 5: Departmental Copy

1. The departmental copy is sent to the departmental or school library placing the order. These may be used as temporary slips by the library. They should be matched with any duplicate slips made by the ordering library so that entries will be uniform.

Form 6: Rider Copy—Order Information Service

1. All Rider copies are to be placed in the Order Processing File along with the Outstanding Order slip until the books arrive.
2. When a book arrives the Book and Rider Copy are sent to the Cataloging Department.
3. The Cataloging Department sends book to Labeler, Rider stays with cards until card work is completed. The department housing the book sends Rider or Order Information Service to faculty member ordering the title.

Form 7: Claim Copy

1. If the book is not received after appropriate period, use Claim Copy to dealer.
2. If the book is obtained, form 8 is returned.

Form 8: Dealer's Report Slip

1. This slip is returned by the dealer with the item ordered.
2. If the item is unavailable or requires further consideration because of format, etc., the report is made on this slip by the dealer.[2]

Columbia has not included a Library of Congress card order slip, because it was found that the Library of Congress could not furnish enough cards to warrant including it. Other libraries, however, have found such a slip useful.

The fan-fold or multiple order form has been used as an effective order device in the larger libraries. Nevertheless, in certain circumstances a list type of order will prove to be better suited, as in the case of blanket orders, Farmington Plan orders, and "locate and quote" lists.

PLACEMENT OF ORDERS. Stipulations which the library makes in its orders are usually printed on the back of the original order slip (if multiple forms are used), or on the letter forms which are frequently sent to dealers. If bids are involved, specific directions for procedure are included. Generally, before preparing the orders, the typist sorts them by dealer so that all items going to a particular agent are kept together. After the typing, the forms are separated and distributed. Copies of the orders are filed in the outstanding order file to await receipt of the materials.

RECEIVING OF ORDERS. An acquisition department, if active, receives materials daily. The department may work closely with a shipping and receiving room, and preliminary sorting of material may relieve the acquisition personnel considerably. Books, periodicals, other serials, microfilms, music, maps, and other items need to be carefully examined on the basis of orders placed. Not infrequently libraries are sent materials destined for other institutions. Errors occur in editions, volumes, and titles.

If the materials are the items ordered by the library, the operations are fairly direct and simple. The order cards are pulled from the outstanding order file and compared with the items received. The order is compared with the bill and the bill is prepared for approval. If a multiple form has been used and one of these is for the permanent order record, the copy of the order is written up in the order book, with receipt date, the bill date, and the cost. The order card is then filed in the "received file." A copy of the bill is sent to the comptroller for payment [3] and another copy filed in the bill record. The materials are then ready to be sent to the cataloging department or other unit of the library.

The work with serials and documents acquisitions may require separate handling in the receiving department. Usually a serials division handles these materials with required separate records (official and unofficial). Serials also involve considerable activity in claiming missing issues, clearing serial bills for payment, and ordering serial replacements. The searching and verification of new serial orders and document orders may well be done by an individual who is not responsible for the book orders.

CLAIMING AND CANCELING. The acquisition department usually is required to follow up on orders which have not been filled after an appropriate period. As a rule, dealers inform libraries of their inability to fill orders. It is necessary, however, to keep a watch over the outstanding order file, and to clear dead wood from it after a reasonable period of time. Correspondence with dealers may be needed in order to clarify certain situations in regard to orders. Sometimes the library will receive materials without the bill or bills without the materials. It is essential that these discrepancies be cleared as soon as possible.

For one reason or another, the library may wish to cancel an order. It is important that this be done as soon as possible, and telephone cancellations should be followed by a written directive. The cancellation operation may be relatively complicated in a library which has its basic bookkeeping records in a comptroller's office, but forms can be worked out which speed up the work. Since the library usually works on a close book budget, cancellations must be registered if the full balance of the budget is to appear in the reports from the financial office. Cancellations must also be made in the order book which the library maintains.

SHIPPING. The library is frequently a sending agency as well as a receiving one. Books are returned to dealers because of errors, because they are not wanted (having been sent on approval), or because of imperfections or mutilation. Libraries may sell certain duplicate or unwanted items to dealers. In exchange programs, there is a constant stream of materials—new publications, duplicates, discards—to other libraries. The shipping operations require an efficient organization if materials are to be sent out promptly and accurately. In the long run it is economical to allow the shipping room to have standard equipment—corrugated paper, rope rolls, adhesive paper, wrapping paper on rolls, paper cutter, wire cutter, proper envelopes, typewriter—so that the work may be done expeditiously and neatly.

RECORDS

Mention has been made of several of the records in the department. Although it is important for the acquisition department to have sufficient and accurate records, it is also important to recognize that it is easy to build up unnecessary ones. Among the common records which are found in the acquisition department are the order record, outstanding order file, continuations file, serials file, periodical file, desiderata file, orders received or in-process file, financial records, correspondence and general records, and a file of dealers' and publishers' catalogs.

ORDER RECORD. The practice in maintaining an order record varies in libraries. Some libraries which maintain the old-style accession book allow this to stand as the order record as well as a record of gifts and exchanges acquired. Libraries using the multiple form system may single out one of the forms for this record. Since the orders are numbered in sequence, it is easy to locate a particular item for any purpose. Usually these are later bound into a permanent order book.

OUTSTANDING ORDER FILE. The outstanding order file is one of the most important records of the acquisition department. It is the file which tells exactly what the library has on order; it is an active file which is used constantly by everyone interested in knowing the status of the orders in the department. In a few libraries, the outstanding order file may be combined with other files, such as items advertised for or desiderata.

In one large university library, orders received are filed together with outstanding orders. Punches on the right side of the card are made to allow for sorting out of a year's receipts of items. It is important that the arrangement of cards in the outstanding order file be done carefully, or unintentional duplication of orders will result. It is also necessary to weed items from this file when orders have been canceled or have not been received after long periods of time. This is especially true of foreign orders, since some dealers in other countries are not as likely to inform libraries of inability to send items as are American dealers.

CONTINUATIONS FILE. In some libraries, the continuations (items which are issued in parts and are expected to be completed) are filed in with the outstanding orders. In other libraries, especially in research libraries, the relatively large number of continuations may make it desirable to maintain a separate file. This facilitates searching, claiming, and billing.

SERIALS FILE AND PERIODICALS FILE. Since serials present problems which are not involved in book orders, many libraries maintain a separate serials file. A number of libraries have placed this file on visible records which are available from the several library supply houses.[4] Form cards are used for checking in issues.

While most serial records in libraries are of the usual 3″ x 5″ catalog card size [5] or the 5″ x 8″ visible file size, punched cards have also been used for this purpose. At the University of Texas Library, the following information is punched on the cards:

1. Title. The title is abbreviated to forty-three letters and spaces because of the printing limitations of the tabulator.
2. Expiration date or volume number. The expiration date is preferable if the subscription can be so placed. Expiration date cards can be reproduced automatically for the following year, while volume numbers must be punched manually in the next year's card.
3. Department benefited.
4. Account charged. Departmental or general library account.
5. Source. The dealer employed or other source.
6. Country of publication.
7. Location in the library (periodical reading room, chemistry library, etc.).[6]

The cards are arranged in alphabetical order after they have been punched. As the invoices are paid, subscription costs and binding costs are posted on the cards in handwriting. The posted costs are punched in each card at the close of the fiscal year. Moffit has indicated that after the cards have once been prepared, they can be automatically reproduced for the following year's record at a rate of from 80 to 100 cards per minute.

The use of the punched cards for analysis of the account, the preparation of bidding lists and renewal orders, and the printing of a union list of serials and continuations has also been instrumental in the adaptation of the procedure for acquisitions work. Used solely as a financial record, it may not be an economical method.

In addition to the card files in the conventional catalog drawer, the visible record, and the punched card record, serial files have also been put on cards mounted on a circular drum. Among the features claimed for the rotary file are that it makes possible faster finding, rapid posting, and easy adding of items, and has extra large capacity, is lower in cost, requires less floor space, is the height of a desk, causes no fatigue or eye strain, has no drawers or slides to open or close, is portable, and has removable segments.

DESIDERATA FILE. It is common practice for libraries to maintain desiderata files, which are records of items subject to possible acquisition in the future. It may be worth while here to refer to a recent study by Lena Biancardo,[7] in which an effort was made to determine the incidence, nature, and use of desiderata catalogs in college and university libraries.

Biancardo gathered data from 68 college and university libraries, ranging in size from a few thousand volumes to over two million volumes. She found that librarians identified their desiderata files by various names: desiderata file, want list, want file, wanted, out-of-print file, out-of-print orders, hold file, and quotation file. She also found that the files were made up in various ways: unfilled order slips, scratch cards (usually submitted by faculty members), publishers' cards (e.g., Macmillan library cards), Library of Congress printed cards or proof-sheet cards, and clipped titles mounted on cards. The files ranged in size from about 500 to 50,000 entries. They included not only items which libraries were unsuccessful in acquiring through dealers, but also desired items not purchased because of lack of funds, titles of secondary importance, out-of-print books, unavailable foreign books, titles which would be acceptable if they could be obtained as gifts, titles of books borrowed for the library's clientele, and rare items.

The files were also arranged in several ways. The kind of arrangement, of course, will be linked with the major purpose of the file. Such factors as the size of the file, the searching procedure of the library, book budget practices, and relations with bookdealers may also influence the arrangement adopted. While a single alphabetical file, including all the types of entries referred to above, may be convenient and may solve filing and searching problems, it lacks a subject approach. As Biancardo points out, "An arrangement by subject will focus attention on major weaknesses in the collection, be useful in apportioning departmental book funds, make the re-evaluation of titles easier to undertake, and be a great aid when a donation is given for books in a specific field." Searching in such a file, however, will be more time-consuming than in an alphabetical file. The use of marginal punched cards to take care of a subject approach to an alphabetical file is a practical application.

Other arrangements which might be useful for particular purposes include filing by (1) priority of purchase, (2) college departments, and (3) language. The latter arrangement may be of some help in ordering from bookdealers who arrange their stock or catalogs by language.

The most common items in the desiderata files were out-of-print books. However, the fact that libraries have used their files for several purposes has sometimes been an obstacle in pursuing such items. Some librarians have made it a practice to have bookdealers come in and examine their files in order that the dealers might have an idea of what the desired items are. Other librarians have copied portions of their files and submitted them to dealers for searching. Usually only one dealer is approached at a time so as to avoid raising of prices.

The files should be revised periodically and items no longer wanted should be eliminated. In academic institutions, faculty members frequently change their minds about titles they order, especially if there is a lapse of several years between initiation of the order and availability of the material. In public libraries, too, items which have been placed in the desiderata file may have been superseded by new titles or new editions. Desiderata files, which can be active instruments in building up collections, must not be allowed to fall into the state described by Christ:

> In general, the libraries scan the dealers' catalogs and try one or two of the above methods [for obtaining out-of-print materials], then the title goes into a non-active desiderata file, where it may remain indefinitely . . . Most of the librarians explained that the cards "just stay there" although two or three have recently revised their desiderata files by referring all titles back to the original requestors for advice. . . . If desiderata files were thus cleared annually, the urgent and important titles would undoubtedly be reduced to a workable number which might then be sought more persistently and with a greater degree of success.[8]

ORDERS RECEIVED OR IN-PROCESS FILES. It is necessary to maintain a record of items received and to know where they are during the period before cataloging and final placement on the shelves. For this, libraries have developed an orders received file, which consists of cards on which are noted the date of receipt of the items, the price, and other relevant information. Usually the outstanding order card is removed, the information is placed on it, and then it is filed into the orders received record. If a book record is kept, the information may be placed on the item in that record.

The in-process file is likely to be a more extensive record, including not only purchased items but also those received on gift and exchange. While the in-process file may be a cataloging department record, in some libraries it is maintained by the acquisition department. Chamberlain [9] and Dewey [10] have discussed this record from the point of view of the cataloging department. Further consideration of this record is included in Chapter XII.

PUBLISHERS' CATALOGS AND DEALERS' CATALOGS. Some acquisition or other library departments maintain files of publishers' and dealers' catalogs.[11] Whether or not a library will maintain such files depends on the use to which these records are likely to be put. Usually, they are kept in alphabetical order by name of dealer or publisher.

DEALERS' CORRESPONDENCE FILE. Every acquisition department carries on correspondence with dealers. In order to be able to produce relevant materials quickly, order librarians generally maintain a file of correspondence, ordinarily arranged in vertical file cabinets by name of dealer. It is important to weed these files periodically in order to facilitate checking for particular pieces of information.

MEASURING PERFORMANCE

It is frequently desirable to measure the achievement of the acquisition department. The studies of Pierce [12] in acquisition performance provide a useful basis for evaluation in that they isolate the activities which are common to acquisition departments of public libraries. Among the measures that were used by Christ [13] in his study of acquisition work in college libraries were the following:

1. Time lags
   a. From receipt of recommendation to placing of order
   b. From placing of order to receipt of book
   c. From receipt of book to completion of acquisition process

2. Discounts received (on current domestic publications)
3. Bibliographical accuracy
   a. Number of unintentional duplicates received
   b. Number of incorrect items received
   c. Number of items rejected by dealers as not identifiable
4. Percentage of successful orders from dealers' catalogs
5. Number of titles and volumes purchased or otherwise processed
6. Expenditure for books

Christ observed that it was not possible to make comparisons between libraries because most did not keep statistics on these factors. The criteria, however, should be suggestive to administrators who wish to test the efficiency of their acquisition departments. Much time, for example, can be spent on placing orders obtained from listings in dealers' catalogs without actually procuring a large proportion of the volumes.

FORMS

Attention has already been called to various forms which are used in acquisitional operations. Most of the library supply houses have available standard order forms, library purchase records, cards for serial checking, document checking cards, and accession sheets. The development of forms was singled out by Morris as an important technique in improving acquisition routines.[14] At the New York Public Library, efforts were made to study carefully the appropriate forms, not only for serial records, but also for orders, gift requests and follow-up letters, and other activities.

Sweet [15] has recently summarized comprehensively the problems in the development of proper forms, particularly in relation to large libraries. The sample forms which are included in Sweet's article should be suggestive to acquisition librarians who have not realized how redesigning can result in economy and acceleration of work. Even in the small library the use of proper forms may make it possible to accomplish more work with less personnel.

The application of the "Photoclerk" [16] should also be noted in connection with forms. The experiments with this machine have demonstrated that it can be used not only in acquisition but in many other library operations as well.

Multiple forms are usually designed for specific libraries. In developing multiple forms it is essential that the librarian consider carefully every use that can be made of the slips which are to be included. It is easy to suggest another slip for a particular purpose, but it is necessary to examine its usefulness in terms of costs. The extensive multiple form of the Columbia University Libraries described earlier in this chapter would hardly do for many public and college libraries.

Another aspect which requires caution is the planning of the forms. Usually the library supply houses and business-form companies will assist the librarian in designing forms so that the space available will be used efficiently.

TOOLS TO FACILITATE ORDER OPERATIONS

Since the acquisition department is engaged for the most part in standard business operations, the librarian will assemble, in addition to any forms needed for records, the tools and equipment which will expedite the work. Such equipment as electric typewriters for multiple forms, correspondence and card cabinets, visible checking records, tables for sorting, shelves for storing and routing received materials, and efficiently designed desks and chairs are necessary for effective performance. Library equipment firms are qualified to assist librarians in the selection of furniture appropriate to the space limitations and purposes of the department.

Another important adjunct to the acquisition department is a collection of bibliographic and other reference tools which are constantly being consulted for information concerning publications.[17] In addition to the files of publishers' and dealers' catalogs, noted above, the acquisition department personnel will need ready access to national book trade bibliographies, which are generally arranged chronologically under country, auction bibliographies, and miscellaneous reference tools, such as directories.[18]

VI. Gifts and Deposits

LESTER CONDIT, in his booklet entitled *A Pamphlet about Pamphlets* [1] wrote that "The collector who is too proud to beg for pamphlets may be passing up excellent opportunities to secure for little or nothing what sooner or later may not be obtained for any price." Any librarian who has worked with scholars engaged in research will immediately realize the truth of this statement. While Condit was referring specifically to pamphlets, the concept may be justifiably broadened to include books, serials, and other materials. The problem of gifts and exchanges in libraries has been one of growing importance to administrators. It is obviously not possible for most libraries to purchase all items they need for their clienteles. Through gift and exchange, some of these items may be obtained. Other titles are sometimes available only through requests for free copies or through an exchange relationship.

EXTENT OF WORK

Many of the older libraries of the country have been built up to their present great proportions through the continual flow of gifts. The tradition of Carnegie and others who have viewed libraries as significant social institutions which could use to their advantage all the aid they might obtain has been of direct assistance to libraries in their struggles to build up their collections. Millions of dollars have been given to libraries in the form of books, money, and other support.

In the *Annual Report of the Librarian of Congress for the Fiscal Year Ending June 30, 1953*, the following statement is made:

More than twice as many gifts, exclusive of manuscripts, were received in fiscal 1953 as in fiscal 1952—a year that marked an all-time high—332,000 items as compared with 152,000. Manuscripts, some 680,000 of which were given to the Library in 1953, and such materials as unbound newspapers received as gifts from publishers are not included in these figures.[2]

While no other library receives quantities of materials as gifts that match those of the Library of Congress, the solicitation and receipt of gifts has become an important activity in many institutions. While the smaller public library may not campaign actively for gifts of books and periodicals, there is usually an understanding in the community that certain types of material will be welcomed by the library staff. This is true despite the fact that much material that is not useful is frequently presented to the library.

The story of gifts to libraries is a long and inspirational one.[3] Yale University Library, long a repository of gifts by interested collectors, friends, faculty members, students, and others, reported the following receipts for 1948–49:

We received 18,184 books, 12,566 pamphlets, and 26,268 serials as gifts. Duplicate books numbered 10,030, and 8,154 were sent to the catalogers. Of the duplicates, 2,562 were selected and added to the college, school, and departmental libraries; 2,112 were donated to other institutions throughout the world; and many of the remainder were sold for a total of $3,075.45 which was credited to our book fund . . .

The Yale Library Associates continue to support the library liberally. Besides books and manuscripts the Associates contributed $20,115.10 in unrestricted funds for immediate expenditure.[4]

In addition to numerous gift additions to existing book funds, Yale also received three new book funds totaling $21,518.02. In 1952–53 the Yale libraries received 17,711 books and pamphlets and 11,112 serials through gift, as well as important additions to seven existing funds.[5]

These two examples may suffice to indicate the extent of gift programs in libraries. While the larger libraries remain magnets for extensive collections which constantly add to their wealth, the smaller libraries also are the recipients of these important donations.

Whether the gifts are the papers of a Boswell or a Jefferson, or merely a few titles of fiction, the act of giving requires the librarian to provide machinery for receipt, record, and preservation.

POLICY

Despite the problems that gift-making and active solicitation have raised for librarians and their institutions in the past, there has been no real systematic study of the effect upon libraries of gift materials. The literature reveals scattered statistics, notices and descriptions of various kinds of gifts to libraries, their origins and sources, how to solicit, and the importance of making due and appropriate acknowledgment of them. There have also been articles about book collectors, collecting, and special collections.

Among the recent articles concerning gifts have been comments regarding the need for a policy in accepting gifts. The time is long past when the efficient librarian will accept anything which is offered. It is well known that the acceptance of a gift will sometimes create internal problems within the library. Stipulations by the donor may negate the value of the gift to the institution. Frequently a donor may offer a gift which the librarian knows with a great degree of certainty will duplicate the library's holdings. There then arises the question of the cost of handling these duplicates and their relative value as added copies, replacements, or materials for exchange. It is important, however, to know just when to reject a gift. The treatment may be different for each case as it arises. The position of the donor and his past and possible future relation to the library should be taken into consideration. A wise donor, however, will discuss these matters with the librarian and will accept his decision when it appears to be more logical to place the materials in another institution.

The factors which arise in the acceptance of a gift include (1) the nature of the gift collection, (2) the restrictions placed upon the gift in its handling, (3) the effects of the gift upon the technical services of the library, (4) the restrictions placed upon the gift in regard to physical accommodations, (5) the limitations which may be placed upon the use of the materials, and (6) maintenance cost.

The policy of the library ordinarily should prevent the acceptance of a gift which bears little or no relation to the book collections of the library or the purposes of a library. A college library would have no use for a run of geological reports if they could not be used in connection with courses in the institution. A public library would normally have little use for a specialized collection on the history of mathematics, while it would be an unusual special library in science which would accept a collection of Dickens or Beowulf.

The librarian, however, must keep in mind the long-range view of the library. A college or university library, for example, might well have need for a particular collection if there are related courses given at present and if there is a likelihood that special courses may be given in the future. This foresight is difficult to exercise, but many of the important institutions have been able to develop instructional and research programs as a result of care in obtaining collections either through purchase or gift. Similarly, the public library has an obligation to obtain materials which may have some relation to developments in the community.

The librarian will also need to consider any restrictions that are placed upon the gift in regard to its handling. Gifts are most desirable if the librarian is allowed to determine whether items in a gift collection should be integrated, discarded, sold, or exchanged. The librarian in charge of gifts should be sure he understands any stipulations made in the acceptance of a collection. Some collectors have been discouraged to find that a library has disposed of their items when they had assumed that the materials would be incorporated into the collections of the institution. The results of such action on the part of the librarian may well be disastrous so far as the future relations with the particular donors are concerned.

Another matter which requires the consideration of the librarian is the possible effect of a gift upon the technical services of the library. This is especially true in a library that has limited staff and has not even been able to keep pace with its acquisitions. Does the donor stipulate special cataloging and classification? Does he insist upon a printed catalog? Few donors have been thoughtful to the extent of providing a fund for the technical handling of the collection. The librarian may well raise the question with understanding donors or at least be aware of the technical implications of a gift. Many gift collections, because of technical complications, have remained stored and useless.

An example of foresight in this connection may be cited. The Yale Library's Coe Collection of Western Americana, about 7,000 items, is said to be "the finest collection of western material in existence, and the finest undoubtedly that will ever be formed. William Robertson Coe began it in 1910, at the suggestion of an impecunious small collector of western books, who recognized the desirability of the formation of a library of Western Americana while early material was still available." [6] Coe not only gave his treasure to the Library, but followed it up with a gift of $7,000, of which $1,800 was "to defray the cost of printing the October, 1949, *Gazette*, which was devoted entirely to a description of the collection. The balance of the money is to be used to defray costs of cataloging this material." [7]

Not infrequently donors will suggest that a collection be given special accommodations. This not only raises a question of space, but also of special catalogs and classification and personnel. A wise librarian will endeavor to remove such stipulations unless the collection actually is of such merit that special housing is generally desirable. As a rule, libraries provide special bookplates which indicate the source of gifts.

Less often there may be restrictions on the use of materials. In the case of special materials which are confidential, such as unreleased papers, this stipulation may be of a temporary nature and would not be a reason for refusal. Gifts which are presented with restrictions against use by certain patrons, however, should be carefully weighed. Rarities, of course, should be protected against abuse by unqualified users, and the librarian would want to impose such restrictions even if they were not made by the donors.

The cost of maintaining a gift is always a factor that should be given attention by the librarian. Special housing or handling will, of course, introduce extra costs. The cost of keeping the collection up to date also should be considered in connection with the purposes of the library. If a special collection of potential minimal use required the diversion of funds from more essential functions of the library, it would represent an appropriate reason for nonacceptance.

SOURCES

Sources of gifts are as limitless as the number of collectors and public benefactors. Many items drift into libraries without any request on the part of the library staffs. Many more are obtained through deliberate solicitation developed from a systematic program. A number of minor publications that can be secured free are listed in *Publishers' Weekly*, *Bulletin of the Public Affairs Information Service*, and H. W. Wilson Company's *Vertical File Service*, *Pamphlet Index*, and library publications. Then there are sample or complimentary copies from authors and publishers; publications and duplicates from other libraries; and books and periodicals from homes of interested citizens, local organizations and clubs, various institutions, scientific and learned societies, governments (domestic and foreign), individual private collectors, philanthropists, and foundations. Academic libraries also acquire materials from faculty members and administrative officers, trustees, alumni, students, and "friends of the library" groups.

The individual librarian's approach in obtaining gifts is described by Thompson.[8] He writes: "There are two keys to successful begging: boldness, tempered by respectful courtesy, and a thorough knowledge of the higher realms of the world of books and the denizens who haunt it." Thompson thus stresses the essential need of librarians to know books and their collectors. He also points up the librarian's obligation to acquire materials, particularly archival items, which are related to the locality and purposes of the institution of which the library is a part.

It has been only in recent years that libraries as a group have tried to obtain gifts systematically through groups of friends or associates. Most of the major libraries, however, have had important gifts come in unsolicited. This is especially true of those libraries which have established reputations for careful handling of gift collections. The genuine bibliophile is anxious that the care he has taken in gathering a collection will be continued. Many libraries have been by-passed because of the insecurity that prospective donors feel about the potential handling their materials will receive.

The late Edward Caldwell, a trustee of Knox College for twenty-six years and long a benefactor of that institution's library, recently gave it a collection of 4,000 volumes relating to the history of the Northwest Territory. The donor was president of the McGraw-Hill Book Company and a noted bibliophile. Of this gift, Van Patten observed: "I doubt if the Knox College Library has ever received more or better publicity . . ." [9] It is to be expected, however, that the materials in this collection will be useful as well as ornamental to Knox.

The results of the work of friends groups have not been systematically evaluated. The Yale Associates, as noted earlier, have been a constant help to the Yale Library. Formed in 1930, the group has as its object to provide "the Library with books and manuscripts which it could not afford to buy out of its invested funds." [10] Membership is open to any person who contributes a sum of money for Library purposes.

Foundation gifts to libraries have not been nearly as extensive as private ones, but their influence has been significant:

> This can be said even though such gifts, when made on an institutional basis, have been restricted to a relatively small number of institutions. . . . Most of these gifts, proceeding on the Biblical principle "to him that hath shall be given," have gone to make already strong, well-established institutions stronger and better.[11]

ORGANIZATION OF WORK

One of the typical arrangements of libraries in so far as acquisitions is concerned is the merger of gifts and exchanges. Lane found that in the most usual type of organization these two functions were combined as a unit in the Acquisitions Department. This seems to be a suitable marriage, for the operations in each of these spheres of work are closely interwoven. Surveyors of libraries have frequently discovered that the institutions weak in one of these areas were generally weak in the other.

It is not uncommon, of course, to find that the librarians of institutions which are notable for their collections are active in gift work. In fact, much of the time of the librarians is spent in making necessary contacts, in sponsoring and actively supporting friends groups, and in effectively making the library known to the public. In libraries which have departmental and branch units, it may be desirable to delegate gift solicitation to the librarians if they have established personal relationships with agencies and organizations.

Earlier, it was suggested that the library establish a clear policy regarding gifts. Northwestern University has sought to do this in a precise manner in a statement issued by this institution and entitled "Opportunities for Giving to the Libraries at Northwestern University." The student will find this a possible model, concise and direct, factual and suggestive. There are some librarians who do not believe that there should be a detailed, written gift policy as it may prove too restrictive.

In the survey of the Alabama Polytechnic Institute Library, Wilson and Orr [12] recommend the establishment of a Gifts and Exchange Section in the proposed Acquisitions Department. It is worth noting that the surveyors further suggest the formation of a Friends Group and also the publishing of a statement concerning the gift policy of the library. Other surveys have made similar recommendations.

Whether or not the librarian is personally active in the gift operations, the personnel concerned with gifts have a strategic place in the acquisition program. The alert staff member in charge of gifts should know how to solicit gifts tactfully, how to acknowledge those items which are sent to the library by generous donors, how to publicize gifts successfully, how to make the most efficient use of duplicate gifts, and how to coordinate the activities with acquisition by purchase and exchange. Thus, the person involved should have qualities of initiative, energy, tact, ability to organize a program, and competence in the handling of clerical assistants.

OPERATIONS [13]

The major activities of the gift unit are solicitation, receipt and acknowledgment of solicited gifts, handling of unsolicited gifts, organizing of materials, and preparing of proper records. Since the work is linked in most cases with exchanges, the unit will most likely be responsible for distribution of materials sent as gifts, especially duplicates. The unit generally has responsibility for the preparation of suitable publicity.

SOLICITATION. Most libraries have worked out appropriate form letters and cards for soliciting items from organizations or individuals. Carbons of letters are commonly kept in a vertical file.

In order to link the work of solicitation with the acquisition program, it has been found desirable to place cards in the outstanding order file or the checking file of the serials division for all solicited items. This prevents the ordering of titles which have been requested by the gift unit. When direct solicitation is delegated to a departmental unit, the central unit should be notified so that a duplicate request will not be made. One of the easiest ways to irritate a prospective donor is to have several units of a library system ask for the same item. For this reason alone, it may be worth while to centralize gift solicitation.

Occasionally it may be necessary for the gift unit to trace items which have not been sent. A form note, indicating the date of the original request and asking if the item might still be available free, is generally sent. To this may be attached a copy of the original request.

RECEIPT OF MATERIAL AND ACKNOWLEDGMENT. The operations involved in the receipt of material include: (1) matching the items with the carbons of the letters, (2) withdrawing the order card if one had been placed in the outstanding order file, (3) dating and filing the card in the received file, (4) noting source and date received on the back of the title page of the item, (5) recording items in gift record on donor's card, and (6) routing the item to the proper departmental library or to the general cataloging department, or searching catalogs and other records in the case of unsolicited gifts.

In the case of serials, the item is matched with the carbon in the vertical file; if the item checks, it is sent to the serials division with the carbon of the letter. If an order card had been made, it is withdrawn from the checking file, stamped with the date of the receipt, and placed in the received file. The item is sent to the requesting library if a departmental unit is involved.

The form of acknowledgment made to donors usually varies according to the value of the gifts. Postal cards are used for minor items, while printed and engraved letters are sent to those who give more valuable materials. For gifts of special importance an acknowledgment from the trustees of the institution may be in order. In some institutions letters are written for all gifts, and carbons are arranged in chronological order to form a gift record.

UNSOLICITED GIFTS. The large institution gets items from publishers, organizations, and individuals without asking for them. They are sent for the purpose of insuring distribution of particular imprints. The gift unit will recognize these and make proper record of them. Generally, a donor card is made and the source and date are placed on the back of the title page of each item. Because there was no previous correspondence or record, it is necessary to check the catalogs to learn whether the items are duplicates of materials which have either been previously purchased or received through gift or exchange. Frequently, it is found that such materials duplicate titles already in the library.

ORGANIZING OF MATERIALS. Control of materials sent in as gifts requires prompt handling by personnel in the gift unit. The recording of solicited gifts provides a control over these until they are cataloged. The unsolicited gifts will require immediate listing if they are to be retained by the library.

The shelving of gift collections will occupy considerable space in the library which seeks materials systematically. The collection of the faculty member who has retired or died, the materials sent in by a neighboring library, or the many single items which accumulate quickly should be placed on the shelves in orderly arrangement until they can be routed to the cataloging or other appropriate department. Since gift materials are of no less importance than purchases in the processing operations, care should be taken to have them move as promptly as possible. The idea that just because an item was not paid for may be a reason for delay in processing is not accepted by the efficient librarian.

RECORDS. For large gift collections, which may be processed either as a unit or piecemeal over a long period of time, effective control will require the making of entries in an in-process file for each of the items; otherwise, the danger of purchasing duplicate copies is great. The use of Library of Congress or other printed cards to facilitate rapid entry in the catalogs is a general practice.

Generally, the gift section should maintain a master gift file. This record should contain information about all gifts presented to the library. So far as possible, entries should be made for items received directly by departmental or branch units. Cooperation by the departmental and branch units through a routine of preparing duplicate slips would provide this record.

The gift record form usually includes such information as the donor's name, address, columns for types of materials and dates they were received, and columns for the date of acknowledgment. The card record is usually filed according to entry under the donor's name, either an individual or a corporate body.

For purposes of efficiency, a current record is maintained on an annual basis. After the accounting year has passed, the cards are removed and placed in the master file.

DEPOSITORY COLLECTIONS

In a few instances, libraries have been designated as depositories of collections. The federal government, and various state and local governments, for example, have selected a number of institutions as depositories for their publications. There are also deposits made by private individuals or organizations. Both governmental and private deposits raise problems for the librarian.

GOVERNMENTAL DEPOSITS. In 1857 the first attempt was made to insure that government publications would be permanently available to the public by the designation of libraries as depository libraries for federal publications. The purpose of this and succeeding legislative acts was to provide collections of government publications throughout the United States. As of July, 1948, a total of 543 libraries in the United States were designated as depositories; 125 were total depositories and 418 were classified as selective depositories. Of this total only 162 were public libraries.[14] By September 1, 1953, the total number of both kinds of depositories in the United States and its possessions had reached 552.

The number of libraries which may be classed as depositories is limited to one for each Congressional district, one to each of the Senators, and one to each territorial delegate. A few other libraries have been designated depository libraries by special acts of legislation. As a result of a survey, R. B. Eastin [15] revealed that there is great variance in the method of handling government documents once they are received by the libraries. He discovered that the lapse of time between receipt of documents in the library and the point where they were ready for use by the library patrons ranged as follows:

1 day or less	224 libraries
2 days or less	45 libraries
3 days or less	49 libraries
1 week or less	51 libraries
2 weeks or less	23 libraries
1 month or less	115 libraries

Some libraries use the *Monthly Catalog of United States Government Publications* for the purpose of employing the classification number that has been assigned by the Superintendent of Documents. Other libraries employ this catalog for part of their classification and Dewey or Library of Congress for the remainder. Some libraries use none of these and espouse the use of indexes such as *PAIS* and the *Education Index* or works such as Hirshberg and Melinat's *Subject Guide to United States Government Publications.*

Two important considerations related to this problem concern the lack of expert staff to service the documents and the lack of space that seems to characterize most libraries. A depository library does not receive federal aid for the privilege of taking charge of public documents. Moreover, the library may not discard any publications provided for it by the depository law without written permission of the Superintendent of Documents. Exceptions are made for those publications which are superseded by others (e.g., slip laws may be discarded upon arrival of the permanent bound volumes), and for material which is available in some form of microfacsimile.

State publications are usually deposited in at least one library within the state that is responsible for the document. This is usually the state library. All other libraries within and without the state must make individual arrangements with the particular department of the state government that publishes the document. Members of the state legislature may often obtain state documents for the libraries within their district. In some states the sending of state documents to requesting libraries outside of the state is done through the agency of the state library's gifts and exchange division.

In general, the institution that most nearly corresponds to a true depository for all of the states is the Library of Congress. The Library of Congress records monthly the titles that have been received by it in the *Monthly Checklist of State Publications*. This is by no means a complete list because states do not always send all of their new publications to the Library of Congress.

No comprehensive catalog exists for municipal publications. Some cities report theirs to the Library of Congress and carry on a sort of exchange program with other cities. Often the public library is able to play an important role, especially if it issues lists of documents available for exchange purposes. The libraries of municipally supported educational institutions may or may not be automatic depositories for municipal documents and in many instances must make their own arrangements to secure these publications.

There is likewise no one listing of current international documents.[16] For the United Nations and its specialized agencies, however, the *United Nations Documents Index* lists UN publications together with those of the agencies which have been received at UN headquarters. The American Library Association and the United Nations have worked out a system of thirty-three depository libraries in the United States for UN documents as part of a group of depository libraries throughout the world.

For the sale of UN documents, official sales agents for each country have been designated, as for example, the International Documents Service of the Columbia University Press. This press publishes a monthly listing of all publications offered for sale under the title *The International Reporter*.

PRIVATE DEPOSITS. The deposit of a collection by a private individual or organization raises peculiar problems. The acceptance of such a deposit should be carefully protected by a written statement as to what is expected of the housing library. There have been cases where certain responsibilities were assigned to the housing library which were not stipulated. For example, the deposit should be accompanied by a statement which contains reservations regarding (1) loss, (2) cataloging, (3) binding, (4) damage, and (5) use. The receiving library should not base its acquisition policy on the fact that the collection is available unless it is clearly indicated that eventually the library will receive title to the collection. Otherwise, the removal of the collection will leave the library in the situation of having hampered its acquisitional program in the field covered. The problem of acceptance of a deposit collection, therefore, is one which requires the careful consideration of the administrative officials of the library as well as the governing authority of the institution.

VII. Duplicates and Exchanges

MOST libraries, even small ones, purchase multiple copies of some titles for the use of their clienteles. In addition, many libraries obtain through gifts, duplicates of books, periodicals, and other items already in the collection. The problem of duplicate copies can be a complex one, and its solution depends on the peculiar conditions of particular libraries.

Many librarians who are aware of the temporary peak demand for certain titles have introduced simplified operations so that there will be no serious "de-cataloging" problem later. Only one or two copies may be entered in the catalog until a decision is made concerning retention of the title in the library permanently. How many copies of a title should a library retain after the immediate demand has diminished? Some libraries dispose of the bulk of the multiple copies, leaving on the shelves a quantity sufficient for foreseeable requests.

Libraries are long-range enterprises, and books and other items are subject to use and deterioration. Consequently it is important to determine how many copies, if any, should be retained for future replacement purposes. The book's content is an essential consideration in this connection. The decision involves cooperation of the readers' service personnel with the technical services staff, since the latter will be concerned with the records of holdings of multiple copies, both of the main collection and of any storage or reserve collection which may be set up.

Any decision to keep duplicates should be made with the knowledge that work on them must be paid for in staff time. Moreover, storage space will entail expense. Any large number of unused copies of titles which have been cataloged and classified and shelved may be an uneconomical use of stack or storage space.

If a decision is made to discard copies of certain titles, owing to cessation of demand or changes in collecting policy, the materials usually are turned over to the library unit concerned with the disposal of duplicates—most frequently the gift and exchange division. These duplicates comprise one of the major resources for the exchange programs of individual libraries.

EXCHANGES

The practice of arranging exchanges between libraries has had a relatively long history. As early as 1694, the Bibliothèque Nationale exchanged duplicates for English and German books.[1] In 1740 German universities were exchanging academic publications, and in 1817 the Akademischer Tauschverein was established. The British government sought to establish an exchange relationship with France in 1832, concentrating on all books published under the copyright laws. The exploits of Alexandre Vattemare in setting up an exchange system for sending Library of Congress duplicates to foreign libraries during the middle of the nineteenth century have been described.[2] Later, the Smithsonian Institution became an important intermediary for the shipment of exchanges between American and foreign libraries.[3]

Several students investigated exchange problems in the late 1930s.[4] Library reports and surveys of libraries also include data relating to exchange programs. Since the end of World War II, the problem of international exchanges has received the special attention of librarians. The destruction of libraries abroad and the inability to obtain new items during the war made it essential to set up exchange programs because of limited funds for purchases. In the United States, "There has been repeated discussion of the desirability of creating some sort of clearinghouse . . . particularly in view of specialization plans and cooperative acquisitions from Europe." [5] The United States Book Exchange, which followed the American Book

Center, is the current effort to assist in facilitating exchanges between American and foreign libraries.[6] It was established in 1948.

> The chief contribution which we [United States Book Exchange] make in the actual handling of exchanges on a current basis is of course that we can offer three-way arrangements which will allow libraries to receive from us items which they could not obtain by direct exchange. It is apparent that the initiation of current exchange, particularly in the international field and under the present chaotic state of publishing and bibliographic control abroad can be a valuable contribution of centralized exchange.[7]

The activities of the USBE are indicated by the following statement from the 1953 report of the Librarian of Congress:

> This nongovernmental organization is operated by a corporation consisting of representatives of 19 sponsoring agencies, of which the Library of Congress is one. . . . The immediate affairs of the organization are conducted by a board of directors . . .
>
> The USBE, which is housed in the Library of Congress, completed its fifth year of service to libraries throughout the world. During the fiscal year, 43 institutions joined the program for the first time, new services were introduced, and existing services were widely utilized. By June 30, 1953, paying members included 352 libraries in the United States and 108 libraries abroad. More than 175,000 books, periodicals, and miscellaneous items were shipped to these libraries during the year. In addition to the exchange program, the USBE sent 75,000 items as gifts to libraries abroad that were unable to engage in exchanges. This gift program was financed through contracts with the Department of State. The first USBE Open House was held in June 1953. It was attended by 42 librarians from 33 institutions in the United States and by one librarian from New Zealand.[8]

In June, 1953, the USBE reported that it had 2,300,000 items available, of which 2,000,000 were periodical issues.[9] Some 16,000 periodical titles were represented in the holdings. The USBE has issued special numbers of its *Newsletter* listing the participating libraries.

Undoubtedly, the possibilities of exchange, both domestic and international, have not yet been fully developed. Librarians will need to work closely with their colleagues and with members of other groups, such as learned societies, if the programs are to function at a maximal level. The profits to be reaped are considerable.[10]

Efforts to encourage international exchange have also been made by the United Nations Educational, Scientific and Cultural Organization (UNESCO) which maintains a Clearing House for Publications that acts as a center for information about material available on exchange. The *Unesco Bulletin for Libraries* regularly contains a section listing materials available on exchange from libraries in various countries. An important source of data on international exchange is the *Manuel des échanges internationaux de publications* (*Handbook on the International Exchange of Publications*), issued by UNESCO in 1950. This manual discusses definitions, historical backgrounds, materials, methods, exchange centers, agreements and regulations, shipping problems, and publications of various institutions.

SOURCES

In his study of exchange work in 85 college and university libraries, Lane found that thirteen different types of material were used for exchange purposes. These were official publications, dissertations (whole), abstracts of dissertations, duplicate books, duplicate serials, nonduplicate materials, university published series, university published journals, university press nonserial publications, instructional department publications, library publications, society publications, and miscellaneous materials (government publications, including state law reports; reprints; experiment station publications; and radio transcripts).

In his tabulation of findings regarding use of these materials, Lane revealed the following:

> Of the 13 types of materials used for exchange which were listed in the questionnaire, 12 libraries used four different types, 10 used three types, and 10 used eight types. Five libraries used 11 types, and no library used more than 11. Duplicate materials, the most popular type of material used for exchange, was checked by 64 libraries. Sixty-two libraries checked

duplicate books and 49 libraries checked official publications of the university. These were the next most popular materials. Complete (unabstracted) dissertations, instructional department publications and miscellaneous materials were each checked by 13 libraries.[11]

While departmental units of academic libraries were considered, Lane did not make a study of the problem of exchange in public, governmental, and special libraries. An examination of the exchange work of these types of libraries undoubtedly would reveal the presence of library publications used especially for exchange work. The Library of Congress, the New York Public Library, the Huntington Library, the Folger Shakespeare Library, the John Crerar Library, and others have publishing programs which provide materials useful in exchange work. Similarly, learned societies and scholarly organizations, as well as industrial and commercial concerns, which maintain libraries or collections of materials relevant to their work, carry on exchanges with libraries. The medical librarians [12] and other special librarians have developed exchange programs which have been profitable to most of the participating institutions.

In past years, dissertations represented an important source of exchange materials. Figures in *American Universities and Colleges* [13] show that 37 of the 105 institutions currently listed as conferring the doctorate require publication of dissertations in whole or in part (in some cases publication in a journal meets the requirement); 43, including some of those which also require printing in fuller form, demand the publication of abstracts. Twenty institutions permit the doctoral student to provide copies of dissertations in microfilm as a substitute for printing. University Microfilms, in Ann Arbor, has taken over the work of providing microfilm copies of dissertations for many institutions.[14]

ORGANIZATION

In the survey of the libraries of the Virginia Polytechnic Institute,[15] it was noted that exchanges had failed to serve the purposes of the institution as effectively as they might. The surveyors made the following observations:

No system of exchanges now exists for the Virginia Polytechnic Institute Library as a whole. Although the institution publishes numerous Agricultural Experiment Station Bulletins and Extension Division Bulletins, the exchanges are carried out by the Publications Office rather than by the Library. No effort is made to obtain a balance in the exchange relations. For example, the Engineering Extension Division sends publications to many institutions in the United States and in foreign countries without getting any items in return.[16]

This particular statement could be applied to many educational institutions. It is significant in that it points out (1) the lack of centralization of exchange work, and (2) the failure to take advantage of the institution's need in exchanges. It also shows a real failure to use the library's facilities to acquire materials through exchange.

In his effort to establish working principles for effective exchange work, Lane set up certain standards relating to its organization and administration. Among the principles was one which stated that "all exchange work should be centered in one division of the library." Of the 81 libraries which provided information to Lane, 39 maintained an organized exchange division. Of the 42 libraries which did not have a formal division, 26 carried on exchange work in some other unit. Generally, the division when centralized is a part of the acquisition department, but sometimes it is a separate unit or serves as part of the reference, circulation, or serials department. As frequently as not, the exchange work may be assigned to the same unit which handles gifts.[17]

On the basis of the experience of libraries which appear to be effective in their exchange work, the larger system might well consider the advantages of a centralized unit for exchange work. In their consideration of exchange activity in the Texas A. and M. College Library, Orr and Carlson found that it was "the weakest phase of the acquisitions program." They write further:

At present this activity consists only in exchanging publications with other libraries through the Duplicate Exchange Union. Although this is important because of the numerous worthwhile publications received, it represents only a minor part of the overall exchanges program which should be in operation.[18]

Since Orr and Carlson have analyzed the Texas A. and M. situation with such care, it may be worth while to consider what they visualize as an exchange program for the institution:

The exchanges program as visualized by the surveyors, would operate as follows: (1) The Agricultural Experiment Station, and possibly other units of the System as well as units of the College, would reserve as many copies of their publications for exchange purposes as might be required by the Library, (2) publications sent out on exchange would be mailed by the issuing units direct to the institutions concerned, (3) all arrangements and correspondence relative to the exchanges program would be handled by the Library, (4) the Library would in each instance determine which publications were to be sent to or received from each institution in an effort to effect a reasonable balance in these exchanges, and (5) the institutions with whom exchanges were made would send their publications direct to the library.[19]

This program provides the essentials of effective exchange relationships. The institution as a whole is part of the program, the publishing units would take the responsibility of direct mailing to the receiving libraries or agencies, the paper work would be centralized in the library, decisions regarding the sending and receiving of certain titles would be made by the library staff, and centralized receipt of the materials would be effected. The results of the program would normally be increased quantity of items received and greater coverage.

Other libraries with effective programs arrange for the materials to be sent to the library for distribution. Direct shipment from the issuing offices has much to commend it, especially if it can be easily arranged and there is close cooperation between these offices and the library. Records of the institutions with which exchange relationships are maintained would be kept in the library as well as in the issuing offices.

Since faculty members are frequently concerned with what the library receives in exchange for the publications of the institution, especially if the publications originate from instructional departments, it is desirable to consult with faculty members in establishing the list of recipient institutions, and in either adding to it or canceling names from it. The library would be in a strategic position to make recommendations on this important matter, while faculty members frequently can assist in suggesting wanted publications.

Similarly, in public, governmental, and special libraries those who use the libraries may on occasion suggest titles which can be acquired through exchange. In those libraries which have departments or divisions, the departmental and divisional heads are in a position to provide information concerning publications which are needed in their work and can be acquired through exchange.

PERSONNEL

Lane found that the typical exchange division in the college or university library consisted of two people, generally a professional in charge, with a clerical or nonprofessional assistant. More than a few libraries with extensive programs of exchange employ larger staffs. The 1953 staff at Columbia, for example, consisted of a professional who had charge of both gifts and exchanges and five nonprofessional assistants. This staff during the last few years handled annually approximately 14,000 pieces of material through exchange (5,000 to 7,000 sent—8,000 received) involving usually over 700 institutions. This is in addition to the gift work and other activities performed by this staff.[20] At the Library of Congress for the year ending June 30, 1949, "The machinery for the exchange of publications handled 3,232,803 pieces . . . a slight increase over the previous year's figure of 3,225,768." [21] For the year ending June 30, 1952, the exchange sections of the Exchange and Gift Division handled more than 2,150,000 pieces, not including the 800,000 newspaper issues and about 1,300,000 pieces determined to be surplus to the library's collections.[22] The Gift and Exchange Division of the Library of Congress in 1952 consisted of 61 people, including the chief, 27 staff members in classification G7 or higher, and 33 in classification G1 to G6.[23] Special units concerned with exchange are the American and British Exchange, European Exchange, Hispanic Exchange, and Orientalia Exchange.[24] It is often difficult to recruit gift and exchange personnel, although their services are needed in the larger libraries. Many surveys of libraries propose the adding of staff members who can handle this area of work.

Lane found that exchange work was an added duty for staff members engaged in other work in over half of the libraries he studied. In a small library, this plan would provide for the handling of the limited number of exchanges which are received. The real objection to this side-show aspect of exchanges in some libraries, however, is the usual resultant inefficiency of the program.

The carrying on of an effective program of exchange requires the constant attention of able staff members. The professional in charge of an exchange program should not be someone who has failed to make good in some other unit of the library. The work requires an aggressive individual, with a knowledge of all kinds of publications and of the nature of publishing programs of educational institutions, societies, organizations, and governments. He and members of his staff should have some knowledge of foreign languages. He must be able to integrate such a program with the general acquisition policy and coordinate it with gift activities of the library. The work demands a businesslike approach, initiative, imagination, ability to clear materials quickly, and a sense of promptness in handling correspondence. The importance of these characteristics becomes apparent when the operations of the exchange unit are considered.

Among the duties of the chief of the exchange unit are the following:

1. Planning and organizing the work of exchanges.
2. Checking in exchanges received.
3. Preparing lists of institutions to which exchanges are sent.
4. Serving as a clearinghouse for all exchange requests.
5. Claiming missing numbers in serial exchanges.
6. Arranging new exchanges.
7. Making contacts with units which provide materials for exchange.
8. Making recommendations in regard to related acquisitional policies.

9. Keeping records and statistics.
10. Examining exchange relations in order to determine whether the Library might not profit more through direct purchase.
11. Organizing and handling duplicates used in exchange work.
12. Visiting other libraries to effectuate exchange relations and frequently to select items to be received on exchange.

In the performance of these tasks, the exchange head requires the assistance of energetic and accurate clerical staff members. One of the most difficult hurdles in the exchange work is the tremendous amount of searching, checking, record keeping, shipping, etc., which should be taken care of promptly. For this reason, some librarians have looked at exchange skeptically and have insisted that it pay for itself. To do this, the exchange personnel must be aware of the economies which may be worked out in the operations.

OPERATIONS

Among the operations which specifically involve the exchange division are: (1) devising the methods of obtaining materials, (2) establishing a sound basis for exchange relationships, (3) selecting the institutions with whom exchanges are carried on, (4) transacting exchanges with domestic and foreign agencies, (5) informing agencies of exchanges available, (6) soliciting exchanges, and (7) maintaining the statistics and records of exchanges.

OBTAINING MATERIALS. Undoubtedly, one of the methods of making exchange pay is to obtain the materials for exchange at the least possible cost. Attention has already been called to the use of publications issued by the institution with which the library is associated. In addition to the original publications so acquired, there are also the duplicate materials which require separate handling.

The ability of the library to obtain a favorable consideration by a press associated with the institution will partially determine the potentiality of the library to obtain materials. Some institutions have been favored with generous allotments of copies by affiliated presses. These have either been gifts or sales at considerable discounts. What this arrangement will be depends on the strength of the press and whether the allotment to the library will cut deeply into the sales of the press publications. In order to offset this competition, an arrangement may be made with the press to distribute publications only after a certain time has elapsed. In at least one institution, an arrangement was set up to take over stock remainders on titles which have been in print sufficiently long to exhaust the domestic market. The remainders can be used profitably for foreign exchanges, especially with libraries which are relatively new, such as those in South America and Australia, and some of the European institutions that were damaged by the war.

As noted earlier, the use of dissertations in exchange has been a standard practice of libraries. Full dissertations or abstracts of them have represented a type of material wanted by research libraries. A number of difficulties have arisen concerning dissertations, however, as Kleberg [25] has pointed out: "The defeat of Germany [which was one of the principal sources of printed dissertations] and the declining number of American universities which require the publication of theses has seriously reduced the theses available for exchange." Moreover, the materials lost as a result of the war, the increasing practice of publishing theses in series (leading to bibliographical problems), the tendency to publish dissertations as articles in journals and use reprints for exchange (less useful to institutions which subscribe to the journals), and the use of microfilm (and possibly, microcards) are creating problems which must be met by libraries interested in exchange.[26] Kleberg also called attention to the need for the clear marking of dissertations as such and to the need for more frequent distribution of them to libraries with which exchange relationships are maintained.

ESTABLISHING THE BASIS OF EXCHANGE RELATIONSHIPS. No matter what basis is selected for an exchange relationship, it is unlikely that an exact balance can be obtained. One of the tentative principles arrived at by Lane was as follows: "In the interests of the sending library, exchange should be carried out on a piece-for-piece basis with an attempt to strike an approximate balance." [27] Many libraries, especially the larger ones, make little or no effort to set up a balanced account, since it is assumed that some assistance to weaker libraries is salutary. In his study, Lane found that of the 78 libraries which supplied information, 17 used the piece-for-piece method as a basis for exchange, one used priced exchange only, and 9 used a combination of these two methods. While 8 libraries exchanged in a lot-for-lot basis, there were 36 institutions which did not try to reach a balanced relationship.[28] Regardless of the nature of the basis, the librarian owes it to his institution to be certain that his library is not losing materials which might be acquired through a systematic program of exchanges.

Priced exchange involves a considerable amount of detailed work with billing, bookkeeping, and recording. For this reason, many libraries, except in cases where rare items or lot sales are involved, do not engage in priced exchange.

It is important that there is common understanding of "piece-for-piece exchange" by the parties involved. One library may send out ten large volumes and, unless stipulations are made, receive ten pamphlets or ten issues of a periodical in return. Categories of exchange may well be set up if it appears necessary to do so. The advantage which may be expected from piece-for-piece exchange is the maintenance of an approximate balance which, ideally, should take place in a well-regulated program.

SELECTING INSTITUTIONS. The names which are placed on lists to receive an institution's publications have sometimes been carelessly selected. In some libraries, the institutions, individuals, and agencies which have been placed on such lists have accumulated over the years, and no effort has been made to weed those which are no longer effective. The intertwining of gift work, which implies a return of some kind, should be carefully examined in compiling a list of exchange partners. Past practice in many academic institutions, for example, has established a precedent for the sending of copies of dissertations to certain institutions or libraries of international importance just to insure proper distribution of the titles. There is no question but that this is a generally desirable practice; but each case should be considered on its own merits. This is particularly true when foreign libraries, which may not have publishing programs, are involved.

Institutions have a way of grouping themselves for certain types of exchanges. Land-grant colleges and universities are interested in obtaining (among other types of publications) experiment station publications, and the agricultural and engineering series are usually sent to other institutions which publish similar series. Law libraries attached to universities exchange their law reviews with other law libraries. Libraries of state universities may also be given an allotment of state publications, statutes, etc., for exchange purposes.[29] In 1946, it was reported "that a recent arrangement in California puts fifty sets of state documents at the disposal of the State Library, with twenty-five each for the Berkeley and Los Angeles Divisions of the State University. Exchange negotiations with foreign governments are in progress at present." [30] State historical libraries exchange their publications among themselves, as also do libraries of scientific institutions. More and more foreign libraries are becoming concerned with the establishment of exchange relations with American libraries.[31]

INFORMING INSTITUTIONS OF EXCHANGES AVAILABLE. One of the regular operations of the exchange division is providing information about materials available for exchange. For institutional publications, new imprints, and stock remainders, this does not present much of a problem. These may be sent automatically to certain exchange partners or may be listed among other exchange items. The real problem centers about the listing and disposal of duplicate exchanges.

Special groups of librarians have been particularly concerned about making exchanges a profitable enterprise. Many items are not bought until it can be verified that they are not available on exchange. Librarians have had varying results in their exchange programs, but apparently have been able to accomplish their ends by organizing the work around their specialized needs. This is perhaps more noticeable in the efforts of the medical, law, and theology librarians than in other groups.

The Exchange of the Medical Library Association was established as early as December 1, 1899, and represents one of the first activities of the Association. The Exchange receives lists of duplicate books and journals from member libraries, mimeographs lists, and apportions the items on the basis of first service to the largest requesting library. The libraries which originally sent in the lists of duplicates are then notified as to where to send the various items. Thus, the Exchange does not have to face the problem of actual distribution, and its expenses are relatively low.

The member libraries of the Medical Library Association are not supposed to circulate lists of unwanted items privately, nor to order any items from the lists for any purpose other than to build up their collections (that is, not to obtain them for the personal use of staff members, patrons, etc.). Libraries are also asked not to request duplicates of materials they already have unless they specify that second sets are contemplated.

Naylor [32] has called attention to the limitations of the system: (1) the "specialty" libraries (ophthamological, dental, etc.) are always small, but have a great need for unusual materials, (2) in theory, the larger the library the less it should need from the lists of duplicates, (3) the largest libraries do not always serve the largest areas, nor the areas in which there are few libraries, and (4) the small library is frequently a new library which has not had time to accumulate the type of material listed and should have preference for at least some types of material.

In this particular system of exchanges, there is no question but that the advantages lie with the larger libraries. As a matter of fact, the larger libraries generally have the greater number of duplicates to distribute. The policy which has been evolved was based on the premise that the exchanges should be as equitable as possible.

The American Association of Law Libraries Exchange is a function of the American Association of Law Libraries. It is composed of some twenty-five participating libraries,[33] and a law library is assigned to take charge of the files and exchange records.

The membership of the participating libraries is limited to institutional members of the Association. Any institutional member may, upon payment of an annual five-dollar participating fee, become a participating member.

The function of the Exchange is twofold: (1) to maintain the listings of the duplicates and wants and (2) to notify a participating library whenever the opportunity for exchange arises. It can easily be seen that unless a participating library lists its duplicates or wants, very few exchanges will take place.

In the filing of listings of materials, the participating libraries customarily list the materials on 3″ x 5″ slips.[34] Such slips customarily contain a notation as to whether the material is a duplicate or is wanted. The slip usually contains an accurate description of the material, the name of the participating library, a date and a notation "oe" if the material is available on open exchange.[35]

The library in charge of the Exchange, upon receipt of the 3″ x 5″ slip with the listing, checks the item against the backlog in the exchange file and, if a matching slip is found, it is removed and either a notice [36] or the slip is sent to the library wanting the item. If, on the contrary, no matching slip is located, the new listing is filed. The slips are filed alphabetically and in the proper numerical order within the class of material. In the filing of complete sets of long runs, the listings are filed immediately preceding the slips covering the individual or odd volumes of the sets.

If matching slips for a newly listed item, or reexamination of old listings, are found, a notice of the matching slip is sent to the library which filed the want slip. The participating libraries, it is assumed, upon receipt of the information, will communicate with the library that has the materials in duplicate and make whatever arrangements are necessary to acquire same.

"Current listings for the American Law Libraries (Central) Exchange files may include any duplicate materials. A listing fee of 10 cents per title will be charged for the listing library and the title will be listed on the next monthly list of duplicate offerings. The list will be distributed to all interested members of the American Association of Law Libraries. The items listed may be offered free, open exchange or carry a price in terms of exchange credits. A library wishing to obtain listed items will forward to the listing library the exchange credits and the listing library will then ship the item." [37]

Some of the problems met by the medical libraries are taken into account by the proposals made by the theology libraries for an exchange program. At the meeting of the American Theological Library Association in Chicago in June, 1948, Ostrander [38] presented a plan for duplicate periodical exchange. Although based on the Medical Library Association program, it included several specific considerations: (1) frequency of issue, (2) limited length of lists, (3) standard form of listing, (4) no preference to be given to any library on basis of size, (5) charges to involve only transportation costs, (6) requests are to be submitted on a standard form, (7) each library shall pay a stipulated fee to defray expenses of sending out lists, (8) each library shall be given a key number to facilitate the work.

At this same meeting, Judah presented another proposal for the theological libraries. The major point made in this plan was the assignment of specific titles to certain libraries in the exchange program. No lists were to be compiled. He wrote as follows:

> A list of the libraries and the specific titles for which each would be responsible would be prepared and circulated to each library for reference. Any library having duplicates would send them to the designated repositories. In reverse . . . any library wishing material of a certain title would make requests of the library assigned to keep that title. The form of request could be standardized, and the request filled at once, if possible; or if not, filed for future fulfillment. Requests would be filled or filed in the order of their receipt.[39]

Although the theological group has discussed exchange programs, the activity has been slight. At the 1953 meeting of the Association, it was recommended that the Periodical Exchange Committee be revived.[40]

SOLICITING EXCHANGES. In addition to such organized programs, libraries carry on exchange work irregularly and sporadically. Libraries in America and abroad that are interested in acquiring specific publications write directly to the institutions and agencies. This is generally done by mail, usually through form letters or cards. It would appear that no categorical direction is necessary as to methods of soliciting exchanges. In large exchange programs, however, the use of form letters and form cards appears to be advisable. Libraries have come to expect such requests, and it would be foolish to spend time composing special letters when they are not needed. More rapid response, however, may be obtained from libraries in some of the foreign countries if the letters are written in the foreign languages involved.

RECORDS AND STATISTICS. Among the operations which commonly are involved in an exchange program is the acknowledgment. This may also be done through form letters or cards. Exchanges of series and journals generally fall into a continuing arrangement, although some libraries may bring up the question of renewal annually. Actually, the exchange librarian may use some judgment in determining whether or not acknowledgments are needed in particular cases.

Lane [41] found that few libraries kept consistent records of materials distributed and received. Fewer still keep records of the value of exchanges or the cost of items in the exchange program, such as personnel, equipment, stationery, packing materials, and the costs of exchange materials.[42] General practice is to keep records of the value of exchanges, if they are maintained, on cards. These are divided into "materials sent," and "materials received," arranged by institution. At a glance, one should be able to tell just what the situation is in regard to a specific institution. A few libraries keep records of the individual series received and sent, the number of serial volumes completed through exchange, and the number of lists received and sent. Most exchange librarians are required to report annually.

BIBLIOGRAPHICAL CENTERS AND EXCHANGE

As a central agency, serving a region, it appeared normal for the Philadelphia Union Library Catalogue to take an early interest in the disposal of duplicates. Actually, it was an outgrowth of the concern of the Union Catalogue to prevent unique holdings from leaving the area, as well as assisting other libraries who were participants in the project as a whole.[43] The major principles of the service were: (1) that no items were discarded or disposed of outside the Philadelphia area without checking at the Union Catalogue, and other libraries in the area had first choice of the material, (2) material is first offered to those libraries whose holdings are included in the Philadelphia Union Library Catalogue, (3) receiving libraries paid for transportation, (4) libraries having large holdings for disposal provided lists to the center and supplied materials directly to libraries wanting items, and (5) materials remaining after libraries had made their choice were made available to individuals. The Philadelphia Center, formerly a depository for duplicate materials for the entire area, now issues only lists.[44]

During the period from March, 1942, when the first list appeared, until April, 1946, when the thirteenth appeared, there was a steady increase in the amount of materials taken. In 1944, when the Special Libraries Association in New York closed its national exchange service, the Philadelphia chapter of S.L.A. joined with the Union Catalogue in its exchange project.

Other bibliographical centers have established programs for the purpose of helping libraries to acquire items which they need. The Pacific Northwest Bibliographic Center and the Rocky Mountain Bibliographic Center have both made an effort to apprize constituent libraries of the existence of duplicates. The Pacific Northwest Bibliographic Center has also inaugurated a systematic program of discarding, so that copies of titles which are held by only one library will not be lost to the region. The mechanics for the plan are simple. "A library planning to discard a group of books sends a list to the center. The list is checked against the union catalog. Those items which are held by other libraries are so indicated and the discarding library is free to pulp them. Those titles that appear to be unique in the discarding library are preserved for the region by being sent to one of the designated repositories, determined according to the subject of the book." [45]

Undoubtedly the development of union catalogs, bibliographical centers, and regional library centers will have increasing effects upon exchange programs of libraries. Although one of the early evidences of cooperation among libraries, exchange has not yet reached the point of effectiveness to which many librarians aspire.

VIII. Catalogs and Cataloging: Development and Functions

EXCEPT for certain types of collections, such as those of special libraries and of some public and small college libraries which weed regularly, library holdings increase from year to year in size and complexity. Evidence of this appears in the preceding chapters on acquisitions. With the accretions, the problem of recording the materials and organizing them for easy use exists. The successful librarian knows that in order to serve his clientele effectively he must control the materials that have been assembled. Catalogs and systematic arrangements, or classifications, of the materials are the means of aiding users to obtain books and other materials promptly.

This chapter considers the development and functions of catalogs. It is the first of several which discuss catalogs and book classification. It is concerned primarily with the growth of the card catalog, its size and form, current developments in descriptive and subject cataloging, and various types of cooperative enterprises.

DEVELOPMENT OF THE CATALOG

With the current interest in book catalogs, one is likely to lose sight of the fact that the present type of card catalog—dictionary, divided, or classed—is an outgrowth of catalogs in book form.[1] The first Harvard catalog, published in 1723, was actually devised for the purpose of informing prospective donors in London of the then current holdings of the college library. The Yale book catalog, first issued in 1745, was aimed more directly at revealing the contents of the library for the use of the students. The first Princeton catalog, dated 1760, had 36 pages and contained entries for 1,281 volumes.[2] This was the first of eighteen catalogs of library holdings produced at Princeton. Columbia College and other schools of Columbia prepared some thirteen catalogs between 1813 and 1875, while at the University of Pennsylvania between 1823 and 1875 seven book catalogs were prepared.[3] The catalogs of the Astor Library, The Boston Athenaeum, the Peabody Institute of Baltimore, and the book catalogs of many other American and foreign libraries are other examples of the efforts of librarians to provide keys to library collections.

The shift from the book to the card catalog need not be traced in detail, but a few high points should be noted. Cataloging was one of the chief topics of discussion at the first American Library Association meeting in 1876. It came to the fore again when the Library of Congress offered printed catalog cards for sale in 1901. It arose once more with the renewed interest in union catalogs and other cooperative plans in the middle thirties. It is an important topic today because librarians are becoming concerned about the high cost of cataloging and the increasing size and complexity of the products that are called catalogs.

The names of Charles Coffin Jewett, Charles Martel, Charles A. Cutter, and J. C. M. Hanson, among many others, in developing card catalogs are significant. Discussions in the literature from 1876 until the present time refer to the need to record the holdings of libraries and to make the contents readily available to users. It should be observed, however, that there was considerable discussion in the period when the transfer was made from the book to the card catalog as to the wisdom of the action. In fact, some major foreign libraries still consider it more desirable to list their holdings in sheet or book form. But the card catalog became the American form, and it is a common tool, varying in size and quality in our libraries. There is no question but that the establishment of the Library of Congress printed catalog card service has been the greatest influence on modern cataloging practice. Whether or not such standardization was on the whole advantageous has been argued. It is generally accepted, however, that Library of Congress printed cards ushered in an era of stabilization in cataloging practice, indeed to such an extent that cataloging practice became largely a process of increased production along established lines for the next quarter-century.

Along with the depression of the thirties there came budget cuts and increased scrutiny of cataloging processes. There was serious concern not only about the expense of cataloging but also about its usefulness. This was aggravated to some extent by the increasing flow of materials into libraries and the accumulating arrears at the Library of Congress and other institutions. Although Ruffin,[4] Corcoran,[5] and Schley,[6] in their studies of early American book catalogs found a gradual evolution of cataloging theory that was later given concrete form in codes of rules for cataloging, the codes were being designed for the card catalogs, which were accepted widely primarily because of the characteristic of easy intercalation. Recently, arguments have been presented that the book catalog, despite certain inflexibilities, can be revised without serious difficulty, particularly through photographic methods, and is not as expensive as the card catalog.[7] The return to the book form for older portions of some large library catalogs is quite within the realm of possibility.

SIZE OF THE CARD CATALOG

What is the nature of the card catalog in so far as size is concerned? Fremont Rider [8] created a stir among librarians and others in 1944 when he speculated, with tongue in cheek, that on the basis of his formula that libraries double in size every sixteen years, the Yale University Library, if it continued to grow at its past and present rate, would in the year 2040 have approximately 200,000,000 volumes, which would fill 6,000 miles of shelving, and a card catalog (although he was not sure that there would be one) that would have 750,000 catalog trays occupying eight acres of floor space. He has also provided us with other fantastic figures, including the one concerning the cataloging staff of over 6,000 to handle the materials coming into the Yale Library annually. Of course, the factors of growth are changing, and various influences such as specialization in collecting and storage centers will affect the growth of individual libraries.

In the *Annual Report of the Librarian of Congress* for 1953, it was noted that the number of cards prepared for the catalogs established a record—more than 1,945,000, an increase of 8.3 percent over 1952—and more than 1,400,000 cards were filed. The estimate of the sizes of the catalogs were as follows: Official Catalog, 9,032,000; Main Catalog, 8,770,000; Annex Catalog, 3,100,000; National Union Catalog, 12,400,000; and Music Division Catalogs, 1,258,000. "The continuing growth of these catalogs has created problems of space and several solutions are being considered." [9]

Figures concerning the growth of other catalogs reveal a similar situation.[10] Columbia University, for example, has a catalog of some 4,100 trays, with an estimated total of 3,500,000 cards. Northwestern University's central catalog contains nearly 3,000,000 cards. Both Columbia and Northwestern are adding about 125,000 cards annually to their public catalogs. The University of Chicago has a catalog of over 3,000 trays, with a total of close to 3,000,000 cards. It is adding about 75,000 cards annually to this catalog. Michigan and Illinois have been adding close to 100,000 cards annually to their catalogs.

The New York Public Library in 1939 had a catalog of 5,752 trays, with an estimated 5,000,000 cards. In 1953, there were over 7,300 trays, containing almost 6,700,000 cards, and increasing by about 150,000 cards annually.

These are just a few examples of the great size that card catalogs of actual library collections are reaching. One has only to project this picture a hundred years, and while there will probably not be catalogs of the size that Rider predicted for Yale, which now has 4,296 trays and over 4,000,000 cards, there is no question that catalogs will be uncomfortably large. The New York Public Library Catalog at its present rate of accretions will have grown to over 20,000,000 cards.

Statistics from the union catalogs are just as impressive. The size of the National Union Catalog in 1953 was reported to be more than 12,400,000 cards. The total number of cards added to the catalog during 1952–53 was 265,243.[11] Sherwood and Campion [12] reported the size in 1950 of the Philadelphia Union Catalog as 4,-500,000 cards; Cleveland, 2,500,000; and Seattle, 1,300,104. The Denver Union Catalog is said to contain about 3,500,000 cards.

There are some individuals who are not particularly concerned about this growth of the catalogs in our nation's libraries. Head catalogers ask their administrators for additional card cabinets each year and are not worried about the future of the situation. Librarians ask their administrative superiors for more card cabinets to keep their head catalogers satisfied. A librarian reports with satisfaction that this year "we filed 25,000 more cards in our catalogs than last year." That there will be a day of accounting few deny—but so far that day has not been reached, although it is rapidly being approached.

Despite these increases in size, there are some librarians who believe that the catalog is not being made as effective a tool as it might be. Berthold, for example, in a paper given in Chicago in 1946 before the regional group of catalogers suggested that libraries will have to give more attention to the cataloging of pamphlets and similar materials. "It is inevitable," he wrote, "that the somewhat neglected practice of analytical cataloging will have to be re-established and developed further without any great regard to cataloging cost. . . . The situation may change," he added, "if and when more, and more adequate, indexes, bibliographies, and abstracts are regularly published." [13]

The discussion up to this point may be considered as being on the negative side in so far as the size of the card catalog is concerned. There is also what might be termed a positive side. There are some librarians who are deeply concerned about the growth of catalogs. They have come to the conclusion that size brings with it complex problems and makes the catalog not only administratively unmanageable but also difficult to use. In an effort to make the catalog more usable, there are a few libraries which have provided "curators of the catalog," who are responsible for the careful editing of the tool. Osborn and Haskins,[14] who recently discussed this problem, also considered the possibility of publication of catalogs in book form as a joint venture of several libraries.

Passing attention should be given to the abortive proposal of Fremont Rider,[15] who in 1940 suggested that the size of the catalog card might be reduced to one half its present size. Indeed, Rider prepared a number of such cards. The physical problems involved, however, were such that the plan has been placed in the discard, even though it is true that many insurance and other business firms use cards of this size for records as extensive as titles on catalog cards.

Two major practices have been used in the effort to keep the catalog from growing excessively. These are eliminating entries for certain types of material and coordinating entries.

A number of libraries, for example, are eliminating entries for such materials as catalogs, directories, pamphlets, dissertations, and documents. In libraries following this practice, the emphasis is placed on the careful arrangement of the materials on the shelves, and supposedly it is not difficult to tell a user whether or not the library holds a certain item. The use of available indexes is also associated with the procedure, particularly in the case of documents and the dissertations of some universities.

The other practice which some libraries are following is to coordinate the editions of a title on a single card. This not only reduces the number of entries under the author, but also under subject and added entries, as single entries are usually made here, too. Of course, it has been common practice in many libraries to reduce subject and added entries for editions by references to the main entries. Whether or not these particular devices really reduce the size of the catalog to any great extent is not known. There has been no carefully gathered evidence on that point.

The introduction of brief cataloging and the use of form cards are not new in American cataloging, but they are being used more today than in the past. They have attained more prominence out of sheer desperation on the part of catalogers to clear the overwhelming mass of materials which libraries have been collecting. This is also true of the device of cataloging related materials of a single author or of a corporate body on single entry cards, rather than providing individual cataloging for each item. The recent action of the Library of Congress in providing for levels of cataloging is in this direction.

THE FORM OF THE CATALOG

The form of the catalog is also receiving attention. This aspect may be considered from two points of view: the physical arrangement in card form and the arrangement in book form.

Most users of libraries have become accustomed to the dictionary form of the card catalog, although there has been continuous criticism of it. Back in 1905, writing on "The Future of the Card Catalog," William I. Fletcher,[16] who had an eye on the probable growing complexity of the catalog, observed: "The dictionary catalog . . . has the character of a superstition in so far as it is accepted and religiously carried out on grounds that are traditional, rather than on any intelligent conviction that it meets present needs and is good for the future needs for which we must make provision."

Fletcher further called attention to the complexity of the dictionary catalog and suggested a division of the catalog (a step that has been taken in a number of libraries in recent years) and other measures which would make the catalog a tool to be used in conjunction with bibliographies. While he did not necessarily disbelieve in the dictionary catalog, he predicted that the leading feature of the library catalogs of the future would be a "straightaway alphabetical arrangement under authors," although rapid growth would even complicate this aspect. His further suggestions are similar to those one hears today and included using the shelf list (with the addition of a subject index) as a classed catalog; using bibliographies instead of burdening the catalog with analytics; using guide cards in the catalog to refer to bibliographies; and even the substitution of lists and references made in each library for the catalog. In connection with the last point, he cited the development of close classification of books on the shelves as a possible substitute for the catalog.

There has been, however, increasing criticism of the dictionary catalog. Fremont Rider, in his "Alternatives for the Present Dictionary Card Catalog," [17] referred to the divided catalog and the classed catalog as possibilities, with broad classification for the books and close classification for the classed catalog. Berthold,[18] in the paper cited earlier, noted that "The dictionary catalog is a public library tool and . . . as such has no proper place in a research library." According to Berthold the worker in the research library comes to the library either to find a specific item, or to find out what the library has on a specific subject. For the first purpose, the author catalog is sufficient; for the second, subject entries as they now stand "are an irritation rather than an answer to the researcher." Like Fletcher, forty years before, Berthold saw two catalogs for the research library of the future: one for authors (or main entries) and a classed catalog, which could be made from the shelf list. Leupp,[19] Butler,[20] and Shaw [21] are among others who have been critical of the dictionary catalog. Leupp prophesied the acceptance of the classed catalog in the larger libraries. Butler and Shaw in their papers at the Chicago Institute in 1940 called attention to the inadequacy of the present dictionary catalog in meeting the needs of scholars in the humanities and sciences, respectively. According to Shaw, the reason why the scientist does not use the catalog, except to locate a specific title, is that the catalog is an organization of physical objects rather than an organization of concepts. "Subject cataloging is a poor substitute for concept bibliography or bibliography of ideas," he wrote. Shaw, however, did not believe that the classed catalog was the answer to the needs of the scholar in the sciences. Recent discussions by Taylor,[22] Dewey,[23] and Herrick [24] suggest that the issue of the classed catalog is by no means silenced. At the present time, a detailed study of the classed catalog at the John Crerar Library is in progress. It is expected that the results of this study will throw some light on some of the problems faced in the consultation of the classed catalog by library users.

Actually, there have been no large libraries changing to the classed catalog. Rather, a movement towards the divided catalog, especially in university libraries, is noticeable. In his study of "The Divided Catalog in College and University Libraries," [25] Ian Thom found that 24 libraries out of 457 that answered his questionnaire had divided catalogs. Twenty of these catalogs developed from the period 1938 to 1947. Many others have changed since 1947. Thom was concerned not only with the prevalence of this type of catalog, but also with some of its peculiar problems and also its evaluation. It is worth noting that despite the fact that the intent of the librarians in dividing the catalog was "simplicity for the student," this important objective apparently was not achieved to the extent that had been expected. Thom also estimated that this type of catalog increased the total size of the catalog by about 5 percent. The divided catalog, then, is not a device for reducing the sheer bulk of the catalog.

A study of user response to the divided catalog was made at the University of California in 1944 by Amy Wood Nyholm.[26] Based on a questionnaire of 1,000 students, faculty members, and librarians, the findings indicated that about three out of every four respondents favored the division of the catalog, and that 62 percent of the users approached the author-title section more often than they did the subject catalog portion.

Markley [27] reported on a more intensive study of the California subject catalog in 1950. Analysis of the opinion of 1,647 persons who used the catalog led to the conclusion that there was 72 percent success (in varying degrees) as against 28 percent failure in finding wanted materials. As Markley pointed out, there was no effort to measure the importance or quality of use. Findings of this type, however, are not necessarily an indictment of the dictionary catalog.

Although Thom, Nyholm, and Markley reach conclusions which appear to suggest the success of the divided catalog, there are still reasons for withholding evaluation of this type of catalog until further studies are made. These reasons concern both costs and success in helping the user, as well as the size and control of the catalog.

Size itself, however, is not considered a handicap by librarians shifting to the divided catalog. Librarians who have divided their catalogs believe that the change has helped users and reduced problems in filing.

Other studies of the use of the catalog are considered in detail in the study by Frarey,[28] and are summarized in Chapter X. Even though Spalding [29] found that the subject entries were consulted as much as main entries by general users at the Library of Congress, Brett, studying the reference staff use, concluded that "While the subject catalog in its present form was the most valuable tool at the disposal of the reference librarians, its use could not be considered as indispensable." [30]

In addition to actual changes in the physical arrangement of the card catalogs, there have been a number of proposals regarding the organization of catalogs into book form. In recent years librarians have become more conscious of book catalogs through the publication of the *Catalog of Books Represented by Library of Congress Printed Cards.* Not so many years ago one might well have thought that the LC printed catalog was an impossibility. With the development of the Rapid Selector and similar devices opening the way to new possibilities in the control and dissemination of information, the future holds promise of important changes to come.[31]

But the future of the card catalog as a basic record appears secure. In a recent paper, Gull [32] discusses the relation of the card catalog to other types of records which have been proposed as substitutes. These include punched cards (fully mechanized), manuscript book catalogs, printed book catalogs, manuscript sheaf catalogs, microfilm, and magnetic tape, wire, and discs. Gull describes each of these types, along with the card catalog, from the point of view of such factors as physical form, arrangements possible, flexibility of interrelating new entries, currency and completion, ease of consultation, widespread availability, and speed of searches in subject arrangements. His final observation, however, suggests that the card catalog is not likely to be replaced as a library's basic record.

The Library of Congress has been giving attention to the possibility of publishing the current author and subject catalogs of American library resources. Spalding's report [33] provides a detailed account of the problems involved, including scope, locations, and frequency. Publication in book form of the National Union Catalog has been discussed recently by David,[34] who refers to an earlier report by Downs [35] which recommended publication. David furnishes an estimate of $5,021,455 as the total cost of 1,000 sets of 164 volumes in three-column publication. Actually, the National Union Catalog was microfilmed in 1952, and can be purchased in its entirety on 2,706 reels at a cost of $10,824 for use in any microfilm reader accommodating 16 mm. film.[36]

DESCRIPTIVE CATALOGING

In the discussion above, consideration has been given to the more general problems of the catalog, its size, and its arrangement in card and book form. At this point some of the proposals and activity in the area of descriptive cataloging, which may be defined as including both the entry and the body of the card, may be treated. In a paper [37] presented in 1942, it was observed that procedures in descriptive cataloging were fairly well standardized. A current review of developments in descriptive cataloging, however, reveals significant modifications. For example, since that date important changes have been made in the body of the card, and these are represented particularly in the 1949 Library of Congress *Rules for Descriptive Cataloging.*

Probably more important than the changes in the body of the card are those associated with the entry. The important "Processing Memorandum No. 60," dealing with the establishment of the entry on the basis of "no conflict" in the catalog, represents a step that has far-reaching implications. This principle is discussed more fully in a later chapter.

Another problem of importance under the rubric of entry is concerned with the entry for corporate bodies. In his review of the 1949 edition of the ALA *Cataloging Rules for Author and Title Entries,* Andrew Osborn [38] observed, among other sharply worded criticisms, that there was an immediate need for rethinking through the rules for corporate entry. Statements by Taube [39] and Lubetzky [40] have created additional interest in the problem. These are discussed in Chapter IX.

SUBJECT CATALOGING

If descriptive cataloging has come to be subjected to examination under the microscope during recent years, it might be said that subject cataloging has probably always been under suspicion. There seems to have been some question from the earliest use of catalogs of the wisdom of placing subject cards in them. It may be assumed, however, that subject cards are needed in card catalogs, and that librarians have not seen fit to eliminate them from their catalogs.

There have been some attempts to reduce the number of subject headings. Harvard, for example, has excluded subject headings for little-used materials. Some libraries have set up a questionable policy of using only one subject or no subject heading to a title in certain categories, such as foreign materials and pamphlets. Brown and Yale have established positive programs in eliminating subject cards, such as overlapping entries, entries for popular and obsolete works, inverted headings, form headings, and the like. Van Hoesen [41] has developed twelve categories that receive special treatment in so far as subject headings are concerned.

More important than the question of how many subject cards are used in catalogs is the problem of the kind of subject headings used. Since this problem is discussed in detail in the chapter on subject headings, reference is made here only to two studies, one dealing with duplication and one with revision.

Simonton [42] selected limited subjects (Shakespeare and Chaucer as represented in the Columbia University Library catalog and in certain outstanding bibliographies) and carefully analyzed the duplications and comparative coverages of the subjects from both quantitative and qualitative points of view. Simonton's first conclusion, drawn from his analyses of the data collected, was as follows: "The practice of assigning subject headings to all items cataloged as separates in the Columbia University Libraries has resulted in files of titles under certain broad Chaucer and Shakespeare headings which represent almost complete duplication of the entries in certain basic bibliographies of the same subjects." He concluded that 91 percent of the Shakespeare headings were duplicated, and 94 percent of the Chaucer headings. A further conclusion, also supported by similar studies, notably one by Swank, is that the bibliographers have used more appropriate subject headings than have the catalogers. Simonton makes the obvious suggestion of removing these unnecessary cards and referring the reader to the bibliographies. In this, there is a similarity to the suggestion made by Fletcher in 1905.

A study of subject heading revision was made by Frarey.[43] From an analysis and tabulation of the additions and changes made between 1941 and 1950 to a 4 percent sample of the headings and *see* references in the fourth edition of the LC list of subject headings, this study endeavors to test the validity of criticisms generally made of LC subject headings, to determine whether there is any emergent pattern in Library of Congress practices to suggest trends in the structure of the subject catalog, and to point out adherence to or departure from established patterns and practices in subject heading assignment.

Revisions to LC headings noted in this study suggest that there is a significant effort to improve the subject approach to books and that libraries generally should endeavor to effect similar changes in their subject catalogs. Since the quantity of revision indicates that proper catalog maintenance may be relatively expensive, there is some reason to believe that additional studies of traditional techniques of subject analysis are desirable and that explorations of more economical methods to achieve the same ends are urgently needed.

As a matter of fact, there are some libraries which do not make changes consistently in their catalogs. The practice of making cross references from old to new headings is usually followed.[44] Other recommendations, including those made at the Army Medical Library's symposium on subject headings in 1948, adhered to this pattern. Justification for this practice is based on the assumption that most library users are interested in current material, and only a small minority would be inconvenienced by having to look in two or more places in the catalog to find material on a given subject.

Another solution to the problem of quick revision of headings has been suggested by some libraries with divided catalogs. In the subject portions of some of these catalogs, headings are not written on the catalog cards but only on guide cards which precede the entries for each subject. A change in a subject heading requires only a change in the guide card and in the tracings on the corresponding main entries (and also perhaps in the penciled indication of the subject entry usually added on the verso of each subject card to assist in filing). It is apparent that the size of the catalog is increased by this particular practice, since each subject requires a guide card. In a large catalog this might make some difference. There is need for a careful study of the use and operational problems of a catalog of this type.

The catalog of the new Lamont Library of Harvard [45] provides an example of directed effort to provide a simple tool for those in the process of being trained in library usage. The author catalog contains brief entries, prepared essentially without research. Pseudonyms are frequently used. The subject catalog, which consists of about twenty trays for a collection of 80,000 volumes, does not attempt to duplicate the classification. If a particular title has a definable subject through classification, no subject entries are made for the subject catalog. The latter is reserved for multiple subjects not covered by the classification. The open shelf arrangement of materials has made the special classification, which is based on Dewey, important in this respect. Entries are not typed on the subject catalog cards; they are filed behind guide cards.

RELATION OF SUBJECT CATALOGS TO BIBLIOGRAPHIES. The relation of subject catalogs to bibliographies has been a topic of discussion and study since the last quarter of the nineteenth century. Swank has done such an excellent job in reviewing the critical discussions in his paper, "Subject Catalogs, Classifications, or Bibliographies, A Review of Critical Discussions, 1876–1942," in the July, 1944, *Library Quarterly*,[46] that it is unnecessary to spend much time on the subject here. The fact remains, however, that this problem has been discussed at length without anybody doing much about it. The important question, as phrased by Ellsworth, is as follows:

> If, for example, what we need is less subject cataloging in card form and more printed bibliographies of various kinds for various purposes, then instead of maintaining hundreds of small groups of catalogers all over the country, why not group these people together in a few centers and put them to work compiling bibliographies? [47]

COOPERATIVE AND CENTRALIZED CATALOGING

Jewett proposed in 1851 an organization of libraries in the United States, with the Smithsonian Institution as its center, which would engage in cooperative enterprise, including cooperative cataloging.[48] The Smithsonian authorities declined, but the idea was revived when the American Library Association was organized. The development of a cataloging code and the adoption of the 3″ x 5″ card were the principal steps toward uniformity of practice before the twentieth century.

Centralized distribution of cards was first authorized in 1902 at the Library of Congress. An agreement was made to acquire card copy from other governmental departmental libraries. In 1910, this scheme began to include libraries outside Washington. In 1926, the ALA Cooperative Cataloging Committee was established, but it disbanded in 1940 when LC took over the cooperative efforts the Committee had been created to develop.

The Library of Congress issued its *Cooperative Cataloging Manual* [49] in 1944. The handbook describes briefly the beginnings of cooperative cataloging and the relations of the ALA and of LC to this activity, in addition to outlining the procedures which have been set up to guide libraries which supply copy for this joint effort.

Studies which have been made of cooperative and centralized cataloging indicate that centralization, carefully organized and administered, probably has more to offer than cooperative cataloging.

Morsch considers "cooperative cataloging as part of centralized cataloging as long as it is coordinated by a central agency and its product distributed from a single point." [50]

Osborn [51] suggests that, although cooperative cataloging avoids sending books to a central location and permits consultation with subject specialists who have special collections in their own libraries, it does not function as well as centralized cataloging. A well-organized centralized plan provides for: (1) a concentration of expensive cataloging reference tools; (2) a concentration of able catalogers; (3) shortened lines of communication, with corresponding efficiency of administration; (4) greater use of standardized, coordinated rules and practices; (5) elimination of extra revising and editing; and (6) greater ease in maintaining a sustained policy in classification and decisions on subject headings.

How far the Library of Congress could serve as the center of a unified cataloging program is conjectural. Many librarians have been impatient with the inability of the Library of Congress to issue cards for more titles. MacLeish acknowledged the seriousness of arrears in cataloging in the Library of Congress and in other large libraries. He suggested that

> The profession . . . candidly face the fact that present cataloging methods are nineteenth century methods devised for forms of print which no longer constitute the bulk of library accessions, and for categories of readers who constitute a part only of present and potential library clienteles.[52]

Studies have been undertaken at the Library of Congress and elsewhere to test various solutions. A number of libraries have already instituted simplified cataloging rules for certain types of materials, and the ALA Division of Cataloging and Classification is sponsoring a study of the need for revision of the 1949 ALA *Cataloging Rules for Author and Title Entries.* The Association of Research Libraries has also been considering cataloging practice for the particular needs of its members.

Another study in cooperation and centralization was by Altmann,[53] who substantiated Osborn's findings concerning the greater possibilities through centralization rather than cooperation. Altmann concluded that, despite various difficulties, problems of coverage, time, form, and cost could be solved by LC for all libraries, providing it could cover on cards the entire output of American book publishers. Some American publishers aid the cataloging program by sending prepublication copies of new titles to the Library of Congress so that cards can be prepared. The LC card numbers are then included in the books when published. The problem is more complicated for publications of foreign countries.

In extension of the cooperative cataloging sponsored by the Library of Congress, mentioned above, the Armed Forces Medical Library in 1950 assumed the responsibility for cataloging all medical titles acquired by the two libraries. The cards resulting from this plan are published in the *Armed Forces Medical Library Author Catalog* which supplements the *Author Catalog* issued by LC.[54] Another cooperative project, also in medicine, is that undertaken by the medical libraries of Yale and Columbia universities, which were later joined by that of the University of California at Los Angeles. Cards are exchanged for the titles that each library catalogs and responsibility for analyzing series is divided among the participating libraries.[55]

Attempts have long been made to achieve some measure of international cooperation in cataloging, but to date these have had little success. The Anglo-American rules have been used as a guide in some countries other than the United States and England, but the major conflict between the basic entry principles of this code and those of the codes based on the so-called *Prussian Instructions* is yet to be solved.[56]

Cooperation in subject control of materials in libraries was mentioned frequently in discussions at the Institute on the Subject Analysis of Library Materials at Columbia University in 1952.[57] The *Subject Catalog* of the Library of Congress is a step toward this continuing attempt to achieve rational organization of library techniques without waste and without duplication of effort. In Washington, four government libraries, the Group for the Standardization of Information Services, have agreed on descriptive cataloging operations, and are working on coordination of subject work.[58]

In a field related not only to cataloging but also to other library services such as binding, the International Organization for Standardization has drafted a recommendation for uniform layout of periodicals to be submitted to national organizations that work with editors and publishers.[59] This organization has also worked on the problem of uniform transliteration of the Cyrillic alphabets [60] and on the standardization of bibliographical references.[61] The bibliographic problem is directly related to the problem of international unification of rules of catalog entry.

Much more can be done in the area of cooperative and centralized cataloging. Probably both of these approaches are necessary at present. For example, cataloging of local materials, especially manuscripts, by individual libraries, helps materially to build up the National Union Catalog. Any plan for centralization must enlist the whole-hearted cooperation of librarians. If libraries use the cards issued by central agencies, cooperative technical work has a *raison d'être*, but if librarians refuse to accept this standardized product, cooperative and centralized cataloging may not develop to their full potential.

UNION CATALOGS [62]

Although he describes the prewar European scene, Pafford [63] has considered the purposes of union catalogs [64] that are applicable in the United States. Probably the principal motive has been to facilitate the location of specific items. This is the finding-list purpose of the union catalog. But union catalogs may be considered from other points of view. They have helped to distribute the burden of interlibrary loans, to reduce the need of several libraries purchasing rarely used materials, to diminish or prevent duplication of certain types of library materials, to indicate gaps in the holdings of libraries within an area and suggest fields of purchase, to make cooperative purchasing practicable and feasible, and to serve as useful bibliographical tools to various departments of libraries.[65]

The National Union Catalog at the Library of Congress in Washington is the major one of its type in the United States. LC also maintains Slavic, Hebraic, Chinese, and Japanese union catalogs. Work on the Cyrillic Subject Union Catalog was nearly completed by the end of fiscal year 1953. Regional union catalogs, sometimes based on LC depository catalogs, have been developed at Philadelphia, Cleveland, Chapel Hill-Durham, Nashville, Atlanta, Austin, Denver, Seattle, and other cities. Special subject union catalogs, such as the Art Union Catalog in Chicago, are also available.

The development of union catalogs has necessarily raised problems of administration. These may be concerned with the amount of money a library is willing to spend in keeping the union catalog up to date and in maintaining it. The emphasis placed upon the union catalog as a tool for extensive reference and bibliographical service, rather than as a mere finding list, suggests that it is likely to be of greater value when placed under the supervision of a large library or bibliographical center than if it operates as a detached unit. The need of providing space and equipment permitting the use of bibliographical and reference tools for business which is frequently not of local origin is a problem which must be solved. The actual operation of the union catalog is generally placed in the hands of separate personnel.

Union catalogs have been found also as part of the policy of individual libraries, as in the case of Harvard College Library. Harvard had begun the acquisition of cards from other libraries as a means of facilitating its own cataloging, and in 1911 began a union catalog of those cards which it did not immediately need—a catalog which later was combined with Harvard's own official catalog. This combined catalog reached such tremendous size that in 1952 all unused cards from libraries outside the Boston area were removed, so that "spatial limitations and financial considerations have combined with newly devised bibliographical tools to put an end to the earlier ideal of a regional or national catalogue for Harvard." [66]

BIBLIOGRAPHICAL CENTERS

One of the real developments in cooperative enterprise in the twentieth century among libraries is the bibliographical center. The Philadelphia Bibliographical Center, the Bibliographical Center for Research in Denver (Rocky Mountain Region), and the Pacific Northwest Bibliographic Center in Seattle are three examples of this organization for assisting libraries, research scholars, authors, and general readers. Already the centers have assumed a pattern which includes the provision of a union catalog, a collection of working bibliographies, and a trained staff. The union catalog, which has already been described, is the basic tool for locating copies of individual titles. The bibliographical collection is used in identifying and locating books and collections. The staff of librarians establishes and maintains contact with libraries within and outside of the region and with other bibliographical centers and other union catalogs. The major purpose is never overlooked—to get the wanted item into the hands of the user as promptly as possible or to provide such information as the user may wish to have regarding a specific title or group of titles.

Thus, the locating function is likely to be the predominant activity of the centers. However, they do more than just locate items wanted by readers. They facilitate the interlibrary borrowing of books by routing requests to the proper sources; they direct those interested in certain subjects to collections best serving their purpose; they assist librarians and library users in solving their bibliographical problems (identification of authors, editions, etc.); and they serve as a clearing house for cooperation among libraries—in bibliography, book-buying, subject specialization, and cataloging.

INTERLIBRARY CENTERS AND STORAGE LIBRARIES

A number of the large research libraries of the United States, faced with the problem of vast collections which are increasing in size with frightening rapidity, have attempted two programs which promise the opening of new cooperation among many American libraries.

In 1941, a group of libraries in the Boston area founded the New England Deposit Library. A central warehouse, built by the cooperating libraries, provides storage for materials which they expect to be used infrequently, thus freeing space in their own buildings which can be devoted to more urgent demands. The Deposit Library rents shelf space and assumes basic maintenance of the deposits, but each cooperating library retains title to its material, and use of what is stored is subject to basically the same regulations as it would be if shelved in the owning library.[67]

The Midwest Inter-Library Center, opened in Chicago in 1951, adds a dramatic new conception to library cooperation, in its function as a libraries' library.

"The individual library can no longer hope to satisfy the needs of scholarship from its own resources." [68] This idea, and that of the financial impossibility of keeping abreast of current publishing output, were the reasons behind a study financed by the Carnegie Corporation in 1947 to discover what solutions there might be. The resultant proposals led in 1949 to a grant of $1,000,000 by the Carnegie Corporation and the Rockefeller Foundation for the creation of the Midwest Inter-Library Center, with the following definite functions:

> 1. To establish and maintain a Midwest Inter-Library Center for the cooperative custody, organization, housing, servicing (and for some materials, ownership), of little-used research materials. The center will constitute essentially a collection of little-used research materials placed on indefinite loan in its custody, and available on interlibrary loan to member institutions under the terms established by its board of directors. 2. To serve as an agency for encouraging and implementing coordination of collection policies for specialized fields, among the cooperating libraries . . . [it will] encourage libraries to define their acquisition policies in special fields, will make known to the participating institutions these selections, and will attempt to encourage further selection and definition to the end that libraries in the Midwest may provide more adequately and with less duplication for the research needs of the Middle West. 3. To serve as an agency to explore the possibilities for cooperative bibliographical services among the member institutions.[69]

The Center now includes sixteen cooperating libraries, and its program is rapidly reaching the stage where its value can be felt concretely by its members, and where critical evaluation of the idea can be begun.[70]

The movement has spread to New England where a Hampshire Inter-Library Center has been constituted,[71] and a Northeastern Regional Library is under discussion by major research libraries of the region between Washington and Boston.[72]

IX. Catalog Entries and Description

THE making of entries for the card catalog is one of the major responsibilities and one of the most technical operations of catalogers. In contrast to classifying and assigning subject headings, the establishing and making of the entries and the description of the volumes entered are accomplished according to fairly well codified rules. Grouping of subjects may change as new concepts develop, and newer terminology may take the place of old subject headings, but the factors governing entry and description have been for the most part constant. Recent discussion of proposed changes in entry may lead to revision of long-standing rules.

KINDS OF ENTRY

Catalog entries are provided to enable the users of the catalog to find the books or materials they need under any entry where they may reasonably expect to find them, to collect works under the responsible author, and to assemble the variants of a literary form. The approach may be by author, title, or subject. However, the users may have other information regarding a publication and therefore may look under the name of a translator or an editor. Perhaps a series title is known and search made under it; or an illustrator may be the chief interest, and an entry under his name the focal point of search. Thus, there is need, depending on the character and content of the materials to be cataloged, for entry under author, title, subject, editor, translator, compiler, series, and still other possible headings. Some works with which a person or group has had important, yet undefinable relationship are also found. In such cases, a catalog entry is made with no designation of relationship—this is called a general secondary entry.

The main entry is made under the author or the person chiefly responsible, when known, otherwise under title. All other entries are called secondary or added entries. Most libraries have in general adopted the unit card system for making these entries.

Catalog entries may be grouped into three types: author and other name entries, subject entries (other than name), and titles. Subject entries present many and varying problems and are not stable.

Name entries, whether author or secondary, present a common problem in that a single form of name is usually established for each person so that all materials relating to the individual will come together in the catalog and be distinguishable from those by or about any other person with a similar name. Establishing the entry may be a complicated operation. The amount of time necessary to perform this operation varies with the importance of the author, his period and nationality, the information available in the material at hand, and also with the type and size of institution for which the cataloging is done. Variant forms of names of personal authors, differences in national usage, works published either pseudonymously or anonymously, all present their peculiar problems. Materials published by public or private agencies as authors necessitate special care and treatment, so that all of an agency's publications will be found in the catalog under a single form of entry.

The term "author" is used broadly to indicate the person or group responsible for a work. To distinguish between individual authors and bodies which act in a responsible capacity as authors (governments, associations, societies, and institutions) the phrase "personal authorship" is used for the former and "corporate authorship" for the latter.

HISTORICAL BACKGROUND OF RULES OF ENTRY

Before considering problems arising with various forms of name entry and the rules involved, it may be helpful to examine briefly the background of the rules now generally followed in the United States.[1] This is particularly appropriate since current practices are being questioned.

The earliest recognition of the principle of authorship as main entry is found in the Bodleian rules in 1674. These rules recognize that the author catalog has a function beyond that of a finding list, in that its function is to assemble under a single heading all issues and forms of the same literary unit. The most satisfactory way of doing this is through attribution of authorship using the name of a person, or as a substitute, a conventional name not derived from the title page, but from the literary source of the book or document.[2]

In the mid-nineteenth century, Anthony Panizzi's famous 92 rules for the British Museum catalog,[3] printed in 1841, and Charles C. Jewett's code of 39 rules, published by the Smithsonian Institution in 1852,[4] gave impetus to thought on establishment of a code of cataloging rules which might be generally applicable to libraries in this country.

The epochal year of 1876 saw publication of the first edition of Charles Ammi Cutter's *Rules for a Dictionary Catalog,* which Sharp considered "the first code of complete cataloging practice for every kind of entry needed in a dictionary catalog." [5] In the first edition, there were 205 rules. In 1883, the ALA's *Condensed Rules for an Author and Title Catalog* were printed in its proceedings in the *Library Journal* [6] and were later reprinted in Cutter's *Rules.* Dewey published his *Library School Card Catalog Rules* in 1889.

"An important, but sometimes overlooked, contribution to cataloguing practice was made in 1886 by Professor K. Dziatzko . . . which an American librarian, K. A. Linderfelt, translated in 1890 and published, with other rules of his own, as *Eclectic Card Catalog Rules; Author and Title Entries, Based on Dziatzko's "Instruction," Compared with the Rules of the British Museum, Cutter, Dewey, Perkins, and other Authorities.* Next to Cutter's *Rules* this was among the most useful contributions made to the science of cataloguing." [7]

Interest in cooperative cataloging and the decision of the Library of Congress to inaugurate in 1901 a printed card service to other libraries, gave impetus to demands for revision of the ALA rules, with a view to greater standardization of practice.[8] A committee of the ALA was appointed and began to function in 1901 "to formulate standard cataloging rules which would be in accord with the system at the Library of Congress. The chairman of the committee was J. C. M. Hanson, Chief of the Catalog Division of the Library of Congress, who by his position was particularly well qualified for the assignment and who was willing to make many concessions in the Library of Congress practice so that it would conform to the requirements of the A.L.A. code." [9] A draft code was printed by the Library of Congress in 1901 as the *ALA Rules—Advance Edition.* With increasing communication of ideas and criticisms of the new code, both here and in Great Britain where it was greeted with considerable interest, it became evident that a joint code might be possible. Melvil Dewey is given credit for suggesting that the two associations join in producing an Anglo-American code. The definite proposal was sent by the Library Association in October, 1904, and was accepted. Consultation proceeded by means of correspondence, and on September 19th, 1906, John Minto of the British Committee wrote suggesting that "the code should be printed in two editions (English and American) but that the editions should as far as possible be identical in arrangement and wording." [10] The American edition was published in 1908.

Discussion of the rules continued, criticisms and suggestions appeared, but not until 1930 was a definite recommendation for their revision made, when the ALA Committee on Cataloging and Classification suggested it as a project. In the following year, the New York Regional Catalog Group, at their spring meeting, took up the discussion of needs.[11] And in 1932, Hanson further emphasized the situation, suggesting certain additions, expansions, and improvements.[12] He made another of his many important contributions in 1939, with his *Comparative Study of Cataloging Rules,* in which he urged the need for further study of cataloging rules, with a view to possible international agreement.

The publication in 1931 of the Vatican code, *Norme per il Catalogo degli Stampati,* was most timely. Based largely on Library of Congress practice, it suggested possible areas of desirable amplification and the use of illustrative material. This code was issued in English translation in 1948.[13]

The ALA committee had been at work considering the evidence of various groups' reports, and had reached the conclusion that the principal need was for expansion, not change. A Carnegie grant, received in April, 1936, enabled work to proceed more formally. For a fuller statement of the progress toward a revised code, one may consult the preface of the 1949 edition of the ALA *Cataloging Rules.*

The Preliminary Edition, published in 1941, was divided into two parts: Part I. Entry and Headings; and Part II. Description of Book. Criticism was made of overelaboration and possible resultant increased costs of cataloging, so a committee was appointed to consider these and make further recommendations. As a result, work on Part II was deferred, and revision of Part I went on. In 1949, the revised edition was finally published. The principal changes were "a rearrangement of the material to emphasize the basic rules and subordinate their amplifications, and to make the sequence of rules logical so far as possible; reduction of the number of alternate rules; omission of rules of description; rewording to avoid repetition or to make the meaning clearer; and revision, where possible, of rules inconsistent with the general principles." [14]

The publication by the Library of Congress of its *Rules for Descriptive Cataloging,* in the fall of 1949, gave the profession an accepted substitute for Part II of the ALA *Catalog Rules* (Preliminary Ed.). The background of the LC rules and their relationship to the American Library Association code is described in their introduction.

Turning from the historical background and development of the rules which guide American libraries in general, consideration may now be given to specific problems of personal and corporate author entry. Understanding of these is basic to consideration of the lesser problems of added entries, since the forms chosen for main entries govern those used for secondary name entries.

PERSONAL AUTHOR ENTRY

General Rule. In the heading give the author's name in full and in the vernacular form with certain specific exceptions. . . . If the author is known in literature, history or common parlance by more than one name, prefer (1) the most authentic, (2) the best known when the authentic has been but little used and another form has been in use predominantly both by the person concerned and in records and literature. . . . Refer from forms not adopted.—ALA *Cataloging Rules*, p. 82.

For the great bulk of modern writers, no difficulty is presented in deciding the form of name to use. It is usually on the title page. This name is used in conformity with ALA Rule 37: "Enter persons of modern times under the family name followed by the forenames and the dates of birth and death when available." When two authors have the same surname and given name, dates of birth and/or death are in most cases sufficient to distinguish between them. In the past, it has been the practice of most libraries to ascertain variant forms of name, and dates, whenever possible with reasonable effort, for all new personal name entries. Morsch has said, "a reasonable effort cannot be defined in terms of time limits because of the varying reference sources, and the greater need for authors' dates in certain cases. For example, a common surname requires more specific identification by means of forenames than an unusual surname . . . [and] the cataloger must keep in mind the law of diminishing return in determining how much research is reasonable in any given case." [15]

The cost of this research has increased considerably the cost of original cataloging, often needlessly and with no definitely beneficial results. The value of the information obtained, and its use by the public, have long been questioned in relation to the cost. Morsch reports that in 90 percent of the books in a group selected for a study at the Library of Congress, the form used in the book did not conflict with other already established entries.[16] The Library of Congress, considering these and other facts, has recently adopted the following rule:

> New personal name entries to be used in all cataloging shall hereafter be established on the basis of "no conflict," that is, a personal name shall be established in the form given in the work being cataloged without further search, provided that, as given in the work being cataloged the name conforms to the A.L.A. rules for entry, and is not so similar to another name previously established as to give a good basis for the suspicion that both names refer to the same person.[17]

Undoubtedly this will save time and cost and will influence other libraries to follow suit. Certain reasons for not accepting the name as given on the first piece cataloged should be kept in mind, and the results of this new LC policy watched. Morsch gives the following reasons which may be advanced for doing research before establishing an author entry:

> (1) The catalog is constructed on the basis primarily of bringing together in one place all the known works of one author. Authors, or their publishers, are known to use varying forms of their names.
> (2) Unless some investigation is made, cross references from other forms, when these exist, would not be known to be necessary and the reader's search under a variant form would be without results.
> (3) Names in the most common and generally accepted form have a more lasting value and are unlikely to have to be revised as later publications are received.
> (4) Names in the most complete . . . form are very unlikely to conflict with entries previously established in the catalogs of our card subscribers who now in most cases accept our entries without question or further investigation.[18]

It remains to be seen whether the new policy will, in the long run, actually save appreciably. On the surface, it would seem that for the great majority of new personal author entries, conflicts would seldom occur.

AUTHORITY FILE. Some cataloging departments maintain an authority file in which are recorded the accepted forms for all names appearing in the catalog as entries. This file serves as a record of authorities consulted in establishing the form of name accepted, of references made from other forms of name, and of the name forms already in use in the catalog, thus saving time in checking for conflict, especially when the cataloger does not have quick access to either a public or official catalog. Forms of authority cards may be found in such publications as *Sample Catalog Cards*, Numbers 32–36.[19]

As was noted in Chapter V, the catalogers use a system of abbreviations for the reference authorities consulted in establishing entries. Many of the major reference works are included in the *Co-operative Cataloging Manual* of the Library of Congress. The checks of identification are as follows:

√ = name found
√d = name and date found
√√ = name and title of book being cataloged found; date not found
√√d = name, date, and title of book cataloged found
o = name not found

PROBLEMS IN NAME ENTRIES. The problems most frequently encountered in personal name entry work are those of married women's names, compound surnames and those with prefixes, titles of nobility or religion, and pseudonyms.

A married woman is usually entered under her latest name, followed by her forenames and her maiden name in parentheses. Reference is made from her maiden name. If, however, she is better known by her maiden name, entry is made under it, with a reference from her married name (e.g., Du Maurier, Daphne, with a reference from Brown, Daphne (Du Maurier)). This seems simple. Problems arise, however, because of divorce with resumption of a maiden name; because of remarriage and possible continued use of a previous husband's name in writing; and because of foreign usage of a maiden name compounded with a married name, particularly in Spanish, Portuguese, and Brazilian names, where the usage is not always consistent.[20]

Compound names are usually entered under the first part of the name, with reference from the second (e.g., Kaye-Smith, Sheila, with a reference from Smith, Sheila Kaye-) unless the author's or national usage prefers otherwise. Spanish, Portuguese, and Brazilian names cause more problems, chiefly because of our unfamiliarity with the national customs and because of their apparent similarity, although they are often treated differently.

The question of national usage also contributes much toward the variations found in names beginning with prefixes. Those which begin with an attributive prefix are always entered under it (e.g., Fitz-Gerald, Edward; Santa Anna, Antonio Lopez de). Difficulty arises with those which begin with a preposition or an article, because of three factors: language differences, change of citizenship, and established usage contrary to the rules. ALA Rule 39B clearly states the forms preferred in the various languages. When a person changes his citizenship, his name is entered according to the rules for the language of his adopted country. Thus, Hendrik Willem Van Loon is entered, according to the rules for English language names, under Van Loon, with a reference from Loon, Hendrik Willem van. Had he remained a Netherlander, the entry would have been under the second form with a reference from the first.

PSEUDONYMOUS WORKS. Titles issued pseudonymously are generally entered under the author's real name when known, with exception generally made if the pseudonym has become better known in literary history (and the author has never written under his real name); if the author does not wish to have his real name known to the public; and if two or more persons have written together using one pseudonym (e.g., Meg, Elizabeth, *pseud.* for works written jointly by Elizabeth Wenning Goep and Margaret Webb). In any case, reference is made from the pseudonym to the real name, or, in the exceptions, from the real name or names to the pseudonym.[21] Practice varies somewhat, with public libraries entering modern authors under pseudonyms more frequently than do scholarly libraries. However, if an author has used more than one pseudonym, it seems wise to use the real name, even if one pseudonym has become well known (e.g., Goodchild, George, with references from his pseudonyms Alan Dare, Q. R. Wallace, and Jesse Templeton).

CORPORATE AUTHORSHIP

General Rule and Specification. Governments and their agencies, societies, institutions, firms, conferences, etc., are to be regarded as the authors of publications for which they, as corporate bodies, are responsible. Such material as official publications of governments, proceedings and reports of societies, official catalogs of libraries and museums, reports of institutions, firms, conferences, and other bodies is entered under the heading for the corporate body, even though the name of the individual preparing it is given.

Monographic works by individuals, officials, officers, members and employees of corporate bodies when these works are not clearly administrative or routine in character, are preferably to be entered under personal author, even though issued by the corporate body.—ALA *Cataloging Rules*, p. 126.

The treatment of corporate authorship, although discussed in detail in the second edition of the ALA *Cataloging Rules*, apparently has not met with general approval. Increasingly, discontent with the existing rules has led to questioning of the practice of the Library of Congress and other large libraries.

Government publications are entered under the country, or other governmental area, responsible for their issuing. The name of the responsible government agency is used as a subheading. A bureau subordinate to an executive department is used as a direct subheading, unless its name is not distinctive (e.g., U.S. *Office of Internal Revenue*, not U.S. *Treasury Dept. Office of Internal Revenue*; but U.S. *Dept. of State. Office of Public Affairs*, not U.S. *Office of Public Affairs*, because several departments might have such offices). This exception causes some inconsistencies in interpretation. Form subheadings are used with the name of the jurisdiction for "laws, decrees, and other acts having the force of law," (e.g., New Zealand. *Laws, statutes, etc.*; South Africa. *Constitution*).[22]

The chief cause of inconsistencies is the distinction made between societies and institutions. The ALA rules define a society as "an organization of persons associated together for the promotion of common purposes or objects, such as research, business, recreation, etc." and an institution as an entity "whose functions require a plant with buildings, apparatus, etc., as distinguished from bodies, organized groups of persons such as societies, associations, etc., whose duties may be performed equally well in one place or another."[23] A society, according to Rule 91, is entered under the first word other than an article, of its "latest corporate name, with reference from any other names by which it is known, and from the place where its headquarters are established." An institution, according to Rule 92, is entered under the name of the place where it is located; an important exception however, is made for institutions in the United States or Great Britain which have names beginning with a proper noun or adjective—these are entered under the name with a reference from the place. It is the possible and frequent confusion between an institution and a society, in practice, which draws most severe criticism of the rules.

Osborn, speaking before a meeting of the International Federation of Library Associations at Oslo in 1947, said:

> The most notable problem with which American libraries are faced is the corporate entry. In 1935, J. C. M. Hanson drew attention in the *Library Quarterly* to the need for a thorough re-examination of the whole question of corporate entry. He felt that he had been as influential as anyone in developing the use of the corporate entry, but now, toward the end of his career, he had to shake his head and wonder whether we had been on right lines after all. An examination of our professional literature will disclose that no thorough study of the corporate entry has ever been made, and that after half a century of use no attempt has been made to get the situation in hand. We have to admit in the first instance that we are not clear in our minds about the fundamental theory of the corporate entry. We are not sure, for example, when to use the official name of a body and when to use another form, commonly the popular name. We are very unsure about subdivisions of corporate names, that is, when to subdivide and how far to carry the subdivisions. When there is a choice of entry between a corporate and a personal name, we do not always know which is the form to prefer; and it is not an uncommon experience for us to find that we have cataloged one copy of a work under the corporate name, and a second copy under the personal name. In these and in other respects then, we have not achieved any such measure of objectivity as to make us

feel satisfied with the results. We are sure that the corporate entry is sound in theory but we are not sure when it comes to individual cases.[24]

The matter gains further importance because of world-wide interest in greater uniformity of cataloging practice and the fact that in the area of corporate entry we find the greatest divergence of practice. The library world is divided into two groups, those following the Anglo-American rules, and those following the German practice as exemplified in the *Prussian Instructions,* which do not recognize the principle of corporate authorship. In the second group, only personal authorship is recognized and publications of societies, institutions, governmental agencies, etc., are considered as anonymous works to be entered under title (the exact practice varying).

Hanson points out that there is evidence of greater economy in the use of title rather than corporate entry, but notes that title main entry also presents difficulties and results in large accumulations of material in certain areas of the alphabet.[25] It does not collect materials of a responsible publishing agency in any one place.

The need for revision of the ALA rules of entry, particularly the corporate entry, was underlined by Taube in his criticism of the present code and his presentation of the three rules for corporate entry as used in the Science and Technology Project of the Library of Congress.

(1) Enter the publication of a corporate entity under its name.

(2) The form of the name is to be determined by information available in the work being cataloged and in authority lists available from cataloging previous works and from these two sources only.

(3) If the title-page or other parts of the work being cataloged disclose that a division or part of a corporate body was responsible for the report, entry should be made under the division or part unless the name of the part is contained in a standard list of names not suitable for entries. In such cases entry is to be made under the next largest administrative unit or part. Names not suitable for entries may be used as subdivisions for filing purposes at the discretion of individual institutions.[26]

Lubetzky [27] pointed out important merits and defects in Taube's suggestions and subsequently prepared a "critique of the ALA rules for entry and a proposed design for their revision," [28] which devoted considerable attention to the problem of the corporate entry and which is now receiving close attention from members of the profession, both in the United States [29] and abroad. The purpose is to prepare a more satisfactory code of rules than now exists.

If the basic rules of corporate entry can be simplified and the illogical applications removed, it seems quite probable that some further step toward international acceptance of the theory may be expected. Ansteinsson, at the London meeting of the International Federation of Library Associations in 1948, remarked that "the idea of corporate authorship is logically consistent with the principles governing the treatment of publications of personal authors, and the adoption of the principle of corporate authorship is a sound basis for any efforts to unify the rules." [30] He then went on to discuss the difficulties of selecting correct forms of names.

Encouragement toward the goal of an international code of cataloging rules, including rules for corporate entry, comes from Sigmund von Frauendorfer. This writer has pointed out that, while the *Prussian Instructions* do not accept corporate entry, they do accept commercial firms as the authors of sales catalogs which they issue. Frauendorfer notes that the principle of corporate authorship has the following advantages: it reduces the number of anonymous entries; its basic principles are simple and easy to apply except for the Anglo-American code distinction between societies and institutions. The present, he suggests, is an opportune time to press for an international code, because of the war's widespread destruction and disorganization of libraries, which necessitate reorganization and often recataloging.[31]

TITLE MAIN ENTRY

For certain types of material (anonymous classics, other works published anonymously and for which the author cannot be ascertained, and publications for which responsibility cannot be attributed to an author, editor, or compiler, personal or corporate) the main entry is frequently under the title. The last-mentioned group includes some forms of composite works, collections, and serials (newspapers, periodicals, yearbooks, etc.).

The remaining group, which is not entered under title, receives what is commonly known as a "form heading" or "subheading" (e.g., Great Britain. *Laws, statutes, etc.;* United Nations. *Charter*). Ellinger has commented on "non-author headings" and some of the problems which they present.[32]

Anonymous works are entered under author whenever identification is possible, and either an added entry or a cross reference is made for any phrase or initials the author may have used in place of his name. Those for which authorship cannot be established are entered under title, with an added entry for any phrase indicating authorship.

Anonymous classics are defined as works "of unknown or doubtful authorship, commonly designated by title, which may have appeared in the course of time in many editions, versions and/or translations." The general rule is to enter "editions of anonymous classics and their translations under a uniform heading consisting of the traditional or conventional title of the work in the language of the original version if known" [33] (e.g., Chanson de Roland, Beowulf). When the classic is well known in several languages, entry under an English form is preferred (e.g., Bible, Arabian Nights). Many public and school libraries prefer the English form in general. The Bible, because of special problems of parts, versions, language of text, etc., receives separate treatment in ALA Rule 34.

A composite work [34] is entered under title when the chief responsibility is not clear and whenever there are more than three collaborators. An added entry is made for the first author mentioned, and for others if they are important for the particular situation. If there are not more than three, the entry is made under the first author.

A collection,[35] if it has a collective title page, is entered under title only when "the work of the editor or editing body seems to be slight and their names do not appear prominently, or if there are frequent changes of editor." [36] The editor receives an added entry.

Periodicals and newspapers are generally entered under their latest titles, with references from any earlier titles they may have had. This includes those periodicals issued by societies, institutions, and government bodies, providing they have distinctive titles. Otherwise, entry is made under the issuing body (e.g., Institute of Production Engineers, *London.* Journal, *not* Journal of the Institute of Production Engineers).

Series are entered under title unless more familiarly known by the name of an editor or publisher (e.g., The Rural Science Series, Harper's Modern Science Series), or unless the series has no distinctive title. In such cases, entry is made under the issuing agency (e.g., Brookings Institution, *Washington, D.C.* Publications).

Some types of material raise special problems: music and recordings, because of questions of authorship or versions and forms of titles; maps, because of the problem of deciding whether to make the entry under cartographer, sponsoring body, or geographic area; foreign publications, because of questions of transliteration and other aspects of language.

ADDED ENTRIES

The problem of what added entries should be made is of the utmost importance because the usability of the catalog is determined nearly as much by the added entries as by the main entries. Also, the whole question of cost of upkeep is involved because of possible growth in size by inclusion of unnecessary or little-used added entries, and the additional card stock and clerical service needed to maintain an expanding catalog.

Subject entry will be covered more suitably in connection with the discussion of classification at a later time. There remain three types of added entry to consider: title, name, and series.

Title added entries should always be made for those titles which are distinctive since this is the first point of search for many users. Space may be saved, and good service still maintained, by including in the catalog only one title added entry per work, if there are several editions of a work available. A note on this entry may refer readers to the main entry for information about other editions. Titles which begin with a common phrase, such as "Outline of" or "History of" should not as a rule be given added entry. Care must be taken to avoid using title entries which are similar to, or identical with, the wording of a subject entry. Works of literature usually are given a title entry. Mann summarizes the problem of title added entry and lists the types of material customarily given such treatment.[37]

Persons having important connection with the production of a publication, although not the authors, often are of interest and should be entered in the catalog. A general secondary entry is made for such persons, if the connection is not definable by some term. Editors and compilers may be either main entries or added entries, depending on the nature of the book and of their services. Added entries for translators are sometimes made, the practice varying with the importance for the needs of the library. Increasingly, libraries are omitting such entries unless it seems likely that the users will refer to a work by the name of its translator. Added entry is made for illustrators only when their work is an important feature of a book.

A series added entry is made for works belonging to series, but the general practice is to omit such entries for publishers' series. Many libraries do not follow the unit card system for such entries, but prefer to use a combined series card,[38] thus saving space in the catalog.

Recently, the Library of Congress, in an effort to speed up cataloging, has changed its rules and has eliminated many of the kinds of entries discussed in the preceding section, when the information is of seemingly little value.[39]

The ALA *Cataloging Rules* are widely used in the United States and many other countries. There are indications of further simplification for the future. There is a wholesome questioning of the present practice in regard to corporate entry, and thus an encouraging outlook for possible reconciliation of rules for a future international code. Cutter's statement, in his *Rules for a Dictionary Catalog*, expresses the relation of the catalog to the user. He wrote in the preface as follows:

> The convenience of the public is always to be set before the ease of the cataloger. In most cases they coincide. A plain rule without exceptions is not only easy for us to carry out, but easy for the public to understand and to work by. But strict consistency in a rule and uniformity in its application sometimes leads to practices which clash with the public's habitual way of looking at things. When these habits are general and deeply rooted it is unwise for the cataloger to ignore them, even if they demand a sacrifice of system and simplicity.

DESCRIPTIVE CATALOGING

The rules for descriptive cataloging as practiced in American libraries have followed rather closely those of the ALA and the Library of Congress. In fact, the ALA, rather than continuing the development of a separate set of rules, has adopted as official the *Rules for Descriptive Cataloging in the Library of Congress.*[40] The ALA, through its Division of Cataloging and Classification, and the Library of Congress work together in developing new rules or changing old ones.

The Library of Congress includes in its definition of descriptive cataloging both the identification and description of books and other materials. The major principles which LC has set forth in connection with descriptive cataloging are as follows: [41]

> Principles of Descriptive Cataloging. The following principles provide a common basis for the rules for the descriptive cataloging of all library materials. By their use it is possible for the cataloger, when faced with problems not specifically provided for, to solve them in the spirit and intent of the rules given below. It is recognized that descriptive cataloging is not the only method of making library materials accessible, and that, in dealing with some types of them, guides, calendars, indexes, inventories, etc., may be preferable.
>
> *Objectives of descriptive cataloging.* The objectives of descriptive cataloging are: (1) to state the significant features of an item with the pur-

pose of distinguishing it from other items and describing its scope, contents, and bibliographic relation to other items; (2) to present these data in an entry which can be integrated with the entries for other items in the catalog and which will respond best to the interests of most users of the catalog.

Description of a perfect copy. An attempt is made to describe a physically complete copy.

Extent of description. The item is described as fully as necessary to achieve the objectives stated above, but with economy of data and expression.

Terms of description. The terms used by the author, composer, publisher or other issuing authority in or on the item generally form the basis of the description. Ambiguous or unintelligible statements used in the description are followed by explanations. Inaccuracies are indicated and corrected when necessary.

Organization of the description. The descriptive elements are given in the entry in the order that will best meet the needs of the users of the catalog and will facilitate the integration of the entry in a catalog with entries for other items.

Documentation. The source of information contained in an entry need be specified only when the information is questionable or the source is unusual.

Style. A uniform style is adopted for all catalog entries, covering spelling, capitalization, punctuation, abbreviations, use of numerals, indentions, and in certain instances, type faces.

It does not seem necessary to discuss in any great detail here the procedures for cataloging as outlined in the LC *Rules.* However, it should be repeated that some libraries do not follow LC to the letter. Simplifications of various kinds, such as shortened titles and omission of imprints, collation data, and notes of various kinds have been introduced in many small libraries and some of the larger libraries.[42] As noted by Morsch in the foreword to the LC *Rules,* "The fact that the Library of Congress is cataloging its materials to integrate them in a large general collection and in large special collections, e.g., maps, music, etc., and is printing its catalog cards, is often a deciding factor in the adoption of certain rules; other libraries using the rules will have to decide for themselves at what point they wish to depart from them." [43]

The elimination of cataloging and most preparational operations for certain types of materials—mystery and western stories, romances, paperback books, and some pamphlets—has met with success in a number of public libraries. A few college libraries have also provided for immediate circulation of paperback books. These materials, which receive minimal handling, are considered expendable.

Attention should be called to the developments in the cataloging of technical reports. Because of mode of origin and security restrictions, these materials present an operational problem somewhat different from the usual book or monographic publications. Adequate records and controls, however, are essential, and some efforts are being made to codify practices.[44]

PERIODICAL INDEXING

In some libraries, periodical indexing may be an important assignment of the technical units, or it may be performed by the staff connected with the reference or bibliographical departments. Regardless of the location of the staff involved in this operation, periodical indexing requires considerable reliance upon the general methodology of cataloging—entry and subject analysis. The *Current List of Medical Literature* of the Armed Forces Medical Library and the *Periodical Index* of the Air University are examples of such indexes. Other governmental, special, and academic libraries prepare indexes of varying scope. In some instances, an effort is made to supplement the several available commercial indexes, particularly those issued by the H. W. Wilson Company.[45] The *Periodical Index* of the Air University is a result of this effort. The Avery Architectural Library of Columbia University prepares periodical analytics for its architectural card file, emphasizing items not included in the *Art Index*. The practices of libraries differ in some respects in the detail and the form of indexing, but on the whole they are similar in style to the commercial indexes. The subject headings in the Air University *Periodical Index* have been developed according to the peculiar needs of the clientele working in the field of aeronautics and related areas. Various tools have been prepared for assisting librarians in their work of compiling indexes.[46]

x. Subject Headings

THE present tendency to assign all cataloging operations to one of two major categories—descriptive cataloging and subject cataloging—has been noted. Descriptive cataloging contributes to the identification of a particular book and to distinguishing that book positively from all others. Therefore, it requires the determination of an appropriate entry according to the principles which underlie ALA cataloging rules and the formulation of suitable descriptive data according to the standards prescribed in the LC *Rules for Descriptive Cataloging*. Subject cataloging, on the other hand, involves analysis of the subject content of the book and the expression of that content in terms of appropriate classification numbers for arrangement and shelving purposes, and of suitable subject headings to provide for an alphabetic or other approach through the library's catalog.

These operations are not wholly separate, and the one activity may, incidentally, achieve the end objective of the other, either in whole or in part. This is more true of descriptive than of subject cataloging, since the description of a particular book may, at the same time, give expression of its subject content. Many of the objections to schemes for simplifying descriptive cataloging operations which have been made by reference librarians reflect this awareness of the dual function performed by good descriptive cataloging. An obvious case to illustrate this point would be the collected literary works of a single author, to which subject headings are not usually assigned. The rules for entry provide first for primary entry of the book in the library's catalog under the author's name; those for description require that the title of the work be transcribed essentially the same as it appears on the title page. Thus, a volume of *The Plays of William Congreve,* when entered and described in a library catalog according to these rules, will also have its subject content sufficiently described. The book will require an appropriate classification number so that it may be shelved with related material in the English literature section of the library's collection.

To take a less obvious case, it is possible for the collation statement, when considered with the rest of the description of the physical book, to contribute to a statement of its subject content. For example, a book on architecture entitled *French Gothic Cathedrals,* and described as "50 p. and atlas of 300 plates," will be recognized without further subject heading as being chiefly pictorial representations of French cathedrals built approximately from the twelfth to the sixteenth centuries and concerned in part, at least, with some representations of architectural details, since there are not 300 French Gothic cathedrals to require that number of plates.

Effective access to the content of most books, however, requires some subject analysis. Classification partly achieves this, but since classification has developed in American libraries as much to determine the location of books as to describe their subject content, it has certain limitations which will be discussed in the next chapter. The other common method by which a subject approach is provided to a library's collection is the subject catalog.

KINDS OF SUBJECT CATALOGS

Subject catalogs,[1] in their historic development, have evolved in a variety of forms. Perhaps the earliest in point of time is the classified catalog which represents, in effect, no more than an inventory of the classified arrangement of materials on the library's shelves. In such a catalog, many titles are likely to be recorded under a relatively few general headings, which may or may not be subdivided. The basic arrangement in the pure classified catalog is not alphabetical, but follows the order of the classification scheme used. Such an arrangement has the limitation that its user must be familiar with the scheme in order to make the most effective use of the subject catalog. If the user has access to the shelves, the classified catalog in this form provides him with no additional approach to the subject content of the library. An obvious extension of the pure classified catalog is one to which an alphabetic subject index has been added.

This is the classified catalog in its simplest form. In the few American libraries where classified catalogs are maintained, the actual catalog is more complex, since multiple entries for the same title are made to provide for as thorough subject coverage as is necessary and feasible. Typically, arrangement is by classification number, not by subject designation, so that instead of having many titles listed under a few broad subjects, relatively few titles are found listed under the minute class numbers. In such a catalog the alphabetic subject index becomes of first importance, and in itself resembles a list of subject headings similar to those found in a typical alphabetical subject catalog as described below. The best-known examples of this kind of catalog are to be found in the John Crerar Library in Chicago, the Engineering Societies Library in New York City, and the Science and Technology Department of the Carnegie Library of Pittsburgh. Boston University Library has recently established a classified catalog based on the Library of Congress system.[2]

An alternative form of the classified catalog, and one which has had some popularity recently and whose influence on present subject-heading practices is easy to identify, is the so-called alphabetico-classified catalog. In this arrangement, instead of having only a few major subject categories arranged according to the classification scheme, a somewhat larger number of main categories are employed, and these are arranged alphabetically. Topics subordinate to the main subjects are listed as subdivisions. For example, if Chemistry is used as one of the main subjects, a book on the chemical properties of sulphur might be listed under Chemistry—Inorganic—Nonmetallic elements—Oxygen group—Sulphur.

The alphabetical subject catalog, in contrast to the alphabetico-classified catalog, utilizes direct and specific subject headings, and these are arranged in one alphabet. The example cited above would be listed in the alphabetical subject catalog under Sulphur. While direct and specific headings represent the ideal, compromises have been necessary for practicality and usability. In American libraries, the alphabetical subject catalog is the most common, although it is usually an integral part of a dictionary card catalog which includes, in one alphabet (though frequently with conventional departures from strict alphabetical order) all entries for authors, titles, and subjects. Within the last two decades, however, a number of libraries have introduced divided catalogs, separating authors and titles from subjects on the theory that the resulting catalog is more easily understood and used. As noted earlier, such analyses as have been made appear to support this contention.[3] Since the alphabetical subject catalog, either as an element of the dictionary catalog or a segment of the divided catalog, is the dominant form in American libraries, this discussion of subject headings will relate almost entirely to their use in an alphabetical subject catalog.

The foregoing types, together with various permutations of them, are based largely on the use of some conventionalized verbal expression of the subject idea. The formalism of these expressions is greatest in the alphabetical subject catalog and least in the alphabetical subject index to the classified catalog. The other type of subject catalog has never been popular in this country and is rarely found here except in early printed catalogs. The catchword subject catalog, called by the Germans *Schlagwort,* makes use of verbal expressions of subject content taken directly from the title of the book being cataloged. This may result in entry for the same subject material under different headings when the authors of books on that subject used different terms. The importance of "catch-subjects," or "catch-titles," lies not in the frequency of their use in modern library catalogs, but rather in their influence on the development of subject heading forms and expressions, as Pettee has demonstrated.[4] Some thought also has been given recently to the usefulness of catch-title entries in lieu of subject headings, particularly when the subject idea is one not easily expressed within the conventions of standardized subject heading practices.[5]

The alphabetical subject catalog discussed in this chapter is composed, then, of a number of distinct subject terms, each of which will be as direct and as specific as possible, and under which will be listed the various books and other materials relating to that subject. Since verbal expressions of subject concepts can take a variety of forms in the English language, the varieties in form of subject headings will be just as many as the language allows. Haykin [6] has described the major types of headings in detail and has indicated the distinctions which the Library of Congress intends to make in its choices among alternate expressions. Some indication of the relative extent of the various types is reported by Frarey.[7] In addition to independent subject headings, subject catalogs regularly include subdivisions of these headings, which may be by subject, by form, or by geographic location or chronology. These are discussed in detail by Haykin.[8]

TERMINOLOGY

In virtually all languages, and certainly in English, there are various synonyms for many words. It is impossible to determine which of several equally familiar terms will occur first to the catalog user. It is, however, undesirable to use more than one subject heading to express one idea; if there were not some limitation, the bulk of the subject catalog would become too great for easy and effective use. Therefore, subject catalogs regularly include references (called *see* references) from terms not used to the equivalent term which has been accepted for use as a subject heading.

Another kind of reference is generally found as well. Since it is necessary to be economical in supplying subject headings, but essential that the subject content of the library be expressed as fully as is practicable and feasible, some general limitations have had to be placed upon the number of subject entries provided for any particular item. While few libraries have prescribed a maximum number of subject entries to be used—and such arbitrary rulings may operate to defeat the purposes of subject headings, or, at least, seriously to interfere with their realization—most hesitate to use more than three or four unless there are compelling reasons to do otherwise. The *see also* reference is the device used to circumvent these necessary limitations. This refers the catalog users from one heading to other related headings which are either more specific than the original term (Trees *see also* Elm) or approximately equal in specificity and independence (Trees *see also* Forests and Forestry; Plants; Shrubs).

The remaining portion of this chapter seeks to identify the relationship of subject headings to classification, to describe present practices as found in American libraries, to discuss particular problems relating to subject headings which limit their usefulness or pose particular difficulties, and to suggest trends which seem to be emergent in current approaches to these problems. It does not attempt to describe in detail the techniques of assigning subject headings since these are covered in Cutter,[9] Sears,[10] the Vatican Rules,[11] and, to a lesser extent, by Haykin,[12] Pettee,[13] Mann [14] and others.

The determination of an appropriate classification number and the assignment of suitable subject headings require essentially the same intellectual activity on the part of the cataloger. Both require the cataloger to try to isolate the specific subject matter contained in the book and to express that content in terms suitable for the library's subject treatment. Libraries which separate classification and subject-heading operations are requiring two different people to perform essentially the same operation on each book. This division of duties does not appear to be defensible on economic grounds. When it has been made, various reasons have been given in an attempt to justify it: (1) the library's classification system may be nonstandard, or inadequately indexed, therefore requiring the classifier to have intimate knowledge of the detailed content of the classification schedules and how they are applied; (2) the library's standard for subject headings may be unique or complex; (3) the librarian or head cataloger, aware of the inability of catalogers to be specialists in all fields of knowledge, may hold that there are advantages to be derived from having the opinions of two nonspecialists as a precaution against inadequate or inaccurate subject analysis;

(4) the organization of work space in the catalog department or the impossibility of providing suitably annotated copies of the classification schedules for all cataloging assistants may dictate the advisability of separating the two activities; or (5) the requirements of the library may demand complete consistency in assigning class numbers, or even subject headings, and this consistency is easier to achieve, though not always so achieved, if only one person bears responsibility for classification.

Some of these reasons can be compelling in certain library operations and may dictate a need to sacrifice economy in favor of some more important objective. Yet money available for cataloging is allocated jealously in most libraries, since each dollar spent for organizing and processing new materials will be unavailable for the development of the library's collection. Consequently, no library which maintains separate classification and subject cataloging units is receiving the maximum return on its investment and probably is paying an excessive price for cataloging.[15] This division of labor within catalog departments is not widespread, and within this discussion it will be assumed, unless otherwise clearly stated, that the assignment of subject headings to a book is the task of the same persons who assign classification numbers.

SUBJECT HEADINGS AND CLASSIFICATION

Bliss [16] has examined the relationship between subject headings and classification. While classification has the limitation of linearity, discussed in the following chapter, subject headings do not. As many subject headings may be assigned to a single book as are necessary to express its subject content. There is no need to obscure subordinate or coordinate ideas in the interest of selecting the most specific class number which encompasses all of the subordinate topics or which represents the dominant subject treated. In practice, of course, most libraries establish some generalized standard to limit the number of subject headings to be supplied for any one book. Special libraries are likely to have less restriction on the number of headings than have general libraries.

Bliss suggests further that there are some concepts which cannot be expressed in classification terms. The topic "Youth," for example, may be considered biologically or sociologically, to mention but two possibilities, and while these two separate concepts of youth can be provided for within a classification system, a book which deals with both cannot be classified in both places. Yet the simple subject heading Youth will encompass both of these, as well as any other meanings of the term, and will provide a suitable subject approach.

The summary of the differences between subject headings and classification by Bliss concludes that subject headings are more complete, more inclusive, more expressive for many general concepts, more capable of minute and meaningful subdivision in many cases, and more plastic in showing interrelationships than are any of the classification systems presently known. Thus he is led to observe that adequate subject approach to the content of recorded knowledge cannot be had except through the use of both classification and subject headings.

Bliss' conclusion is not accepted by all writers on these questions, and many have affirmed the greater usefulness of the classified catalog, either alone or as an adjunct to the regular alphabetic subject catalog. The use of classification for the arrangement of a card catalog does not exhibit the same limitation of linearity that its use to arrange a book collection does. It is just as feasible to supply as many classification numbers for one book as it is subject headings when the same medium for expressing the subject is used: the unit catalog card. Yet the elimination of this shortcoming of classification as applied to books does not answer fully the other points raised by Bliss: that the effectiveness of the alphabetic subject catalog has not been demonstrated and that among many scholarly users a preference for a classified approach to subject material can be observed. This point of view is expressed more strongly in countries outside of the United States. Ranganathan,[17] the eminent Indian librarian, is one of the most outspoken of this group, and his faith in the potential of classification, properly devised and developed, has led him to the observation that the dictionary subject catalog—that is to say, the alphabetic subject catalog—has proved so ineffective that it ought to be retired from the roster of library devices. Not all critics are so extreme, but the literature on the alphabetic–classified controversy is voluminous. Recently, some revival of interest in and perhaps recognition of the need for properly constituted classified catalogs can be observed.[18]

What the ultimate resolution of this controversy may be cannot be predicted, but it does not appear likely that there will be any immediate wholesale alteration of the alphabetic subject catalog now found in most American libraries. Every cataloging department now makes some provision for a subject approach to books in addition to classification.

SUBJECT CATALOGERS

Although properly qualified subject specialists are needed to handle subject cataloging,[19] they are not easily recruited, since many specialists find it economically more advantageous to pursue their specialty than to become subject catalogers. This is particularly true in scientific and technical fields, notably medicine and law. Difficulty in procuring properly qualified personnel has meant either that the progress of subject cataloging in particular fields has been slowed unduly because of staff shortages, or, more frequently, that specialists in other fields have been required to do subject cataloging outside their specialty. To be sure, a biologist may be expected to understand medical concepts better than one who has no training in biology, and a political scientist legal concepts better than one who has not made such close study of government, yet neither the biologist nor the political scientist is a specialist in medicine or law and apparently neither has been able to produce the kind of subject cataloging that properly qualified specialists might achieve.

MacDonald[20] has pointed to another problem which arises from this use of specialists: a lower production rate resulting from too intimate a knowledge of particular subject concepts and the accompanying identification of more controversial problems to be explored before decisions are made. Moreover, subject specialists frequently disagree with one another. This disagreement among experts points to the improbability that anyone's subject cataloging will be entirely satisfactory to all users, and suggests that one whose knowledge and understanding is more general may be able to suggest more satisfactory subject terms for all classes of users in a high percentage of cases. MacDonald has indicated that the Armed Forces Medical Library has accepted this point of view and permits most subject cataloging to be done by descriptive catalogers whose subject background is primarily derived only from some general scientific training. Progress of work has been speeded up and the medical specialists who are using the products of these cataloging operations have not expressed dissatisfaction with the results. Further evidence is necessary to resolve the question of whether subject cataloging should be performed by specialists or by nonspecialists. Nor does it follow necessarily that a decision in favor of nonspecialists should lead to any modification in those organizational plans which now separate descriptive and subject cataloging activities. More efficient operations may still result from this division of labor into two categories of closely related operations. In the last analysis, the local library situation should determine the type of organization.

ASSIGNING SUBJECT HEADINGS

The process of assigning subject headings has been discussed fully by Cutter and others. In brief, this requires the determination of the most specific subject idea which expresses the content of the book and the subsequent expression of this idea in appropriate terminology. This has meant the development of standard subject heading lists to guide the selection of terms, since individual opinions and judgments vary too greatly to dispense with a uniform standard. These lists are discussed below. What the rules for assigning subject headings have failed to do is to provide a suitable code to guide decisions in controversial cases; for example, shall a particular subject be subdivided by country, or the country subdivided by subject?

Generalized practices have been developed, yet most subject catalogers express a need for a code of practice which will do for subject entry what W. S. Merrill's *Code for Classifiers* provides for classification.

One of the difficulties which has prevented the development of such a code results from a general lack of agreement among subject catalogers, reference librarians, and catalog users as to the proper subject entry for these controversial topics. Not only does this lack of agreement prevail among users of general libraries and makers of general catalogs, but also between special and nonspecial libraries and even between different kinds of special libraries. It is not realistic, for example, in the library of a teacher-training institution, to follow the same practices for entering education materials as are followed in the general public library. In the public library, Education is a meaningful subject heading; in the school of education it is virtually worthless, and direct entry under the particular aspect of education is indicated if the subject catalog is to be useful. A sound code of practice must take cognizance of all these essential variations if it is to achieve its purpose; alternatively, several codes for different types of libraries may be necessary.

Such codification of practice as has been developed finds its expression in the several standard lists of subject headings which are now employed in American libraries. This discussion will limit itself to such lists, but it must be observed that other standard lists have been devised for use in other countries, particularly in those using a language other than English. Sometimes these non-English lists have been translations of an English language list; sometimes not. Usually, direct translation of an English language list is less successful than the development of an original list in the foreign language, since variations in idiom and meanings will often require another approach than that represented by the English. This, incidentally, points up a weakness of subject headings not inherent in classification, for the same classification term and its relationships to neighboring terms can be understood universally, since its meaning is independent of its verbal expression.

STANDARD LISTS

Standard lists of subject headings used in American libraries fall into two major groupings: those intended for nonspecialized libraries and those developed for special libraries or for special collections of materials. Historically, the first of the standard lists of subjects headings was the ALA list, first published in 1895 after many years of preparation and study.[21] Designed to meet the needs of medium-sized public libraries, the list was constructed from the headings used in the catalogs of a number of cooperating public libraries and edited to achieve uniformity at the same time that it followed closely the pattern established by those libraries. Between 1895 and 1911, the list went through three editions and met with enthusiastic response from most libraries, which were then in the midst of developing their modern card catalogs. As might be expected, the headings reflected relatively close, but by no means universal, conformity to the principles set forth in Cutter's *Rules*. The list was widely used and adopted in American libraries and has never been entirely supplanted even though the two later lists have become the standards and the ALA list itself is now hopelessly out of date. Its importance derives from the disposition it created toward the use of standard lists of subject headings and from its influence on the forms of headings to be found in later lists.

Beginning in 1909, the Library of Congress published a list of the subject headings used in its new catalogs, and the first edition of its list appeared in parts between 1909 and 1914. Unlike the ALA list, this reflected the practice of only one library, but its compelling importance stems from the fact that these were the headings printed on Library of Congress cards then, as now, available for sale to any library. In general, Library of Congress headings conformed to the pattern of ALA headings, and by making some modifications it was possible to use both lists side by side. The comprehensive nature of the Library of Congress collections was reflected in the list of headings, which included many more terms than were to be found in the ALA list, and therefore provided better subject coverage for larger libraries. The publication of the Library of Congress list sounded the death knell of the ALA list. Both were aimed so nearly at the same group of libraries that there was little need for the continued maintenance of both. From the beginning, the Library of Congress utilized the device of bringing out auxiliary lists to supplement the main list of headings, and four such auxiliary lists have been published up to the present time.[22] In 1948, the Library of Congress published the fifth edition of its list, which included approximately 60,000 subject headings,[23] and a sixth edition is in preparation.

One feature of the ALA list which users of the Library of Congress list found wanting, and for which they often had recourse to the out-of-date ALA list, was the record and listing of *see from* and *see also from* references. The Library of Congress did not include these until 1943, in the fourth edition. Without this record, it was not always possible to interpret Library of Congress practices well enough to make the most efficient use of Library of Congress printed cards. This insistence by American libraries that these references be included reflects relatively complete dependence upon the Library of Congress. Since no other library will have need for all of the headings used by Library of Congress, this dependence can and does result at times in too precise and ill-advised adherence to the Library of Congress pattern, which may not be the most satisfactory for another library catalog. Particularly, it seems to have resulted in a welter and confusion of *see also* references in most library catalogs and limited evidence suggests that they are more likely to be perplexing than helpful to many catalog users.

One compelling advantage of the Library of Congress list over its predecessor and competitor was its continual revision feature. Changes and revisions were published periodically and made available so that each library could keep its subject headings up to date if it chose to do so. This pattern of revision has been maintained through all editions and monthly supplements have been published regularly since July, 1947, with semiannual, annual, and larger cumulations.[24]

By the early 1920s, however, some voices of complaint were heard from smaller libraries which found the Library of Congress list too comprehensive and detailed for their needs. In 1923, Minnie Earl Sears published the first edition of her list of headings for small libraries, compiled, like the ALA list, from lists used in a number of such libraries. This list found immediate popularity. Unlike the Library of Congress list, the Sears list makes no provision for revision between editions except as new headings or changes in old ones may be developed for use in publications of the H. W. Wilson Co. where Sears headings are the standard. Beginning with the third edition, the list has included *see from* and *see also from* references. The seventh edition of the list, compiled by Bertha M. Frick, was published in 1954,[25] and its scope has now been enlarged to meet the needs both of medium-sized and of smaller libraries for which the LC list appears unsuitable.[26] The Sears list now follows the LC list closely in form of heading, terminology, and subdivision, and achieves its smaller size through the elimination of many specific headings, the use of more combined subject heading forms, and the specification of fewer subdivisions for subjects. It is now possible for a small library with a special collection in some subject field to use the Sears list as its general standard and to supplement that list by using the more comprehensive Library of Congress list for the materials included in the special collection without doing violence to its entire pattern of subject headings.

No accurate count has been made of the amount of use of these two modern standard lists in American libraries. It appears, however, that the great majority of American library catalogs are now based upon one or the other. Notable exceptions include the New York Public Library, which has developed an independent list of headings for its Reference Department along lines somewhat different from those reflected in the Library of Congress and Sears lists.[27] Harvard University also has developed its own headings which do not conform in every respect to those established by the Library of Congress. Most libraries which have established some variant standard for subject headings are now concerned with finding solutions for their subject cataloging problems because of growing costs. However, these libraries are now unable to take advantage of the savings offered by the use of printed catalog cards and centralized subject cataloging without costly changes in their existing catalogs.

More or less coincident with the development of these standard general lists of subject headings has occurred the development of special lists for particular categories of library users, or for particular special libraries. Earliest in this group of special lists was Margaret Mann's *Subject Headings for Use in Dictionary Catalogs of Juvenile Books,* issued in 1916 by the ALA. Others include Pettee's list of theological headings,[28] Pettus' list of headings in education,[29] Voigt's list for physics,[30] and other lists for technical libraries, for chemistry, and for music and many other subjects. The Special Libraries Association maintains a file of subject heading lists in special subject fields and publishes a periodic listing of those which it has on file.[31] The increased interest of librarians, documentalists, and scholars in improving subject access to research materials has resulted in several attempts to identify and study the host of special lists which have been developed in various libraries and by individual scholars through the years, and one may hope for some reasoned reports on and comparisons of these lists within the next few years.[32] In general, special lists tend to follow the pattern established by the Library of Congress in its own list. Variations in terminology, intended to bring the special list more nearly into accord with the vocabulary of the specialist group for which it is intended, are common; greater specificity in subject headings is frequent; and the provision for more detailed subdivision of general subject headings is characteristic. In some cases, more careful attempts to define headings or to distinguish between closely related terms enhance the usefulness of the special list. Pettus' list in education deserves special mention, not only because it demonstrates the value of definition and distinction in a fine way, but also because it illustrates the usefulness of a classified approach to a body of knowledge in clarifying subject heading terms and their meanings.

One special list deserves particular attention chiefly because of the manner in which it has been compiled. The Armed Forces Medical

Library list of headings for its *Current List of Medical Literature* reflects a new approach to the construction and editing of subject heading lists. For this compilation, all of the headings used in the *Current List* were transferred to punched cards, and these cards were then coded as belonging to one or more of a relatively limited number of "categories," e.g., Parts of the Body, Diseases, Drugs. From the punched cards, lists of headings within each category were compiled and examined for consistency, duplication, and overlapping. The same treatment was accorded the cross references used and after all indicated revisions were made, the entire corrected list was reproduced in its proper alphabetic order from the punched card records.[33] Through the use of mechanical devices such as punched cards and allied IBM equipment, frequent revision and reproduction of the complete list of headings have been possible, and the advocates of this method point out that greater internal consistency and better selected subject headings should result. If their claims prove to be justified, the alphabetic subject approach to medical literature will have been improved, and some of the criticism directed in the past to ill-conceived, inconsistent, and out-of-date headings will be allayed.

Where libraries adopt one or more standard lists of subject headings, relatively little work needs to be done locally in establishing subject headings for concepts not represented in the standard lists. However, every library will need to do some of this work, since no list is likely to be equal to all of the local demands made upon it. The selection of the appropriate wording and form for new subjects is a specialized activity requiring care, judgment, and knowledge on the part of the cataloger to whom it is entrusted. Dictionaries, special dictionaries, encyclopedias, glossaries, gazetteers, periodical indexes, treatises, and magazine articles are only some of the sources to be consulted if the new heading is to reflect current and common usage at the same time that it provides for the most direct and specific approach to the subject idea. Once the heading has been selected, similar care must be exercised in determining what references to and from the new heading are required and what distinctions must be made between the new term and others to which it may be closely related.[34] Haykin[35] has described a sample authority card by which the record of such a search is kept. These authority cards, like authority cards prepared for name entries in the catalog, form the basic record by which entries in the subject catalog are controlled.

AUTHORITY FILES

The subject authority file on cards is not maintained in all libraries. For many, an annotated and checked copy of the standard list of subject headings used suffices. Such a record will have the headings and references that are used marked in an appropriate manner, and headings used but not printed in the list will be written in. Similarly, revisions and corrections to the list made since its publication will be recorded. Such a record will soon become confused and difficult to use unless it is maintained with care, and unless multiple copies of the annotated record are kept, it may not be equally convenient for all catalogers to use. Moreover, the nature of all printed subject heading lists is such that whole categories of subject headings are indicated only in part or by example. The resulting record cannot give complete and effective control, therefore, and it soon becomes unwieldy when library collections grow to any size. Where cataloging departments can be located in close proximity to the public catalog, the catalog itself is likely to provide a more usable record, except, perhaps, for cross references; where the catalogers cannot be near the public catalog, many libraries have constructed authority files on cards.

Ideally, the subject authority file will include a record of all terms used as subjects in the library's catalog, with the exceptions of names of persons and of organizations—since these will be recorded in the name authority file, if one is maintained. It will record also the subdivisions used under each heading. Definitions and distinctions will be given, all cross references traced, and all local variations in practice from the standard subject heading list will be noted and described so that each cataloger will know the pattern being followed.

Further refinements might include a record of subdividing forms, together with a list of the headings under which each has been used, and a similar record of geographic subdivisions. The initial cost of such a record is high, but once the file has been constructed, its maintenance can be entrusted to competent clerical personnel who will make corrections and additions to it under the supervision of a professional subject cataloger. Some of the techniques involved in building and maintaining subject authority files on cards have been described by MacPherson,[36] Buelow,[37] and Frarey.[38] No one has made a careful study of the relative costs of either kind of subject authority file nor has anyone attempted to measure in any precise fashion the efficiency and effectiveness of each in relation to costs. Further study of the need for subject authority files in cataloging departments and of the most suitable form for them is needed. In view of the supposed high costs of subject cataloging operations, however, it seems likely that some measure of careful control over subject heading practices is indicated if costs are to be kept to a minimum.

PROBLEMS

The use of standard lists does not eliminate subject heading problems, however, as even casual examination of the literature of subject cataloging will show. No objective and rational study of needs has preceded the development of any of our standard lists. In fact, no clear and unequivocal definition of the function of the alphabetic subject catalog has ever been made so that need could be defined in any meaningful way. Standard lists of subject headings, like subject heading practices and techniques, have merely developed, and these standards have been subjected to considerable criticism, just or unjust.

The first and foremost criticism of standard lists of subject headings is that they are not comprehensive enough. A characteristic of a good classification scheme is its comprehensiveness; that is, it must provide for all knowledge. Ideally, a standard list of subject headings which is intended to complement classification, as explained earlier, ought to do the same thing. Practically, however, this is impossible, as Haykin has pointed out.[39] There is always need in some library for subject headings not included in any standard list, and there is continuing need in all libraries for additional subject headings. Some measure of the amount of this need can be obtained from an examination of the monthly supplements to the Library of Congress list. Not all of the subject headings recorded in the supplements relate to new developments in knowledge. Many reflect time-honored concepts which may not have found their way into the books owned by the Library of Congress. The more comprehensive a subject heading list, the greater is its size, and size usually imposes some limitations upon the usefulness of the product. Both Sears and the Library of Congress have endeavored to reduce the size of their lists by defining certain classes and categories of headings omitted. But the fundamental question of how comprehensive a standard list ought to be has not been answered, and criticism of these lists for their lack of comprehensive coverage may be legitimate.

Another question relates to the proper degree of specificity for subject terms. Subject heading practices rest on the principle of expressing each subject idea in the most specific terms possible. This presupposes that the user of the catalog will be most likely to remember the specific term. Yet such measurements of catalog use as have been made point almost universally to the conclusion that catalog users do not understand the principle of specific entry and that a sizable majority of their problems in using library catalogs comes from this lack of understanding. Knapp [40] has observed that the principle of specific entry is basic to the functioning of the alphabetic subject catalog and that any abandonment of this principle would result in no subject heading standards at all and virtually complete subject chaos in our catalogs. Increasingly, however, critics of subject heading practice have raised the question of how specific headings should be. There is some reason to suppose that they have perhaps become too specific in some fields while they are not specific enough in others. As yet, no solution to this problem of specificity has been suggested. An important question which should be answered in this connection is, "How specific is 'specific' for a particular purpose or reader?"

Allied to the problem of specificity of terms is its corollary of *direct* versus *indirect* entries. Ought a heading to be phrased Bridges, Suspension, or should it be Suspension bridges? The former is an indirect heading, the latter direct. In general, direct headings will tend to be more specific than indirect ones, merely because they get to the heart of the matter at once instead of leading into it gradually. In so far as there is evidence, users of library catalogs show a preference for direct headings when questioned about the matter, but in their actual use of catalogs are as likely to approach a heading indirectly as directly. Frarey [41] has shown that this presumed preference for direct form of subject headings is reflected in the changes in and the additions to the Library of Congress subject heading list which were made from 1941 to 1950. Admittedly it is more difficult, if not impossible, to specify standards and to develop subject heading codes if direct headings are to be the norm, for almost the only standard which can be stated is that subject headings shall be stated directly. Prevost has discussed the problems in practice and particularly in teaching the use of the subject catalog which this kind of subject heading presents,[42] and she has advocated that subject heading form be standardized so that the noun will nearly always come first. There is no question but that her method would result in introducing some features of the alphabetico-classified catalog into the alphabetic subject catalog, and most writers from Cutter to Rogers are agreed that this is not desirable.

Another problem closely related to that of specificity is that of terminology. Should popular or scientific terminology be the standard for the expression of a subject heading? Traditionally, it has been maintained that the general library should use popular terminology, while the research and special library ought to use scientific and exact terms. There are two difficulties in this proposal: first, popular terminology tends to change frequently in its meaning and to become obsolete and imprecise, and second, scientific terminology is not always universally recognized and accepted by specialists nor understood by nonspecialists. It too tends to change, though perhaps not so frequently in established disciplines as does popular terminology. Rogers [43] has suggested fairly rigid adherence to standard scientific nomenclature when that nomenclature has been recognized and generally adopted by specialists. Knapp [44] and Rue [45] have indicated that we may be attaching too great importance to the supposition that the layman does not understand the scientific term. Certainly in this age of widely popularized science, the extent of a layman's understanding of scientific terms is greater than it may have been when Cutter and others first formulated the principles by which our present subject heading terms have been developed.

A more serious problem arises from the need for definition of subject heading terms. Haykin [46] has argued that definition is needed only for those terms which are not properly defined in a good dictionary, and points out that it is undesirable for a list of subject headings to develop into a dictionary in its own right. His argument does more to confuse than to clarify the issue. For many terms, the unabridged dictionary gives several definitions, each conveying a distinctive meaning. Obviously there will be many instances where doubt as to which is intended will result unless the subject heading term is defined. Pettus has demonstrated the value of good definition practices in her list of subject headings for education, as has been noted, and most subject heading lists would be easier to use effectively if similar high standards for definition were followed. Unfortunately, the Library of Congress appears to be reducing the amount of definition in its list at the same time that it admits a need for more of it.[47] More careful study of the need for definitions is required, and perhaps cooperative efforts by many libraries will enable the Library of Congress to provide more definitions and distinctions in meaning than it is able to do at present.

The obsolescence of subject terminology is a recurring problem and one to which the authors of any subject heading list must give continuing attention. In recent years there is evidence to suggest that criticism directed against the Library of Congress for perpetuating obsolete terms is ill founded, for the revisions which had been made to both the fourth and fifth editions of that library's list reflect a continuing concern and a determined effort to revise terminology as rapidly as the need develops. Library of Congress subject catalogers have had an unusually big problem here, and their progress has not always been as rapid as users of Library of Congress headings would like. The magnitude of this task results from an earlier preference at the Library of Congress for so-called "cataloger's choice"—subject headings for concepts for which standardized terminology was slow to develop. Since many of these older headings have had to be changed, the revision process seems at times to have moved more slowly than is desirable.[48] Frarey's study suggests, however, that the Library of Congress is aware of its responsibility and is making substantial progress in changing obsolete terms as rapidly as their obsolescence is recognized.[49]

If all of these changes in form, terminology, and up-to-dateness of subject headings are made, the resulting burden upon subject cataloging departments will be sizable. Frarey has suggested the scope of these changes in two of his studies. How they are to be managed by cataloging personnel is a recurring question and one which appears not to have been answered satisfactorily by any library. Relatively few libraries make any definitive effort to keep up with those revisions which are made, not to mention others for which recurrent demands are heard. The maintenance of subject catalogs and their management is a problem deserving more careful study. Some of the problems and techniques will be considered in Chapter XII.

The multiplication of special subject heading lists is creating another problem for subject analysts. A list prepared by specialists for specialists is more likely to meet the needs of these users better than is any general list. Unfortunately, however, the special library whose collection is limited exclusively to one specialty is rare, and the special librarians must draw upon other lists to supply subject terms for concepts not represented in their special lists. The problem is to find a list, or a combination of lists, which will fit together well enough to provide the total subject coverage required by the collection. No doubt many general libraries having special collections in fields for which a special subject heading list has been developed would use these to advantage if they could be fitted into the framework of the general subject heading list used. Since compilers of special lists have not always taken account of other lists in fields closely related to their own nor considered the broad pattern into which their lists should fit, the present array of special subject heading lists is not uniform and displays divergent patterns of approach to subject analysis. A refreshing approach is reported by Benjamin in her description of the method by which the special subject heading list for industrial relations collections was developed,[50] and her suggestion that special lists be extensions of standard lists, to be used as needed, seems more reasonable than to continue haphazardly to develop special lists to take care of individual special needs. Even the Special Libraries Association has been unable to assemble a complete collection of all special subject heading lists thus far developed, in spite of determined efforts to do so.

Ladenson,[51] MacPherson,[52] and others have pointed out that the cross-reference structure of the subject catalog has become so complex that it may serve more to confuse than to assist. Through the years, there appears to have been a tendency to introduce *see* references from virtually all synonymous terms without sufficient regard for need or probable usefulness. The multiplication of *see also* references has been so profuse that under some general subjects they have become virtually worthless. To refer any patron to sixty or more alternative subjects under which he might find additional (or the same) material on his topic is to provide him with service which his own fatigue and frustration will prevent him from using. Some reevaluation of the need for cross references is necessary, and a new standard must be developed to govern their use. Rogers [53] has suggested that a new standard should strive to avoid archaic and purely dictionary *see* references and should give greater emphasis to the proper use of *see also* references, avoiding them except to express necessary relationships and preferring separate headings when relationships are only incidental.

Frarey's summary of the content of twenty-seven studies of catalog use [54] synthesizes the extent of present knowledge of how subject catalogs are used. He observes that the findings of these studies suggest that: (1) users of the subject catalog are more likely to be nonspecialists than specialists, (2) most use of the subject catalog is made either to identify a few "best references" on a topic, or to discover the shelf location for books relating to that topic, (3) most use of the subject catalog is for English language material of relatively recent date, (4) relatively little of the bibliographical information supplied on cards in the subject catalog is used, (5) most difficulties in subject catalog use stem from failure by the user to understand the principle of specific entry, from inconsistent applications of this principle by catalogers, from practices in entry under subject or place which are at variance with users' approaches, and from obsolete terminology, (6) title entries, cross references, and filing arrangements are unusually confusing to most users, (7) the subject catalog is effective in assisting its users to find material about 70 percent of the time, (8) modifications of the subject catalog to provide selective instead of comprehensive coverage seem to be in order, and (9) the need for instruction in how to use the subject catalog is great. Frarey points out, however, that these conclusions come from very small samplings and cannot be accepted without further testing. Studies of catalog use have not, as yet, pretended to evaluate the quality of that use, so there is some danger that significant values of the subject catalog as it is presently constituted may be obscured in the findings of these studies because they do not loom large in the quantitative measurements thus far made. However, evidence points to a likelihood that modifications in subject cataloging practices are needed so as to bring them more nearly in line with the uses made of the catalog.

Merritt's study of catalog use [55] is one of the few recent publications to take note of the costs of subject cataloging. It is not easy to isolate unit cataloging costs in any library, and most cost figures are little more than careful estimates. Just what portion of this total represents subject cataloging costs is not usually stated, but as Merritt points out, it is probably sizable. In all probability it represents a cost in cataloging where savings are most possible and most necessary. Administrators who welcomed the development of the revised code for catalog entry and the new code for book description during the forties, because they were expected to contribute to reduced cataloging costs, may have become disillusioned in the fifties when these costs have not become noticeably lower. Unquestionably there is need to give more study to subject cataloging costs if demonstrable economies are to be obtained. Merritt has demonstrated how savings of approximately 65 percent in subject cataloging load can be realized at the University of California through the elimination of subject cataloging for all foreign language materials and for all English language materials more than twenty years old. That this large saving will reduce the effectiveness of the subject catalog by no more than 20 percent is added evidence that some sound modifications of subject cataloging practices are necessary. Libraries whose budgets are never large enough cannot continue to offer their traditional high quality of service if their processing costs continue to approximate the cost of the books processed.

FUTURE OF SUBJECT CATALOGING

This last consideration—that when more money must be spent to make a library collection available, less can be spent to develop and improve that collection—is fostering increased interest in the traditions and techniques of subject analysis. There is considerable feeling that traditional methods no longer meet the subject needs of effective bibliographical control. This realization has been emphasized by the increased demands since the close of World War II for better subject analysis.[56] Scholars, specialists, philosophers, documentalists, and librarians all have been drawn into these discussions and investigations, and some trends which may be indicative of the future of subject cataloging are already clear.

First, specialists in scientific and technological fields are seeking a level of subject analysis which is more analytical than traditional cataloging methods have provided. Ideally, this level of analysis presumes the identification and description of every concept appearing in any record of human knowledge. Such "depth analysis" may lie beyond the practicable limits of the alphabetic subject catalog, though perhaps not of the classified catalog. The need for mechanizing subject searches through large masses of material, if this kind of depth analysis is achieved, is leading to extensive study of classification schemes and to the development of new ones which will lend themselves to coding for use on punched cards or on film. A master subject index to any large collection of material will be expensive to construct, and even though such tools may be developed to facilitate research in certain definable scientific fields, it is not likely that this kind of depth analysis will come to occupy any large role in the subject cataloging operations of general libraries.

Second, the usefulness of classification schemes in providing access to ideas and concepts, and their adaptability to coding for use with punched cards and other mechanical devices, is resulting in renewed interest in classification. At the same time, clearer recognition of the limitations of classification is contributing to a more careful study of the potentialities of subject headings and to refinements and improvements in subject heading practices and techniques.

Third, this reexamination of subject heading principles and practices points up more clearly the need to define the functions of the present subject catalogs. No positive statement of function has ever been developed, and library subject catalogs attempt at one and the same time to serve the purposes both of a comprehensive and of a selective subject bibliography without succeeding too well at either. Thus far, most interest has been shown in proposals which will operate to make the subject catalog a more selective bibliography and which suppose that printed subject bibliographies will be used more extensively in connection with library subject catalogs in the interest of better and more economical service. It is almost certain that more selective subject catalogs and more extensively used subject bibliographies will characterize subject analysis in the immediate future.

The studies of catalog use referred to, moreover, indicate that no valid definition of the function of the subject catalog can be made except in terms of the use to which it will be put. The limited knowledge relating to catalog use which has been developed only serves to emphasize the need for more such knowledge before functions can be described, principles and techniques developed, and modifications instituted in subject catalogs to improve service and reduce costs. Until these basic problems are studied there can be no meaningful improvement in subject catalogs. All other efforts will produce no more than a remodeled product whose exterior may be bright and shining but whose inner mechanisms will be no more efficient than they were when the present techniques for subject analysis were developed in the early years of this century.

XI. Classification

IT IS essential that a library have a system that makes it possible to find quickly and easily the books it has acquired. As described in preceding chapters, catalogs provide information about the holdings of the library. In addition to bibliographic information, the catalog cards bear a number (or numbers), commonly known as the call number, consisting of a class designation and an author number to indicate the location of the book in the library. This number generally may be translated into a definite subject and serves as an abbreviation for the name of the subject it represents. It is the purpose of this chapter to discuss the purpose, characteristics, and types of classification.[1] Several classification systems are considered in some detail.

PURPOSE

A book may deal with a specific subject or with several areas of knowledge or its form may give it its chief interest or character. The placing of that book by its dominant interest is the problem that faces the classifier, who must grasp the author's purpose for each book and give to each its proper location in relation to the book collection that the library is building. Thus, after the classifier has determined the subject of the book, the topic is located in the classification schedule used by the library and a symbol which stands for that subject is assigned to the book. The problem is to place the books on the shelves in an order which will be recognizable, be in harmony with current studies, and enable the user to find together books which treat of the same subject. If books are to follow the order of current studies or the vocational activities and interests of man, the groundwork of the outline of principal divisions or main classes and their important subdivisions will be in the order in which those engaged in the various branches of knowledge work.

Classification schemes vary from those which aim at ideal schemes of arrangement of knowledge to those which are completely utilitarian, that is, concerned only with the arrangement of books. Since the value of a classification scheme to the user is its cardinal quality, it follows that in constructing schedules examination of the material to be classified must be of first importance. Librarians think this is especially true of books, but no arrangement of books which does not follow the principles of logical classification is likely to meet general needs or to endure for long. That there are differences between knowledge classification and book classification is obvious, but the resemblance between them is even greater. So while an examination of books precedes the final order of the classification, a scheme must first be known at least in outline. Even in roughly arranging a group of books the classifier follows some order in his mind prior to the act of arranging.

The organization of books into well-ordered groups eliminates for the user of the library the necessity of extensive and frequently fruitless examination of a great many volumes when a definite subject is desired. Thus the library should employ a system which will be conducive to prompt and effective service, not only for one book but also for groups of books. If the books are so arranged that they may be used in relation to one another, the person who wishes to know what the library has on a certain subject may select from among many books those which will best meet his needs. If every book on the shelves is placed in the best position (from the user's point of view), it will stand among others with which it can be correlated. In this way one subject leads into another, related topics bearing on a main class are brought into relief, and the reader is led from one subject to the next most closely related to it. The arrangement in the smaller sections of the classification is as important as that of the main divisions, for the arrangement of the scheme as a whole contributes to ease in finding subject material in all its ramifications and relations.

The shelf arrangement should be flexible, that is, the arrangement should permit the insertion of new titles in their proper places among other similar works, and the arrangement should permit continual moving of books from shelf to shelf without destroying the logical order. Thus the place of each book on the shelf is always the same in relation to the books on either side of it, however its actual position on the shelf may vary as books are added, moved, or withdrawn.

Libraries are concerned with so many aspects of books and reading that the use of different schemes of arrangement is necessary in the grouping process. By arranging together on the shelves materials which are similar in subject or in form their use is facilitated. However, direct consultation of the books under class numbers which were meant to cover the specific fields of interest furnish only a starting point in revealing the resources of the library on a particular subject. Use is not always the primary principle governing the placement of books. Some factors limiting this placement may be the classification scheme itself, the separate shelving of selected titles as in a reference or special collection, or the size of the book; these and other factors are discussed later in this chapter. Furthermore, while classifiers attempt to place a book where they think it will be most used, failure to achieve this purpose is often the result of the fact that they are not familiar with many of the fields handled and cannot always determine what its actual, major use will be.

It has been noted that classification of knowledge is the basis of library classification; the method and much of the class-making of the philosopher inevitably lies behind every well-constructed scheme. To be practical, it should have an order of classes that is useful to those for whom it is devised. Librarians, therefore, have made their systems to fit the needs of readers. Having books together in classes in which they are used together may save considerable bibliographical work in gathering and using material and in providing an incentive to the user to get a full view of his material. Any variation from scientific order may be permissible if it serves this end. However, as a rule, the closer classification follows the real order of things, the more fully it serves the purpose of grouping together the books and ideas which are related.

MAJOR CHARACTERISTICS

Mann has defined classification as "in its simplest statement, the putting together of similar things, or, more fully described, it is the arranging of things according to likeness and unlikeness. It is the sorting and grouping of things, but, in addition, classification of books is a knowledge classification with adjustments made necessary by the physical form of books." [2] Sayers defines it as "the intellectual process by which our mental concepts or pictures of things are recognized to have likeness of unity and by this likeness or unity are set *in relation* to one another; [3] [and] the arrangement of things in classes, and when our classes are made and these are themselves arranged we have produced some sort of a classification system or scheme." [4] Bliss defines it thus: "A classification is a series or system of classes arranged in some order according to some principle or conception, purpose or interest, or some combination or such. The term is applied to the arrangement either of the class-names, or of the things, real or conceptual, that are so classified." [5] Richardson gives as "the fullest and most exact form of the definition of classification the 'putting together of like things.'" [6] Kelley has indicated that "the classification of books in libraries . . . is mainly utilitarian in nature, being carried on by one group of persons for the purpose of aiding others in the subject-approach to books. Its meaning and purpose, obviously, cannot be determined by *a priori* assumptions as to worth but can actually by arrived at only in terms of its resulting usefulness for those who use the books so classified." [7]

With these definitions as a basis, the major characteristics of classification may be examined. It should be kept in mind that the characteristic by which material is separated into groups determines the nature of a classification.

TYPES OF ARRANGEMENT

NATURAL CLASSIFICATION. "The arrangement of books by subject is called a fundamental, or natural classification." [8] Here the books are arranged in series according to degree of likeness, from the most complex to the simplest, in logical order. Richardson calls it the logical order or "the inverted evolutionary order . . . because the most complex books containing the greatest variety of subjects should precede instead of follow their inclusive subdivisions in the book classification." [9] He states, however, that the evolutionary or historical order is more useful in subordinate parts. In a natural classification there are found grouped together by subject books of all sizes and kinds, scholarly and popular, regardless of language or date written.

ACCIDENTAL CLASSIFICATION. An accidental classification is a supplementary arrangement of material "in a sub-order according to the time or period in which the subject is considered, or according to the place with which it is concerned." [10] This arrangement is sometimes used as the main device to bring together diverse subject materials concerned with the same geographic region or chronological period.

Geometrical classification is the arrangement according to the order of position in space, its commonest form being the geographical, which arranges together all kinds of things. As a subordinate principle it is used in most classification schemes or systems.

Chronological classification (by subject) is the arrangement according to position in time. Richardson calls it "the position of only a single thing in space though showing it at different instants of time." [11] Its commonest example is a table of dates. This principle is used in most classification systems as a subordinate arrangement.

ARTIFICIAL CLASSIFICATION. "An artificial classification is one in which some accidental property of the things classified is adopted as the characteristic of arrangement." [12] It may be based on alphabet, language, numbers, form, chronology, size, or other characteristics.

Alphabetical classification is the arrangement by authors or subjects in alphabetical order. Almost all classifications have this element, the former in collections of fiction, and the latter in biography, where books are arranged alphabetically by the name of the person written about.

Linguistic classification is the arrangement by language throughout. Thus books are separated first by language and then are arranged by subject within the language. This principle also comes into use when an author's works are separated into editions and translations.

Numerical classification is the arrangement according to the order of numerical symbols (called by Richardson "the prince of artificial classifications and servant of all the natural classifications" [13]). This is used for arranging collections of records, slides, films, museum specimens, and other materials for which the elimination of handling is important.

Classification by form is the arrangement by type of publication. It is used in all systems where all encyclopedias, directories, dictionaries, and periodicals are picked out from the other books in their subjects and put in a separate section or department.

Chronological classification (by books) is the arrangement by publication date or date of first edition of the works of any individual author in his particular language. It may also include the arrangement by accession to the library.

Other arrangements which should be mentioned include arrangement by color, binding, financial value (rare books), fragility (papyri), genetic relationship (likeness of origin, e.g., family history), and fixed location.

Classification by size separates books into categories according to their physical dimensions, usually in four groups: portfolios, folios, quartos, and octavos and smaller. This system is used as a means of conserving space, and has been employed in the United States largely in older libraries, storage collections, and in simplified cataloging and classification projects; its use in European libraries, however, is more frequent. Within each size group, another classification system is used, often arrangement by order of acquisition by the library, which in turn becomes a fixed location classification. To help solve the problem of size, the "dummy," a wooden block or a piece of heavy cardboard shelved in place of the book in its normal order in any one of the several classifications, is frequently used to refer the reader to another shelf location when the book is too large to be put in its regular place. The "dummy" also may be used when the book is so small as to be easily lost, or for other reasons such as rarity or restricted circulation.

Reader interest classification is "a plan to arrange books on the shelf in terms of use and interest by the potential reader rather than strictly by subject content." [14] In this system, broad interest categories are set up, such as Current Affairs, People and Places, and Personal Living, and these categories may themselves be subdivided if desired. Into these groups is placed relevant material from any part of the library's collection, without regard to the exact classification of the book. This scheme is of use chiefly in the public library or in the browsing room of a college or university system.

"All of the various methods of arrangement may be found in a good classification using a basic arrangement by subject matter. Primarily, library materials are useful because of the subject with which they are concerned. One exception to this generalization is the literature class, in which form is more important, e.g., fiction, essays, letters, etc." [15]

DEGREE OF CLASSIFICATION

The application of the classification schedules down to the most detailed or minute subdivision is termed close classification: the general books treating the large, more inclusive subject standing first, followed by those treating special details grouped in order of subdivisions of the larger subject. This minute or close classification is useful in large and special libraries, which will have a large number of books treating the smaller and specific details of the larger subject, and where it is desirable to have these specific details shelved together. By their very nature, certain subjects concerned with concrete, descriptive, scientific, and historical topics require more detailed subdivision, and this consideration should be taken into account. Bliss has observed that "the confusions of close classification *without proper subordination and collocation* should not mislead us to discredit specific classification in science and history, where *proper subordination and collocation may serve with maximal efficiency*." [16] Close classification is also useful in libraries having closed stacks

(stacks not open to the general public), where it is desirable to have specific topics shelved together rather than under the more inclusive general topic—and here the length of the notation usually is no problem.

The frequent objection to close classification is the length of the notation symbols involved. Kelley concludes from her experience that "less effort should be made to place books in accordance with minute subdivisions which might tend to be of temporary value, and which . . . may conform to the needs of very few readers." [17] She contends that the average reader is confused by a classified array of books and advocates broader classification with more detailed cataloging. The suggestion is that close classification is less appropriate for libraries having open stacks. This is not the point of view of many researchers who use books in the stacks.

Broad classification means the use of only the main sections of a classification schedule or the omission of any very detailed subdivisions. It is of value in small and medium-sized libraries which will have but a small number of books treating the more specific details of the larger subject. It is more satisfactory for the classification of abstract, philosophical and literary topics where it may become burdensome when carried out in minute detail. Broad classification is also useful in dealing with any particular section of the library for which the schedules are more detailed than the collection demands. If the size of these holdings should increase considerably or the literature of certain subjects becomes more extensive, the notation may then be expanded. Some librarians, however, prefer to classify minutely from the beginning in an attempt to avoid the eventual task of reclassification.

THE CLASSIFICATION SCHEME OR SCHEDULE

A classification scheme has been defined by Mann as "a schedule which maps out the fields of knowledge in ways that are suitable for library purposes; main classes are followed by divisions and subdivisions of these classes; and the gradation of subjects is so arranged that specific subjects grow out of general subjects." [18]

COMPLETENESS. Since a classification of books should be based on the order of knowledge, or on the order in which the library users in the various branches of knowledge work, it should be complete for the subject involved. While a classification of knowledge is concerned with the arrangement of knowledge itself and its substances, it should be remembered that a classification of books arranges the *expression* of knowledge in written or other form. It is a method of approaching knowledge. The system should thus display the entire field of human knowledge or of a subject with such clarity that one may see subjects in their relative values, their extent, varying aspects, interrelations, sequence and gradations. Its divisions and subdivisions should be all-inclusive. Further, it should be flexible so that new subjects may be added in relation to subjects already in the schedule. This is one of its prime requisites. If this requirement is not met, continual readjustments will have to be made as new discoveries, developments, and changes take place.

CLASSES AND THEIR DIVISIONS. The order of the main classes, their divisions and subdivisions should be a logical process, the subdivision proceeding gradually step by step, showing as far as possible the hierarchy of the subject. Sayers explains the process thus: "When we made our main classes we separated by the class name an area of knowledge from all other classes, and as we progress with our subdivision, at each stage the difference by which we subdivide marks off the divisions from other divisions, and so with the subdivisions."[19] The order should be systematic, proceeding from the general to the special, and should be sufficiently detailed to represent all degrees of generality. It should allow for classifying from several points of view, and for the combination of ideas. The arrangement of the main classes in the large library is less important, since each main class may be shelved in a separate room or on a separate floor in the stacks; the small library, however, will wish to shelve related groups of books together for the convenience of the users. The important factor is that all of the books in a specific subdivision should be shelved together or in convenient adjacent shelves. The classification scheme, as Mann suggests, "should be printed in a form which will give one a quick survey of the field covered by the system." [20]

The "generalia class" is "a class for containing works which are so varied in their content that they will not fit into any class of the scheme that deals with a subject, but overlap all or many departments of knowledge." [21] Every class, and many subdivisions, will have books treating a subject broadly, without giving excessive emphasis to any one particular phase of the subject, as well as books treating of three or more phases. Since these are common types, they must be provided for in a classification scheme. The contents of such books cover a field more or less inclusively; therefore, their logical place is at the beginning of the class or division. For this reason, a good classification scheme will provide a general class for general books, and will also provide for books treating subjects in a general way in any class or division of classes.

Most subjects will include books which organize their material in special ways or may be written to show the history of a subject, the end being to give them a specialized use. Provision is made for such books by the inclusion of form classes in the classification scheme. Thus books are provided for in which the main interest is the pattern in which the matter is presented, such as poetry, drama, and fiction. Frequently these form classes are contained in separate tables, have a constant meaning, and may have symbols which are also constant. They may be applied throughout the classification scheme where the subject matter lends itself to such treatment. General and form classes, Sayers says, are "necessary practical, and in the main accidental and artificial auxiliaries of that classification called for in the form of books." [22]

TERMINOLOGY. A classification scheme might be called a statement of knowledge in terms. A term is a name for a class; whether it is one word or a phrase, it must be an exact description of that class and must clearly indicate what material is excluded as well as included. It must be used unambiguously and consistently, and represent that thing and that alone in the class. Because of these exact requirements, the terminology should be chosen by authorities in the subjects covered. The terms may be technical or popular, words or phrases, provided they effectively describe the material represented. There should be no question about the meaning of the terminology if the classification is to be most effective.

INDEX. The need for an index to the classification scheme should be obvious. It should include all topics covered in the tables of the classification arranged in alphabetical order, giving the notation for each topic so that the user may easily find it in the schedule.

An index may be specific or relative. A specific index attempts to give *one* entry to each subject; the theory being that since a subject has but one place in the classification it can have only one place in the index. A relative index, first used in a book classification by Melvil Dewey, gives the one entry, but also indicates all relationships between topics representing various phases of a subject and the relation of these topics to those in other subjects, synonymous words, and "everything that may form a sub-section of the subject indexed." [23]

The purpose of the index is to enable the user to find specific subjects rapidly in the classification scheme, and should not be used for the actual process of classification itself. The subheadings under the subject in the index serve merely to indicate relationships. One should always turn to the tables in the schedule before assigning a number to a book.

NOTATION

Notation is the symbol which stands for the classes and their subdivisions: a shorthand sign or symbol standing for the name of a term, forming a convenient means of reference to the arrangement of the classification scheme. It has no bearing on the preparation or the logic of the classification, but rather is an important addition to the scheme. Notation is necessary to hold together the tables of the classification scheme, and should convey a representation not merely of the division, but also of the sequence, logical or artificial, so far as it can be expressed. The shorter and simpler the notation can be, so long as it indicates all the necessary differences in the grouping, the more it adds to the usefulness of the scheme.

In addition to providing for the arrangement of the books on the shelves by subject, a further function of classification is to make it possible to return these books to their relative position on the shelves whenever they are removed. The call number, which consists of the classification notation and the book number, serves this purpose.

PURE NOTATION. A notation which consists of one consistent kind of symbol, whether numbers, letters, or other, is called a pure notation.

MIXED NOTATION. A notation is called mixed if two or more kinds of symbols are used, such as numbers and letters together.

FLEXIBLE NOTATION. A notation is flexible when it expands with the classification. The notation is so constructed that by the addition of a symbol or symbols any new subject may be inserted into any place in the classification without dislocating the sequence of either the notation or the classification itself.

MNEMONIC NOTATION. A mnemonic notation is one in which the same elements always indicate the same meaning. This feature is most useful in smaller libraries and in those with open access to the shelves. This will be discussed more fully with the Dewey Decimal Classification.

ELEMENTS AFFECTING USEFULNESS OF CLASSIFICATION

Thirteen elements which affect the usefulness of classification have been set forth by Kelley.[24] The first six are inherent in classification and therefore cannot be changed; the rest, which arise from methods of usage, can be modified to some extent to improve service to readers. The elements are as follows:

a. The changing order of knowledge, which makes impossible the static perfection of any classification scheme.
b. The inadequacy of any single linear representation of subject-matter for expressing the variety of its relationships.
c. The nature of systematic classification, which separates parts from the

whole, and which sometimes results in forced and useless subdivisions.

d. The general obscurity and complexity of any systematic order in comparison with other more easily comprehended orders, such as the alphabetical or chronological.
e. The tendency of any student or specialist, or even the interested reader, to organize a field of subject-matter about his own special and immediate interest.
f. The content make-up of books, which, as written and printed, interferes with the satisfactory application to books of any system of classification.
g. The general impracticability of re-classifying old books on any wide scale, as new expansions and reconstructions appear.
h. The inadequacy of present training in librarianship for preparing students to recognize and to cope with many of the difficulties met with in the actual work of classification.
i. Poor and faulty work of the classifier in difficult and unfamiliar subject fields.
j. The too-frequent tendency to determine classification by the use or purpose for which the book was written.
k. Inaccurate and make-shift decisions due to poorly constructed and out-of-date tables of classification.
l. Absence of books and groups of books for various reasons from their positions on the shelves; also the unavoidable and marked disorder of books which are used frequently.
m. Long and confusing notation for very specific subjects.

CLASSIFICATION SYSTEMS

The rest of this chapter is devoted to consideration of the background, arrangement, and characteristics of several classification systems which are available for organizing library materials. The systems discussed are the Dewey Decimal Classification, the Universal Decimal Classification, the Library of Congress Classification, the Bliss Classification, the Colon Classification, the classification of the Harvard University Graduate School of Business Administration, the Lamont Library Classification of Harvard College, the Union Theological Seminary Classification and the Glidden Classification.

DEWEY DECIMAL CLASSIFICATION

HISTORY

Melvil Dewey first formulated his Decimal Classification in 1873 to counteract the inefficiency of the almost universally adopted fixed-location system of classifying books in libraries. His purpose was to devise a scheme which would be simple and which could be adopted in most libraries because of its ease of application, expansibility, and general appeal. The scheme was first applied in the Amherst College Library in 1873, and in 1876 it first appeared in print. The publication consisted of 12 pages of introductory matter, 12 pages of tables, and 18 pages of index. Since that date, fourteen editions have been published and each except the latest has shown an increase in size. The 14th edition, published in 1942, consists of 1,927 pages. The latest, the Standard (15th) edition, published in 1951, consists of 55 pages of introductory matter, 466 pages of tables, and 190 pages of index. There is an abridged edition for small libraries, the 7th edition of which was published in 1953. The scheme, the oldest of modern bibliographical schemes, has had considerable influence on later systems.

ARRANGEMENT

The arrangement of the main classes is based on the W. T. Harris classification for the St. Louis Public School Library, which is in turn derived from Bacon's Chart of Learning. Dewey divided knowledge into nine large classes and added a tenth class for general works, following no strict logical order:

000	General works	500	Pure science
100	Philosophy	600	Useful arts
200	Religion	700	Fine arts
300	Social sciences	800	Literature
400	Philology	900	History

No one type of arrangement is followed throughout the scheme, rather one will find a number of arrangements—natural, accidental, and artificial. However, the logical process of division and subdivision is carried out in most classes.

A typical example of arbitrary arrangement may be found in the 100 or Philosophy class.

100 Philosophy	150 Psychology
110 Metaphysics	160 Logic
120 Other metaphysical topics	170 Ethics
130 Physiologic, abnormal, and differential psychology	180 Ancient and Oriental philosophers
140 Philosophic systems and doctrines	190 Modern philosophers

Here the method of subdivision and the choice of terminology is somewhat confusing. The exact differences in meaning between 140 and 180–190, and 130 and 150 are somewhat difficult to ascertain. An alternative scheme in the 13th edition combines the material in 130 and 150, but this is omitted in the 14th and 15th editions.

In spite of his "practical usefulness" claim, Dewey employed an arbitrary arrangement in a number of cases where an alphabetical arrangement would have been preferable. Instances may be noted in the tables where an alphabetical arrangement might be used in place of the one given, such as under 546, Chemical elements, and 546.3, Metals. Another example of inconvenient arbitrary arrangement is the table for 780, Music. The chief objection is that the order of the numbers does not correspond to the importance of the classes. Furthermore, these groups are very tightly packed, resulting in fairly long numbers.

THE SCHEME

COMPLETENESS. Inclusiveness and receptiveness to new subjects are well illustrated by the increase in the size of each edition, each of which is, on the whole, an orderly expansion of the original outline. Revision of the scheme rarely passed beyond expansions of existing heads with their original notation until the 13th edition which broke away from the earlier practice and included an alternative schedule for Psychology at 159.9 in place of 130 and 150 which were considered obsolete and confusing. In the 14th edition sections which had been subdivided out of proportion to their importance were drastically reduced. Expansions "include 301.15; 312; 325; 330–339 expanded to 39 pages; 355–359, 12 pages; 364–365, 10 pages; 659.1, 4 pages; 700–779, 147 pages; 931 and 951; and important expansions from 975 to 979."[25] In addition, there is a skeleton schedule for World War II at 940.53–.54, based on 940.3, World War I.

The Standard (15th) edition, published in 1951, follows the form of the earlier editions. Designed to meet the needs of small to moderately large general libraries, it has undergone a complete revision by librarians and subject specialists to bring it up to date and to conform with changing concepts and terminology. The tables are evenly and broadly expanded and liberal use is made of definitions and scope notes. Simplified spelling has been abandoned. The length of the notation, in most cases, has been limited to four decimal places, notably in the 621s, 629s, and 900s. Much unnecessary material has been omitted. Numbers for which no books were found have been dropped. No drastic changes have been made, but recommendations are made when the possibility of alternative numbers has arisen, or when it has been necessary to make a correction. In this case, the new classification is built upon an unused number. In 1930, the Library of Congress began including Dewey classification numbers on its printed cards. In 1954 it assumed general responsibility for the scheme as a whole and has now begun work on the 16th edition.

CLASSES AND THEIR DIVISIONS. Each main class has ten divisions (usually a form subdivision and nine subject subdivisions) and every division ten subdivisions, each of which may be further subdivided ten times, and so on. Where more divisions are needed, the difficulty is overcome by grouping in single numbers the subjects most closely allied, or by assigning 1–8 specifically to major subjects and grouping minor subjects in 9 as "Other," e.g., 299, Other non-Christian religions. Since any of these groups may be further subdivided as needed, provision is thus made for an unlimited number of subjects. Wherever practicable, headings have been so arranged that each subject is preceded and followed by its most nearly allied subjects.

Throughout the subdivisions practical usefulness generally has been given prior consideration over philosophical theory and accuracy. Many minor subjects have been grouped under general headings with which they do not strictly belong, the rule being to assign these subjects to the most nearly allied headings, or in cases where it was felt they would be more useful this way. An important feature of the printed schedule is the use of various type sizes and indentations to indicate relationships between subjects.

GENERAL CLASS. This class is a mixture of subjects and forms. The specific subjects included are here because of their so-called pervasive and general nature. The main divisions are used as a basis for the common form divisions throughout the scheme.

000 General works
010 Bibliography
020 Library economy
030 General encyclopedias
040 General collected essays
050 General periodicals
060 General societies. Museums
070 Journalism. Newspapers
080 Polygraphy. Special libraries
090 Book rarities

SUPPLEMENTARY TABLES. Four additional tables are included in the 14th edition: (a) Geographic divisions, (b) Uniform subdivisions (Brussels form marks) complete with a special index, (c) Languages and literatures, and (d) Philological divisions. These tables have been omitted in the Standard (15th) edition.

TERMINOLOGY. The terms used to designate divisions and subdivisions are both scientific and popular. As a rule the popular terms are supplemented by more specific terms used in the index, which bring out all phases of treatment and points of view concerning a subject. The index also lists synonyms, pseudonyms, and different forms of names. Simplified spelling is used in the tables of the 14th and preceding editions.

INDEX. The index, a relative index, was the first example of this type to be appended to the schedules of a book classification. Dewey claimed that it was the most important feature of the scheme. It is arranged in alphabetical order, and attempts to include all topics expressed or implied in the main tables, together with every likely synonym. It shows the relations in which subjects in the various tables are to be found and the aspect of the subject which a number indicates. It does not include all names of countries, towns, animals, and plants, and in many instances the full subdivisions are not included. To keep the bulk of the index to a minimum, topics that are further subdivided in the tables are entered in boldface type, and superior figures are used to refer to the special tables in the appendix following the index. Examples of entries in the index of the 14th edition follow:

Jet			
	carving		736.2
	geology, economic		553.22
	mining		622.332
	pumps	prac. chemistry	542.9
	relay	radio recorders	621.3841365
Nouns[3]	English etymology		422.5
	other lang.		—25
	English morphol.		425.15
	other lang.		—515
	English syntax		425.5
	other lang.		—55

The index of the 14th edition is prefaced by a detailed explanatory introduction. For this edition, the index was entirely reset and standardized spelling used.

NOTATION

The notation is a pure one, consisting of Arabic figures used decimally. The first three figures serve as a numerical expression of the arrangement before further decimal division has to be used. The notation is infinitely expansible; if there is no unused number available at a desired point, any new topic may be combined with the nearest allied subject, or when it is sufficiently important, a new number may be created by the addition of another decimal. Any division after the first three figures is accommodated by use of the digits 1–9 following a decimal point. A typical example is:

600 Useful arts. Applied science
610 Medicine
611 Anatomy
611.1 Circulatory system
611.11 Pericardium
611.12 Heart
611.122 Left heart
611.124 Ventricles
611.1242 Right
etc.

The length of the notation to be used must be determined by the individual library, taking into account its size, character, and probable rate of growth. The small general library would use a brief notation of three to five figures. The longer numbers, however, are difficult to print on the spines of books, and to use on catalog cards and other records. In cases where special collections require long numbers, this difficulty is sometimes obviated by using only the portion of the notation which follows the decimal point.

Mortimer Taube and others have pointed out that while Dewey used numbers in a decimal arrangement for his notation, the scheme is by no means decimal in the real meaning of the term. In a true decimal scheme the subdivisions of a number must each be of equal value, i.e., they must have the same relative meaning to the whole or "parent" number of which they are subdivisions. Furthermore, they must be integral *parts* of the parent number, which, when added together, will form the whole number. This is rarely the case in Dewey, even in theory, and it is not the case in practice.

For example, under 720, Architecture, 721 is Architectural construction, 722–724 are Architectural styles, 725–728 are Special types of buildings, and 729 is Architectural design and decoration. These are not actually integral parts of architecture, but rather ways of approaching consideration of the subject. All architecture can be considered from the point of view of style as well as the type of building in which this style happens to be manifested. Styles of architecture and types of buildings are not of equal value as parts—they are quite different topics.

That Dewey is not truly a decimal system will be obvious when the simple matter of shelving books is considered. If the classification were decimal, all books in architecture (720 and its divisions) would be shelved *inside* those books classed in the 700s, just as 720 is a part *inside* 700. This is a physical impossibility bordering on the ridiculous. That the scheme is not decimal also can be seen by looking at any shelf list or classed catalog. Here, as on the shelves, it should be as easy to reach 840 after consulting 800 as it is to reach 810, which immediately follows. But this is not true, since 840 is separated from 800 by 810, 820, and 830 and their divisions, and it certainly is no more possible to file the 840 cards *inside* the 800s than it is to shelve the 720 books inside the 700s.

Mathematically, of course, the numbers used above as illustrations are whole numbers, but in the Decimal Classification, Dewey began utilizing the decimal principle before actually reaching the decimal point in the notation.

MNEMONICS. The Dewey notation makes considerable use of the mnemonic principle. By a mnemonic notation is meant one which has the same significance wherever it appears in the classification. It is used in Dewey principally for form divisions, geographical divisions, and language divisions. The use of the four supplementary tables noted above aids in the application of these devices.

FORM DIVISIONS. Dewey employs a series of nine form subdivisions. With minor alterations these are used with the same meanings throughout the scheme wherever specific instructions appear, and in practice may be added to other numbers, if the bulk of the literature on that subject requires it. The form divisions are:

01 Philosophy
02 Compends
03 Dictionaries. Encyclopedias
04 Essays
05 Periodicals
06 Societies
07 Study and Teaching
08 Collections
09 History

The notation of these divisions is used also with other divisions and sections, e.g., Political science, 320, has the same form divisions with the same notation; International law, 341, has .01 Philosophy, .02 Compends, etc., in a similar manner. The zero here is necessary in order that the power of the number 341 may be increased and .1–.8 may be used for subject divisions of International law.

These numbers are added to the subject in the following manner:

355.04 Essays on military science
549.03 Mineralogy dictionaries
622.05 Mining engineering periodicals
653.07 Study and teaching of shorthand

If the subject number already ends in "0," the "0" from the form division is dropped, thus: 630.3 (not 630.03) Dictionary of agriculture. In some cases the form divisions assume a slightly different function, and the numbers are assigned to aspects more applicable to the specific subject. Under 510, Mathematics, 510.8 is Logarithmic and other tables, not Collections; 520.1 is Astrology, not Philosophy of astronomy. There are a few places in the schedules where the form divisions cannot be applied, chiefly under the history of a country, e.g., 942.05 is English Tudor history, not English history periodicals; 946.06 is Spain, Peninsular War, not Spanish historical societies. To augment these form divisions, the 13th and 14th editions include a supplementary table, Table 2 in the appendix, listing a selection of the common viewpoints, forms, and subdivisions of the Classification Décimale Universelle of Brussels, complete with a separate index. These may be used where applicable throughout the scheme.

GEOGRAPHICAL DIVISIONS. Another mnemonic feature of the system is the use in other parts of the classification of the numbers given to the arrangement of History, 930–999. Where the note "divided like 930 [or 940] –999" is found, it means that the appropriate number is taken from the History class and incorporated in the subject number. Thus 398.0944 stands for Folklore of France; 379.744, Education in Massachusetts. Occasionally no directions are given in the main tables, but the subject is placed in Table 1 in the appendix, which is a full list of topics in the scheme where geographical subdivision is possible.

In addition to the geographical divisions in the History class,

Dewey provides period divisions, which are placed at those numbers usually occupied by the common form divisions in other sections of the scheme:

943 Germany and Austria
943.01 Formative period
943.02 Empire before the reformation
943.03 Reformation to 1618
943.085 German republic
943.1 Prussia and Northern Germany
943.11 East Prussia
. . .
943.6 Austria

LANGUAGE DIVISIONS. These divisions are mnemonic to a certain extent in that they are systematic in regard to the subdivision of European languages, and occasionally for books in these languages. However, although the languages always bear these numbers, the numbers (i.e., "2," "3," etc.) do not always indicate the languages.

2 English	420 English language	820 English literature
3 German	430 German language	830 German literature
4 French	440 French language	840 French literature
5 Italian	etc.	etc.
6 Spanish		
7 Latin		
8 Greek		

The order of these main divisions bears some resemblance to that of the geographical divisions.

The national literatures in the 800s are divided by eight common form divisions. French literature is subdivided thus:

840 French literature	845 French oratory
841 French poetry	846 French letters
842 French drama	847 French satire and humor
843 French fiction	848 French miscellany
844 French essays	

Every literature, except Greek and Latin, is divided in this manner.

In Philology, the only division worked out in full in the schedules of the 14th edition is English, 420; all other languages are subdivided mnemonically in the same manner. The divisions of this class also have considerable mnemonic value, for in addition to this internal use of the mnemonic principle and the use of the linguistic numbers in Literature, they are used frequently in other classes for obtaining further subdivisions. Thus 220.5, Versions of the Bible, is subdivided by languages like 400; 220.52 is English Bible, 220.53, German Bible, etc.; in 572.8, Races, and 299, Other non-Christian religions, the linguistic divisions are used to subdivide according to race.

In many classes the subdivisions of one topic are used in the arrangement of another, e.g., 346, British statutes and cases, may be divided like 345, U.S. statutes and cases; 621.72, Woodworking shop, may be divided as 621.71, Drafting room; 745.52, Textile arts, may be divided like 677, Textile manufactures.

USE IN LIBRARIES

An indication of the acceptance and use of the Dewey Decimal Classification scheme by libraries is given in the Standard (15th) edition. It reports "96 percent of the public libraries, and 89 percent of the college and university libraries, and 64 percent of the special libraries reporting used the system. Use of the classification has spread outside the United States to Latin America, Europe, Asia, Africa, and Australia. In part, it has been translated into Chinese, Japanese, French, German, Italian, Spanish, Portuguese, Norwegian, Russian, Hungarian, and Bohemian."[26]

UNIVERSAL DECIMAL (BRUSSELS) CLASSIFICATION

This classification is a development of the Dewey Decimal Classification distinguished from Dewey largely by extensive expansions and by the use of various symbols in addition to Arabic numerals. The classification was first published in 1905, by the International Institute of Bibliography at Brussels. Revision has been continuous, and a complete English edition and the fifth international edition[27] are in process; it has been issued also in German, and in an abridged form. The scheme is intended less for books than for the classified arrangement of cards representing a comprehensive bibliography of universal knowledge. It is, however, used in libraries, particularly in Europe, and in the United States has been adopted by the United Nations Library.

The general principles of the classification are similar to those of Dewey, and the use of symbols in the scheme may be illustrated as follows: [28]

Symbol	*Meaning*	*Classification Number*	*Explanation*
+	Addition and	631.312 + 631.331	Plows and seeding machines
/	extension	631.312/313	Plows and harrows
	Basic number	**631.312**	**Plows**
:	Relation	631.312:631.411.3	Plows for clay soils
=	Language	631.312 = 3	Plows (written in German)
(0)	Form	631.312(021)	Manual on plows
(1/9)	Place	631.312(42)	Plows in England
"."	Time	631.312"17"	Plows in the 18th century
A/Z	Proper names	631.312Lanz	Lanz plows
	Analytics		
—	Special	631.312 — 78	Security devices for plows
.00	General	631.312.0046	Defects in plows
.0	Special	631.312.021.1	The colter of a plow

The Brussels scheme facilitates systematic detailed classification, but its conscientious application rapidly leads to exceedingly long notation. However, the expansions which have been developed in the system can be utilized with profit by a library using Dewey and wishing to have a more detailed classification at some particular point in its collection, or by a special library.

LIBRARY OF CONGRESS CLASSIFICATION

HISTORY

The development of the present Library of Congress classification scheme was begun in 1897 when the Library was reorganized under the direction of Dr. Herbert Putnam, then the librarian. Previously, the scheme devised by Thomas Jefferson (based on Bacon's classification of knowledge, divided in forty-four groups) was followed, since his collection, after its purchase in 1815, formed the nucleus of the Library of Congress collection. Many additions were made to the scheme in subsequent years until 1897, when it was decided that the scheme was not adequate for the growing collection. Existing systems such as the Dewey and the Cutter were carefully considered, but were not found suitable. It was decided to formulate an entirely new scheme based on the actual collections, and at the same time incorporate the best features of other schemes, taking into consideration the special nature of the Library, the character of its collections and probable growth and use. The individual subject schemes were devised by subject specialists on the Library staff, and have been published by the U.S. Government Printing Office since 1901; revisions are made as necessary, some schedules already being in their fifth edition, e.g., Q, Science, while other schemes or subdivisions are still in process of development, e.g., K, Law. Full prefaces are included in many of the published schedules and give the user a valuable insight into the method underlying the development and subdivision of the schedule.

ARRANGEMENT

The order of the main classes, although somewhat arbitrary, is based on such groupings as social sciences, humanities, and natural and physical sciences. The outline of the main classes as revised to 1951 is as follows:

A General works. Polygraphy
B Philosophy. Religion
C Auxiliary sciences of history
D Universal history
E–F American history
G Geography. Anthropology
H Social sciences
J Political science
K Law (in process)

L Education
M Music
N Fine arts
P Language and literature
Q Science
R Medicine
S Agriculture
T Technology
U Military science
V Naval science
Z Bibliography and library science

"The block of letters QS-QZ and W, undeveloped in the Library of Congress scheme, was assigned to the Army [now Armed Forces] Medical Library for its use in preparing a classification system for its books on medicine and related sciences." [29]

The order is based on that used in Cutter's *Expansive Classification.* Instead of utilizing a single method of grouping topics, arrangements—natural, accidental, and artificial—are used according to the particular needs of the subject. In some schedules related subjects have been combined in the same group, e.g., Language and Literature, Geography and Anthropology, and Philosophy and Religion.

THE SCHEME

COMPLETENESS. The field of knowledge is divided into twenty large classes with an additional class for general works. Allowance has been made for the addition of new classes by omitting the letters I, O, X, and Y. Its inclusiveness and its receptiveness to new subjects are illustrated by the increase in size of new editions of the various classes. The schedules undergo constant revision, with changes and additional numbers assigned being circulated quarterly in the form of *L.C. Classification—Additions and Changes.* These lists are arranged in the order of the main classes and include entries for the individual indexes of the scheme.

CLASSES AND THEIR DIVISIONS. The classifiers at the Library of Congress, after making a general conspectus and an outline of each class, took account of the way in which actual books grouped themselves together, and then designed the detailed schedules to fit this arrangement. Theoretical considerations were largely disregarded. The classification schedules have been built up steadily as material has been added to the collection and has required new subdivisions or revisions in the existing schedules. Thus the classes, divisions, and subdivisions have been developed to meet the needs and use made of large collections. The fact that some sections of the scheme are still in process of completion is an indication of the considerable study and work which goes into the building of a classification system. A number of the schedules reflect the specialized knowledge of the compilers, and in this way theory and practical purpose have been combined.

However, this method of creating a classification "from the books" can be used only once with the same materials. When the scheme has been completed and put into actual use, it then is frozen (with its attendant merits and defects) into the pattern designed by its creators. Its subsequent value rests largely on the skill with which its authors provided for flexibility and expansion.

Each main class is provided with a synopsis which also serves as a guide to the contents; those of some of the larger classes show the main divisions. A synopsis also precedes the larger divisions showing how they are subdivided. The complete tables usually are followed by an index. There is no general index to the entire classification system.

The general principle of arrangement within the classes or under individual subjects is as follows:

1. General form divisions, i.e., Periodicals, Societies, Collections, Dictionaries, etc. (These divisions are more detailed than in the Dewey scheme and have no mnemonic features.)
2. Theory. Philosophy
3. History
4. Treatises
5. Law, Regulations, State Relations
6. Study and Teaching
7. Special subjects and subdivisions of subjects.

This sequence is not strictly adhered to and is an indication only of the main groups into which the typical class has been divided. The resulting order is roughly from general to specific and from the theoretical to the practical. Chronological sequence is normally introduced.

Following the form divisions are the general works, which are usually divided by date so that earlier material may be separated from the more recent. The year 1800 is frequently employed as a dividing date, but other dates and centuries are used according to the nature and adaptability of the subject. Differentiation is often made between general and "general special" works. The term "general special" is used for books concerned with the general subject, but treating it in a special way or having a special bearing on it. General books lending themselves to geographical treatment are often divided by country, state, or city, either by means of an alphabetical arrangement under one number, or by means of special numbers.

The schedules provide for minute grouping of subjects, and in many cases include places for individual titles in the arrangement of special collections or the works of prolific individual writers. Examples are found in class B, Philosophy, and especially P, Literature. JC, Theories of state, provides a special table at JC177–178 for the works of Thomas Paine, in which over thirty places are provided for editions of a single work.

An important feature is the inclusion of certain phases of a subject which may preferably be classed with other groups. The same topic may be included in a number of schedules, but the entries are enclosed by brackets to show when the entry is secondary. Frequent use is made of references to related topics in other classes, and definitions of the meanings of the terms are given freely.

Another feature of the subdivision is the use of an alphabetical arrangement where the hierarchical order has no further usefulness. This method is used effectively in many classes, e.g., Philosophy (BF575, Special forms of emotion, A–Z; e.g., .A5, Anger; .A9, Awe; .B3, Bashfulness), Literature (PN57, Special characters in literature, A–Z; e.g., .F3, Faust; .G3, Galahad; .G7, Grail), and Science (QD181, Special elements; e.g., .U7, Uranium; .V2, Vanadium; .Z6, Zinc).

The association of subjects by country rather than by topic is made a feature in such classes as Philosophy, Social sciences, and Political science.

Many classes are equipped with special tables and directions for subdividing the general tables more minutely. These tables are peculiar to the one subject to which they apply and can seldom be used to subdivide other topics, and thus have little or no mnemonic value.

GENERAL CLASS. This is a conventional bibliographical general works class, similar to that of the Cutter and Dewey schemes, and provides only for polygraphical books. The subdivision is frequently the first letter of the name of that subdivision. The outline of the class is:

A General works
AC Collections. Collected works. Series
AE Encyclopedias
AG General reference works (other than Encyclopedias)
AI Indexes
AM Museums
AN Newspapers
AP Periodicals
AS Societies. Academies
AY Yearbooks. Almanacs
AZ General history of knowledge and learning

FORM AND GEOGRAPHICAL DIVISIONS. This scheme provides no common form and geographical divisions which may be used throughout the classification. Divisions are repeated throughout the individual classes with little or no attempt to give them mnemonic significance; this is done to clarify every variation that may be applied to individual subjects, since some are best outlined by a different set of subdivisions designated to suit that particular topic. However, alphabetical order is frequent and is a useful "memory aid."

One of the most general series of form division in use is:

1. Periodicals
2. Yearbooks
3. Congresses
5. History
6. Local
7. Directories, Lists
8. A–Z Individual societies (arranged by Cutter marks)

Throughout the classification, geographical division is made in one of the following ways:

1. By a series of numbers assigned to a place in the regular sequence of the notation.
2. By leaving a series of numbers vacant and referring the classifier to a special table where the countries are listed with numbers that fill the vacancies.
3. By subdividing alphabetically by country.

Examples of these special geographical tables may be found appended to G, Geography; H, Social sciences; T, Technology; and U–V, Military and Naval sciences. The minuteness of the geographical division is dependent on the subject. The student is referred to the discussion and explanation by Grout of the tables used in the Library of Congress Classification.[30]

All literary forms are ignored and the arrangement within the literary periods in the P, Literature, class is alphabetical by author, with these exceptions: Elizabethan drama is recognized as a special study and is given a separate section in English literature, and fiction in English may be classed in PZ3.

Collective and individual biography is classed in the subject it illustrates or it may be classed in CT as an auxiliary of History. CT3910–9995 are provided in brackets to class biography by subject, but this is a secondary grouping, arrangement under individual subjects being preferred.

TERMINOLOGY. The terms used for headings are exact and explicit, scientific and popular, having been chosen by authorities in the various fields. In many instances, definitions are given of the sense in which the headings are used, which is a definite aid to classifiers using the scheme.

INDEXES. Most classes have their own alphabetical index, the fullness of each varying considerably from class to class. Each index is meant for the particular class to which it is appended, but there are occasional references to related topics in other classes. The entries include geographical names, personal names when used as subjects, references from different forms of names, names of battles and other topics often omitted from indexes. The printed list of subject headings used in the Library of Congress may be used to supplement the individual indexes since class numbers are given with many of the headings.

NOTATION

The notation is a mixed one consisting of capital letters and Arabic numerals, and as a rule, each division is numbered from 1 to 9999, according to the detail of the division. Single capital letters are used for main classes (e.g., M, Music), and double capital letters are used for main divisions (e.g., DG, History—Italy). These capital letters are combined with numerals, used integrally, in conventional sequence (e.g., E151, JX1901). Expansion is provided for by leaving gaps in the sequence of the notation (e.g., omission of X, omission of LK, omission of TK9146 to TK9899), by the use of decimals (e.g., E462.1; D353.3), and, in author numbers, by the possibility of adding a lower-case letter in conjunction with the existing capital letters and numerals in the scheme (e.g., PZ3.S848Dy). The notation therefore is not short, but neither is it excessively long; however, it is as short and simple as is possible considering the scope and detail demanded by the scheme. It is a flexible notation with little or no mnemonic value, in that the relation of classes, divisions, and subdivisions cannot be shown.

USE IN LIBRARIES

In whole or in part the scheme has been adopted by approximately 300 university, special, and governmental libraries in the United States and abroad. A complete list of libraries using the list was published in the *Annual Report of the Librarian of Congress* [31] for the years 1936/1937, with additions in later reports. The scheme does not lend itself easily to abridgment for use in libraries with small collections, and serves best in libraries with large collections or special libraries which require minute subdivision of limited subjects.

Valuable aid in classification by this scheme is available through the Library of Congress printed cards, which include the LC classification number for all classes which have been completed. However, these numbers should not be accepted without examination by classifiers in libraries using the scheme, because these may not always fit the special needs or follow the established practice of the local library.

BLISS CLASSIFICATION

HISTORY

A *System of Bibliographic Classification*, by Henry Evelyn Bliss, published in 1935, introduced a new system of arrangement to the library world. Developed in the library of the College of the City of New York, the scheme, like the Colon Classification of Ranganathan, is intended primarily to be what its title indicates, a bibliographic classification, and not necessarily a library classification. However, the system has met with considerable interest and approval, and has been adopted by a number of libraries, particularly in the British Commonwealth. A group of American libraries use it for the purpose of getting suggestions for organizing materials in special subject fields. A considerably larger and revised edition, with complete tables, was issued in 1952–53.[32]

ARRANGEMENT

The scheme is divided into thirty-five main classes as follows:

1 to 9 Anterior Numeral Classes (primarily for collections and locations)

A Philosophy and general science

B Physics
C Chemistry
D Astronomy, geology, geography, and natural history
E Biology
F Botany
G Zoology
H Anthropology, general and physical (including the Medical Sciences)
I Psychology
J Education
K Social sciences
L History, social, political, and economic
M Europe
N America
O Australia, East Indies, Asia, Africa, and Islands
P Religion, theology, and ethics
Q Applied social science and ethics
R Political science
S Jurisprudence and law
T Economics
U Arts: useful, industrial arts
V Fine arts and arts of expression, recreation, and pastime
W Philology: linguistics, and languages other than Indo-European
X Indo-European philology, languages, and literatures
Y English language and literature
Z Bibliology, bibliography, and libraries

THE SCHEME

The classification has been commended on "the excellence and simplicity of its notation and the fact that being the latest system in a long series of similar attempts, it is more up to date and represents, more adequately, current fashions in the grouping of ideas and the arrangement and subordination of various subjects." [33]

The notation relies largely on the letters of the alphabet, both upper and lower case, with the addition of Arabic numerals which represent major fixed categories or common subdivisions. The comma (,) is used to separate adjacent letters or groups of letters which, when combined from various parts of the scheme into a single class mark, might be read as a single unit; the apostrophe (') is used preceding a number which may be confused with a letter, as 5 for S, and 2 for Z. Class marks are generally quite short. Some examples are:

BOYy,U	Television in the United States since World War II
JTL,C7,J	The Library of the Columbia University Law School
QYO	The United Nations
XTZ	History and criticism of French Canadian literature
DDT,P4,R'5,5	Photographs of the Nova Persei in 1905

One of the distinctive features of the scheme is the profusion of alternative possibilities and the liberal cross references which indicate these in the schedules. In addition, forty-six auxiliary schedules are available for use in one or more places in the classification system.

COLON CLASSIFICATION

HISTORY

General classifications of major stature are much less frequently developed than are those which apply to specific subjects. Fewer still are those which employ a principle representing a definite departure from the basic concepts of the Dewey or Library of Congress classifications. Such a scheme is the Colon Classification. It was first published in 1933 and had reached the fourth revised edition by 1952.[34] It was developed by S. R. Ranganathan, of India, who used the collections of the University of Madras Library in constructing his system. Study and development of the classification is going on at Delhi University.

ARRANGEMENT

The Colon Classification consists of thirty-three main classes and ten generalia classes, broadly divided between the sciences and the humanities: [35]

z Generalia
1 *to* 9 Preliminaries
A Science (general)
β Mathematical sciences
B Mathematics
Γ Physical sciences
C Physics
D Engineering
E Chemistry
F Technology
G Biology
H Geology
I Botany
J Agriculture
K Zoology
λ Animal husbandry
L Medicine
M Useful arts
μ Humanities and social sciences
Δ Spiritual experience and mysticism
ν Humanities
N Fine arts
O Literature
P Linguistics
Q Religion
R Philosophy
S Psychology
Σ Social sciences
T Education
U Geography
V History
W Political science
X Economics
Y Sociology
Z Law

THE SCHEME

"The particular contribution of Ranganathan has been his idea of fundamental categories. He contends that if one goes beneath the surface of specific subjects he finds them made up of parts which correspond to the five fundamental divisions of Personality, Matter, Energy, Space, and Time. . . . A classification which is to reflect knowledge accurately would need to allow for these categories. Colon Classification follows such a pattern," [36] each of its main classes being considered to admit of five compulsory facets corresponding to the five fundamental groups. Ranganathan likens the scheme to a child's Meccano set, with standardized parts (or categories) which are linked together by bolts (the colon, :) to form the whole. Thus, instead of lengthy schedules such as those of the Dewey or Library of Congress classifications, which in principle attempt to provide a number for every topic, the Colon Classification consists of a series of short tables, from which the component numbers are chosen and compounded part by part into a single classification number. Dental surgery, for example, is L214:4:7 (L Medicine, plus 214 Teeth, plus 4 Diseases, plus 7 Surgery); a particular title, such as Theodore White's *Fire in the Ashes,* is V5:1:N5 J3 (V History, plus 5 Europe, plus 1 Political and general, plus N 1900 to 1999 A.D., plus 5, the initial digit of the last decade under discussion). The book number is considered an integral part of the call number as a whole, and special instructions are given as to its construction. In the White title above, J represents the decade 1950–1959, and 3 is the last digit of the year of publication.

The facets and foci appropriate to each main class are given in the schedule with that class (e.g., O Literature, contains facets called Language, Form, Author and Work), and in some cases these are applicable also in other main classes (e.g., I Botany and K Zoology refer to G Biology, where the necessary foci are listed). In addition, there are four "floating" tables, which can be used whenever so directed in the main classes; these are the common subdivisions (i.e., bibliography, periodicals, etc.—the usual form divisions), geographical, language, and chronological divisions.

Expansion may occur at any colon, whether within a number or at the end, and the colon may be omitted at points where the nature of the system itself or the subject make expansion impossible or undesirable. Further expansion of the main classes would be possible. Within each main class, however, many numbers are vacant and could be supplied if needed for new materials.

The notation is mixed, and utilizes lower- and upper-case Roman letters, Arabic numerals, marks of punctuation, and Greek letters.

The schedules are indexed by the terms used in the scheme, and as a general rule composite ideas are omitted (e.g., the terms "dentistry" and "dental surgery" do not appear in the index as a key to the classification number illustrated above).

While most classifications of importance are revised continuously so that they will remain useful, Ranganathan has revised the Colon Classification perhaps more extensively than is usual. The fourth edition saw the addition of seven main classes, and a "depth classification" for documentation is planned for the next edition.

HARVARD UNIVERSITY GRADUATE SCHOOL OF BUSINESS ADMINISTRATION CLASSIFICATION

HISTORY

With the expansion of the Harvard Business School Library in the 1920s and the rapid growth of its collection, existing classification schemes were found inadequate, and the decision was made to formulate one which would satisfy the particular needs of the library, and which would reflect modern analysis of the profession of business. It was to be a well-rounded, self-contained scheme, one that would also include various related subjects such as economics, technology, and social psychology. The major compilation was undertaken by W. P. Cutter, with the aid of many members of the School faculty and experts in librarianship. The scheme is based upon an analysis of business functions, with subordinate industrial and geographical approaches, being influenced by the trend of thinking and writing in the field of business, and by the systems of instruction adopted in the leading schools of business administration. The scheme was put into actual practice in the Library where the several sections were correlated into a consistent whole and inconsistencies and detailed inadequacies were removed.

ARRANGEMENT

The internal structure of the classification scheme involves four distinct elements: the relation of business to other subjects, the element of time, the functional divisions of business activities, and the relation of business functions to particular business institutions. It is basically a natural classification, being arranged by subject, with accidental and artificial arrangements interspersed.

When conflicts arose—when it was necessary to choose between alternatives that seemed of equal force, or where items were of interest from more than one point of view—the compilers attempted to make clear the aspect of a given subject to which a specific entry pertained, and where possible followed the lines of decision indicated by the business school curricula or by the trend of writing in the literature itself.

THE SCHEME

COMPLETENESS. The basis for the classification is the analysis of the business profession together with its important related subjects, taking into account the actual literature of the subject and the systems of instruction in the field in actual practice. The subject is treated systematically and space is left for the addition of new subjects as needed. Provision is made for the treatment of various relationships of the many phases of the subject.

CLASSES AND THEIR DIVISIONS. The general scheme of the classification is made up of three distinct elements: the subject analysis, an Industries List, and a Local List. Each of these sections has its own index. In addition, an alphabetical List of Cities in the United States and an alphabetical List of Foreign Cities are appended. Additions and changes have been issued.

An outline of the subject analysis section follows:

A Business: generalia and general relations to government
B Business and economic theory
C Social theories and problems
D Methodology of research and control
E Economic resources
F Business and economic conditions
G Business and economic history
H Business organization and administration
I Industrial management
J Money, banking, and finance
K Financial institutions
L Insurance
M Land and land economics
N Labor and labor organization
Q Primary industries and engineering
R Manufacturing industries. Construction. Services
S Marketing

T Foreign marketing
V–Y Public utilities: transportation, communication, etc.
Z Non-business and non-economic items (used with the Library of Congress classification)

The letters O, P, and U have been omitted to allow for the addition of new subjects should the need arise. Subdivision of the main classes varies in minuteness from class to class depending upon the nature of the subject matter. A series of five indentions is used to indicate subdivisions. The letter Z is used as a prefix to precede the classification schedules of material outside the field of business. By use of this prefix, all the material may be brought under a single notation system. Thus, ZJK2408 is used for American state government; ZQD40 for general chemistry. Many references to related topics are included.

The Industries List follows an arbitrary arrangement, treating first the agricultural industries, then in order, animal, forest, marine, mining, manufacturing, printing and publishing, recreation, construction, communication, marketing, professional, personal service occupations, etc., and ends with government services. An arbitrary arrangement has been followed within the various industries when an alphabetical arrangement might have been used to good advantage. (Some use, however, has been made of the alphabetical arrangement.) In addition to this list, the industrial approach is occasionally provided for in the several schedules to facilitate the convenient classification of books written from the industrial point of view.

The Local List provides for the geographical approach, by means of which books relating to a given country or selected subdivisions of a country may be brought together. Occasionally the subject schedules include entries for special foreign material wherever a considerable number of items relating to such topics are likely to be available. The entries in this list follow a logical arrangement of the geographical and political divisions of the world. The supplementary lists of Cities in the United States and Foreign Cities may be used when direct subdivision is desired, or may be used in conjunction with the Local List.

The Local List uses Arabic numerals decimally in sequence, 11–9940, two to five figures to a number. The List of Cities in the United States, on the other hand, uses the 700 and 800 series of Arabic numbers plus capital letters, some having Arabic numerals following the capitals. The List of Foreign Cities uses from two to four Arabic numerals followed by a capital letter or a capital letter and a figure. In each section gaps have been left in the notation for the addition of new subjects or subdivisions. Thus, the notation of this scheme is flexible.

USE OF SUBJECT, INDUSTRIES, AND LOCAL LISTS IN COMBINATION

To divide the material on a certain subject by the industry to which it relates, the numerals of the Industries List are appended to the appropriate letter notation of the Subject List, separated by a colon (:), e.g.:

IL:601	Production management in the stone industries
SLJ:64	Pricing control in the leather manufacturing industries
JDA:11	Financing grain elevators
NZF:45	Employment conditions in the clothing industry

To divide the material on a certain subject by country, the numerals of the Local List are utilized. In practice, the Harvard Business Library uses no punctuation mark between the letter and the decimal notation. The following examples illustrate the use of this list:

QCP61	Cotton growing in Egypt
MLD75	Regional land planning in the United States
EH911	Agricultural resources of Brazil
KBNR764B	History of the First National Bank of Boston, Mass. (Use of Cities of the United States list)
F36B	Survey of business conditions in Berlin (Use of Foreign Cities list)

Both the Local and Industries Lists may be used for an individual call number; however, such cases will not be numerous. Such items would only be found in the largest collections; the length of the notation might be excessive. Such relationships would best be brought out in the subject catalog.

FORM LISTS AND THEIR USES. Two form lists are provided in order to simplify the handling of the varied items of business literature and to bring together such similar materials. A decimal notation is employed in each list in conjunction with a decimal point to separate the form from the main letter notation.

The Material-Form List relates to the physical character and the source of the material:

.1 Bibliographic
- .12 Bibliographies
- .14 Abstracts
- .16 Indexes

.2 Encyclopedic
- .22 Encyclopedias
- .23 Dictionaries
- .24 Handbooks
- .26 Yearbooks. Almanacs
- .28 Directories

.3 Collections. Symposia

.4 Illustrative
- .42 Prints. Photographs
- .44 Films
- .46 Maps. Charts
- .47 Mechanical drawings. Plans, Blueprints

.5 Manuscript
- .52 Administrative documents: directors' records, etc.
- .54 Account books
- .56 Letters and correspondence

.6 Promotional
- .62 Trade catalogs
- .64 Price lists
- .66 Advertisements

.7 Corporate publications, non-business, and government
- .72 Universities. Colleges. Schools
- .74 Congresses. Conventions
- .76 Societies. Associations. Institutions
- .78 Government publications, business

.8 Corporate publications, business
- .82 Corporations
- .84 Trade associations
- .86 Labor unions

.9 Periodicals

Examples of the application of this list follow:

AU.24 Tariff handbook
KDB.12 Bibliography on bank holidays

The Subject-Form List pertains to the inner character of the books and the treatment to which the data of the volumes have been submitted:

.01	Theory	.06	Law. Regulation
.02	History	.07	Finance
.03	Biography	.08	Accounting
.04	Statistics	.09	Costs
.05	Education. Textbooks		

These lists are mnenomic, since they may be used throughout the scheme where the subject matters lends itself to such treatment.

RELATIONSHIP NOTATION. Material concerning the relationship of certain business functions to subjects not covered by the main functional classification is provided for at the beginning of each major section by the entry "Relation to other subjects," e.g., "M.A–Z Land and land economics; Relation to other subjects." The period is used to indicate relationship. The letters "A–Z" may be used to designate any series of relationships that are found important for a particular main subject.

Another feature of the scheme is the fact that its technical structure permits a more flexible arrangement than is at first apparent. A library with a primary geographical interest and a secondary functional or industrial interest may subdivide its collection first by use of the Local List with a secondary subdivision for the functional analysis together with the Industries List. Similarly, a library may subdivide first by the Industries List and subordinate both the functional and geographical analyses.

RDCK.62	Trade catalogs of air-conditioning apparatus
ANM.9	Periodical devoted to counterfeit money detection
G.23	Dictionary of business history
NEB.84	Publications of an association of employment agencies
RND.46	Chart showing statistics of building operations
I.76	Proceedings of the American Management Association

TERMINOLOGY. In the main the terminology is popular, with a smattering of scientific or technical terms limited to the field, and consists of words and phrases. Some scope notes are given where clarification is necessary.

INDEXES. Each section of the classification has an independent, alphabetical index. The indexes for the subject analysis and industries sections are relative while the others are in strict alphabetical order.

NOTATION

The notation used is mixed, and consists of capital letters and Arabic numerals. The subject analysis section employs only capital letters in expansive sequence, ranging from one to four letters in length, A–YRX, as in the following examples:

B Economic theory. Economics (general)
BAC Economic thought prior to 1500 A.D.
JVK Speculation in securities
LGTC Pumping systems (water supply)

The Industries List employs only Arabic numerals in decimal sequence ranging from one to four figures in length, :1–:98, as in the following:

:54 Railroad equipment manufacturing and repair
:541 Motive power. Locomotives
:5412 Steam
:5413 Gasoline. Diesel
:542 Rolling stock

HARVARD COLLEGE LIBRARY. LAMONT LIBRARY CLASSIFICATION

HISTORY

This scheme was "drawn up to suit the needs of an open-shelf collection of not more than a hundred thousand volumes" [37] and "to meet the special requirements envisaged for a library devoted entirely to undergraduate use." [38] Since no available scheme suited the needs for such a collection, the Dewey Decimal Classification was used as a base, but "was regarded as inappropriate in various aspects, and the Lamont scheme finally adopted actually in many instances bears slight resemblance to Dewey." [39] A provisional scheme was formulated and changed to suit the needs of the collection as it was being amassed, and then published as a "provisional edition" in 1949. The present scheme represents a considerable revision of the former one, being based on the actual needs of the collection. Subjects have been transferred from one class to another in some instances, others have been omitted, and new ones added, thus bringing the scheme up to date.

ARRANGEMENT

Although the arrangement of the main classes is based on Dewey, the sequence has been changed to provide for a more even distribution of books throughout the entire classification. The scheme is not a classification of knowledge, for "an alphabetical arrangement of topics has frequently been preferred to a classified one," [40] and thus it is strictly utilitarian. Examples of this alphabetical arrangement will be found under games and sports, authors' names in art, literature, music, philosophy and religion, and names of countries and individual states of the United States in the History class.

As in the Dewey scheme, knowledge is divided into ten main classes:

Lamont	*Dewey*
000 General works. Amusements	000 General works
100 Philosophy and psychology	100 Philosophy
200 Religion	200 Religion
300 Government and economics	300 Social sciences
400 Social Relations. Education	400 Philology
500 Science	500 Pure science
600 Applied science	600 Useful arts
700 Art and music	700 Fine arts
800 Language and literature	800 Literature
900 History	900 History

THE SCHEME

COMPLETENESS. It is inclusive and flexible; new subjects may be added by inserting them in their alphabetical or logical place within the larger, more inclusive subject, with or without a decimal number. Gaps for expansion have been left in the notation in many subjects.

CLASSES AND THEIR DIVISIONS. This scheme is a broad classification consisting of main classes and their major divisions. There is little or no detailed subdivision. "One major decision was to have one location only for material on any topic." [41] All aspects of a subject are placed together in one number rather than separating, for example, the economic from the technical aspects of a subject as is done in Dewey. Similarly, language and literature are classed together; works of artists and musicians are grouped together with books about them, and biographies are classed with the subject or in the historical period in which the person flourished. Unlike the Dewey scheme, which provides each main class with nine divisions, each division with nine subdivisions, and so on, Lamont uses an entirely different principle. A group of numbers appears in each main class (the number varying from class to class), and follows the usual numerical order. Thus under Commerce and Communication are found:

380 Commerce
380.5 International trade
381 Tariff
382 Weights and measures
385 Communication
385.2 Codes, cryptography
386 Postal service. (For stamp collecting see 051.7)
387 Telegraph, telephone, cable
388.4 Records and recording devices
388.6 Telecasting

The number of decimal subdivisions used varies from class to class depending upon the nature of the subject. Furthermore, the decimal subdivisions do not always indicate a smaller subdivision. They are often used together with an alphabetical arrangement—personal names, names of countries, or names of topics—or are used simply to provide more numbers within the sequence allotted to the particular subject.

GENERAL CLASS. This class is a mixture of subjects and forms:

000–099	General works
000–009	Books and printing
010–015	Bibliography
020–022	Libraries
030–045	Quick-reference books
050–051.7	Amusements
052–079.8	Games and sports
080–086	Photography
090–099	Theater, moving pictures

Provision is made at the beginning of most large subjects for General works, Bibliography, Collective biography, Dictionaries and handbooks, Readings and collections, and History.

FORM DIVISIONS. No form subdivisions are used, except those just listed. These are not used with every subject, but only with the more important ones and with those which lend themselves to such treatment; the notation has little mnemonic value.

LITERARY FORM DIVISIONS. The following form divisions are used only under English (832), American (851), French (871), and Spanish (882) literatures:

832	English poetry
832.1	English poetry collections
832.2	English drama
832.3	English drama collections
832.4	English fiction, short story
832.5	English fiction, short story collections
832.6	English humor, satire
832.7	English humor, satire, collections
832.8	English addresses, essays, letters, diaries, etc.
832.9	English addresses, essays, etc. Collections

TERMINOLOGY. The terms used to designate divisions and subdivisions are popular terms. Since the scheme was devised for the use of undergraduate students, highly technical or scientific terms are not necessary.

INDEX. The index is a strictly alphabetical or specific one. No attempt is made to indicate relations between topics or individual phases of a subject. The classification number for the topic is given first, followed by the name of the subject:

031	Abbreviations
120.2	Abelard, P
167	Abnormal psychology
478.2	Academic costumes and degrees
478	Academic life
651	Accounting
699	Acoustics
092.4	Acting
854.2	Adams, H
etc.	

NOTATION

The notation is a pure one, utilizing Arabic figures arranged decimally. Decimals are employed whenever necessary under any of the thousand main classes, but no more than one decimal place has been used. The numbers have been kept short so that students using the scheme may remember them easily.

Little or no use is made of mnemonics in this scheme, except for the principle of alphabetical arrangement, which is used whenever possible throughout the scheme.

UNION THEOLOGICAL SEMINARY LIBRARY CLASSIFICATION

HISTORY

The early classification of the Library of the Union Theological Seminary was a fixed-location scheme. This proved inadequate, and in 1909 Julia Pettee was invited to reclassify the Library. The classification was constructed by working from the actual collection of books in the Library rather than from a theoretical classification of knowledge. It was first issued in mimeographed form in 1924 in a limited edition of 100 copies. After being tested in actual practice, changes were made, new tables developed, and it has been revised and enlarged in accordance with existing needs.[42] Subject specialists of the Seminary and others were consulted about various portions of the scheme and their recommendations have been incorporated. A supplement, prepared by Lucy W. Markley, was published in 1945.

ARRANGEMENT

The scheme covers all fields of knowledge from the point of view of theology. "The Christian point of view is presented in all its relations to the problems of living, an arrangement philosophically justifiable and practically convenient." [43] Many nontheological subjects are included, each in relation to theology. Some are treated broadly, e.g., Mathematics and Medicine, while others, e.g., Sociology and Music, owing to their closer affinity to theology, are developed in more detail. The arrangement is by subject, and the scheme may be termed a natural classification.

The field of knowledge is divided into six broad groups:

General and Introductory Group

AA–AZ	General works

Literature Group

BA–BZ	Philology and literature
CB–FY	Bible
GA–GW	Christian literature, patristics

Historical Group

HA–HZ	History
IA–K	Church history, general
LA–N	History by country, both Church and political history
OA–OZ	Comparative religion

Group of the Sciences

PA–PZ	Sciences

Philosophical and Systematic Group

QA–AZ	Philosophy
R	Systematic Christian theology

Practical Group

SA–SZ	Sociology
TA–TY	Education
UA	The Church, its constitution, orders and ministry
UB–UF	Church law
UG–UU	Church worship
V	Music, hymnology
WA–WW	Practical church work

XA–XW	Care and culture of the individual religious and moral life, devotional literature
Y	Fine arts, practical arts, medicine
Z	Polygraphy and miscellaneous special collections

Throughout the classification use is made of chronological and alphabetical order wherever applicable.

COMPLETENESS. "The groups covering theology fall in line, in the main, with the accepted categories of theological encyclopedia." [44] Thus church history and political history are grouped under country; religious education is treated as a topic under the broad heading, Education; the relation of Christianity to social problems is found under the heading, Sociology. The arrangement of the major classes is worked out on a generally sound basis; however, some classes seem illogically placed, e.g., J (General history of doctrine) is placed between I (Church history, General) and K (General denominational history), when it might more logically be closer to H (History). Church history, which is classed apart from secular history in the Library of Congress scheme, in this scheme is related to the political and social history of each particular country —an attempt to surmount the difficulties of handling materials on this topic. Many definitions, scope notes, *see* references and directions are given to aid the user, including occasional directions for preparing Cutter numbers. However, adequate directions are lacking in some places.

CLASSES AND THEIR DIVISIONS. The classes are subdivided logically; some are broad while others are divided more minutely, depending first upon the nature of the subject matter itself; second, its relation to theology; and finally, on the literature itself (since the scheme was built with an actual collection at hand). Thus not all classes are subdivided evenly. Examples of minute subdivision include the extensive list of post-Apostolic Greek and Latin fathers (GM–GN), and the tables for Hymnology (VK–VR). The scheme is flexible and lends itself to the insertion of new subjects when the need arises. Provision is made for various points of view on different aspects of subjects.

GENERAL CLASS. The first group, the General and Introductory Group, provides for material which is all-inclusive or so general that it cannot easily be classed in the more specific groups. The main divisions of this class are:

General Works

AA–AJ Bibliography
AK–AN Book arts, libraries, journalism
AQ–AZ Encyclopaedic works and reference books

FORM CLASSES. Union uses a series of nine common form divisions which may be incorporated in the scheme in this order with the given notation, wherever the material requires it. "The general symbol of the group without further notation is usually reserved for periodicals,"[45] and 1, Periodicals, is used only where no other provision is made. Similarly, 8, Collected works, and 9, History, maps, biography, will seldom be used since place is provided for this material in most classes. The form divisions are:

1 Periodicals
2 Societies, conferences
3 Bibliography
4 Dictionaries, encyclopedias
5 Hand-books, compends, outlines, statistics, year-books, tables
6 Study and teaching, methodology
7 Source material, museums
8 Collected works
9 History, maps, biography

Six supplementary tables are included consisting of (a) Country subdivisions, (b) Notation for states, (c) Denominational table, (d) Societies, (e) Schools, Colleges, Seminaries, and (f) Number scheme for individual authors. These may be used throughout the scheme as directed.

TERMINOLOGY. The terminology consists largely of popular words and phrases, and such technical terms peculiar to the subject as are needed. Many personal names are included, together with birth and death dates. The numerous scope notes, definitions and directions are invaluable.

INDEX. The index is a relative index. It contains numerous cross references, both *see* and *see also*, and some instructions for classifying certain phases of subjects:

Discalced religious orders and congregations
  Classify by order, under Augustinians, Carmelites, etc.
Monasteries (Roman Catholic)
  Class under division for Catholic church in church history of the country where monastery is located.

NOTATION

The notation employed is a mixed one, consisting of two letters and one or two figures. It "combines the advantages of an expansive base for the main topics and the convenience of a decimal notation which may be used mnemonically for sub-topics." [46] All the figures in the notation are read decimally. The notation is relatively simple and the numbers are short.

GLIDDEN: A LIBRARY CLASSIFICATION FOR PUBLIC ADMINISTRATION MATERIALS

HISTORY

This scheme was undertaken by the Public Administration Clearing House as a result of the great expansion in the field of governmental activity and the development of public administration as a recognized body of knowledge. An earlier scheme, *A System of Classification for Political Science Collections*, by William Anderson and Sophia Hall Glidden, had been a standard guide for libraries in the fields of political science and public administration, but was inadequate in view of the rapid developments in these fields. The present classification is based in part on the earlier scheme; it has been expanded considerably, some new classes have been added, a class letter transposed, and the Form List enlarged. "The task of revision was conditioned at the outset by two main considerations which at times presented conflicting points of view: on the one hand, as close as possible adherence to the pattern of the Minnesota edition [Anderson and Glidden] without, on the other hand, restricting currently organized libraries by too inflexible an adherence to the old scheme." [47] The scheme is based on an analysis of the subject matter of public administration and its various aspects, and not on a particular library collection. "The Classification is the result of contributions from a large number of sources," [48] for both subject authorities and librarians were engaged in the project. Many libraries were visited by the compiler, and suggestions made have been incorporated whenever feasible.

ARRANGEMENT

The main classes of the 1928 edition were retained with the following exceptions: the old S class has been shifted to Z (Agriculture), and four new classes have been added—J (Planning), OA (Recreation), U (Government and Business), and XA (Housing).

The outline of the scheme follows:

A General reference
B Society. The State. Government
C Constitutional history and law
D International relations
F Citizen participation in government. Politics. Elections
G The Legislature. Law
H The Judiciary. Courts. Legal profession
I The Executive. Public administration. Administrative law
J Planning. Zoning
K Personnel administration
L Public finance
N National defense. Law enforcement. Police. Fire Protection. Safety
O Health. Medical profession. Sanitation
OA Recreation. Commercialized amusements. Clubs
P Education. Libraries
Q Welfare. Dependency. Social insurance. Crime

R Labor
T Economics. Industry. Business. Finance. Standardization
U Government and business. Public Enterprise
V Public utilities
W Transportation. Traffic. Communication
X Public works
Y Natural resources
Z Agriculture

The letters E, M, and S have been omitted to provide for future expansion. The arrangement is by subject, and the scheme may be termed a natural classification. The tables are printed only on the left-hand page; the right-hand page is left blank for the insertion of notes and new subjects.

THE SCHEME

COMPLETENESS. The broad field of public administration is divided into twenty-four main classes covering all important divisions and relations. Each subject is treated systematically, and provision is made for the insertion of new subjects and subdivisions.

CLASSES AND THEIR DIVISIONS. The classes are subdivided from the broad subject to the smaller, specific subtopics. The degree of subdivision varies from class to class depending upon the nature of the subject matter. The method of subdivision for a portion of the L schedule is:

L Finance
  2 Revenue Taxation
    The Form List, L21 and L22 relate to the whole subject of taxation and not to specific kinds of taxation.
    200 Tax departments and commissions
    206 Tax reports
      2065 Tax rolls Assessments rolls
      (2069) Tax maps Assessment maps Prefer A714
  21 Tax policy
      211 Direct and indirect taxation Sources of revenue

Incidence of tax burden Diversity Earmarking of revenues

212 Intergovernmental problems: State-administered locally-shared taxes, Reciprocal taxation, Retaliation in taxation, etc. See also L2285, L69

2123 Conflicting taxation Double taxation

Throughout the schedules, numerous *see* and *see also* references will be found, together with scope notes and special directions. "Prefer" indicates that alternate and more appropriate positions are provided elsewhere in the classification. Where this is used, the number is enclosed in parentheses.

GENERAL CLASS. Class A, General Reference, consists of the usual subject and form books which are too general to be placed in specific classes. The outline of the nine main divisions is:

A1 Library tools
2 Bibliography
3 Literature
4 Public documents
5 Periodicals
6 Histories. Chronologies
7 Atlases. Geographies
8 Statistical material
9 Biographical dictionaries

FORM LIST. This is a mnemonic device which may be used throughout the scheme where the subject matter lends itself to such treatment. Occasionally these form divisions have been included in the main tables. The form divisions are not limited to the eleven headings listed below; further breakdowns have been provided utilizing three and four digits, e.g., 015, Federal supervision of state operation; 0751, Statistical methods.

0 History
00 Administration
01 Supervision. Regulation
02 Powers and functions
03 Laws and legislation
04 Finance. Costs

05 Directories
06 Reports and records
07 Equipment and supplies
08 Education
09 Associations

FORM LETTERS.

f Federal
s State
c County
m Municipal
mt Metropolitan
r Regional
t Territorial
p Private
x Foreign

These form letters may be used where it is necessary to indicate the various levels of governmental or nongovernmental organization. They are added to the notation of the subject to be subdivided, e.g., K2f, Personnel classification plans in the federal service. "The following alphabetical progression is recommended for the form letters: c, f, m, mt, r, s, t, x, and combinations x, as x, xc, xm, xr, etc. With this arrangement, material about the United States for each class will precede material about foreign countries: e.g. L (Public finance) L1; L1c; L1m; L1x; L106f; L106m; L106s; L106xc; L106xm, etc."[49]

CUTTER NUMBERS LISTED BY STATES AND TERRITORIES. This is a list of the 48 United States and Alaska, Guam, the Hawaiian Islands, the Philippine Islands, Puerto Rico, Samoa, and the Virgin Islands. The Cutter numbers consist either of two letters and a digit, or one letter and two digits, e.g., AL1, Alabama; M38, Massachusetts; H31, Hawaiian Islands.

TERMINOLOGY. With few exceptions, general terms have been used. This has eliminated the use of names of specific organizations or departments.

INDEX. A brief index is provided for the Form List, and is arranged in strict alphabetical order. The subject index, a relative index, is arranged in two columns; the subject headings, with their corresponding classification numbers, and the cross references, with their classification numbers, appear in the left-hand column; the "refer froms" are placed in the right-hand column opposite the subject headings to which they pertain. Many *see* and *see also* references are given both in the index and in the schedules. Besides serving its function as a finding list to the classification, the subject index may be adapted and used as a subject heading list. "Each subject is here stated in what may be accepted as a fairly standard form. Since *Public Affairs Information Service Bulletin*, the Library of Congress *List of Subject Headings*, and the various Wilson indexes are most frequently used in American libraries, weight was given to the form of subject headings used in those indexes. Nevertheless, standard sources have been supplemented by the fresh thought of special authorities who have been focusing attention upon the evolution of more precise and acceptable terms." [50] Should the terms be used as subject headings, more cross references than are given here would need to be employed.

NOTATION

The notation is mixed, and consists of one or two letters for the main class, and from one to four digits arranged decimally. The notation is not excessively long. It is flexible, and has mnemonic value, in that the relation of classes, divisions, and subdivisions may be shown.

SPECIAL LIBRARIES ASSOCIATION LOAN COLLECTION OF CLASSIFICATION SCHEMES AND SUBJECT LISTS

The Special Libraries Association maintains a collection of classification schemes and subject heading lists which are available on loan. A listing of material available in this collection is issued from time to time.[51]

XII. Pre-Cataloging and Post-Cataloging Operations

THROUGHOUT this text the need to distinguish between professional and nonprofessional operations in libraries has been stressed. The economic and efficient operation of a library and the morale of a library staff depend upon a proper segregation and assignment of these operations. This distinction is no less necessary in cataloging than in acquisitions work, though librarians appear to have been less successful in distinguishing between professional and nonprofessional operations in cataloging than in other library units. Chapters IX, X, and XI were concerned chiefly with cataloging operations which may be described as professional. This chapter deals with a variety of additional activities which are common to and essential in most cataloging departments and which relate to the preparation of a book for use. Properly, they are almost all nonprofessional tasks, and in a well-organized library, most of them should be delegated to nonprofessional personnel. However, not all libraries are agreed that they can be performed successfully by nonprofessionals, and the pattern for their assignment varies widely among libraries.[1]

One general observation may be made at the outset. Not all libraries organize and administer these operations in the same fashion, and not all libraries assign them to the cataloging department. Neither do these operations remain the same nor are they organized in the same way in the same library over long periods of time, for new and improved techniques are always being devised to accomplish them and experimentation often produces increased efficiency at lower cost. It will be the purpose of this chapter to give a general overview of various types of pre-cataloging and post-cataloging operations and to suggest the techniques in widest current use without presuming to suggest whether they should be assigned to the acquisitions department, the cataloging department, or to a separate book preparations section. The local library situation will always be the real determinant for their organization.

How they are organized or assigned in a particular library or in a particular group of libraries is not really an important consideration here. Rather it is important to note that they are essential in processing a book and that they represent operations which offer a great potential for savings in processing costs, particularly if they are well organized and properly assigned. Hardkopf [2] has demonstrated how savings in money, personnel, and space requirements resulted from an application of method- and motion-study techniques to just three of the operations considered in this unit (accessioning, plating and pocketing, and edge-stamping), and Stern [3] has reported a reorganization of the processing routines in the New York Public Library to take advantage of the savings which her experiments showed to be possible. Custer [4] has also shown how the realignment of work flow and the reorganization of routines resulted in savings of time and money for the Detroit Public Library.

Since there is no predetermined order in which these activities can be discussed, they are considered here approximately in chronological order; in any one library, each activity is likely to follow another in more or less the sequence adopted for the discussion which follows.

SEARCHING, CHECKING, AND VERIFICATION. Processing activities in any library will include considerable searching and checking in the library's own catalog and other records as well as in bibliographies, trade catalogs, auction records, and the published catalogs of other libraries, to mention but a few of the possible places. This searching will endeavor to discover: (1) the exact title and nature of the item represented by the citation or the order request; (2) its relationship to other editions of the same title; (3) its bibliographical history, e.g., whether it continues another work, is identical with or closely related to another work published under a different title, belongs to a series of works, or represents a part or fragment of another work; (4) whether or not the library already possesses a copy of it, or another edition or translation, or the whole of which it is a part, or the work to which it is related; (5) the source from which it can be obtained and at what cost; (6) what its proper entry will be according to ALA entry rules; (7) whether that entry is already established in the library's catalog; (8) whether the added name or subject entries required have been established in the library's catalog; (9) whether necessary references to and from these entries have been or will need to be made, and (10) whether printed cards for the item can be obtained.

Checking for information described in (1) through (5) above is related directly to the acquisitions process since these things must be known before a particular item is purchased or sought on gift or exchange for the library's collection. Information described in (6) through (10) relates most closely to the cataloging process. All of this information facilitates the cataloging operation, and most of it should contribute to greater efficiency in acquisitions work. Thus it is evident that both the acquisitions and cataloging units will be concerned with searching. This joint concern has led to much irrational organization of the searching process, and frequently to a duplication of this activity in both departments, neither of which pools its information with the other for the joint use of both. It is obvious that the purposes of both units can be served effectively by a single searching operation provided that the standards for searching are set high enough to meet the needs of both departments, and provided further that some conventional method of recording the search is followed so that both departments will be able to interpret the record correctly. One encouraging trend in the organization of processing has been the assignment of searching, checking, and verification activities to a single unit which serves both departments. At Duke University, for example, the Bibliography Section is organized as a subdivision of the Order Department and is responsible for most of the searching activities for the entire

Processing Division. A similar organization exists at Cornell University.

Another question related to searching involves the qualifications of the personnel who perform it. Many librarians have insisted that the complexity of the searching operation dictates the need for professionally trained assistants to do the work. On the other hand, a number of libraries have reported encouraging results from the use of well-trained nonprofessional personnel, and, in some cases, of competent student assistants. At Duke, responsibility for searching is assigned to subprofessional assistants for the most part, with occasional added assistance from senior student assistants, but the work of the entire section is under the direct supervision of a professional assistant who devotes full time to this activity. There is no question but that the quality of searching will depend upon the competence of the personnel assigned to do it, and professional librarians who have a comprehensive understanding of the purpose of the activity should do the best work. Yet it is unrealistic to pay professional prices for all of the work when most of it can be done well enough by nonprofessionals. In any library there will be occasional complex problems to require the attention of a professional, but the bulk of the routine searching does not require professional personnel and should not be assigned to them.

ACCESSIONING. Older library manuals describe in some detail the routines for preparing and maintaining accession records.[5] The accession record, commonly maintained in a standard accession book available from library supply houses, presumes to supply in one convenient place a unique serial identification number for each book added to the library, together with full information on the author, title, publisher, cost, source, binding, and the ultimate disposition of the book when it is lost or discarded from the library's collection. In substantial measure, this accession record duplicates information given on the order card, the shelf-list card, or both. The major purposes of this traditional accession record are: (1) to furnish a complete record on each item added to the library collection which can be consulted when the item itself is not available, (2) to maintain a chronological record of the library's growth, and (3) to provide a direct method for tabulating growth statistics. It is evident that the first and third purposes are served by, or can be served by other library records, and there seems to be none but a sentimental reason for maintaining a chronological record of a library's growth. These realizations are contributing to widespread abandonment of separately maintained accession records, for not only does the record seem superfluous, but in actual point of fact, relatively few libraries have ever maintained full accession records according to the classical rules for their construction.

Unquestionably there are some advantages in having the unique identification of each library item furnished by the accession serial number, but no determination has yet been made that these advantages outweigh the cost of assigning accession numbers to the books. Particularly, such serial numbers are useful in distinguishing between several copies of the same title and in matching library card records and library books quickly. Many libraries which first abandoned accession records in their entirety have since resumed the use of an accession number without keeping a separate record of what the number represents, and others have continued to use accession numbers while giving up the separate accession record. As a result, there are a variety of accession practices in use in American libraries today. Some use serial accession numbers like those derived from the old accession books; some use order numbers assigned by the acquisition department when a book is purchased, some use dealers' invoices or invoice numbers as accession records, and still others use a separate series of numbers for each year, thus making the accession number resemble Library of Congress card numbers.[6]

IN-PROCESS FILES. In normal library operations there will be some kind of order record maintained to show what books a library has ordered but not yet received and a catalog which shows what books a library has received and processed for the library collection. Unless some kind of intermediate record, for example, an "orders received" file is maintained, there will be no record of the library's ownership of a particular book between the time it has been received from the publisher or dealer and the time it is cataloged and the catalog records filed. The interval between receipt of the book and filing of catalog records varies in libraries, and even when special efforts are made to reduce the time lag, an interval of a week or more is common. During this time, requests for a particular book may be denied or duplicate copies of the same item ordered by an assistant who does not know that the book has been received. The larger the library and the more complex its processing organization, the greater is the chance that either or both of these will happen. There is more truth than fiction in the ancient joke that books are sometimes lost in the catalog department.

Larger libraries have recognized the dangers in uncontrolled receipts and have developed various methods to provide essential controls over newly acquired materials during the processing period. The purpose of in-process records, whatever form they may assume, is to provide a record of each item between the time it has been placed on order and the time when it has been processed and records for it filed in the library catalog. That order files can be incorporated in more comprehensive in-process files is evident from this statement of function. The form of these process files varies considerably among libraries. Carbon copies of order slips are sometimes used, multiple copies of the order slip are sometimes mimeographed if the library's operations suggest the need for several extra slips (these are kept together in the processing file and the status of a particular book may be determined by an analysis of the number of slips remaining on file for it), and, in some cases, the library's original order card becomes the record for the process file after the book has been received. Chamberlain has described the files used at the New York Public Library, at New York University, Columbia, and Teachers College,[7] and Livingston has described the file constructed at Yale to control the deferred cataloging program.[8] Dewey's pre-cataloging operations anticipate the possible amalgamation of in-process records with the public catalog,[9] and Cooper [10] shows how in-process records are used in a university library to allow books to circulate as soon as they are received without holding them until cataloging is completed.

PRELIMINARY CATALOGING. Some libraries have found that preliminary cataloging slips which are prepared directly from the books themselves by clerical personnel can be used to expedite the cataloging operation and to eliminate all clerical work by professional catalogers. Ordinarily, where printed catalog cards are not available, professional catalogers have prepared the first card for duplication by clerical personnel, or at least, have written out copy for the first card to be typed in final form by a clerk. Currier describes the operation at Harvard where clerks are used to prepare preliminary slips.[11] When the clerks have been given rudimentary training in descriptive cataloging requirements, they may be expected to make such slips complete enough to serve without retyping as the entry for the official catalog or the shelf list. Other libraries which use the multiple order form described in Chapter V assign one of the carbons to serve as a preliminary copy slip even though such slips are not always complete, do not always make use of the correct cataloging entry, and, most usually, do not list the various items of information in proper descriptive cataloging order. Libraries which require careful searching and recording of entry data in connection with acquisition work are likely to find these copy slips most valuable. The system described by Currier and this use of one copy of the order slip result in copy for descriptive cataloging only. Dewey [12] and Livingston [13] have introduced refinements in the processing records which result in preliminary subject cataloging records as well.

It is evident that two variant but not necessarily contradictory functions are now served by preliminary cataloging operations as they have been established: (1) to eliminate clerical routines from the cataloging process, and (2) to make records of newly acquired material available to the public as quickly as possible after it has been received. In some cases where there are large backlogs of uncataloged material awaiting handling and where organized programs of deferred cataloging have been developed, the preliminary slips are intended to serve for some years as the only catalog record. In such cases, preliminary cataloging constitutes a type of temporary cataloging.

Almost all libraries make some use of temporary cataloging for two kinds of material: that for which printed catalog cards are expected to become available and that for which permanent cards may be delayed unduly. Chamberlain reports that at one time as much as six months sometimes elapsed between the time of completing the catalog cards and filing them in the public catalogs at one library.[14] Obviously, in such a case, temporary catalog cards that are filed at once are essential if library service is not to suffer. However, temporary cataloging is an additional operation which should be avoided whenever possible.

SIMPLE CATALOGING. All libraries have established various categories of material for which simple or limited cataloging is utilized in the interest of speeding up operations and reducing costs without hindering service to patrons. Among the classes of material to which simple cataloging routines are commonly applied are fiction, juvenile works, pamphlets and other minor material, material intended for storage, and books procured for reserve book collections when these are administered separately from the rest of the library's collection.

Where libraries make maximum use of printed catalog cards, such as those supplied by the Library of Congress or the H. W. Wilson Company,[15] the descriptive cataloging operations, and sometimes those of subject cataloging as well, can be handled more simply for those items for which printed cards are available. Presumably the printed cards represent finished cataloging done by professionals, and frequently no modification is necessary beyond the addition of the library's call number and added entries. Where this work is assigned to nonprofessionals, the subject cataloging, including classification, is usually done by a professional before the materials are released to the nonprofessional assistants.

ADDITIONS TO SERIALS AND ADDED COPIES. The addition of holdings to cards for serials, continuations, and works appearing in parts represents another class of cataloging operations which can be handled more simply than original cataloging. Adding copies is another activity which can be delegated to well-trained nonprofessional personnel.

It is advisable here to take note of the variety of practices presently followed in libraries in adding to the records of holdings for serial titles. Holdings may be added to the shelf list, the official catalog, the public catalog, a separate serials catalog, a serial check list (which may be a visible Kardex-type file, a rotary drum file, or some modification of the standard 3″ x 5″ catalog tray),[16] or to any combination of these. Some libraries make use of a "traveling card" system so that the catalog entry need not be removed temporarily from the file; [17] some add to holdings on the face of the catalog card, others use a "Library has" card filed immediately behind the entry. Only rarely will a library attempt to record holdings for a work in progress on all the catalog entries for it; generally added entries are stamped to refer the catalog user to the main entry for full information.

When nonprofessional assistants are entrusted with responsibilities for adding copies or for adding to the record of serial holdings, careful attention must be given to their training and adequate supervision of their work must be provided. In each of these operations some exercise of judgment is essential if simple cataloging operations are to remain simple and effective. For example, an assistant to whom responsibility is delegated to add to holdings on open entries must be alert to the possible need for changes in the descriptive cataloging occasioned by the addition of a new volume or part, or by the completion of the whole work which will most usually entail recataloging in order to integrate the information which has been added piecemeal from time to time. Moreover, added copies may present problems of variant publishers or imprint dates. Where departmental or branch library catalogs are involved, added copies may require the preparation of another set of catalog cards for the branch or departmental catalogs.

SHELF-LISTING. Preparing the shelf-list record of a library collection involves the assignment of a book number (ordinarily derived from the Cutter or Cutter-Sanborn author tables) [18] to complete the call number and the making of the shelf-list card. A number of libraries, particularly those using the LC classification, employ LC book numbers. The following excerpt, taken from the January, 1948, number of *Cataloging Service,* issued by the LC Processing Department, explains the practice of developing these numbers:

Compared with the numbers in the Cutter Tables, the L. C. book numbers are very short. It is assumed that, since L. C. class numbers are quite specific, the number of book numbers under each would not be great enough to warrant a long author notation. The following table is used:

For names beginning with a consonant the number for the remainder of the name depends primarily upon the second letter, as follows:

Second letter—	a	e	i	o	r	u
Number —	3	4	5	6	7	8

Interpolation is used for letters not given and to provide for the alphabetic order beyond the second letter.

For names beginning with a vowel the following table is similarly used:

b	d	l	m,n	p	r	s,t
2	3	4	5	6	7	8

Examples:

Cox	.C65
Croft	.C73
Allen	.A45
Atwater	.A87

Since Co is represented by .C6, which has already been used for *Corbett,* Cox which follows *Corbett* is given a decimal extension of .C6, or .C65, which will place it before *Crockett* represented by .C7. Similarly, *Allen* is .A45, or halfway between *Aldrich* .A4 and *Ames* .A5.

In the case of names beginning with vowels, the numbers under each consonant in the table must serve the group of letters following it, up to the next one in the tables, *e. g. Ab* and *Ac* would both be .A2, and *Ad, Ae, Af, Ag* would all be .A3. To enter actual names it is, of course, necessary to interpolate. If *Abraham* is .A3, *Acton* would have to be .A35 or .A37. The second letter of a name could be either a vowel or a consonant. *Oats,* for example, could be represented by .O2, or, better, .O17 in order that *Oats* should precede *Ober.*

In some libraries shelf-listing will be a separate operation handled by a clerical shelf-listing staff; in smaller libraries, shelf-listing will be done by the classifier when the classification number is assigned. If unit cards are used in the shelf-list, a temporary shelf-list slip may be filed to protect the new call number from re-use until the permanent shelf-list record is filed; if unit cards are not used, brief shelf-list cards may be made by the shelf listers. In some libraries, the order card is used as the shelf-list record by adding the call number to it and making such other corrections in the data given as may be required. A shelf-list record is an essential component of the library's tools for access to its collection. Since it shows the material assigned to a particular classification number, it is an invaluable aid to classification; its classified arrangement makes it a substitute for a more elaborate classified catalog, and some proponents of the classed catalog have suggested that shelf lists be equipped with alphabetic indexes and made available to the public. It is also an essential record for inventory of a collection since it represents, in general, the order in which library materials are to be found on the shelves.

PREPARATION FOR THE SHELVES. After a book has been cataloged, certain processes are necessary before it can be sent to the library shelves. These include: (1) addition of ownership marks; (2) insertion of book pockets, date slips, and book charging cards as required; (3) labeling the back to show the call number; and (4) collation of the text to cut pages, repair minor tears, etc.

The use of ownership marks is controversial, not because any library believes that they can be abandoned, but rather because there is no universal agreement as to what ownership marks are effective or how they are to be applied. There is considerable evidence in some library collections to support Adams' contention that librarians are enemies of books,[19] and many cases of book mutilation have resulted from overzealous efforts by librarians to indicate ownership permanently. Edge-stamping, rubber stamp markings within the book, perforations, embossing, and bookplates have all been used. Stamping and perforating are the techniques to which most objection has been raised, particularly since these do most to disfigure the text or its illustrations. In almost any library examples can be found of handsome plates that have been disfigured by perforations or rubber stamps. Since there is no evidence to show that such ownership marks contribute materially to any reduction in losses through theft, modern library practice tends to limit the use of ownership markings considerably. Almost all that can be said at present concerning standard practice is that most libraries do agree on the use of a bookplate affixed to the inside of the front cover.

The extent to which book pockets, date slips, and charging cards are used depends upon the charging system employed by a particular library. With the development of new charging techniques involving the use of call slips for charging or of any of the other mechanical or photographic techniques considered in Chapter XIX, the need for these traditional devices has been reduced, and not all libraries are using them. Cataloging departments generally welcome the adoption of one of the newer charging systems since they contribute to a reduction in the number of operations and hence, to lower processing costs.

Call numbers are sometimes gilded on the spine of the book itself by an electric stylus or embossing machine, sometimes pre-embossed on strips of book leather or buckram and affixed to the book, and sometimes written or typed on paper labels which are glued and shellacked to the spine to hold them in place. In some libraries where plastic protective covers are used with paper dust jackets, the book label is affixed to the book jacket and not applied to the book itself until the jacket has been worn out and discarded.

The collation of books to determine their completeness will usually be done early so that imperfect copies can be detected and returned to dealers before marks of ownership are added. The opening of uncut pages is usually reserved for the book preparation section.

In connection with these book preparation activities it is important to remember that various materials in the same library system may be handled differently. Special treatment should be accorded to rare books, fine editions, and collections of art reproductions in order to prevent disfigurement.

PREPARATION FOR BINDING. The real responsibility for preparing books to go to the bindery rests with the bindery division whose function, organization, and activities are described in Chapters XV, XVI, and XVII. Nevertheless, since cataloging departments often handle material in an unbound state or encounter items in need of binding treatment before they are sent to the shelves, they bear some responsibility for binding preparation. Usually this responsibility is extended to include suggesting methods for binding, assembling the various parts in order, and advising on the division of material into volumes and the marking for each volume in a multivolume set. Since this work is incidental to the cataloging operation and will occur irregularly, no special binding personnel in the cataloging department seems necessary, and regular cataloging staffs may be expected to carry on these activities as a part of the normal work load.

CATALOG MAINTENANCE. There are a number of activities relating to the construction and maintenance of the library's catalogs which are common to all libraries. These may be considered together under the heading of catalog maintenance. They include: (1) the final preparation of cards for the catalog, including minor revisions to printed catalog cards, and the addition of call numbers and added entry headings to both printed and locally reproduced unit catalog cards; (2) the reproduction of unit catalog cards in sufficient quantity to meet the requirements of the library's catalog system; (3) filing; (4) routine recataloging of materials as necessary; (5) editorial work on the catalog to correct filing errors, reconcile differences in headings, correct or augment the reference structure, replace worn or soiled cards, and introduce new guide cards and labels as needed; (6) catalog expansion and shifting as required; and (7) subject heading control and revision.

Osborn and Haskins [20] have recently described the problem of maintenance of the catalogs at Harvard. These authors clearly show the importance of a systematic program if the catalog is to be an effective instrument. Budgetary allotments for regular editing of the catalogs should be made if the various irregularities which develop in these records are to be eliminated.

CARD PREPARATION. Printed catalog cards obtained from the Library of Congress [21] or from the H. W. Wilson Company will need to have the library's call number added and subject headings and other added entries typed in on the added cards. The Wilson Company does offer its printed cards with these headings already added, and even with the classification number imprinted, but ordinarily libraries will still need to supply book numbers to complete the call number. Printed cards may not always match the library's copy of the book exactly, and some minor corrections in imprint date, publisher, or other descriptive cataloging detail may be necessary before the cards are used. Some libraries ignore such variations and accept the printed cards just as they come, but most will make such changes as may be necessary to have the description reflect the copy of the book in the library's collection. Locally reproduced cards will usually have the call number already added to the card, but subject headings and added entries usually will have to be typed at the heads of appropriate cards.

CARD REPRODUCTION. Methods for reproducing catalog cards differ among libraries. When only a few added cards are necessary, most libraries have found it more economical to have them typed individually. But if more than four or five cards are required, some mechanical means of card reproduction is generally used. Most typically, the Mimeograph is the duplicating device employed, but in recent years the Multilith has increased in popularity, particularly among those libraries which have a large volume of card reproduction work to do. Some few libraries have continued to print their catalog cards, but rising printing costs are leading most of them to seek other less expensive methods of reproduction. If mimeographing or multilithing is the method employed, stencils must be cut, or if a library has its cards printed, clean copy must be prepared for the printer. Karpel [22] has described how the Museum of Modern Art has its catalogs reproduced photographically by a commercial photographer and presents figures to show that this method compares favorably in cost with present prices of Library of Congress cards. He reports too that these cards on photographic paper are easier to keep clean because of their glossy surfaces. Since the Gary Public Library experimented with the method in the early 1940s, a number of libraries have adopted the Addressograph stencil for reproducing catalog cards.[23] The limitations of the Addressograph stencil, which admits only five or nine lines, have dictated some abbreviation of cataloging detail, but this compression seems not to have affected the usefulness of the card record. Among the libraries using this method of card reproduction are the Grand Rapids Public Library, the Pasadena Public Library, and other public and governmental libraries, including the Veterans Administration. Of all of these, the Veterans Administration's is probably the largest operation.[24] It is sufficient here to note that no universally satisfactory method seems to be available as yet and newer methods are almost certain to be developed within the lifetime of the present generation. Currently, a number of libraries are producing cards by Xerography.[25]

FILING. The filing of catalog cards has occasioned many discussions through the years, and a variety of filing systems has been developed. Theoretically there should be no problem, for whether the alphabetic catalog be divided or in dictionary form, its arrangement is still according to the alphabet. Unfortunately, strict adherence to an alphabetic arrangement has not always proved satisfactory, and certain conventions in arrangement have been introduced. The simplest of these is that when an author entry, a subject entry, and a title entry are the same, they shall be filed in just that order. Entries for government publications, authors entered under their forenames, abbreviations, and foreign languages are representative of the types of difficulty in arrangement encountered. A number of separate filing codes have been developed through the years, and those used by the Cleveland Public Library and the Carnegie Library of Pittsburgh have been among the most popular. The Cataloging Department of the Columbia University Libraries has also issued a filing code for its system. The New York Public Library Circulation Department issued its revised *Filing Code* in 1953. In 1942, after considerable study, a committee of the American Library Association published a new filing code [26] which endeavors to incorporate and reconcile the best features of the most popular systems.

In the last two decades or so, there has been a rising tide of feeling in favor of strict alphabetic order, and many libraries use this arrangement. The ALA rules emphasize this approach either by preferring it or by including it among the optional arrangement schemes suggested. In theory, the strict alphabetical system is presumed to be less confusing to users, but our limited knowledge of catalog use habits does not furnish evidence that this is so. There is some reason to believe that there is no filing system which will eliminate all confusion, for the large library catalog is in itself so complex that any arrangement is likely to cause difficulty to some users. A special committee of the ALA Division of Cataloging and Classification is studying the ALA filing code.

In small libraries, members of the professional staff usually file cards into the catalogs. Sometimes, clerical assistants file "on the rod," and the cards are revised by professionals. In large libraries, clericals may have the total responsibility for filing.

ROUTINE RECATALOGING.[27] Acquisition of new materials, together with changing patterns of library use and changing concepts and emphases in recorded knowledge operate together to suggest the need for some reexamination of the subject groupings of books in library collections and the bibliographical descriptions of materials assimilated into the collections. The development of new areas of knowledge like television and nuclear fission or psychiatry and the new discipline of communications brings about the need to reevaluate older library materials to see whether they may be classified to relate them to the newer materials. Decisions of an author to expand his original one-volume work to two, of a society to issue a series of annual summaries of its activities instead of occasional monographic accounts of its work, or of a university to collect all of its publications in a general field into a series may create situations which require adaptation or modification of original descriptive cataloging. Changes of names of authors, identification of anonymous works, and the revelation of the real names of pseudonymous authors demand alterations in catalog entries.

All libraries must give some attention to such problems if they are to provide the most effective control of their collections, simplify the problems of acquisition and readers' services, minimize the cost of processing, and facilitate the use by patrons. It follows, therefore, that where the methodology of dealing with technical reorganization is carefully worked out, more efficient and economical library service is likely to result.[28]

Whether these activities are best handled by a special staff assigned to these duties, or whether they can be dealt with most economically by each member of the catalog department who first meets them are questions which can be decided only in terms of the local situation. Planning and organizing this kind of work will include clear statements of policy to establish what reclassification and recataloging operations are to be performed, when they are to be done and by whom, what procedures will be followed, and how special matters are to be handled. Normally, these activities are absorbed in the routine work of a small library and no special provision is made for their accomplishment, although one or more professional or clerical assistants may be assigned certain responsibilities with respect to planning, supervising, and performing them. In the larger libraries, however, the problems presented by these activities are sufficiently complex to merit the assignment of all such duties to a special section of the cataloging department.

It should be noted that unlike other catalog maintenance operations, most routine recataloging activities require the attention of professional catalogers. It will be possible to rely upon nonprofessional assistants to help in these operations by assembling books and card records and making the necessary changes in them after the professional assistant has determined what these should be, but responsibility for recataloging is clearly a professional assignment.

EDITING THE CARD CATALOG. The Library of Congress has established a special Editorial Section to deal with problems which arise in the catalogs. Its functions have been described as follows:

1. To edit the general and special card catalogs in the custody of the Catalog Maintenance Division, eliminating unnecessary, duplicate, and superseded entries, correcting inaccurate, inconsistent, and other confusing or misleading entries, and improving generally the integrity and reliability of the catalogs.

2. To study the problem of, and recommend measures for the functional integration of the special catalogs of the Library with the general catalogs, so that the reader consulting the general catalogs will be referred to the special catalogs for the materials in his field of interest which are recorded in these catalogs and not in the general catalogs.

3. To study the problems encountered in the maintenance and use of the catalogs and recommend measures to improve their efficiency.

4. To study the growth and development of the catalogs and plan for their future.[29]

In addition, any such section may have responsibilities for seeing that catalog trays are in good condition, correctly and adequately labeled, and furnished with adequate guide cards to facilitate the use of the catalog entries contained in them. Where the size of the catalog does not suggest the need for a special section, it will be advisable and most efficient to delegate the supervision of the catalog to one person, either a professional or a well-trained nonprofessional staff member, to insure that these matters will be taken care of systematically.

The catalog in any large library represents the accumulation of millions of points of information concerning books and other materials. Even with the greatest caution, it is apparent that such a tool will contain some errors or will require adjustment to changing conditions. Wise administrators have realized that it is necessary to assume an attitude of calculated risk if production is to be maintained on a high level and to make provision for handling such matters as the changes which are needed daily in filing, corrections of call numbers, changes in entries, corrections of errors in the texts of the cards, correcting cross references and subject entries, modifying or adding guide cards, introducing new historical cards, and adjusting the catalog trays and cases. At Columbia University, the various editorial changes which are likely to be needed have been given code numbers to facilitate communication of them between users of the catalog (including the library staff) and the catalog assistant in charge of changes. This method of communication has been so satisfactory that the code is reproduced below.

CODE FOR CATALOG CHANGES[30]

FILING

10. General catalog
11. Depository catalog

CALL NUMBERS

20. Wrong numbers (too general to go in subsequent numbers)
21. Typographical errors, transposition, etc.
22. Former number left unchanged
23. Illegible call number or location stamp
24. Incorrect (or no) location stamp
25. Confusing call number or location stamp
26. University Extension, etc., cards without call number on front (not an error, but a change in practice)

NAME ENTRIES (PERSONAL OR CORPORATE, WHETHER MAIN OR ADDED ENTRIES)

30. Name completions, corrections, etc. (See also 32)
31. Dates to be changed or added
32 Typographical errors (transpositions, misspellings, etc.)

CARDS LEFT IN CATALOG

40. Old cards, tracing overlooked or possibly untraced
41. Old *removal* cards: cataloging oversight
42. Old *removal* cards: filing oversight
43. Old *temporary* cards: cataloging oversight
44. Old *temporary* cards: filing oversight
45. Cards to be removed for Collegiate German Study, etc.
46. Cards to be removed for department library copies at request from the department (request should be made directly to the Cataloging Dept.)

ADDED REFERENCES NEEDED

50. Subject card
51. Title card
52. Editor, translator, etc. (any secondary note otherwise provided for)

53. Series card
54. Analytic card
55. Cross reference
56. Corner mark
57. History card
58. Request for recataloging

ERRORS IN BODY OF CARD

60. Omitted or misleading bibliographical information (too general to fit other categories)
61. Incomplete or incorrect record of holdings
62. Misleading advice on cards
63. Incorrect cataloging information
64. Contents omitted or incorrect
65. Incorrect word or misspelling, mainly typographical
66. Incomplete or incorrect dates, mainly typographical

INCORRECT CROSS-REFERENCE

70. Blind cross-reference (i.e., cross-reference to nothing)
71. Cross-reference to another cross-reference
72. Cross-reference not clear
73. Cross-reference out-moded (i.e., to a new changed location, etc.)

SUBJECT CORRECTIONS

80. Incorrect subject (as *Hungary—Revolution, 1918–1919*, instead of *Hungary—History—Revolution, 1918–1919*)
81. Incorrect technique (as failure to subdivide, etc.)
82. Incorrect concept (misunderstanding of topic of book)
83. Typographical errors (e.g., *Barbers in America* for *Berbers in America*)

GUIDE CARDS

90. Broken guide cards
91. Suggested additional guide cards
92. Misleading guide cards

CATALOG TRAYS AND CASES

95. New labels needed
96. Broken trays
97. Trays needing shifting

CARDS MISSING FOR LONG AVAILABLE BOOKS

101. Cards missing in general catalog
102. Request for temporary cards for general catalog
103. Reference Department catalog omitted
104. Cards not supplied by Law or Medical

MISCELLANEOUS

111. Cards to be stamped: For other copies
112. Cards to be stamped: Current in Periodical Reading Room
113. Cards to be stamped: Continued on next card
114. Reference reserve card to be supplied
115. Temporary removal card too brief
116. Temporary removal card fails to locate all copies
117. Temporary removal card illegible
118. Broken or soiled cards
120. No error

CATALOG SHIFTING. As catalogs grow to keep pace with increasing library collections, the need for more catalog space requires the addition of new catalog cases and the redistribution of the old catalog throughout the additional space available. Such shifts are time consuming and disruptive of library service when they occur, and careful attention must be given to planning the expansion of the catalog to reduce this disruption to a minimum. Some head catalogers have insisted that the redistribution of the catalog is so important that it cannot be entrusted to any assistant and must be accomplished by the department head himself. Behind this assumption lies the belief that tray divisions cannot be arbitrary if users are to be best served, and that suitable divisions can be determined which will take account of the irregular growth of the catalog in different parts of the alphabet. Such a restrictive outlook when dealing with a large catalog seems ill considered, for the minor adjustments which might result from such personal supervision are almost inconsequential in a catalog of any size. If policies to govern the expansion are clearly established, there is no reason why nonprofessional assistants cannot work out the details of the plan.

The advance planning will involve measurements of the existing catalog and redistribution of its cards into as many units as there will be trays in the new expanded catalog. The actual division of the catalog into new trays can be accomplished before any cards are actually shifted, and the new divisions marked in the old catalog trays with colored cards or other signals. If this is done, labels for the new catalog can be prepared in advance and several teams of workers can do the actual shifting simultaneously and independently of each other. Such a plan will make it possible for the physical move to be completed rapidly with minimum dislocation of catalog service. Moreover, the shifted catalog will be ready for use as soon as the move is finished. Almost the only post-shift operation which will be necessary is the inspection of the new trays for added or revised guide cards. This can be done in advance too, but it is probably done more efficiently after the shift has been made. Terry [31] has described the routines employed in the most recent shift of the Columbia University catalog and pointed up the problems which must be solved in carrying out the plans for expansion. Merritt and Frarey [32] have reported on the costs of expanding a large catalog.

SUBJECT HEADING CONTROL AND REVISION. In Chapter X, it was observed that subject analysis techniques for library materials, involving, as they do, the use of standard lists of subject headings, result in recurring needs to revise the subject headings used in a library catalog so that they will represent a modern and rational approach for the user of the catalog. The use of subject authority files either on cards or in the form of checked lists of headings has been noted and their function and the techniques for their construction discussed. It was pointed out that the maintenance of the subject authority file could be a nonprofessional task provided that professional supervision was given to it. In this chapter particular attention is given to the changes which must be made in the library's subject catalog and in its subject authority file.

Changes in the subject catalog include the following: (1) the substitution of a new subject heading term for an older one; (2) the addition of a new subject heading for a new subject concept; (3) the redefinition of a subject heading to limit or expand its meaning; (4) the addition of a new specific subject heading for some aspect of a subject formerly encompassed by the general heading; (5) the addition of new subdivisions to a general heading, including subdivision by subject, aspect, or phase, subdivision by place or locality, subdivision by date, or subdivision by literary or other form; (6) the cancellation of an older subject heading or of a subdivision of a heading; (7) changes in the accepted spelling or form of the subject heading; and (8) the addition or subtraction of *see* and *see also* references.[33]

Where these changes represent no more than the substitution of one term for another, changes in the subject catalog and the authority file are purely mechanical. Old subject headings are erased and the new ones added to the catalog cards, corrected authority cards are made for the authority file, and tracings on the main entries for these subjects are changed to conform to the new headings. Some libraries dispense with the changes in tracings, particularly when the new subject heading resembles the older one closely. Other libraries introduce a simple *see* reference from the old form to the new one in order to eliminate the need for changing tracings. In so far as evidence is available, it appears that most libraries do change both headings and tracings for them when subject headings are revised.[34]

Since these mechanical changes are time consuming, particularly when their volume is great, suggestions have been made to simplify the routines for making them. Starr [35] has proposed that when a subject heading is changed, older literature in the library catalog be ignored and the new heading used only for materials added to the library's collection after the date of the change. This practice recognizes the predominant interest of most library patrons in current materials and presumes that users will not be inconvenienced particularly by it. References to connect the two headings will be necessary, of course. Brodman has also suggested the same practice.[36] As a short cut the practice outlined by Starr and Brodman is satisfactory, but it is highly improbable that it will solve the problem permanently so long as our subject catalogs attempt to serve the purposes they do today, and so long as our revision practices continue along present lines. This reference device will work very well so long as headings change only once. As soon as a heading changes more than once, however, the reference structure of the catalog will become unduly complex. That multiple revision of the same heading does occur has been pointed out by Frarey.[37]

Whenever the meaning of a subject heading is limited or expanded, or whenever new headings or new subdivisions of existing headings are introduced, the revision process becomes more complex. In these cases it will usually be necessary to examine the subject cards under headings requiring change to determine whether they should be kept under the old heading or given a new entry under a new subject. While this determination can be made from an inspection of the cards in many cases, it will be necessary sometimes to reexamine the books themselves. Not all libraries attempt to keep up with this kind of subject revision, but it is an essential activity if the subject catalog is to be maintained at a high level of efficiency. It is obvious that such revision as this will require more professional attention than that described above.

Changes in and additions to the reference structure of the catalog are largely mechanical ones, and responsibility for making new references or eliminating older ones can be given to a clerical assistant who has a thorough understanding of the purposes for which references are made. Reference changes usually require extensive checking and rechecking in the subject catalog or the authority file to insure that no "blind" or "chain" references are admitted to the catalog, and it is essential that all references or changes to them be recorded accurately in the subject authority file.

It is evident from this discussion that there are many routine operations involved in the revision and control of subject headings. Efficient practice requires that the whole program be directed by a qualified assistant who has a full understanding of the mechanics of control and revision. If policies are defined by the professional staff, and if procedures are well organized, most of the revision burden can be allocated to nonprofessional assistants. In a large library, a full-scale revision program may well be a full-time assignment for one or more assistants.

CATALOG MAINTENANCE ORGANIZATION. It remains to consider how catalog maintenance activities are best organized. In practice they have often been absorbed in the routine operations of a library and no special organization has been created to handle them except as responsibility for planning and supervising may be delegated to one or more professional assistants in addition to their regular duties. Larger libraries may well consider whether some more formal organization may not be desirable if maximum efficiency is to be achieved. Probably the most highly organized catalog maintenance operation to be found in any American library is in the Library of Congress. The reasons for the establishment of the Catalog Maintenance Division, together with its historical background and its present function have been stated as follows:

The establishment of the Catalog Maintenance Division, announced in General Order No. 1305, October 22, 1946, reflects the recognition of a new dimension in the cataloging process and a new problem in library management: the problem of the catalog. What should be the objectives of the catalog and what its limitations? What kind of entries should the catalog contain and how should these entries be organized and integrated? What should be the general design of the catalog or system of catalogs, and in what form or forms should it be prepared and maintained? The continued and progressive growth and complexity of the catalog have made it increasingly more difficult to maintain and unwieldy to use. The vicissitudes of the catalog caused by changing vagaries have deeply affected its integrity and made it often confusing, unreliable, and misleading. It has come to require special attention, study, and care, if the ultimate objective of cataloging is to be achieved and not lost in the process.

The larger the library and the more varied its catalog, the more complex is its catalog program. In the Library of Congress, the existence of special catalogs of manuscripts, maps, music, Orientalia, and other materials not recorded in the general catalog calls for the development of methods which will provide for the functional integration of these catalogs with the general catalogs of the Library. The publication of the Library of Congress *Author Catalog* and *Subject Catalog* and the cultivation of their potentialities in the promotion of bibliographical exchange and scholarship represents still another aspect of the Library's catalog program.

Historically, the Catalog Maintenance Division recalls the former Catalog Preparation and Maintenance Division which was created in December 1940 together with, and as part of, the Processing Department, and dissolved in June 1943, simultaneously with, and partly as result of, the formation of the former Acquisitions Department which took over some of its functions. The name of the present Division, and two of its sections—the Card Preparation Section and the Filing Section—are derived from that Division. The principle objectives of the present Division, however, are essentially new and without precedent in the Library. The establishment of the Catalog Maintenance Division follows a growing realization that, while much study and thought have been given to the design and contents of the individual catalog entries, the problem of the catalog as a whole has received insufficient attention. It has grown and expanded without adequate planning and supervision.

Functions.—The general functions of the Catalog Maintenance Division are:

(1) To plan, organize, and maintain the general catalogs of the Library—including the Main Catalog, Annex Catalog, and Official Catalog—the catalogs of the Music Division, and other catalogs which may be assigned to it in the future.

(2) To assist in the organization and maintenance of special catalogs and indexes maintained by the various divisions of the Library.

(3) To provide the functional integration of the special catalogs with the general catalogs of the Library.

(4) To plan, organize, and prepare for publication the *Library of Congress Author Catalog* and the *Library of Congress Subject Catalog* and other catalogs which may be undertaken in the future.

(5) To edit and supervise the catalogs in its custody, and to investigate bibliographical and technical problems related to their development and improvement.

(6) To develop rules for the organization of these catalogs and aids to their use.

(7) To maintain an information service on the receipt, location, and progress of materials ordered or in process and to locate these materials when urgently needed.[38]

This account suggests that there may be a need for similar organizations in other major libraries. It should be observed, however, that major projects which may be undertaken in response to a particular need—recataloging and reclassification programs, extensive reorganization of a library's catalog machinery, movements to new library quarters, consolidation of separate catalogs or the construction of new ones, extended subject heading revision programs, changes in filing practice, for example—sometimes offer opportunities for editorial work on the catalog. Hitchcock and Field have described the results of three such major projects at Yale.[39] Their conclusion that there are advantages to be gained from allowing the catalog to grow uniformly over a period of time and by making periodical frontal attacks on editing it reflects an interesting point of view which merits consideration. In any case, the need for attention to catalog maintenance cannot be denied in any library which is concerned with the effectiveness and integrity of its catalogs.

WITHDRAWALS. Thus far the concern in this chapter has been with routines involved in adding new materials to the library collection and in maintaining the records of the collection complete and up to date. The removal or discard of materials from the collection also involves certain operations which may often be assigned to nonprofessional personnel. Every library loses some books and discards others because they are worn out, have been superseded, or are no longer useful in the collection. In fact, as more and more libraries become concerned with the problem of increasing size, more and more of them are developing organized weeding programs to rid their collections of obsolete material. While the exact routines for dealing with lost books may vary somewhat from those employed for discarded ones, they are essentially alike and will be considered together in this discussion. In essence, they require the cancellation of all library records concerning the item being removed from the collection, and additions to the library's record of lost books if one is maintained. Where a library carries an insurance policy against routine losses, careful and permanent records of lost books are necessary since the annual report to the insurance company must contain information about recovered losses as well as new ones.[40] Shelf-list records and catalog cards must be corrected to give up-to-date information about copies or volumes owned, and all card records must be removed when a title is discarded completely. Corrections to cross references in the catalog may be necessary when all card records for a title are withdrawn. When books are discarded from a library collection, it is important that ownership marks in them be eliminated or obscured in such a way that the book will not be returned to the library later. Usually libraries stamp an appropriate legend on bookplates and adjacent to any other ownership markings indicating that the book is no longer the property of that library or that it has been withdrawn from the library collection. Assistants who work with lost and discarded books must be trained to be careful and accurate for costly confusion can result from slipshod withdrawal routines.

SUMMARY. This chapter has identified a series of operations which are closely related to the cataloging process and are usually performed in conjunction with it. The routines described are not common to all libraries but they are typical of many, and they are not absolute in any sense of the word but vary within a library as time goes by and among libraries at any one time. The proper organization and assignment of these tasks, all of which can be handled by competent, well-trained, nonprofessional assistants who are well supervised, will do much to contribute to the efficiency of the catalog department and to reduce cataloging costs. Moreover the nature of these operations is such that the best way to accomplish them has almost certainly not been discovered. Experiments and improved techniques are reported frequently. By keeping an open mind about the essentiality of any of these routines and the efficacy of any particular organizational setup to handle them, the alert library administrator will be able to take advantage of new ideas, new routines, and new machines as they may be developed and thus contribute to the over-all efficiency of the library operation for which he is responsible.

XIII. Reclassification and Recataloging

SINCE there are many American libraries which have not adopted either the Dewey Decimal or the Library of Congress classification, but have continued to use either a locally devised system or one of the less common standard classifications, there has been considerable interest in reclassification projects. The development of the library survey in the mid-twentieth century has shown the inadequacy of a number of these classifications, and as libraries have attempted to improve their services a number of major reclassification projects have been undertaken. In 1941, a report [1] was made on reclassification projects in sixty academic libraries. Although World War II and rising costs have prevented some additional projects from being started, reclassification has been continued, and several additional projects have been recommended.[2] Among libraries changing to the LC classification in recent years are those of Cornell University, Rutgers, Washington University (St. Louis), and of the universities of Tennessee, Iowa, Miami, and Mississippi. A number of public, special and governmental libraries have also reclassified their collections according to the LC system.

Most libraries which have reclassified their collections have taken this opportunity to recatalog. Since improvement in cataloging is desirable in many libraries, reclassification and necessary recataloging may well be combined, for both require card-by-card removal and modification. Although more time will be required for combined operations, recataloging can be more efficient when it is done at the same time as reclassification. Besides these comprehensive recataloging and reclassification projects, almost every library carries on some sort of continuous classification and cataloging revision, sometimes of individual titles or small collections.

DEFINITIONS

What is meant by reclassification and recataloging? Changing soiled or worn cards, or half-sized or manuscript cards, for new, full-sized or printed cards may be recataloging, but only in a mechanical sense. The actual changing of call numbers on cards and books has been termed reclassification, yet this, too, is only a mechanical phase of the process—in short, renotation. The term "recataloging" as used here means any change made in the original cataloging; that is, in the form or content of the entries of the main or secondary cards, the bodies of cards, the various types of notes, or in the form or terminology of the subject headings. "Reclassification" is meant to describe the regrouping of a collection of books into subject classes different from those previously employed; the term includes the reassigning of a distinctive call number to each item, which indicates the group to which it belongs and the place it should occupy within that group in relation to other books.

TYPES

Complete reclassification may refer to a change within a classification (such as expanding an abridged system) or to a change from one system to another, and involving complete, partial, or no recataloging. Partial reclassification involves the rearrangement of a certain section or sections of the book stock or of a special collection; this may be accompanied by any one of several degrees of recataloging. Incidental reclassification consists of rearrangements within a classification which result from temporary classification or detections of misplacements and obvious errors.

COSTS

Some librarians have estimated the cost of reclassification and recataloging to be twice as much as the original costly processes. Remarking of books, withdrawal of cards from the catalog and shelf list, ordering new cards or erasing old ones, refiling, and changing book cards and pockets all represent added activities which increase the cost. The 1941 study estimated that the total cost of reclassifying and recataloging 5,461,000 volumes in sixty academic libraries ranged between a million and a half and four million dollars. Postwar costs have increased to the point where the upper range of this estimate represents more nearly the actual figure; indeed four million dollars may be a modest guess. Yet in spite of the known expensiveness of reclassification–recataloging projects, librarians are still willing to consider them.

VALUE

Though a librarian may be cognizant of the difficulties and costs involved in programs of reclassification, he may institute the project on the basis of two assumptions: (1) that the use of a classification such as that of the Library of Congress (for most changes have been toward the use of the LC classification), or an arrangement based on reader interest, achieves a grouping of the books in the collection that is of greater educational significance and shows to the users the currently accepted relationships among the branches of knowledge more effectively than did the system that is being replaced, and (2) that the adoption of a new classification, which involves abandoning a system that has been found expensive to handle technically, will in the long run be an efficient administrative device. These assumptions are based on the testimonies of librarians who have grappled with the problem, and on the results of general surveys. Ideally, every librarian who is considering reclassification should test these assumptions for his specific situation by propounding a series of questions which can be answered by a systematic study: Do users looking for a specific title find through classification others which were used in addition to the original item? Are the stacks used directly without consultation of the card catalog? Do the users come to the stacks to examine all items on a certain subject? Is the classification unsatisfactory because the patron finds books which he uses together dispersed in a half-dozen places in the stacks? Questions relating to the administration of the library might be asked: Is the cost of the technical processes higher in a particular library than in other institutions comparable in size, purpose, and conditions of work? Is this a defect of the classification system used? Does the circulation department need to provide extra personnel to locate and shelve books because of complicated notations and book numbers? Does the reference librarian need to give inordinate service to users of the card catalog because of inconsistent and faulty cataloging? What conditions might the librarian expect in the future if the defects of the classification and the catalog are not corrected?

Positive findings in answer to some or all of these questions must govern the decision to reclassify and recatalog. The costs are too great and the inconveniences and dislocations too serious to be discounted.

> The most important thing that can be said about reclassification of a library is, "Don't do it unless there is some really compelling reason." No classification scheme is perfect, and all have quite serious failings in various branches of knowledge, so if you are not satisfied with your present classification, you may be sure a new one will not bring complete relief.[3]

REASONS FOR UNDERTAKING RECLASSIFICATION

The history and growth of a library and its collections, as well as the development of the institution of which the library is a part, are primary factors to be considered. For example, it is far less difficult to explain the need for reclassification of a large collection in a library that has been arranged haphazardly by an inadequate local classification scheme or by a system of fixed numbers than it would be to show why a slowly growing collection, fairly well arranged by the Dewey classification, should be reclassified by the schedules of the Library of Congress. Libraries which adopt subject divisional organization plans and provide information, advisory, and lending services at various service points rather than centrally may find that such a reorganization requires some recataloging and reclassification to make efficient groupings of materials.[4]

REASONS RELATING TO CLASSIFICATION SYSTEMS. If the vague statement that "the Library of Congress system is better suited for a college or university collection" can be disregarded, the principal reasons given for discarding classifications pertain to their completeness, their inclusiveness, the logical order of the classes, the internal arrangement of the classes, and the modernity of the terminology of the system. In the report by Tauber [5] specific reasons, more or less in order of their relative importance, included: (1) classes in the discarded system were too broad; (2) some classes were lacking; (3) no provision was made for modern thought; (4) the classification was not considered suitable for a scholarly collection; (5) the discarded classification was not revised frequently enough or fully enough; (6) classes were poorly balanced in that some subjects were classified closely while others, with equivalent printed material available, were classified more broadly; and (7) classes were not arranged logically. Since all of the libraries studied were changing to LC from some other system, these criticisms are directed very largely against the Dewey, Harris (Cornell), Rowell, Cutter, Harvard, Richardson, Poole, and local schemes. The majority of the libraries used Dewey before the change; thus these criticisms indicate some weakness of the Dewey classification in academic libraries. However, in college and university libraries more importance usually is attached to the classification of materials than in public libraries.

REASONS RELATING TO LIBRARY USERS. Ideally, a study of the uses made by library patrons of classifications and catalogs ought to precede a decision to reclassify. However, the librarians in the institutions covered by the 1941 study seem to have thought less of the users than of the classification *per se* or of problems of library administration.

The data indicated that in six academic libraries, graduate students were active in suggesting changes of classification. These suggestions, in libraries classified by Dewey, were primarily complaints about the structure of the classification, e.g., the separation of an author's works by form. In libraries not using Dewey, criticisms of the whole systems were made. In twenty-eight of the sixty institutions studied in 1941, faculty members recommended adoption of the Library of Congress system. There was a close relation between the institutions which had faculty members active in the reclassification program and institutions in which specific criticisms were made of the classifications which were discarded. The study does not include any information, however, which suggests the whole quantity of criticism or the proportion of critics to the total number of users.

There will always be some patrons who disagree with any classification. The problem which the librarian faces is that of resolving individual dissatisfactions in relation to the whole, not only for the present, but also the future—as far as that is possible.[6]

REASONS RELATING TO LIBRARY ADMINISTRATION. Thirty-five libraries in the same study indicated that their decision to reclassify was influenced in part by administrative reasons. The most important of these were: (1) the need to correct past errors of cataloging and classification; (2) the belief that the LC classification is more effective in providing groupings of material satisfactory to users having access to the stacks, thus minimizing staff attention; that it facilitates the work of the circulation department in locating and shelving books, and that it aids in classification, since there is little difficulty in interpolating large quantities of titles in the various classes; (3) the possibility of adopting LC printed cards, subject headings, and cataloging procedures; (4) the economies to be achieved through the use of LC classification numbers, which are already assigned for a large percentage of titles; (5) the possibility of cooperation with affiliated libraries or consolidation with larger libraries; and (6) the possibility of centralizing the technical processes within a given library system.

If the system of cataloging within a library is consistent and serves the purpose of the library, the need for recataloging is open to question, even though by some standards the library may be badly cataloged. There have been some cases in which recataloging has been used as a pretext for reclassification, rather than as a reason.

Although there is substantial professional opinion that the LC classification provides better groupings of material, facilitates location and shelving, and simplifies the problems of classification, there are no objective studies to prove these assumptions. Mere adoption of LC printed cards, subject headings, and cataloging procedures cannot be accepted as a valid reason when offered alone, for although more than 6,000 American libraries use the LC cards, and a substantial number use the LC subject headings, thus far only about 300 libraries of all types in all countries have adopted the LC classification system in whole or in part.

The most telling administrative reasons appear to be those which relate to economy, cooperation, and centralization. While cost figures are not readily available, there is strong reason to believe that the use of LC classification schedules is less expensive, since the classification numbers for individual titles are supplied on each LC printed card, and unless a library chooses to depart drastically from the LC schedules (in which case there is legitimate question as to why the LC system was adopted at all) these numbers may be used with little or no change. However, LC printed cards also include Dewey classification numbers.

Cooperative classification and centralized technical services both operate most economically and efficiently when all the units involved are using the same classification and are following common cataloging procedures. The Newark Colleges of Rutgers University decided to recatalog their John Cotton Dana Library primarily because the other libraries in the university system were using the LC classification, and because the Dana Library had been designated as the centralized processing center for all of the Rutgers Libraries in Newark.[7] In at least five instances in the 1941 study, reclassification occurred in libraries consolidated or cooperating with other libraries. In these cases, the centralization of the technical operations, or the desire for uniformity for the convenience of students and faculty, were the motivating causes for reclassification. Recently librarians have tended to recognize that cooperative and centralized cataloging and classification projects probably offer the most immediate relief from the high costs of processing done independently. An increase in the number of such enterprises may be expected, and this may, in turn, result in some increase in the number of recataloging and reclassification projects which will be undertaken. It is not likely, however, that the growth of cooperative programs will result in wholesale recataloging projects, since most libraries will prefer to keep recataloging to a minimum in order to realize the greatest savings from cooperation. The degree to which major revisions are made in the ALA cataloging rules will probably have a direct effect on the amount of recataloging which libraries will find desirable and possible.

That administrative reasons have been the most significant in those projects which have been undertaken is not unnatural, yet it tends to support the suspicion that in most libraries, classification is essentially a librarian's tool for aiding the users. When free access to stack collections is denied, as it is in many academic libraries, the value which classification possesses in "educational suggestiveness" or in showing the relationships of branches of knowledge is largely lost to the users. In such libraries, the reasons for reclassification can only be administrative.

ADMINISTRATIVE PROBLEMS

While such matters as the size and type of building, the layout of the technical department and of the stacks, and the complexity of the library's organization introduce problems that make it hazardous to generalize on all aspects of managerial control in reclassification, several factors operate in varying degrees in all libraries. These involve such problems as the execution of a newly defined policy of classification and cataloging; the planning of procedures and techniques; the control of materials and effort; the operation of the processes at maximum efficiency; and the maintenance of all elements in the reclassification project in a state of proper balance with the regular work of the cataloging department and in effective coordination with other aspects of service within the library.

In any reclassification program, cooperative relationships may and usually must exist between the librarian and his trustees, president, dean, or other official to whom he is responsible, between the librarian and the users of his library, and between the librarian and his staff. In academic libraries, similar cooperative relationships will exist with the faculty library committee, the faculty as a whole, and with the students, particularly graduate students. Since reclassification is a process with influence beyond the cataloging room, and since it bears directly upon the service given to users and upon the cost of the operations of the library, such relationships should be clearly defined if the process is to function efficiently. If the various groups involved have a good understanding of the meaning and needs of the reclassification project, and if their active support is enlisted at the outset, even though they may have no direct role in the final approval of the project, there is greater assurance that continuing financial support for the work will be provided and that friction resulting from routine activities and dislocations of service during reclassification will be kept to a minimum. Staff participation in decisions regarding the placement of certain classes of materials is desirable, and consultation and planning with the personnel of the various library departments is essential if work of the cataloging department is to be coordinated effectively with the total library program and if service to patrons is not to be completely disrupted.

PLANNING. Administrators of libraries confronted with the problem of reclassification will need to consider the following steps in an effective program: (1) efficiency in planning, involving such matters as outlining a policy for the technical processes, providing sufficient and efficient supervision, adequate quarters for the mechanical work of reclassification, and probably most important, stated appropriations of funds for the work; (2) efficient techniques and mechanical routines; and (3) efficient coordination of the old work with the new to insure continuous and even service to the users.

The technical problems of recataloging and reclassification are many and complex, and concern policy as well as procedures. In matters of policy, such questions as the following should be considered: Will an attempt be made to reclassify and recatalog the whole collection quickly and efficiently by a special temporary staff, or will the work be performed gradually by the regular staff along with the handling of new accessions? Will the new classification or new subject headings be applied to new books, to books in special subject fields, or to books in the whole collection? The answers must be determined by the funds and the personnel which can be made available and by the size and type of the existing collection.

PERSONNEL. Some of the personnel problems which appear in reclassification projects concern (1) the use of the incumbent staff to do the work along with the handling of current accessions, (2) the use of a special staff to carry on the project, and (3) the distribution of routine and professional activities.

Although there are obvious advantages to be gained from the use of the regular staff on a reclassification project, when all other conditions are equal, experience indicates that a special staff will complete the job in a shorter time and will establish fewer variations for "local conditions" which have long ceased to exist. There is no question but that reclassification offers the librarian an opportunity for critical reappraisal of the technical operations.

Special staffs may be composed of experienced reclassifiers and recatalogers, assisted by clerical helpers, or by such an arrangement as that used in a college library where one professional cataloger supervised the work of a corps of student assistants. Where the largest portion of the special staff is composed of nonprofessional help, close adherence to LC classification and cataloging practices has been observed, since progress is dependent upon maximum delegation of responsibility to the nonprofessional staff. This is possible only when standardized methods are maintained.

The tremendous amount of detail involved in large projects demands a careful differentiation of duties. Available evidence suggests that professional workers have been doing many tasks, such as withdrawing cards and erasing call numbers from cards and books, which should be delegated to untrained or clerical help.

SPECIAL PROBLEMS

INADEQUACY OF NEW CLASSIFICATION SYSTEMS. The librarian who has decided in favor of reclassification is assuming that the new classification provides better groupings of materials than did the old one. Such a decision includes consideration of the provisions made in the new system for the particular kinds of materials which the library possesses. Nevertheless, no system is perfect, and inadequate provisions exist for some classes of material in the best of these. A library which boasts of a single or of several unusually strong collections in special subject fields may find that general classification systems do not make the best provision for some of these materials.

ALTERATIONS OF NEW CLASSIFICATION SYSTEMS. Although it has been noted above that alterations in the newly adopted system may be considered, professional opinion is strongly against such changes unless they are absolutely necessary. Not only do they result in higher costs during the reclassification project and forever afterward, but they also contribute to inconsistencies and errors in classification. Subsequent catalogers cannot be depended upon to view the need for such modifications in the same light as those who decided in favor of them. Such alterations have not been uncommon in libraries, however. In Providence, the 300s and 800s in the Decimal classification were reversed in order to locate literature and philology together.[8] Boisen [9] has reported that in the reclassification of the George Avery Bunting Library of Washington College, a decision was made to telescope the LC classes into smaller divisions in order to give greater unity to the collection. His reported adaptations are numerous, and the regroupings of some subjects are so extensive that the result bears little similarity to the LC classification except in notation. Gerould and Noyes [10] have reported an alteration of the LC schedules for literature which does not do such violence to the original LC plan. At Clark University, they sought a system which would have all of the advantageous arrangements of the LC schedules but which would avoid what they considered to be unduly complicated notation. Thus they retained the LC classification except for the works of individual authors and material about them, for which they introduced a simple scheme using letters for languages followed by author book numbers. Instead of changing the old call numbers on catalog cards they substituted general notices posted over the card catalog and in the stacks called attention to the changes in arrangement.

If modifications of the new system are decided upon, extreme care must be exercised to insure that they fit logically into the new system and that alterations are not so extensive that the integrity of the system is wholly destroyed. Changes introduce higher costs into the project, and if one of the purposes of a classification is that of reducing costs, alterations will be held to a minimum or dispensed with altogether.

CLASSIFICATION OF SPECIAL TYPES OF MATERIALS

Most classification systems provide alternate locations for certain types of materials, and any library beginning a reclassification project must decide how it will handle these items. In libraries where the classification has grown over a period of years, the patterns are usually established, but the adoption of a new system affords an opportunity to reexamine past practices and to decide whether an alternate arrangement may not be preferable.

SUBJECT BIBLIOGRAPHIES. Librarians have never been in agreement as to whether subject bibliographies belong properly in a special collection of bibliography materials or with the subject to which they relate. Reference librarians tend to think in terms of a complete collection of bibliographical aids, and will favor an arrangement which keeps subject bibliographies within the reference collection. Other users relate a bibliography to the subject field to which it pertains and consider that its proper place is with other materials on the same subject. LC makes provision for both arrangements. In order to classify bibliographies with the subject in Dewey, special devices (such as the use of letters) may be introduced.

BIOGRAPHIES. The placement of biographies presents a problem similar to that raised by bibliographical materials. Generally libraries which have followed LC practice place biographies with the subject. For those titles which are difficult to place with a specific subject, the general biography numbers are used (CT in LC, the 920s, or devices such as "B" or 92, in Dewey).

FICTION. An important problem relates to the separation of fiction from other literary works or its amalgamation with the other literature of the country of its author. In the Decimal Classification, the form divisions, if used, serve to segregate fiction as a type of literature from other types. But in the LC schedules no such distinction has been made, and opinion generally seems to favor LC practice. Even though LC has provided the class PZ3 for most of its "non-literary" fiction, those libraries whose practices have been studied seem to believe it more useful to the patron to discard the PZ3 class and place fiction with the rest of a national literature. The practice is by no means universal, as many use the PZ3 schedule. A separate fiction collection, arranged alphabetically by author and frequently marked "F," is found in many libraries.

TEXTBOOKS. The arrangement of textbook collections is rarely a problem except in those libraries which serve teacher-training institutions and maintain sizable collections of textbooks for student use and evaluation. When these collections are assembled for this specific purpose, it does not seem reasonable to obscure the function of the collection by dispersing it throughout a general collection which may number several hundred thousand volumes. Teacher-training institutions have preferred to build special textbook collections, but other libraries not primarily concerned with educating teachers have preferred to class textbooks with the subject. An interesting special classification has been devised in at least one library where the LC class numbers for subjects have been prefaced with the letters LT, thus creating a distinct grouping which maintains subject relationships while it sets the textbook collection apart. Results of this arrangement seem uniformly better than in four other institutions which have devised special classifications based upon broad Dewey numbers prefaced by LT.

JUVENILE WORKS. The presence of juvenile collections which are used in connection with teacher-training schools, by the pupils themselves or by students preparing to be teachers, presents a problem similar to that of textbooks. Alternatives in libraries adopting the LC classification are placement with subject or grouping in

PZ5. In academic libraries, at least, the segregation of juvenile works is probably more effective, for it hardly seems satisfactory to class a work for eighth-graders with a scholarly treatise. In public libraries juvenile collections are generally kept separately and are arranged by broad subjects.

PERIODICALS. Periodicals generally have been reclassified along with books, although in several libraries, this classification has been done for shelf-list purposes only, since the periodicals themselves are arranged alphabetically by title on the shelves. Evidence based on observation alone indicates that the approach to periodicals generally has not been on the basis of subject groupings of the titles but by specific articles. It is probable, however, that subject groupings of periodicals aid the user who is working on a special topic by bringing together a similar group of journals. At least two libraries have decided in favor of reclassification of periodicals after the original decision had been made against it, for experience demonstrated that readers in the stacks found an alphabetical arrangement difficult to use when periodicals changed titles or merged with other titles. Stack attendants encountered similar difficulties in locating and shelving materials. Present evidence is not clearly in favor of either classification or alphabetical arrangement, though there seems to be an emerging tendency to favor the alphabetic arrangement as the one which is likely to be more useful to most readers and as the one which does reduce the processing costs. There is as yet no evidence to demonstrate whether this kind of reduction in cataloging costs is a clear saving, or whether increased costs of servicing an alphabetic collection outweigh the advantages.

GOVERNMENT DOCUMENTS, LOCAL COLLECTIONS, AND DISSERTATIONS. Some institutions prefer to classify government documents and dissertations with their respective subjects. However, the utilization of the Superintendent of Documents classification or a shelving arrangement based on chronology may offer more economical methods of handling large quantities of publications. Chronological arrangements of dissertations under the names of issuing institutions, rather than subject groupings, are not uncommon. From the point of view of use, it seems preferable to adopt subject groupings as far as this is feasible, since this eliminates artificial distinctions of form which usually make little sense to library users who frequently may not be aware of their existence. However, administrative efficiency and economies in processing and servicing may have dictated such special arrangements.

Local collections of archival material relating to the academic institution, to the locality, or to special industries, or activities of major concern to the users of a particular library may also offer difficulties. Sometimes these collections are so large that they cannot be grouped effectively in the sections of the classification appropriate for such material; at other times, this material may vary so much in form or content that strict adherence to the classification schedules will disperse it so as to destroy its usefulness as a special comprehensive collection. In such cases, careful modification or expansion of the classification to provide for suitable groupings of all of the materials in or being added to the collection is desirable and usually necessary. An alternative method is the construction of a special classification system apart from that adopted for the general collection.

DEPARTMENTAL COLLECTIONS. A decision to reclassify a departmental collection will depend largely on its nature, as well as its relation to the central collection. When processing activities for departmental collections are centralized in the main cataloging department, and when the collections are growing and are being used, it seems that reclassification will insure greater technical efficiency and ease of use on the part of patrons and staff. Libraries facing this problem frequently have decided in favor of reclassification for departmental collections, although notable exceptions have been made in medicine and law.

DISTINGUISHING BETWEEN OLD AND NEW CLASSIFICATION. Pearson [11] has reported that one of the reasons underlying the selection of the Dewey Decimal Classification for the new classification system in the District of Columbia Public Library was the need to select a new system which would be markedly distinguishable in notation from the old, in this case, Cutter. There have been other instances in which a major factor in the choice of the new classification seems to have been this desire to distinguish between the notation of the old and the new. This consideration may, in some cases, have been more influential in the choice than the general suitability of the system selected. Such emphasis is misplaced, for the appropriateness of the new classification should take precedence. If extensive reorganization is considered necessary, then it behooves the librarian and his staff to determine which is the best possible new classification for their needs and to work out mechanical details of distinguishing between the old and the new after the decision is reached. It is true, of course, that similarity in notation may require special attention to the old and new groups of volumes during the time that the reorganization is under way.

MATERIAL IN USE

Some technical difficulties result in handling books charged out to users, books at the bindery, and, in academic libraries, books on reserve. The most satisfactory procedure is to wait until this material is returned to the shelves before attempting to reclassify and recatalog it. In academic libraries, where such charges, except for books at the bindery, may be long term, it may be preferable to recall these books at times when their reprocessing can be expedited, so that they can be returned to service with a minimum of delay. The library should strive to serve the users rather than the momentary efficiency of the process; even the best planning and the most careful organization of reclassification projects are disruptive to the easy use of library materials. Every effort should be made to reduce this to an absolute minimum.

ATTENTION TO USERS

All possible methods of maintaining access to materials during reorganization should be explored. These will include the maintenance of proper circulation records while books are being worked on, suitable information in the card catalogs to indicate titles even though these may be temporarily out of active circulation, and suitable guides to the stacks to indicate what sections are undergoing reclassification and that materials on some subjects may be located in more than one place in the stacks. The cataloging personnel or the reclassification staff should maintain appropriate records within the department so that materials which are being worked on can be located readily if need for them arises before the reprocessing is completed.

The whole organization should be so planned that books will be withheld from circulation the shortest possible time. The library must guard against the withdrawal of more of the collection than can be reprocessed within a reasonable time, and insure that remarking and relabeling of reprocessed books is completed promptly so that books can be returned to active circulation.

ORDER OF RECLASSIFICATION

Nearly one half of sixty libraries reporting on their reclassification projects indicated that the most-used classes were selected for reprocessing first, and one fifth indicated that whole classes were handled in the order of the notation. Other choices of the order for reclassification included location of materials, poorly classed sections, subject groupings, recency of material, the appearance of LC schedules, reference collections, fastest-growing classes, and departmental libraries.[12] The same order will not be equally applicable to all libraries, but there is strong reason to select the most-used classes for first treatment. Circulation departments are in a position to suggest what these classes may be, and which may be causing the most difficulty for users, either because of location in the stacks or because of delays in service resulting from the old arrangement.

The amount of time to be taken to complete the reclassification is to be considered in selecting an order of materials. When reclassification is done "in no special order," the implication is that the process has not been carefully analyzed nor has a time limit been sufficiently considered. Reclassification under such conditions usually becomes a fill-in job.

DISPOSITION OF NEW ACQUISITIONS

Some libraries have placed new acquisitions in the old classification —usually with penciled call numbers—until the whole class is worked upon. During the process of reclassification, therefore, the user in the stacks does not have to consult two places each time he searches for material on a subject, except in the class that is in process at the moment. Another advantage claimed is that relationships are seen to exist in groups of books which are not observed when individual books are reclassified. While this may be true, if the LC classification—which was developed from books on the shelves—is being applied, the need to see all books within a class at one time is not important.

However, it is usually less costly, and in the long run more convenient to most library users, to place new acquisitions in the new classification. A second marking of new books and the withdrawal and retyping of cards are thus eliminated. By judicious arrangement, newly classified materials may be made easily accessible to the clientele using the stacks. For example, if the collection is being reclassed from Dewey to the LC system, there is no reason why materials going in the "L" schedule could not be placed adjacent to the 370s.

RECATALOGING

Recataloging may mean a number of things, such as eliminating obsolete main and subject entries, revising descriptive information on cards, abandoning the use of one subject heading list for another, introducing a new system of cross references and information cards, and subdividing subjects which have grown rapidly. It may also refer to such activities as substituting standard-sized cards for odd-sized cards and replacing handwritten and worn cards with typed and printed ones. These activities are usually present in a general recataloging project which may have as its goal a complete editing of the catalog.

In most recataloging programs attention should be given to such matters as (1) the type of catalog to be maintained, (2) the methods of ordering LC printed cards, (3) the use of LC printed cards, (4) procedures relating to LC assignment of class numbers and subject headings, (5) main entry assignments, (6) added entries, (7) analysis of series, and (8) routines concerned with catalogs, cards, and filing.

The following suggestions, based on experience in reorganizing libraries, are offered in connection with decisions which are necessary to carry on controlled operations:

1. Large-scale use of printed cards may be profitable, but these are not essential for certain types of material such as fiction, textbooks, and juvenile materials.

2. Policy regarding the acceptance of classification numbers and main, subject, and added entries on printed cards should be determined at the outset. The greatest degree of efficiency usually results from the fewest possible variations.

3. Policy should be established for the cataloging of materials for which no printed cards are obtainable or desired.

4. Series which are adequately indexed should not be analyzed.

5. Authority files, shelf lists, and intralibrary union catalogs should be made, if these do not already exist.

6. It is probably more effective to begin a new catalog during reorganization. This should reduce errors to a minimum and will aid in catching untraced items in the old catalog. The presence of the two catalogs—old and new—makes it necessary to provide explanatory guides to aid patrons and staff.

ORGANIZATION OF THE WORK

The principal consideration in the organization of a project is whether or not to maintain a separate unit. Data indicate that where libraries have maintained special units, the work of reorganization has proceeded more rapidly and more smoothly than when the project was conducted on a fill-in basis. If a separate department is established, particular questions relating to its organization, the number and kinds of personnel, and the relationship of the special unit to the permanent classification and cataloging work must be answered. Provision must be made to insure the availability of funds to support such a special unit.

Careful planning will take into account the physical arrangements of the work in order to insure the most efficient operations. Suitable quarters must be provided, and work space assignments made carefully.

Ideally, reclassification will be handled most efficiently if the working quarters can be located in close proximity to the card catalogs and to the stacks, since any arrangement that will facilitate the constant traffic to and from the catalogs and the stacks will expedite the work. Of paramount importance is the utilization of space so that no confusion will result in the handling of new acquisitions and the rehandling of materials from the stacks. Some libraries have preferred the obvious arrangement of confining technical reorganization to the cataloging department.

A second arrangement calls for the separation of the work on books, which is performed in the stacks, from that with catalog cards, which is performed in the cataloging department. This has the obvious advantages of reducing traffic through the technical departments as well as keeping the old stock separated from new acquisitions. It helps to keep crowding and confusion in a cataloging department at a minimum. However, catalogers may be handicapped by their lack of special reference tools in the stacks, by the difficulties of providing adequate equipment in stack areas, and by their distance from shelf lists, authority files, and other records.

Some libraries have preferred to maintain separate reclassification rooms where the work on the older stock can be effectively segregated from the current work. Where current programs are sizable and thousands of volumes must be processed annually, this arrangement offers particular advantages. The special room, however, should be in close proximity to the regular catalog room, to the card catalog, and to the stacks. Separation may also require some duplication of equipment and reference tools.

The bindery has also been used as a place to carry on the routines of reclassification and recataloging. This arrangement has one advantage not found in other accommodations; that is, facilities for the quick repair of torn books and for the marking or stamping of volumes.

Still another method which has been used in smaller libraries with limited staffs is to have the work done in various parts of the building. In libraries using this procedure, reclassification is usually carried on in slack times, becoming busy work for attendants who are not charging books or answering reference questions. This method, although it offers opportunities for the effective utilization of spare staff time, requires a high degree of careful planning and coordination if it is to work successfully. The possibilities of error, inconsistency, and duplicated effort are high. To use student assistants or clerical workers concentrated in the cataloging department appears to be a more efficient approach to the problem in the smaller library. In academic libraries, where the institutions do not maintain summer sessions and where the service load on the library is likely to be very slight during vacation periods, it is possible to carry on reclassification projects with the whole staff participating during the summer months and holiday periods.

A careful study of the flow of work in order to determine the proper sequence for the various units of work is requisite to efficiency. Well-designed layouts which contribute to the continuous flow of the books and cards being reprocessed will pay handsome dividends in speed, improved service, smooth operations, and minimum confusion and disruption. They contribute to the more effective use of personnel assigned to the project and may reduce personnel requirements.

Departmental manuals which describe the special techniques and routines of cataloging and classification, and particularly of recataloging and reclassification as well, may prove to be useful.

MECHANICAL DETAILS

Reclassification projects involving mass quantities of books require adequate work tables, shelving, trucks, typewriters, marking supplies, and catalog trays. Attention should be given to the possibility of using mechanical aids in reclassifying and recataloging. Experience has shown that lack of attention to these factors often can be serious obstacles to satisfactory completion of the project.

MARKINGS ON EXTERIOR OF BOOKS. To change numbers, librarians have had to contend with various markings on books, such as gold leaf or black ink stamping or lettering, markings by stylus, and lettering with white and black ink on paper or cloth labels. Where gold leaf has been used, the greatest difficulty has arisen. None of the several methods—blacking over the gold stamping with ink or paint (which usually cracks later), removing the old numbers by an electric stylus or eraser, or scraping the numbers off with a sharp instrument—has met with complete success. The use of the electric stylus or eraser obtains more uniform results than other methods, but the risk of injuring the binding exists. Generally, the gold markings are moistened before erasing. In order to remove labels or inks which have been shellacked, it is necessary to use varnish remover (e.g., ethyl acetate) first. It is usually helpful to shellac over the space where the old marking was before the new class numbers are applied to the books.

MARKINGS ON INSIDE OF BOOKS. An electric eraser used to remove the numbers from bookplates and from the insides of the back covers of the books usually results in rubbed patches which cannot be neatly re-marked. Sometimes new bookplates have been placed over the old ones, a procedure which results in a cleaner job. Soaking off each bookplate is a tedious task. The librarian faced with the re-marking of a large collection of books may well reconsider the whole policy of marking.

RE-USE OF OLD CARDS. A question which is relatively important is whether the old cards may be re-used or new ones ordered. With the increase in the cost of LC printed cards and the charges involved in ordering and handling sets of such cards, the usual procedure, if the old cards are standard and represent acceptable cataloging, is to make as much use of the old cards as possible. If the library has been following LC subject heading practice and using other LC entries, considerable retyping can be eliminated by this policy. The electric eraser will aid in making necessary changes in call numbers and entries. The preparation of new cards by mechanical or photographic reproduction, using information on LC cards, is also another possible procedure.

COROLLARIES OF RECLASSIFICATION AND RECATALOGING PROJECTS

When a reclassification and recataloging program is being considered, it is wise to take into consideration other phases of technical reorganization which might be undertaken concurrently. It is often possible to incorporate these supplementary activities into the main project at an expenditure of time, money, and effort which is considerably less than if attempts are made to do them independently.

Study of the use and arrangement of existing card catalogs and their possible improvement may be made. The handling of all catalog cards during complete reclassification and recataloging projects presents an opportunity for introducing major changes in catalog arrangement—establishment of a divided (or classified) catalog, a revised filing code, new policies concerning subject headings and other entries, as well as the possibility of interlibrary union catalog cooperation.

It may also be possible to make a complete inventory of the library's holdings. Rebinding and general improvement of the physical condition of materials may be undertaken. A systematic program of weeding the collections can be included.

SUMMARY

While the primary reason for undertaking extensive reclassification and recataloging projects should be a demonstrable need to improve library service to patrons, the most important reasons thus far advanced by libraries which have introduced such technical reorganization appear to relate particularly to administrative problems. Whatever the reason, careful thinking about the need for such a project is fundamental,[13] since the high cost of accomplishing it and the inevitable disruption of service to users while the project is under way are both strong reasons for exploring other avenues of improved service before deciding to reclassify.

XIV. The Cataloging Department: Administrative Problems

IN Chapters XII and XIII, as well as in some sections of other chapters, various problems which arise in administering a cataloging department have been considered. The concern of this chapter is to review more general aspects of administration with reference to the cataloging department, as well as to discuss a group of special matters which are of importance to heads of catalog units.

The administration of the cataloging department is concerned with the application of theoretical elements and principles.[1] The elements—planning, organizing, staffing, directing, coordinating, reporting, and budgeting—are obviously important in the control and operation of a cataloging department. While in the small library, with one person doing the cataloging, there will be less concern with some of these elements than with others, actually all of them are involved. In the larger cataloging department, they play a more significant role. Each of these elements may be considered briefly in connection with the cataloging department.

No cataloging department can function effectively without careful planning. The planning concerns not only the internal aspects of the department, involving the handling of current acquisitions, but also the external relationships. The head of the cataloging department should be aware of the activities of all departments of the library if he is to plan the work so that materials are made available promptly and economically. This will involve close coordination with the acquisition, reference, circulation, and serials departments, as well as the departmental or branch libraries. It will also involve efficient use of personnel, equipment, and physical facilities.

The setting up of precise relationships which facilitate management and operation is reflected in organizing. This is the element which is directly associated with the establishing of operations and techniques in the department.

The head of the cataloging department has an important responsibility in the staffing of his unit. The efficient management of the department will depend on the recruiting of qualified personnel, as well as on the proper disposition of work among the professional and clerical staff members.

The need for making specific orders and arriving at decisions is involved in the element of directing. Head catalogers are constantly called upon to issue orders which determine the current and future policies of the department.

No department's work is more concerned with the work of other units than is that of the cataloging department. The element of coordinating is reflected in the activities of the head of the department which are involved in relationships with other departments of the library. Unless the work of the department is closely associated with that of the acquisition department, for example, much waste can result.

The cataloging chief is required to report on his work as are other heads of units of the library. The general practice in the cataloging department of keeping accurate and full records of work accomplished and the time it takes to do it provides the basic material needed for these reports.

Because the cataloging department requires a fairly large part of the budget of the library, it is necessary to analyze carefully the budgetary needs of the unit. A relatively large number of cataloging departments spend $50,000 a year or more for the recording of books. It is as essential to justify expenses in this unit as it is in others. This is especially true since administrators have been conscious of the growing costs of cataloging activities.

BUDGETARY PROBLEMS

Generally, the budget of the department is distributed among the salaries of the professional and clerical staff, the cards purchased from the Library of Congress, the cards used in the work of the department, and equipment of various kinds. Salaries of catalogers vary from library to library and from locality to locality. However, there has been some standardization in the salaries of catalogers. In libraries having classification schemes of service, the junior or beginning catalogers generally receive the same salaries as other junior librarians entering the service. Cost of printed cards has increased considerably in recent years. The cost of rag-paper card stock, usually employed in cataloging departments because of its durability, has also increased considerably in recent years.

Equipment is an important part of the cataloging department's work. The typewriters, duplicating machines, card cabinets, book trucks, microfilm reader, and other apparatus needed in the department are relatively expensive pieces of equipment which need careful examination before purchase. Posture chairs for catalogers, for example, are useful if the fatigue of these workers is to be kept at a minimum.

PERSONNEL

The need to distinguish between professional and clerical operations in the cataloging department has been recognized by the modern head cataloger. In some of the more efficient libraries, the distinction between professional tasks in the department and the clerical activities is direct and definite. The professional librarian is concerned with the establishment of the entry, the making of the unit card, the classification of the book, and the assignment of subject headings. The making of decisions on these matters is an important responsibility of the professional cataloger. A recent statement regarding the cataloging division in the Stanford University library reveals the following organization:

The staff of the Bibliography Division now consists of fourteen persons, or seventeen if the Education catalogers and their clerical assistant are included. The Education catalogers work in the Education Library but are responsible to the chief of the Bibliography Division. Of the fourteen persons in the Main Library, six are professionally trained. Student help equivalent to about one and one-half full-time persons augments the subprofessional staff of eight persons. Certain individuals here classed as subprofessionals do now perform, however, and are qualified by experience and background to perform professional work, although they have not had professional library training.

The balance between professional and clerical staffs in this division is good. Additional staff is needed, however, if the department is to expand its services to departmental libraries and to undertake new projects in the cataloging of special types of materials such as microfilms and rare books. It is recommended that one additional cataloger be added to assist with the cataloging of the Hoover materials, which . . . is badly in arrears, another to catalog materials in the Special Collections (12,000 volumes in arrears) and another to concentrate on the improvement of the departmental catalogs to which the Bibliography Division has thus far not supplied cards. If two additional clerical assistants were then provided, one for searching and another for preliminary cataloging, it is estimated that the productivity of the professional staff would be sufficiently increased to handle the present and suggested volume of work.

Despite the very low salaries paid to members of the cataloging staff, the morale of the Bibliography Division is reasonably good. Under its new chief, a capable and experienced cataloger recently added to the staff, the Division is doing a job which deserves recognition from the University—that of incorporating new materials into the incredibly complex structure of a million-volume library in such a way that the University's resources on any subject can be commanded for educational and research purposes.[2]

The size of the staff, the problem of arrears, the unfinished projects and the morale of the staff, have been discussed in the preceding quotation from the Stanford survey. The size of staff is, of course, dependent upon the amount and type of work to be done. If cataloging is complicated, if the materials are diverse and in difficult languages, the need for more staff with experience and background will be evident. Under ordinary circumstances, the competent cataloger, using printed cards as much as possible, can do as many as 3,000 titles per year. In some institutions, catalogers have prepared from 4,000 to 5,000 a year. In two hundred working days, a cataloger doing 4,000 titles would do approximately twenty titles per day. Using LC and Wilson cards is essential to a high rate of production.

Dean,[3] studying catalogers in academic libraries, found that in 19 libraries, the cataloger's average annual production in number of volumes was 1,485. Dean found that libraries generally do not keep a record of titles cataloged; the number of volumes handled is usually reported. This can be misleading, especially if equated in terms of costs. A large library once reported that cataloging costs had been reduced to 50 cents per volume. This sounded like progress until it was learned that included in this average were some 40,000 serial items which were merely checked in on serial cards. Actually, this library was spending $3.53 to catalog each new title, including those for which there were printed LC cards. Orne has noted a reduction in the cost of cataloging from 61 cents a volume to 37 cents over a three-year period.[4]

In her study, Dean was also interested in the ratio of cataloging to total staff. In the 46 libraries studied, varying in size from 170,000 to over 1,000,000 volumes, she found a range of from 13 percent to 45 percent of staff, with a median of 27 percent. In relation to output, Dean suggested that a library receiving 12,000 yearly accessions should have a staff of eight persons, of whom at least half would be professionals. In the production table in Mann,[5] which also considers 12,000 volumes, a staff of nine, including four professionals is suggested.

Dean points out that the size of staff is obviously conditioned by such factors as the ratio of titles to volumes, the number of serial titles involved, the number of titles in foreign languages, the number of rare items acquired, the number of duplicate or departmental catalogs which need to be made and maintained, the amount of responsibility for checking and searching, accessioning, inventory, and other activities. All of these factors are referred to by Seely in her recent study of cataloging personnel.[6]

Worker satisfaction is highly important in cataloging. Turnover in staff, changing of personnel to non-cataloging positions, and other pressures upon the cataloging department make staff problems in it somewhat more difficult than in other departments. Herrick[7] found that salary was not the most important factor in worker morale. Such things as physical conditions, ability to work independently, and the attitude of the head cataloger and other members of the department are important factors.

PHYSICAL CONDITIONS

Miller[8] has noted some important physical aspects of the cataloging department. Because the cataloger works closely at his work, it is essential that careful attention be given to such matters as location of the department, lighting, ventilation, furniture, and work space. Wheeler and Githens[9] have considered in detail many matters relating to physical needs of the cataloging department.

LOCATION. The cataloging department needs a suitable location to save wear and tear on the staff. If it is not near the reference collection, the general catalog, the stacks, and the circulation department, much time can be lost in walking from one to the other. In some libraries, special arrangements such as providing an official catalog or duplicate reference works may be necessary because of the location of the cataloging department.

LIGHTING. Catalogers should have good lighting. Herrick found that bad lighting was an important reason for catalogers looking elsewhere for positions. The work of the cataloger is mostly visual, and the least the library can do is to make the illumination effective. Good lighting pays dividends in increased production. Kraehenbuehl[10] has indicated that constant work in an office, such as might be done by a cataloger, requires power of 30 foot-candles for effective work. The card catalog itself should have an illumination of 25 foot-candles on the horizontal surface of the file.

VENTILATION. Since the cataloger sits for relatively long periods, the problem of ventilation is also important. Catalogers generally sit close to one another, and this may present problems because of different needs in ventilation and temperature. The wise head cataloger will try to place catalogers in such locations in the department that ventilation does not become a daily cause for personnel friction.

FURNITURE. Mention has been made of the special chairs for catalogers. Supplies of desks and of book trucks are also important for saving the time of the professional cataloger. At one large university library, an effort is made to place physical accommodations on a high level. The cataloging room for professionals is arranged like a well-appointed office, with carefully selected desks and other furniture. No typing is allowed in the room, and the quiet atmosphere is conducive to efficient work. The recent reorganization of the cataloging department in the New York Public Library included installation of new furniture and realignment of work space for the staff.

WORK SPACE. It has been suggested that the desirable amount of space to be allotted to catalogers is 100 square feet per cataloger. Few libraries have allotted this much space; it is generally closer to 50 square feet. However, the need for careful allocation of space is obvious. Crowded and noisy cataloging rooms are not usually very productive. There must be enough space allowed for the desk, chair, book trucks, and shelf space for the cataloger. There must also be shelves available for housing of materials in process and for reference tools.

ADMINISTRATIVE STANDARDS

The operations of the cataloging department should be constantly studied and evaluated. The use of manuals and codes for establishing efficiency in procedures has been recognized. Also, various measures are available for determining the relative efficiency of the department.

MANUALS AND CODES. The extent to which a library department should go in listing procedures depends largely upon the size and diversity of the system, the nature of the personnel, and the types and quantity of materials received. The *Catalog Department Manual* of the Enoch Pratt Free Library [11] is a good example of a well-conceived and relatively complete guide to the work of the unit.

Generally, the manual should include the policies of the unit as well as the routines for specific processes or groups of processes, such as accessioning, inventory, variations in cataloging and classification from generally accepted codes and classification schedules, and filing. Special procedures in recataloging and reclassification should be recorded in order to insure consistency and efficient administration. Libraries cataloging by the LC rules may well use a system of recording their variations by interpolating them in their proper places in the LC rules.

A carefully worked out manual should reduce to a minimum the need to repeat routine directions, facilitate the training of new assistants, and make available to the administrator and other staff members a statement of policy and procedure.

MEASUREMENT OF EFFICIENCY. The work of the cataloging department may be measured both quantitatively and qualitatively. From a quantitative standpoint, such items as arrears, rapidity of processing materials, and success in obtaining simultaneous mechanical preparation of books and reproduction and filing of cards measure the efficiency of the department. The number of titles processed annually may be used to judge roughly the work of the department. Depending upon the definition of "volume," it may be used comparatively. Qualitative measurements may be concerned with the degree of success users and staff members meet in having the catalog answer their questions or with the success with which the classification system groups books to the satisfaction of stack users.

Some catalog departments have been criticized, often with justification, for the delay in processing materials. A system of arranging books received into date periods has been used effectively in expediting the preparation of items which otherwise might remain in the department longer than the allotted time—which may be placed at several days in most libraries. A "fast cataloging unit" makes it possible to process additional copies, editions, and continuations immediately upon receipt. The "jet cataloging" unit at the New York Public Library is based on separating materials on the level of difficulty.[12] Libraries which receive LC card proof sheets can sometimes speed card work by reproducing these proofs in place of ordering LC cards. The use of newer methods of card reproduction should be considered, for considerable savings may be realized in duplicating entries for which printed cards are not available.

OTHER ADMINISTRATIVE PROBLEMS

Other administrative problems to be considered briefly include: inventory, assistance in the use of the catalog, handling of microfilms and other non-book materials, and cataloging for special collections and departmental libraries.

INVENTORY. Responsibility for taking inventory may be delegated to the circulation department. Sometimes it is shared with the cataloging department. Inventories may be continual or may be made at stated intervals.

Inventories usually reveal situations which affect the cataloging personnel and other members of the staff. The administrator must make decisions concerning the withdrawal of cards for books which are missing, stolen, or discarded; suggest replacements with the cooperation of circulation and departmental librarians; and select items for rebinding. Inventories may reveal inconsistencies in cataloging and classification which require correction.

ASSISTANCE IN THE USE OF THE CATALOG. Assistance in the use of the catalog is usually an activity of the reference department, although it may involve the circulation and cataloging departments as well. In some libraries a member of the cataloging department is stationed near the card catalog to advise and help users. Close cooperation between the reference and cataloging personnel should result in the discovery and elimination of difficulties. Any aid the cataloging department can give by posting directions or exhibiting samples of entries, should be valuable in assisting the user.

MICROFILMS AND OTHER NON-BOOK MATERIALS. The inclusion of such materials as microfilms, music, phonograph records, manuscripts, maps, and archives in library collections usually carries with it problems for the administrator of the department. The situation has been clarified to an acceptable degree in the handling of most of these types of materials. The professional literature on the cataloging of such materials is voluminous and various methods are suggested.

DEPARTMENTAL AND SPECIAL COLLECTIONS. The maintenance of special collections within a library raises problems for the cataloging department administrator in the form of special catalogs, special types of cataloging, and, often, special systems of classification. So far as the historical situation will permit it, the administrator should insist upon uniformity unless it can be shown that special treatment is essential in facilitating use.

Preparation and servicing of departmental and branch library catalogs is often the responsibility of the central cataloging department. One may easily see its possible ramifications by an examination of the following table showing the departmental and school library catalogs in a university library system:

Table 1. DEPARTMENTAL AND SCHOOL LIBRARY CATALOGS COLUMBIA UNIVERSITY

Libraries	*Author Catalog*	*Dictionary Catalog*	*Shelf List*	*Serials Catalog*	*Other Catalogs and Indexes*
Avery (architecture)		x	x		x
Barnard (general)		x	x		x
Burgess (social sciences)	x				x
Business		x	x		x
Carpenter (English literature)	x				x
Chemistry		x	x	x	x
Classics	x				x
College (general)		x			x
Columbiana		x	x[a]		
Dramatic	x		x		x
East Asiatic		x	x		x
Egleston (engineering)		x	x	x	x
Fine Arts		x	x		x
403 Low (science)	x		x[b]		
Geology		x	x		x
Journalism		x	x		x
Law		x	x		x
Mathematics		x			x

Libraries	*Author Catalog*	*Dictionary Catalog*	*Shelf List*	*Serials Catalog*	*Other Catalogs and Indexes*
Medical		x	x	x	x
Modern Languages	x				x
Music		x[c]			x
Paterno (Italian)		x	x		x
Periodical Reading Room				x	x
Philosophy	x				
Physics		x	x	x	x
Psychology		x	x		x
Reference	x				x
School of Library Service		x	x		x
Special Collections					
B (general)		x[d]	x[d]		x
Book Arts		x	x		x
Bronson Howard (drama)	x		x		x
E (incunabula)	x				x
Joan of Arc	x				
Mary Queen of Scots	x				
Park Benjamin (general)	x		x		x
Plimpton-Dale-Smith[e] (general textbooks—weights and measures—mathematics)		x	x		x
Seligman (economics and finance)		x	x		x
Typographic	x	x	x	x	x
X (mss.)	x		x[f]		
Ware (Working coll. for School of Architecture)		x	x[g]		x
Zoology—Botany—Agriculture		x	x[h]		x

[a] Incomplete—not current.
[b] Kept in Egleston.
[c] Two sections: author-title and subject.
[d] Incomplete.
[e] Dale—author only.
[f] Incomplete.
[g] Kept in Avery.
[h] Zoology only and incomplete.

SOURCE: Mildred Straka. "An Historical Review of the Cataloging Department of the Columbia University Libraries, 1883–1950." (M.S. Essay, Columbia University, 1951), pp. 56–58. Also issued in mimeographed form. Some changes have been made since the completion of this study.

Problems which arise in the handling of materials for departmental or professional school libraries in the academic library system and branch libraries in a public library system have been discussed by Dickson and Fresch.[13] Many systems provide a complete catalog for each departmental library, but a general practice is to prepare only an author file through the central cataloging department and permit the departmental unit to make subject and other cards as they are needed. In recent years more librarians have recognized the values to be obtained by having at least an author union catalog of all library holdings in the central building. Not only is duplication in acquisition kept at a minimum, but patrons are provided with one source of information concerning the entire resources of the library system.

Figure 3 is a flow chart indicating many of the technical operations performed in the Brooklyn Public Library. The chart shows the relatively complex organization that is involved in a centralized plan for the cataloging and preparation of books for use in a large system with forty-four branches and ten sub-branches or deposit stations. Cards are prepared for 110 different catalogs.

COSTS OF CATALOGING

Studies of the cost of cataloging, arrived at by dividing the total salaries by the total number of volumes cataloged, or by more exact time and production studies, have been made by librarians.[14] What is the purpose of these studies of cataloging costs, be they exact, approximate, or rough? The values of cost studies, either of cataloging or of other services, center about the need of the administrator to know the expenditures of certain departments in order to determine which units are functioning efficiently. The knowledge of cataloging costs may specifically enable the administrator to determine whether or not a large gift of books may be processed within the limits of the departmental budget. It is also evident that funds put into cataloging or other routine processes reduce the total sum available for purchasing books or other materials. This does not mean that cataloging has no value. Obviously, service costs of other departments would rise if cataloging and classification were discarded. But the administrator who is interested in an efficient organization will, through knowledge of costs, be in a position to be critical of established library operations, to review routines in relation to objectives, and to consider new methods of doing things.

The cost of cataloging perhaps has received more attention than other costs of library services, but as Leigh has pointed out in the Public Library Inquiry, these costs have been somewhat exaggerated.

FIGURE 3. FLOW OF WORK IN THE CATALOGING DEPARTMENT OF THE BROOKLYN PUBLIC LIBRARY

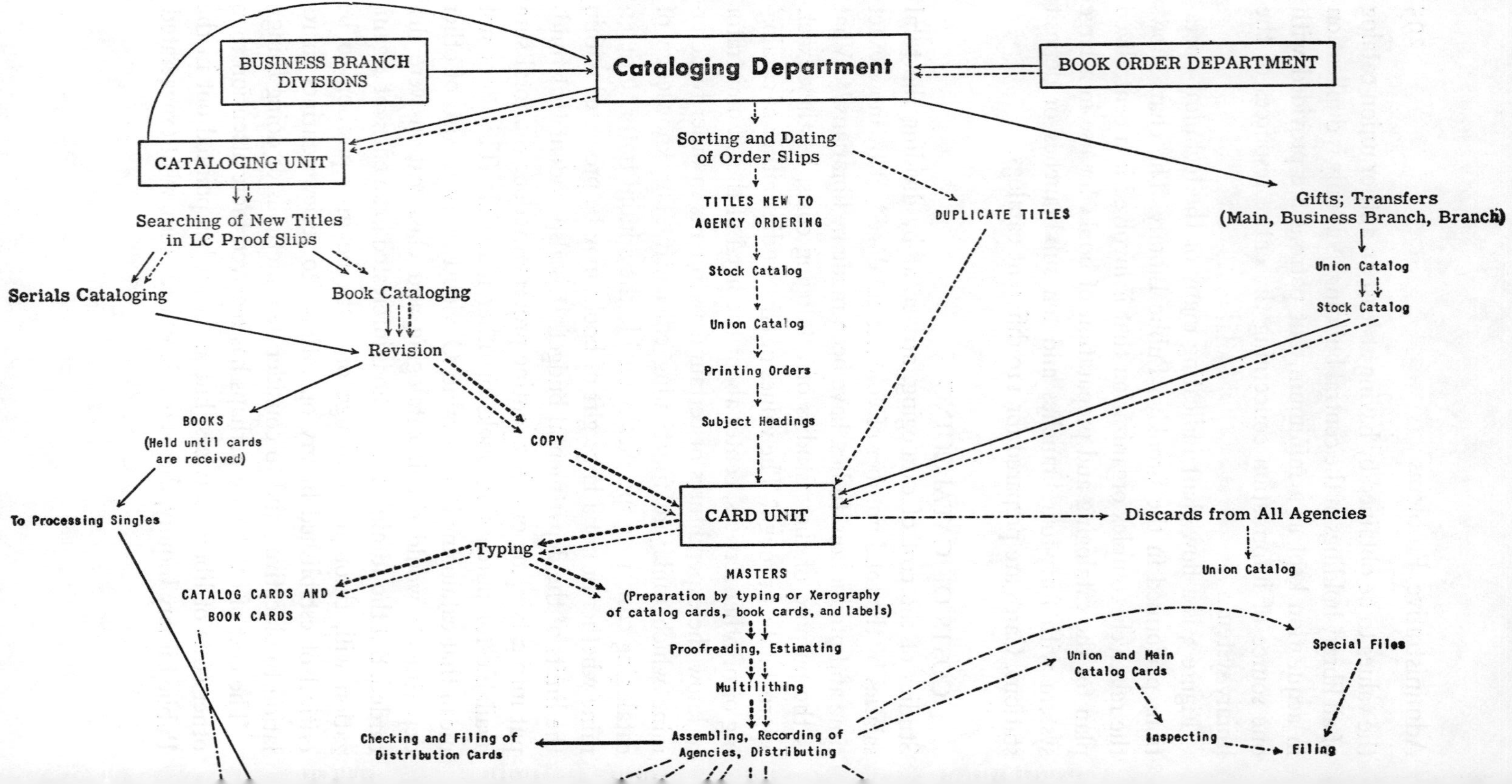

BUSINESS BRANCH DIVISIONS

Cataloging Department

BOOK ORDER DEPARTMENT

CATALOGING UNIT

Searching of New Titles in LC Proof Slips

Serials Cataloging

Book Cataloging

Revision

BOOKS (Held until cards are received)

To Processing Singles

COPY

Sorting and Dating of Order Slips

TITLES NEW TO AGENCY ORDERING

Stock Catalog

Union Catalog

Printing Orders

Subject Headings

DUPLICATE TITLES

Gifts; Transfers (Main, Business Branch, Branch)

Union Catalog

Stock Catalog

CARD UNIT

Discards from All Agencies

Union Catalog

Typing

CATALOG CARDS AND BOOK CARDS

MASTERS (Preparation by typing or Xerography of catalog cards, book cards, and labels)

Proofreading, Estimating

Multilithing

Assembling, Recording of Agencies, Distributing

Checking and Filing of Distribution Cards

Union and Main Catalog Cards

Special Files

Inspecting

Filing

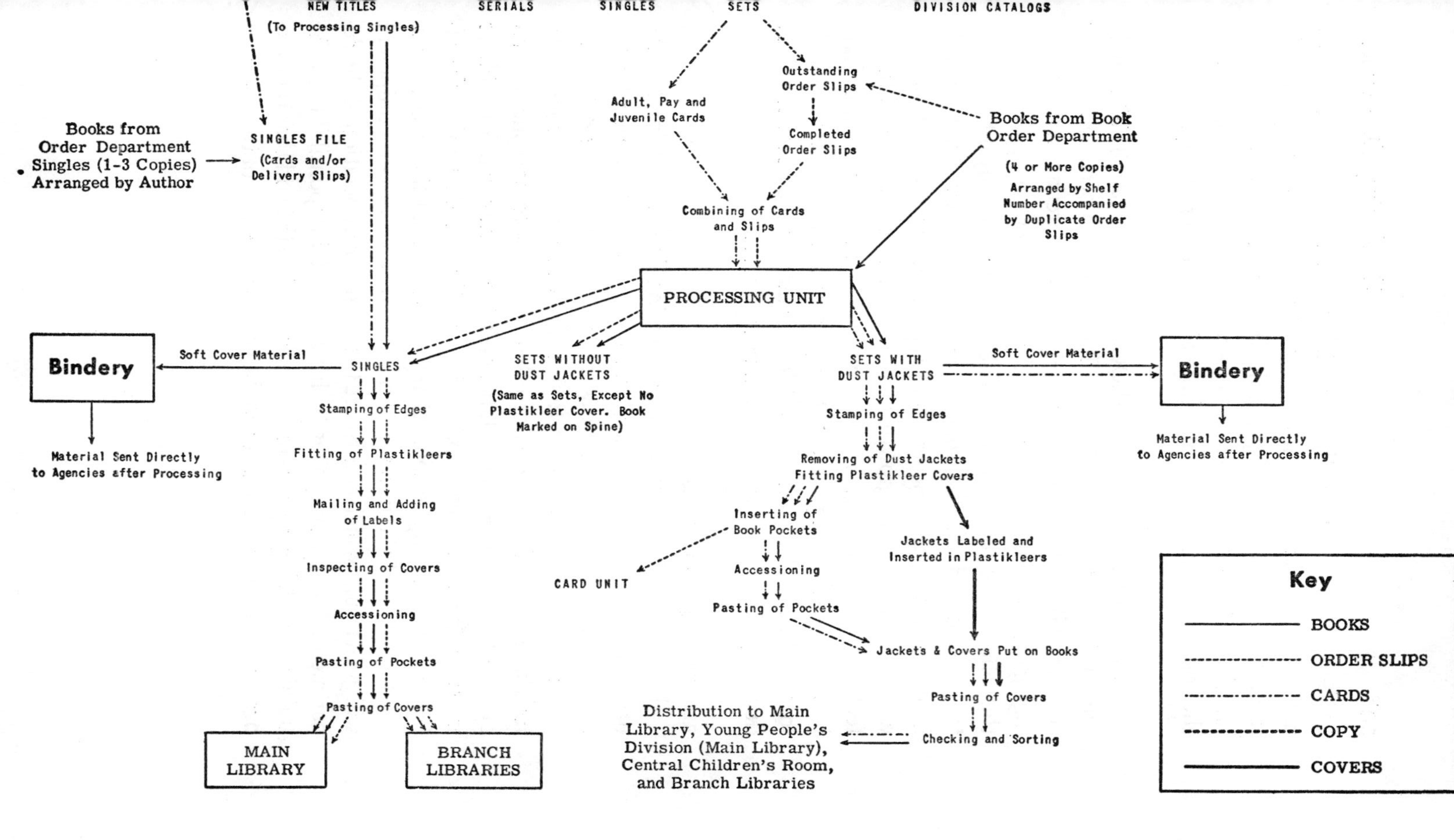
NEW TITLES
(To Processing Singles)
SERIALS
SINGLES
SETS
DIVISION CATALOGS
Outstanding Order Slips
Adult, Pay and Juvenile Cards
Completed Order Slips
Books from Book Order Department
(4 or More Copies)
Arranged by Shelf Number Accompanied by Duplicate Order Slips
Books from Order Department Singles (1-3 Copies) Arranged by Author
SINGLES FILE
(Cards and/or Delivery Slips)
Combining of Cards and Slips
PROCESSING UNIT
Bindery
Soft Cover Material
SINGLES
SETS WITHOUT DUST JACKETS
(Same as Sets, Except No Plastikleer Cover. Book Marked on Spine)
SETS WITH DUST JACKETS
Soft Cover Material
Bindery
Stamping of Edges
Stamping of Edges
Material Sent Directly to Agencies after Processing
Material Sent Directly to Agencies after Processing
Fitting of Plastikleers
Removing of Dust Jackets Fitting Plastikleer Covers
Mailing and Adding of Labels
Inserting of Book Pockets
Jackets Labeled and Inserted in Plastikleers
Inspecting of Covers
Accessioning
CARD UNIT
Key
Accessioning
Pasting of Pockets
BOOKS
Pasting of Pockets
Jackets & Covers Put on Books
ORDER SLIPS
Pasting of Covers
CARDS
Pasting of Covers
Distribution to Main Library, Young People's Division (Main Library), Central Children's Room, and Branch Libraries
Checking and Sorting
COPY
MAIN LIBRARY
BRANCH LIBRARIES
COVERS

In the research library, with its special materials, such as rare books, manuscripts, serials, maps, music, etc., the cost of cataloging is likely to be proportionally more per unit. It is necessary to consider a library's local conditions before any comparisons are made between the costs of its cataloging and those of some other library.

ARREARAGES OF CATALOGING AND CLASSIFICATION

One of the problems with which librarians have been increasingly concerned is the accumulation of unprocessed materials in their cataloging departments. When such materials are not amalgamated into the collection so that they are available for use, not only is the service to users reduced, but the work of the technical services departments is increased and complicated, and the continued presence, or even worse, the continued growth of these backlogs interferes with effective and economical library service. A number of libraries have instituted systematic programs to cope with actual or potential backlogs of material,[15] and it is probable that many more libraries will be devoting attention to this problem in the future.

RECORDS AND STATISTICS

The efficient direction of the cataloging department implies the utilization of such records and statistics as will make it easy for the administrator to report on the work of the unit.[16] Some cataloging departments maintain elaborate statistics which are time consuming for the individual catalogers or other assistants to compile. It may be possible to reduce these statistics if the administrator is able to make spot studies over short periods of time to determine the effectiveness of the operations. Carefully worked out flow charts, constant attention to routines, and the introduction of new equipment will yield results which contribute to the effective operation of the department.[17] The library schools have a special responsibility in the training of cataloging department personnel to the end that they recognize both the educational and the economic results of their work.[18]

XV. Conservation of Library Materials: General Organization and Administration

IN 1937, Randolph G. Adams [1] startled some librarians by describing them as "enemies of books." The arguments which Adams set forth at that time appear not to have lost their point, however, if present practices in conserving materials in many libraries are typical. Although Adams was willing to acknowledge that the present day librarian must be an administrator rather than a bibliophile, he believed that too little attention was being paid by librarians to the curatorial aspect of the profession. He said, in essence, that in order to build up a great library, the librarian should have a knowledge of and an appreciation of the collector's feeling about books, lest potential donors of important books take their gifts elsewhere. Further, he noted that the profession as a whole must demonstrate a greater appreciation of books as objects of art if existing libraries are to continue to be enriched. The librarian's responsibilities in collecting and preserving local imprints, in constantly examining the stock to select those items which have become rare, in singling out rare or potentially rare volumes as they are received by the library, in according special technical treatment to rarities, and in guarding against possible misuse of rare books by unqualified readers are emphasized by Adams in his treatment of an aspect of librarianship that has frequently been neglected.

Care of rarities, of course, is only part of the conservation program of a library. Most libraries, as indicated earlier, acquire various kinds of materials which need special handling and care. Undoubtedly the recent war, which put a premium on many types of library materials —especially books—served to remind librarians of their dependence upon planned conservation. Since the war, the scarcity of certain materials, the rising prices of books, the increasing number of unbound foreign books, and the more than doubling of charges for domestic binding have all tended to develop the concern of librarians toward their function of preserving materials.

What is an adequate program of conservation for a library? This and the two following chapters consider such a program. It is the purpose of this chapter to discuss four topics related to the general problem: the organization and administration of binding work; coordination with other departments of the library; coordination between central and departmental or branch libraries; and the essentials of an over-all program of conservation.

ORGANIZATION AND ADMINISTRATION

Binding does not present a serious problem when materials are not used heavily, where periodicals are not kept permanently, and where special materials are not collected. In the larger libraries, however, which may spend many thousands of dollars annually on upkeep of the collections, it is necessary to provide a systematic organization to insure the proper control of funds allocated for binding. Since the funds available for binding are insufficient, in most libraries, to take care of everything which should be bound, the need for a selective policy is evident. In several recent surveys of libraries,[2] it has been found that serious neglect of the binding activity has resulted in issues of periodicals becoming lost or mutilated, in books being used beyond possibility of repair, in rare volumes being needlessly damaged, in leather bindings being allowed to deteriorate, and in special materials being destroyed. While a library need not bind every item it acquires, nevertheless every item should be maintained in such physical condition that it can be used by patrons without injury to the material.

In the smaller library, where binding funds are meager, it is usually the practice to have a member of the staff, more often than not with primary duties in another department, responsible for the regular preparation of materials for the commercial binder. Sometimes the preparation is done during spare moments, and often only when a reader or a staff member brings a volume to the attention of the person concerned with binding. In the larger libraries, while periodic attention may be given to binding, frequently the organization of the work may be ill considered. Pelham Barr has taken librarians to task for this unsystematic approach to the problems of binding.

> Silence, rarely broken, seems to surround the subject of book conservation and the administration of binding. This applies to libraries in general and to college and university libraries in particular. Discussion of book conservation (under other names) is generally concerned with the techniques of maintenance and the routines of preparing materials for binding. In the literature of library administration, binding receives little mention, and surveys of individual libraries are skillful in satisfying the amenities with the briefest of nods. On organization charts, binding supervision is usually placed in a box in some out-of-the-way corner.[3]

While this may seem exaggerated, Barr is actually correct in calling attention to the haphazard organization of binding in some libraries. It has not generally received the attention that has been given to acquisitions, cataloging, circulation, and reference. In some libraries, binding is combined with acquisitions; in others binding may be the responsibility of the periodical department, the circulation department, or the cataloging department, depending upon the interests of individual staff members. In some libraries with departmental or branch libraries, the several units may be responsible for their own binding.[4] However, Barr's statement of the scope of a well-developed conservation program makes it apparent that control of binding by a department with primary responsibility for another major function may lead to serious oversights. He wrote as follows:

> The scope of book conservation may be outlined by following the essential tasks from the time of receipt of a piece of material (and before) to the time of discard: (1) selecting material before purchase with respect

to usability and useful life; (2) examining condition and probable future condition of all material received, whether by gift or purchase, and prescribing conservation treatment, if necessary, before use; (3) providing proper housing of all material, in accordance with its conservation needs as well as its accessibility; (4) assuming responsibility for its condition at all times; (5) assuring its proper handling by staff and patrons; (6) organizing systematic inspection so that need for conservation attention is promptly recognized; (7) deciding on the proper treatment of all material needing attention; (8) supervising the treatment; and (9) deciding on storing and discarding.[5]

It can readily be seen from the above statement that binding is thus a library problem rather than a departmental problem. For this reason it is not easily integrated into the standard organizational pattern and so has not received the systematic attention given to other aspects of library service. Recognition of binding as a part of a total program of conservation, however, suggests that the care of materials might well be given full status as a separate unit of the library's organization. Such a unit, whether independent or part of a technical services department, should provide for a librarian in charge whose position is high enough and whose authority is adequate to command the confidence and cooperation of all other units. In this way, recognition of the over-all nature of the problem of binding may be achieved. Not only will relations with all departments and branches of the library system be established on a sound basis, but also it is likely that a systematic program of book conservation will be developed, that budgeting and allocation of funds will be carefully planned, that personnel will be carefully selected and adequately supervised, that proper housing of materials will be considered, and that good judgment will be exercised in selecting commercial binders.

Generally speaking, in those libraries which have organized independent or semi-independent binding departments, the problem has been kept under control. There are many functions and activities in which such a unit will participate. Proper safeguards and precautions will be taken to prevent the abuse of materials by readers and to reduce the number of cases of unnecessary wear and tear. Materials will be carefully screened for certain types of conservation treatment. Schedules for binding will be set up to insure the least inconvenience to the patrons. Adequate instructions and specifications will be worked out so that the binder has no trouble understanding them. A businesslike atmosphere will be created, and both library and binder will benefit through economical measures. On the other hand, surveys of various libraries, such as those of the University of South Carolina, Cornell University, and Virginia Polytechnic Institute have shown that many problems connected with binding stemmed from the neglect to provide a formal place for binding in the library organization and program. Too often the responsibility for binding has been given to an individual whose time is taken up with other and seemingly more important tasks.

What are the organizational characteristics of the binding department? Although the Binding Division of the Library of Congress is larger than will be necessary in most libraries, it provides an illustration of the essential responsibilities of a binding unit. Following is a statement describing the scope of work of the Division:

> This [Binding] Division is responsible for binding newly cataloged monographic material received in an unbound state and for preparing for rebinding previously bound volumes in the collections which have become worn or damaged through use and handling. This preparation involves the recording of all such materials and the specification of style of binding, lettering and special instructions to the binder. This Division also reviews serials and other special subject materials prepared for binding in the custodial divisions of the Reference Department and the Law Library.
>
> It maintains current records of material in the process of binding and permanent records of material bound, compiling statistics of binding in terms of the styles of binding and of the divisions from which the material was received.
>
> The Binding Division is responsible for liaison with the Library of Congress Branch Bindery of the Government Printing Office and provides for the limited servicing of materials in the process of binding which are urgently needed for immediate use and are not readily available elsewhere.
>
> Responsibility for fiscal control of the regular binding allotments of the Printing and Binding Appropriation rests upon the Binding Division

and involves the preparation of monthly requisitions for binding, the checking of monthly bills against binding received and the scheduling and preparation of vouchers for payment of bills.[6]

The organization of this work at the Library of Congress called for a staff of eight, including a chief, assistant chief, two serial revisers, a binding reviser, two binding assistants, and a clerk typist. Of these, the chief and the assistant chief were of professional grade, and the revisers and assistants subprofessional. Most libraries with binding departments will have smaller staffs, usually consisting of a head, with one or more assistants to perform the subprofessional and clerical duties.

COORDINATION WITH OTHER DEPARTMENTS OF THE LIBRARY

Since conservation is a library (rather than a departmental) problem, the binding unit must maintain close working relations with other units of the library system. The acquisitions, cataloging, reference, circulation, periodical, and photographic departments all play important roles in the program.

ACQUISITIONS DEPARTMENT. As indicated earlier, attention to binding begins during the acquisition process. The careful selection of material before purchase with regard to usability and useful life will in the long run reduce the binding expenditures of the library. The choice between a well-bound book and one that is not well bound may not seem important at the time of purchase. A careless procedure in this respect, however, will eventually complicate the binding problem. Similarly, accepting materials by gift or exchange without regard to physical condition may result in making serious inroads into the funds allotted for binding.

The acquisitions department is in a strategic position in the conservation program of the library. This has been recognized in some libraries, and specific directions have been established to guide the processes of purchasing, accepting materials, and accessioning. The librarian of the University of California at Los Angeles, in his "Memorandum to the Staff on Rare Books," [7] has included the elements of a screening procedure which could be applied to other situations. It is reproduced below:

RARE BOOK CODE

UNIVERSITY OF CALIFORNIA

MEMORANDUM TO THE STAFF ON RARE BOOKS

The Library has a twofold purpose; to serve people, to conserve books. We are judged by the present on how well we serve from day to day. The future will judge us by how wisely we have conserved the research treasure which we inherited, increased, and willed to our successors.

An evidence of a Library's cultural maturity is the care given to its scarce and irreplaceable materials. Its workers must be able to recognize such books at any point on the belt line of acquiring, cataloging and shelving.

I am asking that every member of the staff share this responsibility of seeing that valuable books be given special handling. Normally the Acquisitions department screens them out of purchases, gifts, and exchanges for review, but the volume handled there is increasingly heavy, and fugitive items will sometimes escape through the finest mesh. Then it is up to the catalogers, and finally the loan and shelf people, to sequester these items which cannot be entrusted to the perils of the stack.

No rules-of-thumb can be devised which will take the place of personal knowledge, intelligence, and discrimination. Attached however is a list of preliminary criteria for recognizing possible rarities which is used by the Acquisitions department. All staff members are asked to study and be guided by it.

RARE BOOKS

Books and periodicals in the following categories may be considered for inclusion in the Rare Book collection and will be held in Acquisitions for review before accessioning. Inclusion in one of the classes is not tantamount to rarity, and the list is not necessarily definitive. The possibility of rarities outside these criteria must always be recognized. Books finally accepted as Rare will be so designated and given special handling (i.e., the legend will be pencilled lightly along the inner margin of the page following the title page; all ink stamping, perforating, etc., will be omitted; the call number, preceded by a triangle, will be pencilled inside the front cover and inked on a small label pasted to the lower right corner of the back cover; special care will be taken in plating, so that, for example, original bookplates are not removed or pasted over). Current Rare periodical issues will not be date-stamped, will be carefully marked with a pencilled triangle, and shelved with the Rare Books. All Rare materials will be given special care in binding, after consultation with the Head of Special Collections. Hand-binding or the use of boxes will be considered; covers, advertisements, etc., must be preserved intact.

This code applies also to Branch Libraries, for it is recognized that specialized Rare Book Collections exist and will develop in Branch Libraries, as in the history of chemistry and medicine. Branch Libraries will consult the Head of Special Collections on matters of housing, care, etc.

1. Books of value due to early imprint date.
   a. All books printed before 1600.
   b. American books printed before 1820.
   In states west of the Appalachians, according to date printing started (California books printed before 1870; Los Angeles books printed before 1900).
2. Books whose irreplaceability or uniqueness makes them rare.
   a. Limited editions (300 copies or less).
   b. Association and autographed copies, when by important or local authors.
   c. First editions of significance.
3. Books of esthetic importance (fine printing, illustration, or binding).
4. Books which cost the library more than $50, or which have a similar auction record.
5. Items of local or archival value or interest, including local fine press books.
6. Erotica, excluding sex hygiene, scientific works on sex, etc.
7. Other books subject to loss or damage.
   a. Volumes or portfolios of fine or loose plates.
   b. Books whose illustrations make them subject to mutilation.
   c. Books of fragile physical make-up.
8. Special collections, i.e., unit acquisitions containing both rare and non-rare material, which need to be kept together.
9. Books with significant manuscript or other materials laid or tipped in.

It is apparent that other libraries will need a code of this kind, modified to fit their particular situations. Although the code is concerned specifically with rare items, the principle of care is important for all materials, though in varying degrees. The personnel of an acquisitions department working under such a directive should soon become accustomed to sorting and segregating materials of all types which present conservation problems.

CATALOGING DEPARTMENT. While the acquisitions department is the focal point for diverting items which entail special treatment, the cataloging department generally takes part in the procedure. Occasionally, volumes which should have been caught during the acquisition process arrive in the cataloging department. The alert cataloging staff will be acquainted with the code as well as with practices connected with it, and will hold out such items. In those cataloging departments which have the responsibility for the physical preparation of books for the shelves, the routines for the marking and labeling of materials will require careful supervision.

The personnel of both the acquisitions and cataloging departments should be aware of the general binding practices of the library. The practices concerning the handling of pamphlets, periodicals and other serials, art books, music, or mimeographed materials should be incorporated into a binding code to guide the personnel in all departments. In some libraries the catalogers have the responsibility for determining the type of binding that a particular item will receive. It would seem that this responsibility might well be delegated to the staff of the binding department.

REFERENCE DEPARTMENT. Hutchins [8] has called attention to the interest of reference librarians in the binding of periodicals. The inclusion of title pages and indexes is essential for the easy use of the bound volumes. The members of the reference staff are also conscious of the inquiries which involve advertisements, even if they are paged separately from the reading text of the periodicals. Although advertising matter adds to the bulk and cost of bound volumes, the many uses made of it by writers, professional people of all kinds, and research workers warrant its preservation in many instances, and particularly when illustrations are involved. Reference librarians, therefore, have an obligation to those in charge of binding to instruct them in the retention of advertisements.

Making certain that indexes, title pages, and advertisements are included in periodical volumes is only one of the problems in preparing them for the binder. The question of when a periodical volume or reference book should be sent to the binder needs also to be considered. This question has been studied carefully over a long period of time by W. R. Thurman, formerly foreman of the bindery of the New York Public Library. Although he was concerned primarily with periodical and reference works, Thurman, seeking criteria for a binding policy, raised the following eleven questions which a librarian might well ask before sending a volume to the binder:

(1) How much use is the volume going to have? (2) In what way is it going to be used? (3) What kind of readers are going to use it? (4) How quickly does such a volume usually get worn out? (5) At what points will it be likely to get most wear? (6) How long are the contents of the book going to be timely and how soon will they have only historical value? (7) How much is the book worth now? How much is it likely to be worth in the future? (8) Can it be easily replaced now? Can it be easily replaced in the future? (9) Is it such a size and weight that it needs special attention of the binder? (10) How about the kind of paper in the volume, plates, maps, inserts, etc.? (11) What is the present condition of the book or periodicals? [9]

Through experience, the person in charge of binding should be able to answer most of these questions. He will, of course, need the help of the reference, periodical, and circulation librarians in determining what might best be done since some questions are concerned with the contents of the books. As for the purely physical aspects, he will need to know the characteristics of book cloths and leathers, papers, adhesives, and sewings. In the problem of getting a durable binding on a book which will be used heavily, some book dealers have tried to assist librarians. These dealers and some publishers have developed library bindings for titles as they have been published. Heavily used fiction titles, for example, as well as children's and school library books, are available in these library bindings. Some of these bindings are called "reinforced," "reconstructed," or "prebound." Publishers of volumes which will receive heavy reference use realize that librarians will pay close attention to the bindings that are placed on their products, and experienced firms match the binding to the book. Reference librarians can be of considerable assistance in the conservation program if they are asked for advice concerning the bindings on various editions of a title that is being considered for purchase.

Hutchins also calls attention to the fact that the reference librarians are required to consider the convenient use of materials as well as their preservation.[10] Indicating to the binder what is contained in volumes of an encyclopedia or yearbook, recommending the use of buckram "pulls" for heavy tomes when necessary, and careful shelving of reference volumes are other ways in which the reference staff can aid the bindery directly in its conservation program.

CIRCULATION DEPARTMENT. The circulation department of the library, by virtue of its constant contact with readers, is in the position of watchdog of the circulating portion of the collections. Through careful attention to each volume as it is returned by the user, through systematic routing of damaged volumes to the bindery, through the exercise of caution in the handling of books on trucks and book lifts, through guarding against abuse of volumes in the stacks, and through proper shelving of books, the circulation department personnel can materially reduce the load on the binding department. With or without the cooperation of the cataloging department, the circulation staff should remove during inventory items which require special handling. Just as the acquisitions department must be watchful of books as they enter the library, so must the circulation department extend every effort to maintain the materials on the shelves in good condition. It is a never-ending task that pays dividends in both service and reduced costs.

PERIODICAL DEPARTMENT. Many of the tasks of the reference department in regard to binding will be minimized if a periodical department exists in the library. Such a department generally maintains close relations with the bindery, and participates in the formulation of binding routines. The periodical department will also have the responsibility for arranging the volumes for the binder and for making certain that title pages, indexes, supplements, inserts, errata sheets, and other parts are included in the volumes. One of the problems of librarians is the satisfactory scheduling of binding. This is especially important for periodicals which are in great demand while they are current. Careful and systematic attention to problems of use will make it possible to send volumes to the binder and to have them returned with as little interruption in service as possible. Hughes,[11] who studied the problem in sixty-three college and university libraries, found that only 7 percent of the libraries have a binding plan based on an analysis of reader service. A large number of the libraries duplicate some titles, keeping one copy available while the other is being bound. This practice, together with making some arrangements to accommodate the working schedule of the bindery and stipulating a definite date for return of the material, frequently constitutes the extent of planning.

Hughes also found that, in the opinion of librarians, present practices should be amplified by one further practice; namely, that of dividing important indexed periodicals into general fields and staggering of the binding schedules for various titles within each division. Six additional procedures were recommended by experts who were consulted and by many of the reporting libraries: (1) formulation of a calendar for binding weeklies, monthlies, and quarterlies at specified intervals; (2) staggered binding for important abstracted or indexed titles in subject fields; (3) staggered schedules for abstracts and periodicals abstracted; (4) sending of titles in class use to the bindery only upon notice from the instructor that they are no longer required; (5) keeping volumes available for a considered interval after the title page and index have arrived; and (6) staggering of schedules for similar titles among various campus libraries. Such scheduling of binding work is also necessary in public and school libraries, especially in the public libraries which provide considerable service to students and scholars.

Both the periodical and reference departments, of course, must be watchful of especially heavy demand made upon single articles or single issues of periodicals. Readings of interest to a large group sometimes will result in the destruction of an issue so that it has to be replaced. Pages or issues deliberately mutilated must also be replaced before the volume is bound.

PHOTOGRAPHIC DEPARTMENT. One of the important tasks of a photographic department is the reproduction either by Photostat or microfilm of articles in periodicals or pages in books. Great care must be exercised by the photographers in the handling of older volumes and bound newspapers, since mishandling of the volumes frequently will break the bindings.

COORDINATION BETWEEN CENTRAL AND DEPARTMENTAL OR BRANCH LIBRARIES

Many of the relationships described in the preceding section also apply to the departmental or branch units of a library system. In libraries having such units, it is usually necessary to establish either a quota (on the basis of number of volumes) or a fund allotment, in order to obtain equitable distribution of the money available. In addition, carefully worked out routines will be needed to insure prompt and economical handling of the binding tasks. One of the important functions of the supervisor of binding will be the minimization of extra operations sometimes insisted upon not only by departmental or branch librarians but also by reference librarians. Since departmental and branch librarians are sometimes charged with preparing specifications for binding, it is desirable constantly to review practices (especially for the treatment of run-of-the-mill materials) which are of questionable value, which contribute to delays in the return of books, and which raise the cost of binding. Some of these practices may be worth while listing, as studies of central library-departmental library relationships show that they exist: [12] (1) unnecessary use of leather labels; (2) excessive use of gold lines and blind lines; (3) exactly matching the binding of other copies; (4) gilding horizontally and vertically on the same binding; (5) gilding of copy numbers; (6) matching publishers' bindings in rebinding; (7) gilding of call numbers on ordinary books; (8) gilding of over-long titles and corporate entries on backs of books; (9) binding non-serial or non-set items according to a color pattern; (10) selecting discontinued buckrams and cloths and demanding that the binder obtain them; (11) specifying colors for single volumes; (12) indiscriminate "stubbing" of periodicals for missing issues (necessitating rebinding); (13) requiring sewing through the fold when not necessary.

Both Barr [13] and Litchfield [14] have raised the question of conflicting authority between departmental librarians and a central binding unit. If the department is working on a fund allotment for binding, it may wish to patronize the cheapest binder, even though the head of the binding department knows that the work of that binder is below standard. On the other hand, a central binding unit may not give full attention to the departmental problems:

> The advantages of centralization may become purely theoretical if the person in charge at the central library is unfamiliar with binding, if centralization involves buying binding through a purchasing agent's office which follows policies not adapted to the task, if the binder selected is incompetent, or if the specific needs of the department are not given attention.[15]

There are likely to be a number of such questions raised in the relations of the central department to departmental and branch library binding work. The administrator of the library should be cognizant of these, and every effort must be made to meet reasonable needs of departmental collections.

ESSENTIALS OF AN OVER-ALL PROGRAM OF CONSERVATION

"Conservation . . . is the only library function which should be continuously at work twenty-four hours a day," writes Barr.[16] He amplifies this statement as follows:

> It is the only function which should be concerned with every piece of material in the library from the moment the selector becomes aware of its existence to the day it is discarded. The reason this sounds so exaggerated is that it is a forgotten platitude. It applies to any library collection,

whether it be of Egyptian papyrus, of the third-grade classroom in an Iowa village, or of a university's incunabula.[17]

Up to this point the discussion has been devoted to the general problems of organizing a binding department and to the various relationships of the binding department to other units of the library system. It is necessary, however, to emphasize the essentials of an over-all program of conservation. Although several of the library surveys which have been made in recent years have singled out the lack of a policy or program in regard to binding, they have not always been emphatic regarding a total plan of conservation for all the materials the libraries collect. Barr is undoubtedly correct in his contention that inclusive studies should be made of conservation problems of libraries, that administrative relationships of the binding department need clarification, and that a full-scale program supported by a proper budget and adequate personnel and supervisory staff is the most effective way of attacking the problem.[18]

XVI. Conservation of Library Materials: Finance, Personnel, and Other Aspects

SOME of the more general aspects of organizing binding in the library have been considered in the preceding chapter. In this chapter, the following phases are treated: (1) financial support, (2) personnel, (3) cooperation with users, (4) housing and handling of materials, (5) selection of a binder, (6) relationships with the binder, and (7) press binderies.

FINANCE

It is sometimes difficult to determine how much a library spends for binding, since the funds are often included in the totals for the purchase of books and periodicals. However, few libraries have the funds to provide the best possible care for all the materials which they acquire. The amounts reported by 63 college and university libraries for 1952/53 showed a range from $508 (University of Massachusetts) to $109,207 (Harvard University). The median for the group was $14,000.[1]

The percentage of the budget which will be needed for binding will depend largely upon the past support given to the preservation of materials, as well as upon the current budget for books and periodicals. In his analysis of funds spent at the library of the University of North Carolina, Kellam estimated that 25 percent of the total book and periodical appropriation was used for binding in 1948.[2] This expenditure was unusually high because of certain backlogs resulting from the purchase of old sets in need of binding. Blanche P. McCrum, in *An Estimate of Standards for the College Library*,[3] analyzed a group of budgets of liberal arts college libraries. Of the total allotment for books, periodicals, and binding the percentage used for binding ranged from 12.8 to 17.4 percent. Inadequate support of the binding needs of a library can seldom be made up later without special appropriations. Periodicals which are not bound when they are first ready for binding not only create difficult problems in care and shelving, but are usually more expensive to handle at a later date. The possibility of losing or damaging issues of an unbound volume increases as time goes on.

Investigation of individual libraries has shown that permitting an arrearage in binding to build up may result in a serious financial problem. The following statement, for example, reveals the extent of the problem at Columbia University:

> In the fall of 1947 the Assistant Director, Technical Services, conducted a survey of the binding arrearages which have been building up in each of the library units over a period of years due to insufficient binding funds. On the basis of the findings of this survey, a request was included in the Budget for 1948–49 which would not only include funds needed for all current binding during the year but also for 10 per cent of the arrearages. It is anticipated that this arrearage of more than 28,000 volumes will be cleared up within ten years and the materials thereby preserved and made more readily available for use.[4]

Estimates of sums necessary for the elimination of arrearages in binding have appeared in several library surveys. Typical of these is the evaluation of the binding problem at Alabama Polytechnic Institute by Wilson and Orr. After pointing to the lack of funds for binding during the 1930s, and the inadequate sums available for binding in subsequent years, the surveyors observe:

> It is established that $10,000 is needed to take care of the arrears in binding satisfactorily. This amount should be made available in equal amounts over a five-year period. It should be understood that the sum mentioned above is in addition to the funds needed for current binding purposes. Beginning with the academic year 1949–50, or as soon as possible, the sum of $10,000 should be made available for current binding needs, ex-

clusive of the funds needed for wages and salaries for personnel to staff the Binding Section of the proposed Acquisitions Department.[5]

It should be noted that ordinarily binding arrears do not present a problem that can be solved by a single large appropriation. The old materials must be carefully prepared for the binder, records must be made, and the binder must not be loaded down with a single huge order if the work is to progress with a minimum of confusion. At the same time, of course, the binding staff must allocate its time and energies so that the current work is handled with dispatch.

PERSONNEL

Assuming that sufficient financial support is given for a library conservation program, what should be considered in selecting the staff necessary to carry on the work? What are the essential qualifications required of the professional, subprofessional, and clerical personnel? What are the duties of such a staff?

Browning, among others, has pointed out that book and periodical collections in public and college libraries have been increasing rapidly in recent years.[6] Despite this growth, he observed, "the care and conservation, including binding, of these materials have been left with assistants with too little training and experience for the task at hand." He noted further that this condition was particularly true of the smaller library. Much of the trouble, according to Browning, has developed from the failure of library schools to give training in problems of binding, as well as the infrequent calls from library administrators for persons who are specially trained for binding supervision and book conservation. As a result, many important binding posts have been filled by individuals who do not recognize the total problem of conservation. The large sums of money put into the acquisition of materials represent an investment that the librarian cannot ignore. Browning also called attention to the development of larger units, such as county or regional libraries, which require centralized binding, mending, repair, or replacement. The implication is that there will be increased need for personnel trained in conservation of materials.[7]

Shores observed that library school courses in binding methods are not entirely satisfactory, and that binders have not been able to provide the information needed by librarians in this phase of their work.[8] The result has been that much of the knowledge of librarians in charge of binding has been acquired through individual experience. What are the special requirements of a head of a binding unit? The chief of the Binding Division of the Library of Congress, for example, must meet the following requirements:

> A minimum of three years of progressively responsible experience in a large reference or research library which demonstrated the ability to plan, organize and administer a binding operation; a broad knowledge of the standards and procedures for binding library materials and of the rules of entry for serial publications; a reading knowledge of three or more foreign languages.[9]

Although the assistant chief must have two years of experience and knowledge of two foreign languages, the other requirements are similar to those of the chief. The qualifications of the revisers are primarily those of general knowledge, such as might be obtained in college courses, some acquaintance with rules of entry for serial publications, standards and procedures of binding, and familiarity with modern foreign languages.

Shores [10] lists some sixteen subjects related to binding which are covered in "required" courses in library schools. These subjects include: (1) preparation of materials for the bindery, (2) forms and records, (3) relations with binders, (4) conservation, (5) Library Binding Institute specifications, (6) policy, (7) mending and repair, (8) format evaluation, (9) history of bookbinding with reference to Grolier and other figures, (10) binding materials, (11) costs and budgets, (12) periodical and serial binding, (13) description of sewing and other processes, (14) distribution of departmental responsibility for binding among circulation, cataloging, and order departments, (15) federal funds for binding, and (16) directions for mounting pictures and caring for pamphlets.

In the section on "Physical Upkeep of Material" in the *Descriptive List of Professional and Nonprofessional Duties in Libraries,*[11] the professional responsibilities outlined for this area of librarianship include: (1) determining methods and techniques for preservation; (2) establishing policies concerning binding, mending, and discarding; (3) preparing binding specifications; (4) making final decisions on items to be bound, mended, or discarded; (5) negotiating with bindery agents, and (6) supervising upkeep processes. Full understanding of these aspects should enable librarians to perform the duties involved in binding and conservation.

The important duties in both of these listings showed up clearly in the job descriptions of the chief, assistant chief, and revisers of the Binding Division of the Library of Congress.[12]

CHIEF OF THE BINDING DIVISION

DUTIES:

Under the general direction of the Director of the Processing Department:

Plans and directs the work of the Binding Division, with a staff of eight, with responsibility for: (1) the preparation of all monographs for binding, except a minor proportion prepared by the Law Library and four of the reference divisions; (2) the preparation of all materials, monographic and serial, for rebinding; (3) the bibliographical review of all serials prepared for binding, involving integration of binding preparation with treatment in classification and with catalog and serial records; (4) maintenance of control of flow of materials to the Bindery and of records of all materials transmitted to and received from the Bindery; and (5) preparation of statistical reports of all material bound.

Coordinates the procedures and technical decisions of all the binding operations of the Library by consulting with and advising all custodial units preparing material for binding and by determining or reviewing binding treatment to be accorded all material bound for the collections, in accordance with Library policies.

Performs all liaison duties (except those assigned to the Supply Office) between the Library and the Bindery and between all custodial units and divisions of the Processing Department in matters relating to binding.

Initiates recommendations for appointments to the staff of the Binding Division; participates in regular conference of the Director and division chiefs of the Department in consultation of problems related to the work of the Department as a whole.

MINIMUM QUALIFICATIONS:

Education: Graduation from a college or university of recognized standing; graduation from an accredited library school or the equivalent in training and experience.

The assistant chief of the binding division, also a college and library school graduate, has full responsibility for the revision of serial publications in all languages, verifies for correct bibliographic arrangement, verifies or adds instructions for binding, corrects discrepancies on the basis of various records and tools, and indicates the routing of serials following binding. He supervises the assistants working with the serials and monographs issued in parts, and helps the binding officer in the training and directing of staff. He is in charge during the absence of the chief officer. Thus, it is evident that he should have not only professional and linguistic ability but also competence in administration.

The binding reviser checks materials sent to the bindery and examines them on return. Instructions concerning the number of volumes, type of binding, special handling, and source are checked by the reviser. Volumes which present no problems are distributed, while those with errors are returned to the binding office. The reviser also participates in the revision of instructions for binding of serials and compiles statistical reports on production. The reviser is required to have a college or university education or equivalent training or experience.

COOPERATION WITH USERS

Closely related to the problem of financial support is the care given materials by the users, both those who use the stacks or reading rooms and those who take the books home for reading. Although most librarians hesitate to bring up the question of mutilation or defacement of materials, it is sometimes necessary to post state laws which stipulate the penalty for such actions. Circulation librarians are in a position to examine materials after use, but they are not always able to detect abuses when they occur.

Mutilation of volumes so that rebinding is not possible, damaging of covers by water-soaking, tearing, or spotting; warping of covers; breaking of covers, removal, loss, or tearing of pages; marking of pages with ink, crayon, or pencil; allowing oil or grease to get on leaves; spotting of edges in various ways—these are the dangers which constantly beset the book. Some librarians have established charges for damages of these kinds. Librarians should take a firm stand on these matters, since it probably is the only way to discourage deliberate mischief, as well as to minimize accidental injury to books and other library materials. A statement is sometimes printed on the date due slip or on the book pocket cautioning borrowers against writing in or otherwise defacing the books.

Users of the stacks and reading rooms also need to be cautioned about possible damage to books. Some libraries prohibit the use of ink for copying purposes in reference and reading rooms. Another practice sometimes employed is the counting of plates in rare and expensive items containing reproductions each time the volume is used. This is expensive and should be done only for especially valuable items.

HOUSING AND HANDLING OF MATERIALS

The contention that librarians have not always systematically cared for the collections under their supervision is a valid one. However, the lack of systematic conservation is often the result of poor layout of the library building and the lack of effective or adequate equipment. In some of the newer buildings, attention has been given to these factors in the hope of preventing deterioration of materials.

Air conditioning has been used to control the deterioration of paper, cloth, and leather resulting from certain factors. In an ideal situation, the temperature of the stacks is maintained at about 70 degrees, and the relative humidity between 50 and 65 percent. The air is washed and filtered to remove any dust and gases which might have damaging effects upon the books. In some libraries which have windows in the stacks, sunshine may have the effect of drying out paper and leather and discoloring the bindings, even though it may help measurably in eliminating certain destructive insects and molds.[13]

Other physical conditions conducive to the efficient handling of materials are the provision of adequate shelving, effective book supports, and satisfactory means of routing and transporting the materials. All of these conditions are ordinarily within the control of the librarian. Lydenberg and Archer, for example, call attention to the dangers of allowing books to sag on the shelves.[14]

Since many libraries have been faced with the lack of sufficient shelf space,[15] it is probable that many shelves are kept so full that bindings are injured in the removal and replacement of volumes. Lack of shelving makes it necessary to shift books constantly from one location to another, and these transfers frequently result in damage to bindings.

Lydenberg and Archer also call attention to the need for proper book supports to hold the volumes upright. Especially is there caution against placing books on their fore edges.[16] After noting that "large books should be stored on shelves deep enough to hold them safely, on shelves fitted with proper supports" they also point out that some of the larger volumes should be housed on roller shelves.[17]

SELECTION OF A BINDER

Earlier, in the discussion of personnel, attention was called to the lack of knowledge of the fine points of binding on the part of many librarians, and the reliance which must be placed upon the binder as a consequence. The selection of a binder, therefore, represents one of the important decisions of the librarian. Generally, librarians like to have binding done by a firm which is close to the library. This makes it possible for the binder to pick up and return materials quickly. In many instances, where no local binder exists, it will of course be necessary to select a binder outside of the community in which the library is located. With public libraries there is a general inclination toward supporting local firms, since they are taxpayers and part of the commercial life of the community. When such binders are qualified to do an efficient job, support should be given to them.

In recent years, the Library Binding Institute, working closely with the American Library Association, has been helpful in establishing standards of binding which guide the librarian in making his selection. The provision of "Class A" materials and workmanship, reliable service, careful handling of books, proper insurance coverage, and fair prices are criteria for appraising the binder. It is assumed that such factors are associated with a binder who maintains satisfactory working conditions for his personnel. The librarian or the person in charge of binding might well visit the bindery for the purpose of observing facilities.

The Joint Committee of the Library Binding Institute and the American Library Association has also guided librarians in identifying binders through the establishment of a certification plan for binderies. In order to be certified, a binder submits samples of his work which are examined by the Board of Review of the Joint Committee. If the samples are satisfactory, and if the binder can meet other qualifications, such as proving responsibility and reliability, providing satisfactory references and sufficient insurance, and maintaining standards, he is eligible for membership in the Library Binding Institute and for certification.

There is considerable competition among binders, and all binders are not members of the Library Binding Institute.[18] The lack of such membership or such certification does not mean that a binder cannot do satisfactory work. It is the librarian's responsibility to see that the binding meets specifications and is done at reasonable prices. If the prices are far below prevailing rates, the librarian may well raise the question as to whether or not the materials or work are inferior. A librarian should be able to detect these conditions without difficulty.

In libraries which have public support, the law may require the librarian to ask for competitive bidding. Some binders do not like to become involved in such jobs because it may mean lowering standards in order to obtain the work through low bids. The librarian is obligated to insist on the maintenance of standards, despite a low bid, and should be in a position to discourage binders who cannot fulfill the specifications. The librarian should also provide specific data regarding the size and condition of the volumes to be bound, so that no confusion will exist as to the type of work that has to be done. Most librarians who have been successful in keeping their collections well bound find that true economy results from selecting a binder who is fair in his dealings and who produces good work. Changing binders will not necessarily mean that the library will benefit financially or otherwise, but changes might well be made if the interests of the library are at stake. It is not unreasonable to believe that binders can improve their operations so that costs will not rise beyond the means of libraries.[19]

RELATIONSHIPS WITH THE BINDER

Reference has been made to standards of binding. During the past twenty-five years, progress has been made in the binding of library materials through the introduction of machine methods. For example, the oversewing machine, which is used in the large binderies for many of the items which libraries require to be bound or rebound, has done much in speeding up the work, as well as aiding in the improvement of binding. Satisfactory library bindings not only permit easy opening, but they wear well and have an attractive appearance that appeals to readers.

The Committee on Bookbinding of the American Library Association [20] was established early, and its suggestions for binding were published as early as 1909.[21] This activity, directly and indirectly, later led to the formation of the Library Binding Institute in the industry itself, and in 1934 a Joint Committee of the ALA and the LBI was constituted. The late Pelham Barr, long a director of the LBI, explained that the "basic purpose of the cooperative program is to raise and maintain the standards of library binding workmanship and business practice." [22]

The Committee will advise as to types of binding suitable for various needs and will check on the quality of binding in compliance with specifications. It is prepared to advise on the selection of a bindery and to arrange for arbitration in case of controversy between the library and the bindery. It will check advertising and sales claims of binderies. It will also present the subject of binding to interested groups, library associations, library trustees, or library schools.[23]

What is probably the most valuable contribution of the Joint Committee is its establishment of specifications for library binding. The *Library Binding Manual* [24] is an elementary guide to the subject, and includes as appendices the Minimum Specifications for Class "A" Library Binding and the Standards for Reinforced (Pre-Library-Bound) New Books. The Library Binding Institute issues a quarterly, *Library Binder*, which contains information useful to librarians.

The librarian in charge of binding has certain obligations to fulfill. Directions must always be clear, each shipment should be examined carefully as to collation, and records should be made for the library. If the books are sent to another community by express or other means of transportation, the binder should be so informed. Many binders supply special boxes or receptacles for convenient shipping of materials from a distance. The binder, when he pays the cost of transportation, usually stipulates the method of shipment.

The binder will usually maintain the "rubbings" which are used in the uniform preparation of serial publications or sets. He will also maintain in his stock the types of cloths and buckrams which the library prefers. He will generally call attention to items which cannot be bound for certain reasons, such as incompleteness of the volume, poor paper, or insufficient binding margins. In cases where special work has to be done, the binder should notify the librarian before any work is performed on the items.

PRESS BINDERIES

In some universities, libraries have had their binding problems, particularly those relating to books, pamphlets, and periodicals, taken care of by the institutional presses. The librarian will need to work closely with the personnel of the press if the binding is to be done expeditiously and economically. Many of the problems of press binding for libraries are discussed by Wright and Barnes.[25]

XVII. Conservation of Library Materials: the Bindery within the Library and the Handling of Special Materials

IN ADDITION to the problems of organizing binding work in the library and of creating an effective relationship with commercial binders, the librarian may need to deal with several other matters relating to the program of conservation. Consequently, this chapter will discuss some of those subjects under the following headings: (1) the bindery within the library; (2) the repair of books; (3) the handling of special materials, such as periodicals and other serial publications, newspapers, pamphlets, clippings, maps, and music; (4) special processes, such as the preservation of leather bindings and paper; and (5) special conditions which affect conservation, such as the presence of mildew, insects and vermin, and foxing.

BINDERY WITHIN THE LIBRARY

In his book entitled *The College Library Building,* James T. Gerould [1] considered the problem of the library bindery and book repairs. He recommended the operation of a bindery within the library only in exceptional circumstances and for large institutions which spend in excess of $10,000 for binding. He maintained it important, however, for libraries to provide quarters for the repair of materials.

Although Gerould wrote in 1932 when the value of a dollar was higher than it is today, many libraries with much more than $10,000 a year for binding at that time were not equipped with binderies. The question of whether or not a library should operate its own bindery is still an important one, but one which cannot be settled categorically. On the surface, it would seem that a library of moderate size would gain much by the establishment of its own bindery. The matter becomes more complex, however, when the problems which attend the operation of such a plant are considered.[2]

The theoretical advantages of having a bindery within the library may be summarized briefly. The presence of such a bindery allows for personal supervision and the application of special methods to the needs and conditions of the institution. Moreover, it has been found that, under certain conditions, the bindery within a library can reduce the costs of binding. Finally, the materials in process are always within reach, and, theoretically, readily accessible to the users. Gerould regarded this accessibility as a possible disadvantage, since there might have to be frequent searches for unfinished materials on the bindery shelves to satisfy users with immediate needs. Actually, this has not been a problem in libraries maintaining binderies.

The factors which need to be considered in deciding whether or not to establish a library bindery include the amount of work to be done annually, the physical quarters available, the specially trained personnel needed, and the additional financial burden which will result from installing and operating the bindery. Of course, if such a department is established, careful thought must also be given to the planning of routines and schedules if the maximum advantage is to be derived.

WORK LOAD. In order to make a library bindery worth while, it is essential that the binding cost of the library amount to several thousands of dollars yearly. In 1952–53, for example, the New York Public Library, in its own bindery, bound 30,541 volumes, repaired 1,584 items, and performed a wide variety of miscellaneous tasks such as making slip cases, manuscript boxes, and special loose-leaf binders, framing and mounting prints for exhibitions, and repairing and mounting prints, maps, and labels.[3] The bindery in the University of Minnesota Library, during 1951–52 bound 7,475 books, 7,142 periodical volumes, and 3,687 pamphlets. This bindery also furnished various other services, such as book repair, newspaper binding, thesis binding, and special preparation of maps and portfolios. The total expenditure was $39,260.24.[4] To cite yet another example, the Columbia University binding department, during 1952–53, dispatched 23,613 volumes to commercial binders, bound 16,919 pamphlets, manufactured 1,176 board portfolios and 6,750 manila folders, repaired 2,715 items, prepared 73,424 books for the shelves (plating, perforating, and so on), oiled 15 leather-bound books, and performed a variety of other functions, including the preparation of 12,612 binder's slips.[5]

All of these libraries maintain extensive binding programs. It may be well, therefore, to present statistical information pertaining to the bindery operated within the Olin Memorial Library, Wesleyan University, a medium-sized collection. That department, during 1948–49, bound 2,387 books and 1,620 pamphlets, and repaired 1,131 books. The Wesleyan bindery also carried on routines complementary to its main function, such as map mounting, cutting of stock, bottom cropping for the library's unique compact storage project,[6] and call numbering of books.[7]

These examples of work load and activities suggest the need on the part of librarians to study the binding situation before a decision to establish a library bindery is made. In the operation of a bindery, it will be wise to examine in detail the functions being carried out, lest the bindery be burdened with tasks for which it is not adequately equipped or staffed.

PHYSICAL QUARTERS. If the library building was not originally planned to include a bindery, it may be difficult to find adequate space which is well lighted, equipped with the necessary electrical outlets, and provided with suitable connections with the other units of the library. Not only must the internal arrangements of the bindery quarters be suited to the operations to be carried out, but also proper orientation with regard to the movement of material within the library and to and from outside agencies is necessary. Space for shelving, work tables, the rather noisy sewing machines, and other equipment, some of which will require heavy floor loading, must be provided.

PERSONNEL. At least one person in the library bindery should be thoroughly skilled in the details of binding operations. The head of the department, whether he be that skilled person or not, should have an intimate knowledge of binding materials, should be of an orderly nature, and should have the ability to supervise others. While the head of the binding preparation department, described in Chapter XV, should have complete command of the ordinary problems of binding, the chief of a library-operated bindery will, in addition, need to have a sound knowledge of machines, equipment, and techniques. In the decision to set up a bindery within a particular library, the potential supply of personnel may play an important part. Selection and training of subordinates in the bindery will constitute an important function of the department head.

COSTS. Additional investment of capital in equipment, space, and facilities necessary to the organization of a bindery will result in an increased fixed cost to the library. These and other expenses, for example, insurance, will place a burden on the library which it will be difficult to reduce even over several years. All costs, both fixed and variable, must be predicted accurately and then compared with the money spent for commercial binding before it can be determined whether a bindery in the library will constitute a saving or an extra expense. Only in rare instances will it be wise management to allow convenience to outweigh financial considerations.

REPAIR OF BOOKS

Whether or not the library maintains its own bindery, it will have problems of repair. One of the important decisions which needs to be made involves the determination of what to discard, what to rebind, and what to repair.[8] Librarians have not always used the best judgment in singling out materials for these three categories of treatment. Bad condition is not the only reason for discarding materials, though when an item is badly worn it should be considered for permanent removal from the collection. Out-dated books, especially textbooks and technical materials, frequently can be discarded. Special libraries and school libraries generally make periodic surveys of their holdings and eliminate obsolete items. The research library, either public or private, as was pointed out in an earlier section, may have good reason to retain old editions of titles, even if they have been superseded.

Books with missing pages and worn or soiled books which can be replaced and trivial books which are no longer useful to the collection are among the types which can be generally discarded. On the other hand, books which receive hard, continuous use, both fiction and nonfiction which have established value, and expensive items are usually selected for rebinding. Mending is called for when pages are loose, torn, or rumpled; when the back is breaking at the joints at the top or bottom; when super or joints are broken. Usually those designated for mending are titles, especially fiction, which are in too great demand to be sent to the bindery, adult nonfiction of temporary value not to be rebound, rebound items which need slight adjustments, valuable books too old to be rebound, and little-used books retained for illustrations, plates, or because of local interest.

The entire staff needs to be concerned with the inspection of books for early signs indicating need of repair. Loose or torn pages should be mended promptly or loss or greater damage will invariably follow. Alertness on the part of the circulation and other service desk assistants, as well as of the stack assistants, will generally result in catching many items before irreparable injury is done to them.

In the large library, it may be desirable to obtain the services of a professional binder, though the smaller library probably will not be able to support this type of staff member. The literature of book repair is extensive and clearly presented and it should be possible to train an employee without recourse to formal training. In some libraries, assistants work on books to be discarded in order to develop facility in repairing.

The repair unit of the library, if it is to do its work effectively, will need adequate space for equipment and work surfaces. In many libraries, this work is done in an out-of-the-way spot in the basement, or in some other undesirable location. If the morale of the personnel assigned to repair is to be maintained and if the best work is to be done, consideration should be given to lighting, ventilation, and other such factors.

MENDING MATERIALS AND EQUIPMENT. The repair unit will need to have certain essential materials for cleaning paper and covers, mending torn pages, tipping in loose leaves and sections, and strengthening hinges. Stationers, hardware shops, and library supply houses are able to furnish all necessary materials and equipment.

For cleaning, such items as Artgum erasers, ink erasers, steel erasers, and ink eradicators are needed. These will take care of most smudges and pencil and ink marks. Alcohol and gasoline can be used as solvents for the removal of oil spots and stains which cannot be erased. White soap or prepared cleanser can be used, with caution, for cleaning book covers. Vinegar has also been found useful for this purpose. For cleaning edges of books, sandpaper and Artgum have been used successfully.

For waterproofing, shellac and book lacquers have generally been applied to new books. The waterproofing keeps the book covers in good condition, and they are generally safer to clean when they become soiled. A vulcanized brush with metal handle is used to apply the shellac. Plastic book sprays also have been developed for this purpose.

Some of the items which will be needed for repair work are: a pair of general office shears with a six- or seven-inch blade, a sharp-pointed paring knife, two or more bone (or plastic) folders, a straight ruler with steel edge, a paste pot, paste and brushes, dusting powder, blotters, waxed paper, mending papers (transparent tissue and parchment papers), and end and lining papers. Careful repair assistants will save paper from discarded books and from certain types of book jackets; these can be used frequently in mending and are often more suitable than the commercial paper.

While full-scale rebinding requires large pieces of equipment, recasing and repair of contents may frequently be done with a minimum of supplies and apparatus. A large pair of shears (nine-inch blade), a bevel-edged knife for paring edges of board, flexible glue to be used in backs of books for recasing, an electric glue pot, heavy pasting brushes, cloth binders or plain white muslin for recasing, cord for reinforcing upper and lower edges of a new spine, book cloths and buckrams, binders' board, a paper cutter, and a small press are the essential items required for satisfactory performance in this kind of work.

The Indiana State Library, Extension Division, in its *Do's and Don't's of Book Repairing,*[9] calls attention to many cautions which must be heeded if successful repairing is to be done. Among the practices to be avoided are the following: overmending a book that will eventually be rebound, attempting to sew books, using water on glazed paper, cutting feathered edges before mending with tissue, using cellulose tape, fastening in too many sections with binder, allowing tipped-in sheets to extend beyond the margin of the book, and using too much paste.

In the preceding paragraphs, the discussion centered about the practical aspects of repairing the usual type of volume in the library. The discussion would be incomplete without reference to the handling of rare items. Librarians who have regard for books as examples of an art will avoid repairing rare books unless it can be done by an expert bookbinder on the staff. Lehmann-Haupt [10] has commented fully on this point. He especially cautions against the procedure of placing strictly utilitarian new bindings on old volumes.

SPECIAL MATERIALS

PERIODICALS AND OTHER SERIALS. Discussion of some of the problems relating to the binding of periodicals is included in Chapter XV. The binding of these materials in the research library represents an important segment of preservation, and planning and care are necessary if appropriate and economical binding measures are to be insured. It is essential that libraries prepare manuals of procedures [11] so as to minimize errors and to facilitate the training of new employees. In addition to procedures, such manuals should provide information regarding bases of decisions for binding or not binding (thickness, quality of paper, format, intrinsic value, and possible or probable use).

Very thin items, for example, especially if they are in a homogenous series, may be held, tied in boards, until thick enough to be combined into a regular cloth volume; but if they deal with varied subjects, they may better be put into individual volumes. Some items are printed on paper too poor or fragile for regular binding. If these materials are to be retained permanently, they may have to be Japanese-tissued or otherwise protected and then bound; or, they may be placed in cloth portfolios and marked to match other parts of the sets if these have been bound. Materials, such as press releases, which have awkward formats or insufficient margins will also need special attention. As noted earlier, distinction should be made between items which are rare and those which require less expensive treatment. Finally, consideration should be given to the probable use of materials. Items that are to receive heavy use may be bound in separate pamphlet style, even though their size may suggest holding for combination with others into a larger format; on the other hand, items that are likely to get little use may be kept unbound indefinitely.

NEWSPAPERS. Neal Harlow, in proposing a cooperative program for conserving the newspapers of California, wrote the following:

> Of all the source materials bearing upon the life of a community, the local newspaper is probably the most comprehensive, the easiest to secure, and the most evanescent. Collected today, tomorrow it is scarce, later, perhaps, rare or unique. The scope of information contained in a well run sheet is astounding, and even against its own editorial will it reflects the conditions, events, and forces of its time. Bulky, yellowing, unmanageable by usual library methods, files are more easily ignored than stored, and because their value is likely to be cumulative, a steady, long-term policy regarding them is required.[12]

Since newspapers have been printed on wood-pulp stock for many years, files tend to disintegrate regardless of the use they receive. Too, each newspaper file is expensive: the cost of subscription, the cost of checking in each issue, the cost of binding, the cost of storing the bulky volumes, and the cost of servicing the collection may quickly take up a large part of the library's budget. Although the library may save some money for the moment by using various "temporary" bindings on newspapers, such methods are usually not satisfactory for long-range conservation, and may actually increase the cost of later handling.

The small or medium-sized public library and the school library probably will be concerned with relatively few newspapers except for more or less immediate use. Where the library's responsibility for preserving local materials is taken seriously, of course, the number of local newspapers purchased may create an acute problem. Too, most libraries will find it necessary to maintain a file of one of the large metropolitan dailies. Rag-paper editions and microfilm editions of these publications tend to simplify this part of the conservation program.

As Paine has pointed out,[13] microfilm offers a possible solution for the library which is obligated to preserve a considerable number of newspaper files. After concluding that the small library usually cannot afford to establish its own photographic laboratory, Paine wrote:

> Several alternatives were immediately apparent. First, the library might purchase outright or rent the necessary equipment from the Recordak Corporation and employ an operator. Second, a contract could be entered into with the Eastman subsidiary, under which the library would ship the material to be photographed to the company's plant, where all of the work would be done. Third, we might find a professional operator *properly equipped* for microphotography and near enough to make it possible to set up a camera in our building, or to whom we could get the materials to be filmed without elaborate packing and high transportation costs. Obviously the criteria for choosing from the above methods must be the quality of work obtainable and costs.[14]

While any extensive program of microfilming will be expensive, the construction of additions to the stack area and meeting the problem of deterioration of paper will ordinarily cost considerably more. There are several catalogs or check lists which provide information as to what newspaper files are already available on microfilm,[15] so the alert librarian will not attempt to finance an independent project without first determining whether the files considered for filming have already been reproduced.

PAMPHLETS. Most libraries collect pamphlets, and if these materials are to be used to best advantage, considerable attention must be given to proper care. Some research libraries, and most libraries at various times, bind pamphlets much as they bind books—in boards with cloth or paper covers. A few libraries group pamphlets on special subjects and bind them into volumes. Other libraries place pamphlets in vertical files, boxes or envelopes, or wire-staple them into manila covers. The decision as to which method a library should follow will depend upon the emphasis placed on preserving pamphlet materials, upon the nature of the pamphlets collected, and upon the probable use to be made of the pamphlets, both at present and in the future. It is possible for a library to follow several of these methods.

Note should be taken of the practice of binding several pamphlets into a single volume. While the practice has as its primary advantage the grouping of like materials on the shelves, it is important to consider such matters as the size of the pamphlets and the nature of the paper on which they are printed. At the New York Public Library, where the practice is followed, it has been found that as a pamphlet on poor paper deteriorates it may be necessary to rebind the entire volume. The binding of pamphlets of various sizes into a volume may also result in an awkward volume, especially when several of the pamphlets extend an inch or more beyond the others. In some cases, bindings which include items of various sizes will not retain their shape.

The practice of putting pamphlets into vertical files is common in many libraries, though the value of such an arrangement in a research library has been seriously questioned.[16] In general, pamphlets in vertical files are placed in folders, and the entire file is alphabetically arranged according either to a standard subject heading list or to a list devised to suit the particular needs of the library. Files such as these are especially valuable for the library with a special clientele or for the library which finds that it must supplement its collection with printed information which has not yet been consolidated into book form. Material appearing in pamphlets is often of ephemeral interest and can be discarded after a period of time. Thus, systematic weeding is essential both to keep down the bulk of the file and to discover those items which appear to be of permanent value, so that they may be bound or otherwise preserved.

Condit's statement on when pamphlets should be discarded and bound is of interest at this point:

> The purpose of many pamphlet collections is to supplement knowledge obtainable elsewhere in bound volumes, to keep readers supplied with up-to-date information or with data pertaining to the current calendar year or fiscal year, and to demonstrate by examples the newest processes of printing and engraving. Since the space for housing of the pamphlet collection is limited, pamphlets may be transferred or discarded as soon as the information which they contain is superseded by material in bound volumes, as soon as the fiscal or calendar year has come to a close, or as soon as certain technological processes have become historic rather than representative of newest developments. Whenever a society or organization disbands or unites with another, its pamphlets may be collected and bound. Whenever an author dies, the time is ripe to collect and bind his available reprints and pamphlets. Whenever an invention passes from the experimental to the practical stage, pamphlets dealing with pioneer researches in the field may be collected and bound. Whenever a political movement of social significance has its fruition, the time is at hand to collect and bind pamphlets dealing with its rise, its growth, and its eventual culmination.[17]

CLIPPINGS. Separate files of clippings from newspapers and periodicals (usually duplicate copies are clipped) are useful in libraries where materials of current interest are needed and in certain specialized libraries such files will be of considerable historical value.

At times, the pamphlet file and the clipping file are consolidated. Ireland [18] advocates clipping local newspapers, pointing out that a well-indexed paper (such as the New York *Times*) need not be clipped to make it more readily useful. Although Ireland also advises mounting clippings on a good grade of typing paper, if the file is weeded systematically and is ephemeral in nature, this is an expense which may be avoided. Ordinarily the clippings may be filed in manila folders and indexed by subject as is done with pamphlets.

Newspaper and journalism libraries, which maintain extensive clipping files as a primary source of material have been comprehensively treated by Desmond.[19] The author deals in detail with the supplies and equipment used in the "morgue" and with its organization. He also describes a practical method of determining when to discard clippings.[20]

MAPS. World War II brought to the attention of many librarians the importance of maintaining collections of a wide variety of maps. The demands made upon the map resources of the nation by the armed services and, especially in the public libraries, by the families of individuals in the services pointed up the lack of well-organized collections of this type of material. Storage and equipment represent major problems of map administration. The wide differences in size and form of map material, such as globes, relief maps, sheet maps, roll maps, folded maps, and maps enclosed in cases require special storage facilities.[21]

In a most useful pamphlet Le Gear discusses the care and treatment of maps under the headings of (1) Preliminary processing, (2) Secondary processing, (3) Atlases, (4) Mounting and reconditioning maps, (5) Map filing equipment, and (6) The map room.[22]

MUSIC. Since music scores generally are used for performance, binding must allow for easy, flat opening on a music stand. This requires sewing along the signatures. Some music for ensembles cannot be bound at all, but must be conserved in folders or boxes of various types. Only experienced music binders should be employed. An adequate conservation program for music is usually expensive.

SPECIAL PROCESSES

CARE OF LEATHER BINDINGS. Few surveyors of libraries have failed to observe the general lack of care of leather bindings in libraries. In some of the larger libraries of the country, thousands of leather-bound volumes are gradually deteriorating. The effects of heat and dryness in stacks on leather bindings have made it necessary for librarians to introduce systematic care of these books in order to preserve them. In one library, for example, once each year the many hundreds of leather bindings are given a treatment to prevent drying and cracking. In another, newly acquired titles with leather bindings are treated. Depending upon the climate and upon whether or not stack conditions can be controlled, such treatment should be given to these bindings if rotting is to be prevented. Rare book curators of the larger libraries have recognized the dangers to expensive leather bindings and are usually rigorous in their care of them. Lydenberg and Archer have assembled a number of formulas which are useful in decreasing "the harmful effects of modern conditions on leather bindings." [23]

The experience of a number of libraries, especially the New York Public Library, has clearly indicated that animal and vegetable oils are superior in their preservative effects to the mineral oils that some librarians have been inclined to use. Archer's tests at the New York Public Library [24] provide evidence on this point. Various bookbinding materials were tested on a set of *The Century Dictionary* from 1925 to 1935. The set was bound in several leathers (Persian Morocco [domestic], Turkey Morocco [German], Oasis Morocco [English]), and buckram. The leather bindings were three-quarter style with buckram sides. Except for three volumes which were untreated, the leathers were treated with neatsfoot oil, castor oil, lanolin, vaseline, and neatsfoot oil combined with castor oil. The conclusions of the study were as follows:

1. There's nothing like leather—well-tanned leather—for book binding.
2. Domestic leather of bark tannage is not good for binding.

3. Animal and vegetable oils applied to leather bindings are beneficial, while mineral oil seems to be harmful.
4. Increased volume-weight adds much to wear and tear, and decreases the life of binding; volumes of moderate weight last longer.
5. The continued application of oil to leather seems to soften the size and to cause the gold lettering to rub off.[25]

Some mention should be made of the limitations of the tests. While an effort was made to study the bindings under actual conditions of use in the library, it cannot be described as a scientific study, since there was no control for certain types of bindings; i.e., both volumes bound in full buckram weighed eight pounds, while some of the leather bound volumes weighed four pounds.

Among the formulas listed by Lydenberg and Archer is the one consisting of four parts of lanolin and six parts of neatsfoot oil.[26] This preparation has been used with good results by a number of libraries.

REINFORCING AND LAMINATING PAPER. The preservation of archival and manuscript material has always been a problem to librarians and custodians of records. Various practices have been developed in the effort to prevent deterioration, and special attention has been given to the economy of such programs. Minogue, in a section in *The Repair and Preservation of Records* devoted to the reinforcement of paper, has listed several methods.[27] These include "framing" or "inlaying" a sheet of paper into another sheet of more durable paper; mounting on another sheet (if one side is blank); glazing (mounting in a frame or between two sheets of glass); resizing in order to regain the original strength; lacquering; or covering with a transparent, flexible material.

In the last instance, crepeline (a silk gauze), Japanese tissue, or transparent cellulose sheeting have been used. If cellulose sheeting is the material to be used, it may either be applied to the paper with an adhesive or applied by melting the foil under heat and pressure so that it forms a bond with the document to be preserved. The last method is generally described as "lamination."

According to Minogue, the material or sheeting must be such that it will flow at a low enough temperature so that the paper being treated will not be injured, it must be permanent, and it must not be subject to discoloration with time or exposure. Cellulose acetate, cellulose acetate-propionate, cellulose acetate-butyrate, and nylon films are all suitable. Cellophane, cellulose nitrate, ethyl cellulose, and the vinylite resins are either not sufficiently plastic or are not permanent.

The equipment used consists primarily of a press which may be heated to 300°F., and which will produce up to 1,000 pounds pressure per square inch. The press may be either flat-bed or roller. A number of polished and flexible steel plates are needed, together with a fine wire screen, blotters, and other miscellaneous apparatus. The press, obviously, will be relatively expensive.

In his review of the Minogue monograph, D. L. Evans pointed out that lamination is as yet unproven, except by laboratory experiments which may not have tested the ability of the cellulose sheeting to last long periods of time without becoming brittle or discolored. His concern was over the fact that the process of lamination cannot be undone. All other means of preserving records (tissue, silk, etc.) can be taken apart and done over; lamination is permanent.[28] Evans advocated lamination for records which are badly in need of repair, and which are not unique. Newspapers and other records which exist in multiple copies are fit material for this process; unique records are not. Evans made much of Barrow's treatment of paper [29] before lamination to remove acidity.

SPECIAL CONDITIONS

MOLD OR MILDEW. Lydenberg and Archer describe mildew as "a thin, whitish coating consisting of fungi of many kinds." When it takes hold in a library its action is rapid. While it is well known that light and good ventilation will tend to prevent mildew, it is not always possible to combat the encroachment of this enemy of books. Various authorities, including Lydenberg and Archer, suggest the use of artificial heat to drive away the humidity which encourages the growth of fungi. If the books are affected only on the covers or on the outside of the paper, the stains can be removed with alcohol. There seems to be no cure once mildew gets into the fibres of the paper. Thymol has been used for sterilizing.[30]

Hetherington has recommended a solution which has been used successfully to prevent the growth of mold. The ingredients of his formula are thymol crystals (10 grams), mercuric bichloride (4 grams), ether (200 cc), and benzene (400 cc). He points out that one application of this solution to books was sufficient to stop the growth of mold. The solution, however, is both poisonous and inflammable and must be used very cautiously. It is best applied in open air or in a well-ventilated room and with a piece of cotton held in forceps so as to keep it off one's hands. It is damaging to wearing apparel. Hetherington notes that the solution needs to be applied only once; books may be returned to the shelves immediately. It is suggested that each binding be tested with a small amount of the solution to see whether it will cause the color to run.[31]

INSECTS. Librarians are not only faced with possible damage to books from human hands, they have also to be watchful of the harm that can come from insects. Weiss and Carruthers, in their extensive study, call attention to the nature of the attacks on books by insects:

> Various species of insects attack books, and their activities may show injury to wood, leather, parchment, or cloth bindings, to paper or to paste, and almost any part of a book is liable to be damaged. The injury may vary from slight feeding marks on the sides, pages or backstrip to more or less complete riddling of the covers and leaves, resulting in the book's almost falling apart when it is opened. Some infestations may be so severe that the shelves on which the books are standing become covered with excrementitious frass, and dust. Books remaining in piles or on stacks for long periods of time, without inspection, are particularly subject to injury.
>
> Certain conditions favor the multiplication of various species of insect. Many flourish in the presence of excess moisture, of darkness, etc. Many of these adverse conditions have disappeared within recent years, and more and more attention is being paid to light, cleanliness, ventilation, temperature, etc., of places in which books are kept.
>
> However, if certain species of insect gain access to libraries, they may flourish in spite of cleanliness, and ideal temperature and moisture con-

ditions of books, because after all, paper, leather, wood, parchment, etc. are their natural foods and while the food supply lasts, so does the species.[32]

The authors describe a dozen or more insect species which may infest books, and, where possible, indicate methods of control. Among the insects and the controls described are the following:

Insect	*Method of Control*
Book lice	Destroy source; clean, air, and dry storage space.
Silver-fish	Mixture of 12 parts of sodium fluoride to 100 parts of wheat flour placed on the shelves.
Cockroach	Sodium fluoride scattered on runways.
Drugstore beetle	Fumigation under vacuum.
White-marked spider beetle	Fumigation as for drugstore beetle.
Larder beetle	Fumigation or raising temperature to 125° F.
Mexican book beetle	Fumigation with carbon bisulphide, at a dosage of 1 pound to 1,000 cubic feet, for 24 hours; frequent dusting will prevent activity of this insect.
Brown house moth	Fumigation with a mixture of ethylene dichloride, 3 parts, and carbon tetrachloride, 1 part; 14 pounds per 1,000 cubic feet for 48 hours at 80° F. is one remedy.
Termites or white ants	Carbon bisulphide or carbon tetrachloride will kill them in soil; concrete and steel buildings needed to prevent termite infestation.

FOXING. The term "foxing" is used to describe the dull rusty patches which appear frequently on pages of old books. Iiams and Beckwith [33] have made intensive studies of foxing in books, and their experiments are worth noting. While emphasizing the inconclusive nature of their experiments directed at detecting the possible causes of foxing, they indicate that foxing is caused by the action of enzymes produced by fungi on the iron contained as an impurity in paper.

The hygroscopic qualities of some types of paper or excessive humidity (75 percent relative or over) demonstrably fosters the growth of fungi. Therefore, the most effective means of retarding the spread of foxing is to maintain ideal temperature and humidity (70 degrees of temperature and 50 percent of relative humidity) in book storage areas. This can be best accomplished through air conditioning.

Once foxing has affected a book, there appears to be little success in arresting it. However, foxing does not operate like insects or mildew; only those books with paper stock containing chemical impurities are affected by foxing. "There is little, if any, danger of its spreading from one book to another, unless the paper came from the same run of paper." [34]

XVIII. Circulation Operations: Registration

A LOAN department, or, as it is frequently called, a circulation department, is responsible for the services relating to the loan to the library's clientele of books, periodicals, maps, music, prints, microfilms, and other materials. In addition to serving regular patrons, the department may also be called upon to provide materials requested by telephone or by letter. The department usually maintains a record of these loans, recalls overdue items, assesses fines, accepts reserves for titles in demand, supplies information for the replacement of lost items, supervises the arrangement of materials on the shelves, and makes provisions for readers to use materials in the library stacks. All of these activities require careful planning if maximum service is to be provided. Many readers are critical of the apparent "red tape" which sets up problems in borrowing books, but experience of librarians has demonstrated that systematic procedures are necessary if control of materials is to be maintained.

The organization of the circulation department will differ from library to library, depending upon its scope of work and the degree of departmentalization which exists. A centralized organization will provide for uniform loan practices in all units of a library system. It will also be the center for a constant review and appraisal of the operations, devices, forms, and records which are used in circulating materials to readers. Public libraries differ somewhat from college, university, and special libraries in their relations with their clientele; consequently they have developed certain approaches to fit their particular needs.

PURPOSES OF REGISTRATION

The fundamental reasons for registration in public libraries are the need to know who has borrowed materials and what are the general characteristics of the clientele.

The identity of the borrower must be established in order that the library may know where to seek the item if it is not returned. This involves a contractual relationship between the library and its patron, a responsibility on the part of the library to safeguard the property entrusted to it, and the protection of the rights of other individuals in the community who may wish to use the material.

The library staff is also concerned with the extent to which it is reaching its patrons. Wilson, in his book entitled *The Geography of Reading,* states that "the principal data upon which the library depends in measuring its social significance to its patrons are the number of volumes circulated and the number of borrowers served during the year." [1] How many take advantage of the library's service, who are they, and where do they live? The American Library Association has recognized the number of registered borrowers as a quantitative standard for public libraries. The minimum standards based on a three-year registration period are: Adult borrowers (15 years and over), 20–40 percent of the population; Juvenile borrowers (5 years through 14 years), 35–75 percent of the population.[2]

In addition, information taken from registration files has been used in studying the strength of a library, in analyzing its relation to various segments of the population, in showing why it should have an increased appropriation, in making comparisons with libraries of similar scope and program, and in giving proper value to circulation figures. For example, in a study at the Montclair (New Jersey) Public Library, it was found that about three fourths of the books were borrowed by less than 5 percent of the total adult population; this amounted to about 20 percent of the actual borrowers and to only 10 or 12 percent of the persons registered in the library.[3] Such information should be useful in the development of the library program in relation to community needs.

GENERAL REGISTRATION PROCEDURE

The steps in registration are fairly well standardized. The borrower-to-be is given an application blank to fill in. The information usually requested is the name, residence and telephone number, business address and telephone number, occupation, and the name, address, and telephone number of a reference or guarantor. A borrower's number is sometimes assigned to this application form and is also entered on the card given to the borrower; this is omitted in the transaction charging system which is explained later. In libraries where the borrower's number is used in book charging, an additional card may be made with the borrower's name, address, and number. These cards may be filed numerically and form a numerical record of registration, though in some libraries the numerical file is kept in book form instead of on cards. The original application card is usually filed alphabetically and serves as an alphabetical registration record.

Registration is usually for a definite period—three years in many public libraries—and borrowers' cards are issued free to all residents of the area served by the library.

BORROWER'S REFERENCE OR GUARANTOR

Many public libraries still require the borrower to name a reference or a guarantor. When a reference is given by an applicant, the name and address of the reference is usually verified in the telephone book or in the city directory. The older practice of requiring a guarantor to sign an agreement to assume responsibility for the borrower has now largely disappeared. In 1887, Carr [4] indicated that the signature of the guarantor was required for its moral effect upon the borrower. The usual reason advanced today for the use of a reference is simply that, in the event the borrower should leave the community in possession of property belonging to the library, it is presumed that the person who is listed as reference may know the whereabouts of the delinquent borrower.

If an applicant is unable to furnish suitable personal identification, some libraries mail a postal card to the address given on the application form. The return of the postal card to the library by the applicant is usually considered presumptive evidence that the address given by the applicant is the correct one.

ELEMENTS OF A REGISTRATION SYSTEM

1. The alphabetical registration record will tell who is registered and if that person has been registered before.
2. The numerical file, used in some circulation systems, will tell how many registered borrowers the library has.
3. When the charging system employs a borrower's number instead of his name, the numerical file will show to whom any given material is charged.
4. The same registration plan may be used in various departments by adding symbols to the registration number, such as "J" for a children's department.

JUVENILE REGISTRATION

Juvenile registration is kept separate from adult registration in most libraries. To be eligible for a children's card, a child must have reached a certain level in school. Many libraries require only that the child be capable of signing his name; an alternative requirement is that the child be in the third grade in school. Some libraries stipulate that the child's parents must sign his application as guarantors.

In handling children's registration, most public libraries observe one or more of the following practices: (1) the borrower's registration on a juvenile card may bear a distinguishing symbol; (2) a block of registration numbers may be assigned for juvenile use; (3) the borrower's card used by juveniles may be of a different color than the adult card; and (4) the registration period for juveniles is sometimes only one year instead of the three years for adults.

Children are generally entitled to adult borrowers' cards when they reach the age of fourteen, or when they enter the ninth grade in school. When a change is made, the records of the juvenile borrower may be transferred to the adult registration files, and notation of the shift made for statistical purposes.

NONRESIDENT BORROWERS

Each library system must determine what persons, although not legal residents of the area served, still may have the privilege of using the library. Two classes of nonresidents who are usually entitled to library service are students attending local educational institutions and nonresident employees of business concerns in the area. A third class is the nonresident taxpayers. Because these people contribute to the support of the library they are usually entitled to library service. The New York Public Library [5] states that any person with a home, business, or school address in New York city, or any nonresident owning city real estate, may receive borrowers' privileges. The Carnegie Library of Pittsburgh [6] issues a special borrower's card to business concerns in the city and recognizes only authorized persons from those concerns.

Most public libraries have a system whereby other nonresidents, upon the payment of a fee, may be granted borrower's privileges in the library. There does not seem to be any standard fee, and the range is usually between $1.00 and $5.00. This fee is subject to certain variations—for example in St. Louis [7] the nonresident adult fee is $2.00 and the nonresident children's fee is $1.00. Pittsburgh [8] charges a nonresident fee of $3.00, except for study clubs outside the city, for whom the fee is $5.00.

Various devices of color, specified blocks of numbers, and symbols such as N.R. are used to indicate the nonresident borrower's card. Because these cards normally are issued for one year (instead of three), and the application blanks represent a fee paid into the library, some method of keeping these applications must be devised in order that they may serve for auditing purposes.

TEMPORARY BORROWERS

Borrower's privileges are usually accorded to temporary residents upon payment of a deposit fee. This fee varies between $2.00 and

$5.00 and allows the borrower to withdraw up to three books at a time for home use. A borrower's card with some special number or symbol to indicate the temporary nature of the card is issued and often serves as a receipt for the deposit. This is returned in full or in part when the borrower leaves the community, after any unpaid fines or losses are charged against it.

Rochester Public Library [9] has a special card for transient borrowers, which carries a stub that may be detached to serve as a numerical borrower's record. The card, issued for a three-month period, serves both as a borrower's card and as a receipt for the borrower's deposit. The deposit is filed in an envelope which is used as a part of the alphabetical borrower's file or alphabetical registration record. Both the card and its stub carry a registration number in a special block of numbers known as the "T" series.

BORROWERS IN COLLEGE AND UNIVERSITY LIBRARIES

College and university libraries grant borrowing privileges to all faculty, staff, and registered students. The method of student identification differs among institutions, but it usually assumes one of the following forms:

1. The student is required to show an identification card received at the time of entry into the current academic period. This card is used more in university libraries than in smaller college libraries.

2. An alternative to the above method is to require the borrower to show his bursar's or auditor's receipt.

3. Sometimes used in conjunction with the first two systems is the practice, common in many public libraries, of having the borrower sign his name on the book card.

4. A variation of the third system is the visible file of registration. This is kept at the circulation desk and each time a call slip is presented the visible file is referred to: (a) to see whether the borrower is registered; (b) to check his signature; (c) to see if the borrower owes any fines.

NONSTUDENT BORROWERS. In general, college and university libraries also grant the privilege of using their libraries to the residents of the community surrounding the institution. Oberlin College Library [10] has a contract with the village for library service. The library at Alfred University is also a registered public library under the New York State Education Law. At the University of Illinois,[11] residents of the community may obtain a permit at the circulation desk to withdraw books for home use on a two-week loan. Antioch College [12] keeps a file of names and addresses of townspeople who are permitted to use the library. Wesleyan,[13] in addition to keeping the same kind of file, searches the voters list for townspeople who may have been excluded from the file. If the would-be borrower is a nonvoter, the signature of a voter in the town is sufficient endorsement. The University of Texas [14] asks the local residents for suitable identification and a $5.00 deposit.

TRANSIENT BORROWERS IN COLLEGE AND UNIVERSITY LIBRARIES. There is no definite policy with respect to the handling of loans to this group. Antioch charges a deposit of $2.00; Temple asks a $2.00 deposit from students without bursar's receipts and a $5.00 deposit from others, including alumni. In his study of 71 state universities and land-grant colleges, Miller [15] listed four other types of temporary or transient borrowers who received no standardized treatment in the institutions studied. (1) Part-time students. Because these students tended to be local residents, they were given borrowers' privileges in all but one of the institutions studied. (2) Correspondence or extension students. These were given service directly or by mail in the thirty institutions that offered extension courses. (3) Nonregistered graduate students. This group includes those students who have finished their course work, but are working on their dissertations away from the university. Fifty-one of the 62 institutions giving graduate work make loans to these individuals. (4) Alumni. Very few institutions give special service to alumni. In general, they are offered only the same privileges that other citizens of the community or state may enjoy.

DUTIES RELATING TO REGISTRATION

TEMPORARY BORROWER'S CARD. One of the arguments against the use of a borrower's card or borrower's identification card is that the borrower may forget to bring the card with him when he wishes to withdraw a book. Since this is not an infrequent occurrence, libraries must make some provision for those registered borrowers who find themselves in this predicament. If it is a small library where the patron is known, a common procedure is to allow him to sign his name to the book card and withdraw the book.

The Milwaukee Public Library [16] asks the person to fill out a special card to which the patron's number is added from the alphabetical registration file. This temporary card is good for that day only and applies only to the main library. Branch libraries may not issue temporary cards. A patron who has forgotten his card may be permitted to withdraw a book if he knows his card number, or presents adequate identification.

The New York Public Library [17] requires the borrower to deposit $.25 for a temporary card good for immediate use. The Carnegie Library of Pittsburgh[18] will issue no more than three temporary cards in a year free. After three such cards have been issued, a five-cent charge is made for each temporary card.

LOST BORROWER'S CARD. When a patron loses his borrower's card, he should report the fact to the library. The desk assistant follows a fairly standardized procedure in issuing a duplicate card:

1. The patron fills out either a lost card form or a new application blank; or, a note is made on the original registration that a duplicate card has been issued.

2. The information is verified and the patron is issued a new borrower's card.

3. A fee of between ten and twenty-five cents is charged for the first duplicate and each subsequent duplicate card.

4. The fee is usually less for duplicate cards for juvenile borrowers; in some cases there is no fee.

In photographic charging, only a slip with the signature and address of the borrower is sufficient to complete a transaction. This is for temporary use; a permanent card is subsequently issued.

CHANGE OF ADDRESS. A registered borrower who reports a change of address is issued a new borrower's card containing his new address, and the address is changed in both the alphabetical and numerical registration records. If the change of address makes the borrower a nonresident, then the procedure for persons of that status is put into force.

CENTRAL REGISTRATION

Central registration is a complete list of all persons registered throughout a library system. In the case of county libraries, the central registration file is maintained at the headquarters of the system. County library systems generally use the borrower's application form for the alphabetical file and a second card file or a loose-leaf registration book for the numerical file. When a borrower is registered at a branch library or with a bookmobile, his registration application is sent to headquarters for checking. There his records are placed in the numerical and alphabetical files and a borrower's card or borrower's identification card, along with duplicate cards for the branch alphabetical and numerical files, are sent to the branch. Larger bookmobiles that are self-contained to the point where they resemble mobile branches are usually supplied with these same records. The use of most of these records in smaller bookmobiles is optional.

Sandoe [19] mentions that when deposit stations are used in connection with county library systems, borrowers are not always registered, although a notebook may be placed near the collection and new borrowers asked to register when they withdraw a book.

Where a county is supplied with library service on a contract basis with a large public library, some symbol or device is sometimes used to distinguish between the city borrowers and the county borrowers, or between those receiving library privileges as residents and those whose privileges are furnished by virtue of a contract.

Schenk has called attention to the efforts of Los Angeles and San

Bernardino counties, among others, to reduce registration records to a minimum. "The borrower signs a single application which is sent to a central agency, checked against a blacklist file, counted, and returned to the branch or station. Withdrawals are counted by subtracting the number of borrowers which were added during the same month three years before." [20]

If registration is to maintain its value, it must represent borrowers who have borrowed books within a definite period (usually three years), and it must exclude those borrowers who have moved away or who are deceased. To keep such a record, the library must provide for re-registration or renewal of borrowing privileges, either on a current, staggered basis, or by establishing arbitrary dates when registration expires and new cards are issued.

With continuous registration, the borrowers' cards expire on a day-to-day basis—usually three years from the date of issue. For this purpose a block of numbers is usually assigned to a definite period of time and all borrowers holding those numbers would re-register during that time. This method of re-registration has the advantage of being continuous and affords a convenient means of distributing the work load.

One method of registration illustrates the continuous system and, in addition, has a device whereby the borrower's number conveys a warning of the expiration date.[21] In this system, the cards are numbered successively through one year. The first numeral indicates the year of expiration and the second is the borrower's number. At the start of a new year a new prefix number is used. This helps clear the files automatically every three years.

Borrower's Name	*Registration Date*	*Card Number*	*Expiration Date*
A	January, 1953	6-1	January, 1956
B	January, 1953	6-2	January, 1956
C	April, 1953	6-26	April, 1956
D	December, 1953	6-336	December, 1956
E	January, 1954	7-1	January, 1957
F	January, 1954	7-2	January, 1957

In smaller libraries, re-registration is often done at stated periods, rather like the registration for classes in a university. An arbitrary period is set aside and all borrowers are asked to re-register at this time.

With transaction charging, annual or quarterly re-registration is preferable, since there is no numerical key to the expiration dates.

STATISTICS

The registration records of a library generally provide the following information:

1. The number of registered borrowers.
2. The number of borrowers registered at the various service points in the library system.
3. Separate totals for:
   a. Juvenile borrowers
   b. Youth borrowers
   c. Adult borrowers
   d. Subscription borrowers
   e. Re-registered borrowers (in any category)

Registration applications are sent to central registration daily. A monthly compilation is made, which, in turn, is used in making the library's reports.

Other records, pertaining to registration, that may be kept are:

1. Transfers from juvenile to adult department.
2. Transfer of borrowers from one branch to another.
3. The number of temporary borrowers' cards issued.
4. The number of nonresident borrowers registered.

Registration figures will not be of as much interest to the librarian of a college or university library as will figures on how much the students are using the library. Statistics for these purposes may be obtained from circulation figures or by counting attendance.

XIX. Circulation Operations: Loans

REGISTRATION enables the patron to take advantage of the privileges of the library. The form of registration is directly influenced by the type of circulation system. Circulation is the activity of certain types of libraries whereby library materials are loaned to borrowers and records are kept of these loans. "Of all library activities," wrote Berelson recently, "the circulation of books for home use represents by far the major public service provided by the American public library." [1] A study of thirty-seven public libraries by Baldwin and Marcus [2] revealed that 29.5 percent of the staff time was allocated for circulation work. In addition, 17.8 percent of staff time was devoted to the care of the collection, which includes the shelving of books, getting books from the shelves, keeping shelves in order, preparing periodicals for use, mending library materials, discarding materials, and maintaining contacts with the bindery. These duties are usually the responsibility of the circulation department, since this activity generally involves more than the control of the charging and discharging of library materials. The introduction of work simplification programs, including transaction charging, has been designed to reduce the amount of professional and clerical time spent on circulation operations.

In order to provide maximum service and to protect property, it has been deemed essential that the librarian or the custodian of the library materials have some method of keeping an accurate record of these materials when they are withdrawn from their assigned places in the library. Some librarians, particularly those in academic libraries, must be in a position to know which materials are on loan, when they are due back in the library, and who is responsible for them while they are out of the library. To answer these questions, the librarian generally keeps one or more of the following records:

1. *Time Record.* This record (frequently called the "date due" file) shows when the books are to be returned. This record is necessary so that materials for which the loan period has expired or, in other words, which are overdue, may be recalled so that they can be made available to other users. It is claimed that this record is of greater use in a public library, where demand may exceed the supply, than it is in a college or university library, where the demand for certain materials can be more easily anticipated and the supply regulated accordingly.

2. *Book Record.* The book record serves to show who has a particular item. In practice, this is often combined with the time record in order to provide a complete check of items.

3. *Reader's (or Borrower's) Record.* A record which is sometimes used to indicate the number of books a borrower has out at one time is known as the reader's record.

CHARGING SYSTEMS

The urge to experiment and develop has been especially apparent in the matter of charging systems. Melvil Dewey [3] may have explained it when he observed, "There is nothing in library economy that influences the opinion of the borrowers as to the management so much as the system of issuing and charging books. This is the one thing that every reader has to do with on every visit." Besides the impression which the charging system makes on the public, it was found by Baldwin and Marcus [4] that the average time required for charging and discharging a single book was 2.1 minutes and the average cost was 1.8 cents. Therefore the elements of time and cost also must be considered as possible reasons for librarians to seek to modify charging systems.

The earlier charging systems may be divided roughly into five groups in the order of their development: ledger systems, dummy systems, indicator systems, temporary slip systems, and the permanent slip or card system.

LEDGER SYSTEM. The original method of charging for a volume borrowed was a daily record of transactions called a day book. The difficulty of searching through this type of book for a single entry led to the use of a ledger wherein accounts were kept under the borrower's name. The pages of the ledger were numbered and the page number became, in effect, the registration number of the borrower. A book was charged by noting its call number and the issue date under the borrower's name. A line through this entry served to discharge the book upon its return to the library.

DUMMY SYSTEM. Small libraries sometimes used a dummy book with the borrower's name on the spine. The dummy was maintained in an alphabetical file and was used as a substitute for the book on the shelves when the book was withdrawn for use. The call number and the date of issue were written on the cover of the dummy. A variant of this method is the use of a duplicate call slip or card, which is left on the shelves in place of the book when the latter is in use. The slip is destroyed when the volume is returned.

INDICATOR SYSTEM. A large wooden frame was used, which contained many pigeonholes in which could be inserted blocks, pegs, or cardboard slips representing books in the library. Each end of the insert had a call number of the book; one end had a blue background and the other red. The public was able to look at this indicator for their book and if the red side of the insert showed, they knew the book had not been charged out. The actual charging was done by means of a ledger. Libraries of this period were of the closed-shelf variety.

TEMPORARY SLIP SYSTEM. Because the ledger system was inflexible, many libraries adopted a temporary slip system. The slips were used to keep an account with the reader just as was done with the pages of the ledger. Some variations which were introduced here find a counterpart in present-day systems. For example, in many libraries a slip was made out by the borrower and on it were listed the borrower's permanent registration number, the call number of the book or the author and title, and the date of issue. These slips were arranged at the loan desk in one of three ways; by date (this forms the equivalent of the day book and there is an advantage over the day book in that the slips may be subarranged by call number or by borrower's number); by borrower's name or number; or by call number. A book was discharged by destroying the slip when the book was returned.

PERMANENT SLIP SYSTEM. The next step in the development of charging systems was the permanent slip or card system. The first type of card used seems to have been the book card, where each book had its own card. This system can be viewed as a development of the dummy system except that the book is represented by a card instead of by the borrower's dummy, and a trip to the shelves is eliminated by keeping the card at the loan desk.

The use of a permanent book card for each book brought the book pocket into use. In larger libraries the problem of increasing reader patronage brought about the use of an identification card which soon became amalgamated into the record system of the loan desk as a borrower's or reader's card. Thus the borrower's card records the call number of the book and the date of issue, while the book card has the borrower's number and date of issue. This is the beginning of the two-card system, an important step in the evolution of the charging system that is used in many libraries. This system is known as the Newark charging system.

NEWARK CHARGING SYSTEM

The Newark system is primarily a single-entry time record with an incidental book record. The essential components are: borrower's card, book card, book pocket, and date slip.

Charging a book under this system involves a series of definite steps. The borrower presents to the loan desk a borrower's card containing name, address, and registration number, and an item of circulating library material that he wishes to withdraw. The desk assistant removes the book card from the book pocket. This card will represent the book in the library after it has been withdrawn, and will give the author, title, copy number, and call number of the book. Special symbols are sometimes used to indicate the period of time the book may be loaned, or a type of book, such as a juvenile or young adult's book.

The other steps, in usual sequence, include the following: stamping the date when the book is due in one of the left-hand columns of the book card; writing in pencil the borrower's number opposite the date due in one of the right-hand columns of the book card; stamping on the borrower's card the date when the book is due; stamping the date due on the date slip that is pasted opposite the book pocket in the book; inserting the borrower's card in the book pocket, after which the borrower is free to leave the circulation desk. The book card goes into a file which is kept at the circulation desk, usually arranged by date, and within this date by call number (except for fiction which may be filed alphabetically by author).

WHAT DO THE RECORDS SHOW AT THIS POINT IN THE PROCEDURE? The records in the library files will answer questions concerning the books that are loaned on a given date, the readers who are in possession of the volumes that are not in the library, and which books may be expected back in the library on any given date. The records of the transaction that are in possession of the borrower are his borrower's card and the date slip. The former shows how many books he has charged out and when these books are due. The date slip in each book indicates when that particular book is to be returned.

The circulation of a book is not finished when the book card is filed. To complete the cycle, a book must be returned. Discharging a book is fairly simple. The borrower brings the book to that section of the loan desk that is devoted to book returns. The desk assistant, after opening the book to the date due slip to see when the book is due, searches the file under that date for the book card. When the book card is found, it is compared with the information that is on the book pocket with respect to call number, copy number, and author and title. When the book card is found to be the correct one for that book, the card is returned to the book pocket.

The borrower's card is taken from the book pocket, is stamped with the date of return in one of the right-hand columns, and is then returned to the borrower. The date of return which has canceled out the date due serves as a receipt to the borrower for the return of the book. The book is then set aside until such time as it can be returned to the shelves.

Because many of the methods of charging in use today in American libraries are based upon the Newark system, it may prove useful to examine the other operations involved. These operations are found in some form in the other methods, and often the departure from the Newark system lies only in a single point.

GROUP RESERVES. In college and universities, instructors will request that certain books be reserved for class use. In a public library, this is paralleled by adult education group activities. In response to such requests, the desk assistant collects the specified books from the shelves. The book cards are removed from the volumes, charged to reserve, and filed by call number in the circulation file. A reserve slip is inserted in the book as a substitute for the regular book card during the period of reserve. The reserve books are then shelved in a special location and when a reader requests one of these for use in the library, the reserve book card is withdrawn and filed behind a time guide.

If reserve books are loaned overnight, the date slip and the book card are stamped as being due the next day. Sometimes the hour due is recorded, but overnight loans are generally due back in the library during the first hour of opening the following day.

INDIVIDUAL RESERVES. The desk assistant may note a patron's request for a book that is currently charged out by having the borrower fill out a postal card containing the author and title of the book, as well as the borrower's name and address, or by filling out a reserve slip, or by writing the borrower's name on the book card. An indicator (often in the form of a colored slip) is attached to the book card to indicate that there is a reserve against this particular book.

When the book is returned to the library, the postal card or reserve slips are found in the special file where they have been filed under author and title. More than one reserve for a given book would mean that a further arrangement by date (date when the respective reserves were made) would be necessary. The borrower's name is placed in the book, and the book is placed on the "books held shelf" for a specified length of time. If a postal card has been filled out, it is then mailed to the borrower. If a reserve slip or the borrower's name on the book card is used (more common in school and college libraries than in public libraries), notification is sent to the borrower's home room or placed in the student's mailbox. The book is circulated in the regular manner if the borrower calls for it within a stipulated length of time. A book not called for during this holding period is allocated to the next person on the reserve list or is sent to the shelves if there are no further reserves on it.

With transaction charging, a list must be maintained of those books for which reserves have been placed. As volumes are returned to the library, they are checked against this list, before reshelving, so that the reader can be notified that the volume he desired is now available.

RENEWAL. A renewal is an extension of the loan period of a book. Books may be renewed in one of three ways: (1) with the book and the borrower's card; (2) without the book; or (3) without the book and borrower's card, on personal, mail, or telephone request.

In the first type of renewal, the borrower presents both the book and his borrower's card. The book card held by the library is removed from the file, and the borrower's card, the book card, and the date slip are stamped for a new charge period.

In a renewal without the book, the book card must be traced in the files under the date indicated on the borrower's card. The borrower must give the author and title as accurately as possible and, if need be, the call number may be obtained from the card catalog in order to find the book card. The book card and borrower's card are then stamped for a new charge period. Some method of filing the renewed book card must be used in order that it may be traced from the date due slip (which, in this case, has not been stamped with the new date due) when the book is returned. For this, there may be a special renewal file, an arrangement under the new date with a reference to the original date, or an arrangement under the original date. The first method, even though it means questioning the borrower about particulars concerning the book, seems to eliminate some of the searching necessary when the book card is removed from the date file corresponding to the original date stamped on the date slip. Renewals based upon mail or personal requests also may be handled in this way.

The telephone renewal request requires a slightly different technique because in a busy library it is undesirable to keep the telephone out of service in order to complete the searching necessary to renew a book. The simplest method is probably to write the information on a slip of paper and complete the renewal later. Not all libraries will honor a request for renewal by telephone.

OVERDUES. The date file is searched regularly for books which are overdue. The book cards for these are withdrawn from the file. A search is generally made for the books on the return shelf and on the "snag" shelf, and if there is any doubt as to whether the book may have been returned a check should be made on the regular shelves. If the books are not found, overdue notices are written and mailed. It will be necessary to look in the registration files for the name and address of the person in order to send the notice. The book cards are filed in the renewal file and small colored clips are attached to cards to indicate that overdue notices have been sent.

MODIFICATIONS OF THE NEWARK SYSTEM

IDENTIFICATION CARD. In an effort to eliminate one step in the Newark system an identification card is used instead of the borrower's card. When a book is charged, discharged, or renewed, the borrower's card does not have to be stamped. The disadvantages of the modification are that the borrower has no record of the number of books he has out, the library has no way of knowing or controlling the number of books held by a borrower, and the borrower has no receipt in the form of a stamped date in the return column of his borrower's card when he has returned a book.

DETROIT SELF-CHARGING METHOD. The borrower writes his number on the book card and passes the borrower's card and book to the desk assistant who stamps all three and files the book card in the usual way. This attempt to speed the charging process does not eliminate one disadvantage of the Newark system, namely the danger of copying the wrong number onto the book card.

OTHER SELF-CHARGING METHODS. A further modification of the self-charging system in a college library works as follows:[5] Four divided boxes are placed on the circulation desk. The boxes are for fourteen-day books, seven-day books, three-day books, and for books to be used in reading rooms. The patron signs the book card and places it in the appropriate box. From the rear of the same box he removes a prestamped date-due slip and places it in the book pocket. At the end of the day the cards are removed from the first three boxes, arranged by call number, and placed in the date file behind date guides that correspond to the date the book is due. This method would seem to overcome the disadvantage inherent in the Newark system when a patron lacks his borrower's card when he wishes to withdraw a book.

Another method of self-charging, designed to eliminate the use of borrowers' cards, is the use of a visible registration index of borrowers' signatures.[6] The borrower signs his name to the book card and hands it to the desk assistant who verifies the signature with the visible index and then stamps the date due and files it in the usual way. This does not eliminate the need for stamping the date due on the date-due slips of the book. This method might be improved by having the patron stamp the date slip with the date due or by having the patron insert a prestamped date card into the book pocket as he hands the book card to the desk assistant.

A method of self-charging used in the children's department of the Edmonton Public Library requires the children to write their own registration numbers on the book card.[7] The desk assistant removes the book card, stamps the borrower's card, and slips a prestamped date-due card in the book pocket with the borrower's card.

A number of the devices being used today in libraries, especially in college and university libraries, are not actually new, but rather are adaptations of the old temporary slip system. To this system has been added the concept of self-charging. That is, by the use of printed signs the borrower is directed to perform certain steps in the process of charging a book. This introduction of so-called "self-charging" methods has simplified some circulation operations from the point of view of the librarian, but it must be borne in mind that self-charging has not changed any basic principles. It means only that the patron has assumed some part of what traditionally has been the librarian's work. The extent to which borrowers will accept this depends largely on the local situation.

By the use of a McBee Keysort card, printed as a call ("C") slip, a college library combined the time record and the book record on just this one card.[8] The C slip is filled out by the patron and is stamped by the desk assistant as is the date slip in the book. Before the C slip is filed, one of the holes on the side of the card is notched by a punch according to a prearranged schedule which lists the holes corresponding to the dates due. The C slip or Keysort card is filed by call number in the circulation file. Overdues are found by running a sorting needle through the appropriate date holes on the card. All cards representing books that are overdue on the given date will fall off the needle and out of the group because that particular date hole had been notched or cut out when the book was withdrawn. This is a rapid process and the circulation staff at Harvard has been able to sort from 60,000 to 90,000 cards per hour. Reserves are indicated by stapling a call slip to the back of the charge card. A renewal is made by stamping a new date on the charge card and by stapling a blank Keysort card to the back of the charge card in order to cancel the notch representing the expiration-of-the-loan date. A new notch is made through both cards.

FURTHER ATTEMPTS TO SIMPLIFY CIRCULATION OPERATIONS

Librarians have exercised considerable ingenuity in devising circulation systems which do not require expensive equipment. Basically, the problem is to have one file tell what books are charged out, to whom they are charged, and when they are overdue.

COLOR KEY AND TAB SYSTEMS. A system involving a color key has been placed in use at the University of Pennsylvania.[9] The call slips are filled in by the students and are stamped by the desk assistant to fall due on a Monday or a Thursday, one week, two weeks, or one month from the day of withdrawal. The call slips are sorted according to the loan period and small areas of the slips are painted in predetermined positions with colored ink. The colored portions of the slips (which are filed by call number) constitute a visible date-due record. Thirteen positions on the card are employed, and four different colors are used, thus giving a coverage of fifty-two dates.

Steel signal tabs have been used in a college library.[10] The library has open shelves and the books contain both book pockets and book cards. A single record is maintained by filing the student-signed book card by class number and indicating the date due by means of small colored slips which extend one eighth of an inch beyond the card. This library added another step to the self-charging method by having the students stamp both the book card and the date-due slip. The loan period of the library was for two weeks and overdue notices were sent semiweekly. At least one university library employs a system which uses colored Scotch tape instead of clips or colored ink.[11]

Date tabs represent another circulation device in a college library.[12] The essential feature is the use of a tab which extends above the top of the 3″ x 5″ combination call slip and book card. The tabs are numbered from 1 to 31 and fall into six positions across the top of the cards. The one circulation file, arranged by classification, serves as a date-due file. There is some overlapping of numbers: for example, 1, 7, 13, 19, 25, and 31 have the same location on the left-hand side of the card. Actually, because most charges clear every two weeks, there are seldom more than three of these overlapping dates in the file at the same time. Overdues are withdrawn by checking the column in which a given date appears.

GAYLORD ELECTRIC-AUTOMATIC BOOK CHARGING MACHINE. Although the method of charging is changed slightly because of the equipment used with the Gaylord charging machine, its use does not involve any change in the basic Newark circulation system. The machine is rented to libraries by the manufacturer.

Every registered borrower is issued either an identification card or a borrower's card. The borrower's card has space for recording the date for every book charged, while the identification card does not; otherwise they are identical and carry the name, address, and registration number of the borrower and the expiration date of the card. The borrower presents his card to the desk assistant together with the book that he wishes to withdraw.

The card, which has an embossed metal number plate attached to it (the same as the printed number on the front of the card), is inserted in an open vertical slot in the top of the charging machine. The book card, taken from the pocket of the volume that the patron wishes to use, is then inserted in a curved chute in the top of the machine. Automatically the machine prints the date (which has been set for the desired loan period by means of a small knob) and the borrower's number on the book card. At the same time a corner on one side is clipped from the book card so that the next time it is used the card will be inserted a little farther into the chute. In this way, the next charge will automatically be printed just below the previous one.

The borrower is given back his card, and the book card is filed under date. A date card printed with the same date as the book card is slipped into the book pocket for the borrower's information. This date card replaces the date slip. It fits into the same curved chute as the book card, so both are registered with the same date. Since the borrower's number is not required, these cards can be predated for different loan periods and prepared before books are charged.

DICKMAN BOOK CHARGING MACHINE. This is a mechanical stamping machine which works on the principle of a hand stapler. Except for the operation of the machine, the system is exactly as described for the Gaylord system. The borrower's card is inserted in a slot on the right-hand side of the machine and the book card is placed on a platform. The knob of the machine is depressed and the book card is stamped with the date and the borrower's number.

TRANSACTION CHARGING SYSTEMS

PHOTOGRAPHIC CHARGING

Two of the disadvantages attributed to the Newark system are the danger of mistakes in copying the borrower's number on the book card and the time involved in stamping. In order to avoid copying mistakes and to minimize the time spent in these operations as well as to gain other advantages in simplified operations, a system known as transaction charging has been developed.

In 1941, Ralph Shaw [13] announced that a method of photographic charging had been in use at the Gary Public Library for about a year. The idea of using a camera was not an unusual one, since as Shaw observed, this was an era of mechanization and no new charging systems had been developed. The more spectacular efforts had been the introduction of machine operations for manual manipulation in the basic Newark system. Shaw, however, did introduce a new device in charging systems—the use of a transaction number. Each record of a book borrowed is given a serial number which is used to connect all of the elements of the charging process.

A borrower presents a book to the charging desk, where the assistant removes the book card from the pocket and places it in the proper location to be photographed. The borrower's identification card is placed beside it, together with a predated and prenumbered date-due card. This number on the date-due card is the transaction number. The exposure button is pressed, thus making a complete photographic record of the transaction number, the book card, and the borrower's identification card. When the book is returned, the assistant removes the borrower's card and returns it to him, and the date-due card is placed in the file. The book card remains in the volume, which is then ready to be shelved or to be borrowed again. At regular intervals, the files of accumulated date-due cards are checked and missing transaction numbers noted. These numbers are searched in the film record, which provides the information necessary for overdue book notices. The transaction number cards may be devised so that they can be used repeatedly.

The fundamental difference between this and the basic Newark system is the use of the transaction number for each withdrawal. The system may also modify other features of the Newark system: (a) the substitution of a flexible means of borrower's identification in the form of a driver's license or Social Security card for the conventional borrower's card or library identification card; (b) the possible elimination of the book card if author, title, call number, and copy number of the book can be photographed together; (c) the use of a camera instead of a mechanical or electrical charging machine; (d) the elimination of the charge file by call number, or by author and title under date due, while the book is out of the library; (e) the numerical filing of the serially numbered date-due cards after the book is returned to the library; (f) the missing numbers which represent books that are overdue, and the photographic record which must be checked to find out who has these books.

The advantages of the operation are: (a) speed of charging and discharging books; (b) returned books are available immediately for reissue; (c) the numerical registration file is done away with; (d) it is easier to count circulation, since the first and last numbers on the date-due cards issued for that day indicate the amount of circulation; (e) reduction of error; (f) reduction of staff necessary to man the circulation desk; and (g) there is a permanent record on film of what is borrowed.

Problems involved in photographic charging include: (a) eyestrain which may result from reading film, (b) difficulty in making a classified circulation count, (c) difficulty in handling reserves and renewals, (d) the reader has no receipt to show that his book has been returned, and (e) to find who is responsible for books overdue it is necessary to run through the whole film for the period in question. Many library systems have introduced photographic charging and regard the time-saving and public relations factors as definite advantages. Photographic charging machines generally in use are the Recordak Book Charging System and the Remington Rand Photocharger.

OTHER TRANSACTION CHARGING SYSTEMS

AUDIO-CHARGING. An innovation at the St. Louis County Library [14] and at the Charlotte Public Library [15] that is similar to the photocharging method, in all respects but one, is the audio-charging system. Here a sound-recording medium—disc, cylinder, tape, or wire—is used to record the charge. This method was employed because it was found that reading the photographic charging record was causing eyestrain, with a consequent loss of personnel. The procedure for audio-charging is the same as for photographic charging except that the date due and the first and last transaction numbers are written or marked on the record medium. A book is charged by having the desk assistant dictate the transaction number, author and title, name and address of the borrower, and telephone number of the borrower. The Charlotte Public Library found that patrons objected to having the titles of their books read aloud, and a system of dictating the accession number of the book was used instead. This was found to be faster. No processing is necessary for the recording medium, and unlike film, most records may be reprocessed and used over again.

The Erie County Public Library [16] found that they were able to record up to 300 charges an hour by using a photographic charging machine in their bookmobile. The bookmobile of the St. Louis County Library [17] found the audio-charging method speedy enough to circulate 700 books in five hours.

INTERNATIONAL BUSINESS MACHINES. The use of IBM machines in the loan of books by libraries was started as a joint effort of the International Business Machines Corporation and the Montclair Public Library.[18] This system reduces the time and effort involved in record keeping to a minimum, through automatic recording of the transaction and automatic sorting of IBM cards.

The borrower presents to the desk assistant a filled-in C slip along with his borrower's identification card. The C slip differs from the C slips discussed previously in that the call number of the book is not required. Only author, title and the borrower's name and address are included. The desk assistant inserts the C slip in an IBM

Stamp Machine. This machine automatically prints the date of withdrawal, transaction number, and branch or charging station identification. A prepunched and prenumbered IBM Transaction Control Card, containing this information in a printed form and in a punched record, is inserted in the book pocket. These cards may be reused until they are worn out. The C slip is then filed; filing is done according to numerical sequence. The C slips which have accumulated in numerical sequence are held as a group by date. When the book is returned the IBM Transaction Control Card is withdrawn from the book pocket and dropped, without regard to order, into a box. The book is then ready again for circulation. The collected IBM Control Cards are sorted on an electric sorting machine and the cards that are missing from the numerical sequence represent overdue books. It is necessary to check the missing transaction numbers in the C-slip file in order to obtain the author, title, and borrower's name and address for the preparation of overdue notices.[19]

The transaction card is common to the IBM system, the photocharging system, and the new audio-charging method.

Not all libraries can afford IBM machinery or even the equipment necessary to set up a photocharging or audio-charging system. The medium-sized public library of Mill Valley, California,[20] with an average circulation of 200 books a day, liked the IBM idea but could not afford the equipment. There resulted the following modification of the operation: (a) a numbering machine is substituted for the IBM Time Stamp; (b) a date slip is pasted in the book; (c) the C slip is designed on the model of the McBee Keysort rather than the IBM card, and therefore the sorting and arranging of the C slips (transaction control cards) can be done with a needle instead of an electric punched-card sorting machine; (d) borrowers' registration or identification cards are eliminated by requiring the borrower to sign a statement on the C slip guaranteeing the return of the specific book; and (e) C slips are used to see how many patrons use the library during a given period. For administrative purposes, this figure has probably more significance than merely knowing the number of registered borrowers.

In his study of the use of IBM in libraries, Blasingame [21] found that circulation applications were among the most prominent. His discussion of a college library's use of an IBM charging system for the main library desk (annual circulation, slightly over 350,000) is valuable for a detailed explanation of a comprehensive operation.

COLOR SORTING (SELF-CHARGING). The Wayne County Library [22] employs the transaction procedure. Because it requires no mechanical equipment it is an example of what can be done to improve the circulation routine at slight expense. This system requires the use of a C slip and a transaction card. The important point is that the transaction cards are obtained in six serially numbered decks, each deck a different color. The patron fills in both sides of the C slip. Name and address are on one side and the transaction number and space for four authors and titles on the reverse side. The desk assistant inserts a predated and prenumbered transaction card in the book pocket. The number on this card corresponds to the number on the C slip. When the book is returned, the transaction card is removed. The color of the card will automatically tell whether the book is overdue. The transaction cards are sorted by color for date due and then the particular color group is arranged numerically. A note is made of the missing transaction numbers. The C slips bearing the numbers corresponding to the missing transaction (overdue) numbers are removed and the information there is used to prepare overdue notices.

CIRCULATION (ACCESSION) NUMBER. A different approach to the use of a transaction number is employed at Harvard's Lamont Library.[23] The use of a circulation number is designed to give better service to students because books may be charged out at a number of different points in the library. Each book is assigned a circulation number. This number appears on the book pocket, on the verso of the title page, and on the shelf list (it is actually an accession number). The total number of books in the library is restricted, so that numbers from 1 to 29,999 are assigned to the reserve book collection and the remainder, 30,000 to 99,999, are in the general collection. The student fills out a C slip. The circulation number is written on this slip. The attendants responsible for checking write the circulation number on a predated date-due card which is placed in the book pocket. The C slips are arranged numerically by circulation number under date due. When a book is returned the date-due slip is removed and the book is shelved. The date-due slip, which contains the date due and the circulation number, is used to cancel the C slip which has been filed by that arrangement.

MARGINAL PUNCHED CARDS. College and university libraries introduced the marginal punched card in circulation more than fifteen years ago.[24] McGaw,[25] in his recent study, has assembled a basic body of information concerning the application of marginal punched cards to library operations. The second section of his report, dealing with circulation, includes discussion of such topics as the use of marginal punched cards as call cards, one-a-week due dates, a variant routine for sorting overdues, the use of clips to supplement Keysort, description of call cards, renewals, personal reserves, the master file, room-use charges, carrell charges, location charges, tracing routines, statistics on library use, library registration card, student identification numbers, faculty loans, elimination of book cards and pockets, use of call cards in open-stack libraries, handwritten call numbers, the use of marginal punched cards as book cards, the use of marginal punched charging pockets, and various problems in the use of punched cards in the reserve book room. The discussion by McGaw is especially useful, since he reports on correspondence with a number of librarians who have had experience with the marginal punched cards.

xx. Circulation: Other Operations and Records

WHAT to lend to patrons and for what period of time are problems which are faced by staff members of free circulation departments. Three mutually interdependent factors are the period of loan, the policy on renewals, and the book supply and demand.

The period of loan is determined largely by the size of the library's collection and the number of active borrowers. A library with a small collection and many active patrons will need to use a shorter loan period if the patrons are to receive an equitable service.

Such circumstances also will affect the renewal policy of the library and require some limit on the number and length of renewals that are granted. The renewal policy is influenced by the period of loan which is in effect, in that when books are loaned for fairly lengthy periods of a month or more, it will rarely be necessary for patrons to renew their books. Shorter loan periods are quite likely to bring increased requests for renewals.

LOAN PERIOD

World War II gave impetus to the establishment of a twenty-eight-day loan period in many libraries, because of the shortage of staff. Libraries that have changed from loan periods of three, seven, and fourteen days find that the twenty-eight-day period has several effects: clerical work is lessened, overdues are cut down, and renewals are minimized. Patrons like it because they are spared the inconvenience of having to renew a book. Circulation, however, may tend to decrease.[1]

The period of loan in force in a library is indicated to both the borrower and the circulation staff by the use of colored date-due cards or by indicating the date by rubber stamp. The use of a rubber date stamp shows the date involved in the transaction. This shows the borrower at a glance when his book is due, and allows the circulation staff to renew books and to compute the amount of fine on overdue books with relative ease.

As an alternative, the card may be stamped with the date of issue. Here one stamp serves for both charging and discharging books, and all book cards representing books charged during the day are filed behind the date guide for that day. When book cards are filed in this way, and materials are loaned for varying periods, it will be necessary to indicate the varying periods of loan by means of colored book cards or some similar device. It also is difficult for the borrower to tell immediately when his material is due.

NUMBER OF BOOKS LOANED

Public libraries have often decided it was necessary to limit the number of books that could be withdrawn on one card because borrowers might abuse the privilege of withdrawing books and the work of the loan desk would be unduly increased. However, as an example of the current trend in libraries, the Gary Public Library [2] formerly limited to four the number of books that could be borrowed on one card. In an effort to determine whether or not the imposed limit was justified, the limit was lifted, and a record kept of books taken by each borrower for a two-month period. It was found that the average number of books withdrawn per borrower was less than four; that the median was two and one-half, and that less than one percent of the borrowers withdrew five or more books. As a result, the limit was discontinued. Obviously, the only way to control the number of volumes is through the borrower's card.

RENTAL COLLECTIONS

PUBLIC LIBRARIES. In some public libraries, rental collections are referred to as the "pay duplicate system." In others, some new fiction is purchased for rental only. This is a means of attempting to keep up with the popular demand for current titles, and was tried early in the St. Louis Public Library.[3] Librarians are hesitant about spending public money for duplicates of books that will soon be superseded in popularity. The money received from rental fees of this collection is usually applied to its maintenance. When the demand for titles has waned, the books are usually transferred to the regular shelves.

In charging books of the rental collection it is necessary to remember two points: (a) the amount of fee to be charged is determined by the length of the loan; and (b) to complete the charging process it is necessary that the borrower not only return the book but also pay the necessary fee. The sum paid by the borrower is often entered on the book card and may serve for future guidance purposes. For example, a book by a given author may be expected to more than pay its way in the collection, whereas books by other authors may result in a financial loss.

COLLEGE AND UNIVERSITY LIBRARIES. In university libraries the rental collection was first used as a means of supplementing the reserve book collection. The first reference to the use of this service on a sizable scale is at the University of California in 1929.[4] There the collection included books necessary for collateral reading, as well as some texts. The collection was composed of all duplicate copies in the library in excess of three and was shelved in a separate stack and serviced by a separate circulation desk which worked in connection with the reserve book desk. The fee charged was three cents a day, and coupons purchased from the business office were used instead of cash in order not to complicate the procedure and the records.

A different form of lending library was started at Columbia University[5] in 1940 in order to make available for circulation on the day of publication the latest nontechnical books. This collection is maintained at about 3,000 volumes, about half of which are nonfiction. The service is not designed to help solve the reserve book problem, but was a university librarian's method of supplying the demands for current popular books without added expense to the university. The record of this service is limited to a book card signed at the time a volume is charged out. Identification of the borrower is required.

OVERDUES AND FINES

PUBLIC LIBRARIES. Fines are imposed in most public libraries for books or library materials kept by borrowers past the date due. Librarians usually regard fines primarily as a penalty for interfering with the rights of others. In many cases, fines automatically revert to the financial authority on which the library depends.

Fines are considered by some librarians as a source of income, and in the larger libraries may amount to several thousands of dollars annually. There is no standard fine in use in public libraries, but the tendency is to charge between two and five cents per volume per day overdue. The fine for reserve books and short loan books is usually greater. The custom is not to levy fines for holidays and Sundays, or days that the library is not open. Some libraries have an established maximum fine, but, in general, the cost of the book and the demand for the book determine the maximum fine to be charged. The amount charged may depend upon the ability of the delinquent borrowers to pay, in that the fines imposed upon juvenile borrowers tend to be less than for adults. Some libraries do not impose fines on overdue children's books, and other libraries remit the fines at stated intervals.

COLLEGE AND UNIVERSITY LIBRARIES. In an effort to see if a better method of insuring the return of books could be found, Patterson and Berthold [6] instituted a symposium by mail on this subject with a questionnaire to twenty-three college and university libraries, all of which charged fines.

Forty-eight percent of the libraries reported a fine of five cents a day for circulating books, while 24 percent were found to employ a fine of two cents a day. One library, in an effort to reduce the staff time necessary to administer the collection of fines, has established a system whereby the amount of the fine is reduced if the fines are paid when the books are returned. If they are not paid at the time the books are returned, the standard fee is charged.

A few libraries have eliminated fines for general circulating books. Reports indicate that the action has not resulted in any disturbing effects upon the service of the libraries.

Reserve book fines are usually higher than for ordinary circulating books. Twenty-four percent of the libraries charge twenty-five cents for the first hour overdue and five cents for each additional hour. The highest amount reported was fifty cents for the first hour with rates of five cents, ten cents and twenty-five cents for additional hours. The purpose of reserve book collections is to make books available to all students and the heavier fine is imposed to insure this.

Many college and university libraries, at the end of an academic period such as a semester, notify the college or university administration of students owing fines or other charges, and the administration will then withhold academic credit until the indebtedness is cleared from the records.

RESERVE BOOK SYSTEM IN COLLEGE AND UNIVERSITY LIBRARIES

The reserve book system has developed in college and university libraries, not because librarians desire it, but because the educational practice of "required reading" obliges the librarian to establish some form of control of these books in order to give effective service. Munthe, looking at procedures in American college and university libraries, noted that "over 90 per cent of all library loans are 'required reading,' a mystical concept as far as European librarians are concerned." [7]

Smaller libraries may keep their reserve books near the circulation desk, but the larger libraries require one or more special rooms for this purpose. In a recent study of thirty-two college and university reserve rooms, Lansberg [8] has indicated three standard methods of handling the reserve problem:

1. The closed shelf system, where the reserve books are kept behind a desk and are loaned to the students upon request for a limited period of two hours, with the privilege of an overnight loan to early applicants. This system has the disadvantage of preventing the

student from browsing, but it enables the library staff to exercise an equitable control over books that are in constant demand.

2. The open shelf system, where the reserve books are placed where the students have access to them. It had been thought that such an arrangement would work to the advantage of selfish students who would withdraw more than they needed and thus deprive others. The experiment conducted at the Library of Teachers College, Columbia University, in 1930 indicated that its 13,000 volumes of reserve books could be transferred from closed to open shelves without any great harm to the library or the students.

3. The third is a combination of open and closed shelves. The books in greatest demand are circulated from closed shelves and the others are placed on open shelves. Lansberg reported this to be the most popular method employed in the libraries in his study. Helm [9] lists various factors which appear to determine how many copies of a reserve book are needed by a library, such as the number of students in a class, the number of pages to be read, the number of pages the average college student will read per hour, the number of hours the library is open per day, the length of time allowed for the reading assignment, and the number of titles on the list of readings.

Lansberg found that for heavily used books nearly half of the libraries provided one copy for every ten students. The next nearest figure used by any number of libraries was one copy for six to eight students. The Yale library is reported to provide only two copies of any one edition and if additional copies are needed they must be furnished by the department making the assignment.

Reserve books are often shelved by teaching departments and further subdivided alphabetically by author under the course. Harvard's Lamont Library has 22,000 items on reserve with most of the reserves on open shelves, arranged alphabetically by author under broad subject classifications.

INTERLIBRARY LOANS

Even the largest library can never hope, and usually never intends, to have everything which its clientele may desire. A library serves the majority of its patrons with the majority of what those patrons want and need; limitations due to size, specialization in subject matter, rarity of certain items, cost of certain materials, to name only a few, are usual in libraries and are accepted by librarians and readers alike. Yet the librarians' concept of service as complete as possible makes it essential that a library be able to provide for serious use by its patrons material which the library itself does not possess. The photographic processes discussed elsewhere in this volume have evolved primarily in an attempt to solve this problem of access to documentation more vast than any one library can provide. But the process of interlibrary loan is not only the oldest but the most frequently used method of access to books and other material not immediately at hand. It is probably the earliest form of cooperation among libraries.

Reduced to its elements, interlibrary loan is not basically different from the usual loan from library to reader. In essence, all libraries which are willing to cooperate become a single library with tremendous resources, and that library seeking a particular item for one of its patrons becomes, in turn, a patron of the inclusive system. Thus, in theory, any reader can draw on the resources of any library. In practice, there are certain limitations, based on the necessity for working out in detail the technicalities of the reasonable use of an idea of such vast scope. "The purpose of interlibrary loans is to make available for research and for serious study library materials not in a given library, with due provisions made by the lending library for the rights of its primary clientele." [10]

Interlibrary loan, then, is to be used for research and serious study. It is doubtful that any two libraries, or even two librarians in the same library, will interpret this in the same manner. The Library of Congress, which in 1951–52 lent 32,000 volumes and pieces to nongovernmental libraries [11] has felt obliged to decline requests for material to be used by graduate students in the preparation of theses and dissertations, but there can be no doubt that this practice is generously interpreted and many Library of Congress loans are for this purpose. Many libraries go so far as to recognize that undergraduate students may be engaged in "serious study," but it is customary to refuse to borrow for current class assignments. Whether the study or research is being conducted within the scope of the library's institution or outside, private study, self-improvement, club programs, and similar activities which give little or no evidence of contributing to knowledge in general are usually excluded from interlibrary loan privileges.

Once the reader's eligibility has been established by whatever criteria his library may employ, the material he seeks must undergo scrutiny. The principal categories excluded, except under unusual and explained circumstances, are current fiction, current issues of periodicals, inexpensive items currently purchasable, books for class use, current books for which a recurring demand is anticipated in the borrowing library, extremely rare books, music to be used in public performance, and works difficult and expensive to pack and ship.[12] Substitution of photographic reproductions of the material desired may be mutually agreed upon and prove satisfactory for items which cannot be borrowed.

The library accepting a reader's request must then verify it. It must confirm that what is desired is actually not available locally, and if not, proceed to supply, with the reader's assistance, as complete a bibliographical citation as is possible, with an indication of the source from which the original reference was obtained. The importance of a complete and verified citation for an interlibrary loan cannot be overemphasized, and figures indicate that 55 percent of the libraries in a recent study have found unverified citations the principal obstacles to efficient loaning.[13] Some libraries do not possess the bibliographical tools necessary for verifying all requests which they may need to make, but in such cases it is essential that the citation be clearly marked "cannot verify."

The problem of where to borrow is the library's next responsibility. Major research libraries have automatically attracted an overlarge percentage of requests simply because the borrowing library, with little or no checking, could assume that the material sought would be found there. These libraries have, in general, responded by lending to the extent of their possibilities, but it is unfair to expect them to lend material much of which can be secured elsewhere. The resources of the large library are needed for the book which is truly hard to find, and the requesting library must learn to distribute its requests among other, smaller libraries which have, nevertheless, resources larger than its own.

Bibliographical centers and union catalogs, discussed earlier, offer important keys to locating sources for borrowing. Winchell's *Locating Books for Interlibrary Loan,*[14] the *Union List of Serials,*[15] and *Special Library Resources*[16] are useful as guides in placing requests intelligently and distributing them evenly. The librarian responsible for interlibrary loans needs to be familiar with the collections in his own region, particularly those which may have special interest for his clientele, and should use their resources instead of promptly asking the Library of Congress, the New York Public Library, or a large university library.

"Interlibrary loan service is a courtesy and a privilege, not a right."[17] The requesting library is subject to the lending policies of the library from which it has requested material. The owning library may consider the item too rare, fragile or irreplaceable, and thus not wish to lend it; it may be part of a collection which cannot leave the library; it may be an item in demand by the library's own clientele; the library may have more extensive restrictions on its lending than those suggested by the interlibrary loan *Code*. Thus, the requesting library must be prepared to have some of its requests unfilled, and may be obliged to use photographic reproduction.[18] The lending library, apart from these instances, will now send the material, if it owns it, to the borrowing library, frequently with the restriction that the item be used in the library through which the reader has made his request.

Thus, the major part of the library's work is completed, and the item is at the reader's disposition. It remains only for the borrowing library, which accepts full responsibility for the material during the loan, to return the item at the end of its period of use. Although libraries have developed their own procedures and forms for carrying on this work, the Interlibrary Loan Committee of the Association of College and Reference Libraries has recently introduced a standard multiple-unit request form.[19] The advantages of this standardization are apparent: a saving in typing and filing time, speed-up in the lending operation, and general uniformity. This form is now available from library supply firms, and its increasing use indicates that it should help to simplify procedures that heretofore have caused unnecessary complications and friction.

The borrowing library does the initial and only typing required of the four-copy, carbon-interleaved form. The first copy (white) is kept by the lending library for its records; the second copy (yellow) is returned to the borrowing library for its final record of the loan; the third copy (pink) is an "Interim Report" designed for use in case the item cannot be sent when requested or for making renewals; and the fourth copy (maize) is kept by the borrowing library, since it is a record of the date and method of return of the item.

Questions of mode of shipment (express *vs.* parcel post) and insurance (blanket, coupon, parcel post) must be considered by the librarian.[20] Adequate packing must be assured by both libraries in a loan transaction.

The costs of interlibrary loans vary considerably depending on how they are handled and whether or not they are completed. Columbia University Libraries find that it has cost them $2.70 per volume to borrow, and $1.27 to lend.[21] At present, a general study is going on to determine in detail the costs involved in interlibrary loans.[22]

The collection of fees for interlibrary loans varies from library to library. In many of the academic libraries, transportation charges, either the full sum or a flat fee, are imposed. Libraries are generally hardpressed to find appropriations which would eliminate this fee. It is also thought that the existence of the fee will discourage unnecessary borrowing.

Some public libraries in adjacent communities have made their borrowers' cards valid in any of the cooperating libraries. This reduces interlibrary lending for the libraries in the group.

RECORDS

The records of the charging system used in the library may involve one or more of the records which have already been described—the time record, book record, and the reader's record.

Another record maintained by the circulation staff is related to the collection of fees. In the smaller public library these records will involve overdue books, payment for damage, charges for lost books, rental fees, and notification fees.

The record of fines collected on overdue books is usually kept on a daily cash sheet or a notebook in which the amount of fine collected is entered, and initialed by the circulation assistant making the entry.

The record of the payment for damage to library materials is also a bookkeeping record. Most libraries have a policy of determining the charge for damage to a book which is based on the cost of replacement, the cost of repair or rebinding, and the original cost to the library. Libraries that have circulating phonograph record collections are frequently faced with this difficulty when a record is returned broken. The use of unbreakable records is likely to minimize this difficulty. The payment of any money into the library for damage to library material will require a more detailed record than the entry in the cash book. Information probably will be needed as to the payer as well as complete information about the damaged materials.

The money paid into the library for materials lost by patrons will form another record to be kept at the circulation desk. Because "lost" books are sometimes found by the borrower, it is reasonable for them then to desire a refund of the money they have paid. Many libraries keep a separate record of the money paid for lost books, because of this possibility of having to refund. There is no one treatment of the problem of refunds on lost books. One public library will refund money to patrons on the following schedule for the return of "lost" materials that have been paid for: less than one month, full price is refunded; 1–4 months, 75 percent refunded;

4–8 months, 50 percent refunded; 8–12 months, 25 percent refunded. No refund is granted after the lapse of a year. Another library charges the borrower the cost of the book with no additional amount for an overdue fine. If the book is found, the borrower is refunded the cost of the book minus the amount that would be due on a fine for an overdue book. A third library charges the price of the book less 20 percent and plus the fine for the period the book has been overdue until the date of payment. Children's books are charged only half price.

The collecting of fees for books in the rental collection involves a record which may be kept on both the cash sheet and the book card. The book card record is the more important if the library is interested in whether the books are going to pay for themselves or not. The use on the book card of a date stamp set for the issue date of the book will make for easier computations.

If the library uses postal cards to notify patrons that a book is being held on reserve for them, a fee of five cents may be charged for this card and entered in the cash record.

The above records are kept by the circulation staff only. Certain other records pertaining to registration are kept by the circulation staff in smaller libraries, but in large libraries they may be kept by a special registration section. The first three of these have been dealt with earlier: (a) alphabetical adult registration record; (b) numerical card file, if numbered borrowers' or identification cards are used; and (c) alphabetical juvenile registration record (this is often combined with the alphabetical and numerical records).

Since a fee is usually charged for the replacement of a borrower's card, a record of the fees collected may be entered in the daily cash sheet and combined with the entries for fines. Some libraries do not keep a daily cash sheet.

The fees for nonresident borrowers may be entered in the daily cash sheet, but a separate record should be kept if the number of these is very large. The fee may be entered on the nonresident borrower's application form and the applications filed in a separate section of the alphabetical registration record file.

The fee for temporary borrowers is often entered on the borrower's card and may be also entered on the daily cash sheet (if one is maintained). Because the money is sometimes refunded, a separate system of handling this money may be needed.[23]

STATISTICS

Most libraries produce some form of an annual report covering the activities of the library for the year. In many instances, public libraries are required by law to make an annual report to a state agency or to some local governing body. For these purposes standard forms for statistical presentation are usually required. Statistics, and especially those concerned with circulation, should not be regarded as an end in themselves or even as a complete basis for evaluation or comparison of one library with another.

CIRCULATION RECORD. A count of the book cards for materials that have been withdrawn from the library is made daily. Frequently this is done the first thing in the morning for the preceding day's circulation. One of the easiest methods of keeping this record, especially when the book cards are filed by class number, is to use a printed daily record form of circulation which is arranged by Dewey numbers and may be further divided into adult and juvenile circulation. At the end of the month the total circulation figures from these daily record sheets are brought together in a monthly total. The monthly sheets are used in compiling that part of the annual report devoted to circulation statistics. In transaction charging, it is impractical to break down statistics by classification number. Sometimes a special record of circulation is kept for certain periods of the day when the librarian wishes to study the use of the library for a possible adjustment of hours or a reallocation of the work load of the circulation staff.

Libraries do not usually attempt to count as circulation the books or other materials that are used within the building. An exception may be made when a librarian in a college or university library is studying the use of a given room, or the use of the library at certain hours. Books that are on intralibrary loan—a book sent from one service unit in the library system to another unit in the same system —do not usually count as circulation. However, books on interlibrary loan may be counted.

OTHER STATISTICS. The library that borrows materials from another library should keep a record of the receipt of the book and information concerning its return, including the amount of transportation paid. Some record of this nature is necessary because the borrowing library is responsible for the material borrowed. The library lending the material needs no record other than the book card, on which is written the name of the library to which the material has been circulated.

Registration statistics have been noted earlier.

An attendance count of the library, or of a given section of the library, is not a customary record. When kept, it may form the basis for a statistical report on some special phase of library administration.

Statistics based on the fines and fees collected are often mentioned under income in the library's financial report.

SHELF WORK

An essential step in circulation is bringing together the book and the reader. It is the step toward which the various operations and techniques which have been described earlier are directed. As Jesse has pointed out in his manual,[24] it is the aim of the shelf worker to deliver an item when it is wanted, return it to its assigned place after use, and properly care for it until it is wanted again. Jesse considers such matters as the arrangement of the book collection, various shelving practices for books and non-book materials, architectural potentialities of bookshelves, paging and shelving books (including the tracing of missing books, shelving operations and techniques), shelving and binding, shifting and moving books, stack management and shelving equipment (the bookstack, stack capacity, and types of bookshelves and methods of utilizing them), stack control, care of books, shelf list and inventory, and personnel. In open-shelf public and college libraries, many of these problems are reduced to a minimum.

Librarians maintaining stacks not open to their public have taken much pride in their ability to get items to users promptly and economically. Some studies have been made of the time necessary to obtain a volume from the stacks for a user. One large research library considers it inefficient if it takes more than five minutes to deliver a volume. It is always desirable to tell a patron exactly why a requested title cannot be located.

One of the first applications of time and motion study to circulation operations was carried on in the library of the Bradley Polytechnic Institute [25]—a college library with open shelves containing 53,000 volumes. This study showed that the arrangement of books in the stacks so that those in greatest demand were nearest the circulation desk was an important factor in reducing the time involved. The final stack arrangement was determined by the use of circulation statistics which showed that the books in the Dewey 800, 300, and 900 classes were in greatest demand in this particular library.

Another study involving time studies was recently conducted by Forrest.[26] In order to introduce a new type of call slip (dual slip interleaved with carbon), and use of a transaction card instead of book cards, it was considered important to determine whether or not additional staff time would be required to handle the operations. The new form makes it necessary for the reader to fill out more information than previously, but Forrest reports that in spite of this and the disadvantage of having the assistant who charges books handle two slips, the advantages to the user are: (1) charging is completed at one point, (2) identification is shown only once, (3) name and address are written only once, (4) all books are returned at one point, (5) books are returned to the stacks more quickly, and (6) more books are available because of systematic overdue operations. Advantages affecting the Circulation Department more directly than the user are: (1) elimination of a separate charge desk, (2) elimination of slipping, (3) easier compilation of statistics, (4) control strengthened by systematic overdue operation, (5) more accurate charging with transaction card, (7) more accurate information on charge card, and (8) easier check on slips sent to stack tiers. A recent report indicates that the new operation is more efficient in the return of books to the shelves and in controlling overdue items.

A type of shelf arrangement by time period was started in January, 1950, in the John Crerar Library,[27] to replace the system of shelving books by the decimal system. In this arrangement provision is made for placing non-serial books in three groups: books published before 1800, books published from 1800 to 1899, books published in 1900 and later. Books are first arranged by size and then in shelf-list order. The volumes in the third group are arranged on the basis of their interest to the medical department and the technology department. The subarrangement is by period of publication, size, and shelf-list order. Serial publications are shelved as a separate collection by primary subject interest, size, and shelf-list order.

The staff of John Crerar maintains that by using this type of shelf system (which does not change the basic classification), book lettering is simplified by reducing the number of digits in the call number, the amount of space reserved on the shelves for expansion is reduced by concentrating it to a few time groups rather than among large subject classes, and the time of book delivery is reduced by adapting simpler shelving symbols and by concentrating the most frequently used books on one stack level.

XXI. Photographic Service in Libraries

IN PREVIOUS chapters references have been made to the application of photographic methods to various library operations. Thus, the acquisitions department has sought to obtain materials or to replace out-of-print items through various microreproduced records such as microfilm and microcards or through photographic processes such as Photostat or the preparation of standard prints.[1] Some libraries, especially those associated with governmental and research units, have used photographic techniques in publishing bibliographies and other works.[2] Cataloging departments have used photographic processes for preparing cards or making records of old files; circulation departments have installed photographic chargers, and have been experimenting with the Photoclerk [3] for certain operations; and other units of libraries have employed photography in performing a variety of services.

To give some idea of what goes on in a photographic department of a university library, the following activities represent what might happen on a typical day: (1) photostating statistical tables for a faculty member, (2) photostating an article in a Japanese journal for an oil company, (3) making a film strip of the *Dance of Death* for a library school faculty member, (4) answering queries on reproduction of charts, etc., for a dissertation, (5) repairing reading machines and giving advice thereon, (6) advising on a camera, (7) microfilming a master's essay, (8) answering queries from a Danish librarian on the storage of microfilm, (9) microfilming copies of diaries on deposit in Special Collections, (10) making lantern slides from photographs, (11) enlarging Photostats, and (12) advising on illustrations to be used in an essay. The usual work of microfilming, showing visitors about the laboratory, and answering questions on costs were also included in the day's activities.[4]

In this particular department, about 4,000 orders a year are filled. Some 26,000 Photostats are made and 60,000 microfilm exposures and 1,300 lantern slides are prepared. Work for individuals comprised 59 percent of the activity, and the remaining 41 percent was distributed as follows: library departments, 10 percent; university departments, 15 percent; outside institutions, 9 percent; and corporations, 7 percent. The personnel consisted of a professional head, two technicians, one clerk, and a student assistant.

Undoubtedly, libraries will use photographic techniques for various services for some time to come, even though recently there have been questions raised as to certain procedures in library microtextual copying.[5] Individual projects, such as those enumerated above, will continue to represent a large part of an institutional laboratory's activity. More and more attention, however, is being given to cooperative projects and to making information available to librarians, so that duplication of microreproductions will be kept to a minimum.[6]

It is the purpose of this chapter to discuss the various types of photographic and microphotographic copies used in library services and to point out some of the problems associated with their production and use. There is no intention of describing in detail the chemical and laboratory techniques necessary for the successful operation of a library photographic department.[7]

TYPES OF REPRODUCTIONS

PHOTOSTAT. The Photostat Corporation manufactures the machine which produces the copy known as the Photostat. This name has been used to denote any projection photocopy, as well as the machine. Reproduction through the Photostat involves copying from the original material directly onto paper. Copies can be reduced, enlarged, or produced full size. The first copy appears as a negative but positive copies can be made. Colored paper can be copied by using a color filter. The Photoclerk is built along the lines of a small photocopy camera.

The unit cost in producing Photostats does not decrease as the size of the edition increases. Reduction of the size of pages copied, however, will result in saving in photographic paper used.[8]

Libraries have used Photostats for a variety of purposes. Copies of one or more pages, tabular materials, or illustrations commonly have been made.[9] Photostats have also been made to replace lost pages in volumes.

DEXIGRAPH. Another kind of photocopy similar to the Photostat is made by the Dexigraph, which is a trade name for the equipment produced by Remington Rand. The Dexigraph can make copies ranging from 100 percent to 50 percent of the original size. Berthold pointed out that early in the thirties several libraries had used the Dexigraph to reproduce catalog cards.[10] It has also been used in the making of an official catalog.[11]

Like a Photostat, the first product in Dexigraph copying is produced as a negative. The sensitized paper which is used comes in precut or roll form and varies in weight, size, and type of paper. Remington Rand either sells or rents the Dexigraph or the Junior Dexigraph (which handles copy up to letter and legal size).

RECTIGRAPH. The Rectigraph is a counterpart of the Photostat and is made by a machine produced by the Haloid Company. As in the Photostat, rolls of sensitive paper are fed into the Rectigraph. Exposures can be made as needed. These are cut from the roll and fed mechanically into the developer and fixing solution.[12] The Photo-Flo is a similar semiautomatic machine made by the same company.

DIAZO PRINTS. The Diazo process does not use a photographic lens. Light-sensitive dye papers or dye-coated papers may be handled in ordinary artificial illumination and contact prints can be quickly produced. While Diazo has not been used much in reproduction work in libraries, it has been employed frequently in registrars' offices and business. The Diazo print is positive and the same size as the original, the Photostat print is negative and usually the same size, and the Photoclerk print is negative and 3″ x 5″ in size. The Photoclerk can handle documents 3″ x 5″ or 4¼″ x 7″, or similar sized portions of larger originals. The Photostat can copy bound or loose materials. The Diazo can copy only loose originals. The Photostat and Photoclerk can take opaque and translucent documents. The Diazo works with translucent (or transparent) materials without an expensive foil intermediary. Producers of Diazo equipment are the Ozalid Division of the General Aniline and Film Corporation, the Charles Bruning Company, and the Eugene Dietzgen Company.

OTHER COPYING EQUIPMENT. As Fussler explains,[13] there are other processes of copying with photographic paper which do not require a camera. Among the units are the Photo-Copyist, the Hunter Electro-Copyist, and the Contoura.

The Contoura has been used increasingly by individuals who wish to copy pages or short runs of material.[14] In operation, light-sensitive paper is placed in close contact with the document to be reproduced, and light is allowed to pass through the sensitized paper. The resulting negative reads in reverse. The image may be read in a mirror or by holding it up to ordinary light. The negative, of course, may be rephotographed to produce a positive copy, which reads the same as the original.

Conrad[15] describes other devices for reproducing materials, including the Polaroid Copymaker, which is essentially a framework for holding a Polaroid Land Camera; the Apeco Autostat and the Remington Rand Trans-Copy, which are suitable only for flexible materials and require two kinds of special paper; the Thermofax, which will provide copies of all kinds of materials and contains an infrared light source which sends rays to the black and white material; the Xerox Copier, which makes prints on any paper and utilizes electrostatic forces to lift a dry powder and deposit it permanently on the paper through brief application of heat; and the Stenafax, which brings together into one unit a telefacsimile sender and receiver to provide an office-duplicating machine which makes single copies or cuts Mimeograph stencils of flexible materials.

Experiments at present are going on in the use of Xerography. Xerox can be used for multiple copies when combined with Multilith. An example of a publication produced by the Xerox has been prepared by Hodgson.[16] The copy in the pamphlet was reduced 30 percent. A sample catalog card made at the Denver Public Library is one of the exhibits.

Since librarians are interested in the new devices in printing, it may be pertinent to refer to two other developments—the new method of reproducing type on film known as photocomposition, and the increased use of typewriter composition, often referred to as "cold type" or "near print." Both of these kinds of composition are generally used in conjunction with offset or other planographic printing processes instead of the traditional relief or letterpress printing.

In photocomposition, the letters are reproduced directly on film, instead of being cast as single letters or lines of type in metal. The film is itself used for making the offset plate. Photocomposing machines are appearing with various trade names: the Photon (formerly Lumitype [17]), the Fotosetter (successfully in use in 1954), the Monophoto, and the Linofilm (announced in 1954).

In cold-type composition a typewriter or other office machine produces a single, clean proof which is transferred photographically to the offset plate. This may be made on a regular office typewriter equipped with carbon ribbon, on the Vari-Typer, or on an IBM typewriter. Or it may be made on one of the new office machines (the Justowriter,[18] for example), designed to produce typing that is similar in appearance to printing type.

Both photocomposition and cold-type composition offer methods of producing certain kinds of printed materials at minimum (though not inexpensive) cost. Silver [19] has pointed out that certain other methods facilitate the use of and reduce the cost of offset printing: paper plates, for example, may be prepared directly on the typewriter (as in the Multilith process).

MICROREPRODUCTIONS

The types of reproductions described so far are approximately the same size as the originals, and do not need to be projected in order to be read. Librarians, however, have become increasingly aware of the possibilities of various types of microreproductions, such as the microfilm (roll and strip), the microfiche (or sheet microfilm), the microcard, and Microprint.[20] Miniature facsimile differs from these in that it may be read directly from the page or with the aid of a reading glass, even though there is considerable reduction in the size of the print.

Mention has already been made of some of the uses of microreproductions in libraries. Although microcopying has been practiced in libraries for many years, it has been primarily within the last ten years that important strides have been taken. Fussler's *Photographic Reproduction for Libraries*, published in 1942,[21] pointed the way for library applications on a wide scale. Industrial organizations, research workers, and archivists, as well as librarians, have become concerned about the various applications of microcopying in information services or in the preservation of records.

Major uses of microreproductions for library purposes may be categorized as follows: (1) condensation, as in the case of bulky archives or newspapers, (2) acquisition, especially of materials which are unique, out of print, costly or rare, (3) preservation, as in the case of deteriorating manuscripts, wood-pulp newspapers, or documents of various kinds, (4) distribution, in lieu of interlibrary loans, of materials to libraries and researchers at small cost, and (5) publication, as in the case of dissertations or documents issued in limited editions.

MICROFILM. Microfilm is important for libraries because it represents a medium for producing a single reproduction of an item at relatively low cost. An edition of one copy costs close to the amount charged for a current publication. Microfilms also have been used for producing institutional union catalogs and duplicating card catalogs, for reducing the handling of irreplaceable materials, for completing runs of periodicals, for recovering lost and obscure texts, for storing little-used or obsolete materials, and for implementing general classroom instruction.[22] A number of newspapers, listed in the *Union List of Microfilms,* have been microcopied, and several, including the New York *Times,* are available on film currently. University Microfilms prepares annually several hundred thousand feet of microfilm, particularly of dissertations and periodicals.

A study of microfilm problems in 1949 [23] indicated that in acquisition some difficulty to libraries resulted from (1) the lack of facilities for filming material desired, (2) the question of copyright, especially of foreign items, (3) the slowness in getting film copies from libraries, (4) the high cost of foreign work, (5) the poor quality of work, and (6) errors in orders.

As librarians have made more and more use of microfilms they have insisted on promptness and accuracy in copying and on high quality work. Library personnel qualified to do photographic work are relatively scarce, but several library schools have included courses in microphotography. Major libraries abroad have been interested in microcopying, especially in recent years. The Libraries Division of UNESCO also has become concerned with various types of microreproductions.[24] The Library of Congress has sought to work closely with foreign libraries in exchange of microfilms of periodicals. Cooperative projects in the microfilming of newspapers are also assuming more importance.[25]

Eaton, in writing of the state-wide program of microfilming of newspapers in Louisiana,[26] calls attention to other filming projects by individual libraries, state historical societies, state library associations, commercial firms, individual publishers, and learned societies. The New York Public Library, the Library of Congress, the University of Chicago Library, and others have filmed newspapers from all parts of the country. The Wisconsin State Historical Society has engaged in a filming project of Wisconsin papers, and at the present time is filming over 300 weeklies and about 35 dailies published in the state, as well as 250 labor and trade union papers from all parts of the country. The California Library Association has made progress in developing a state-wide plan for newspaper preservation. The Recordak Corporation, a subsidiary of Eastman Kodak, has engaged in newspaper microreproduction. The New Orleans *Times-Picayune* has undertaken its own microfilming. The American Council of Learned Societies sponsored the filming of Negro newspapers on a nation-wide scale.

The question of the relation between microfilming and binding is a matter with which librarians are concerned. Power [27] summarized his studies of the problem as follows:

1. The purchase of older back files of periodicals, often at premium prices, is not a wise investment. The same needs can be furnished by microfilm copy. In bound form space costs continue at a high rate year after year, whether the materials are used or not; in microfilm the fixed charges are greatly diminished.
2. Storage of newspapers in bound form is not warranted. The space required is excessive, binding expensive, and the use after a short period of time infrequent. Moreover, the cheap wood pulp will disintegrate after 25–40 years and the total investment is lost. A microfilm copy is small, compact, satisfactory to use and permanent.
3. Through the proper use of microfilm pressing problems of space can be substantially eliminated. Files necessary for adequate library service can be kept and maintained without frequent expansion of stack capacity and new construction at the present high building costs.
4. Present library service can be maintained or expanded through the use of microfilm, as publications can be kept on microfilm that otherwise would have to be discarded because of space considerations.
5. As the number of desirable publications is itself increasing in parabolic curve, storage of many titles on microfilm may become inevitable if costs are to be kept within manageable limits. With many libraries it may become a question of using microfilm to give adequate service, or severely curtailing the resources made available to their users.

Rider [28] has indicated that microcards are an adequate and cheaper substitute for "less-used titles," but neither this nor microfilming means that libraries will or should discontinue the purchase of titles in regular book form. Both microcards and microfilms have a role to play in providing materials needed by readers.

Table 2. MICROFILM READING MACHINES

FEATURE	RECORDAK OR KODAGRAPH		GRISCOMBE			SPENCER
	C	*MPE*	16–35A	18 T	*PA or PB*	*Scholar*
Film	16 and 35	16 and 35	16 and 35	16 and 35	16 and 35 (Perf.)	16 and 35
Image Screen	Translucent	Opaque	Opaque	Opaque	Opaque	Opaque
Screen Size	18 x 18	20 x 20	14 x 14	18 x 18	14 x 14[a]	13 x 15
Magnification	12X to 23X	19X	17X, 22½X	17X, 25X	PA-23X PB-17X	15X
Scanning	Full	Full	Full	Full	Full	Limited
Rotation	360°	360°	360°	360°	360°	360° by 90° steps
Lamp	200 W.	100 W.	100 W.	100 W.	100 W.	100 W.
Pressure Flats	Automatic retracting	Rotating	Automatic retracting	Automatic retracting	Tension rollers	Nonautomatic
Heat Filter	Yes	Yes	No	No	No	No
Current	AC-DC	AC-DC	AC	AC	AC	AC-DC
Cost [b]	$725	$350	$300	$380	$165 or $175	$108

[a] May use ceiling or wall [b] As of April, 1954; subject to change

The *Unesco Survey of Microfilm Use* includes data on choice of microcopy processes; microfilm and microfiche cameras; microfilm, microfiche, and microcard readers; processing apparatus for microfilms and microfiches; film printers; and enlargers. Since projectors are important in the use of microfilm, Table 2, prepared by Hubbard Ballou of Columbia University, provides information on several reading machines.

MICROFICHES. The basic difference between the microfilm and the microfiche is that the microfiche is kept in sheet form and usually filed in the same way as index cards. Microfiches, which are on a transparent base, are more popular in Europe, but they are also used in American libraries to a limited extent. Standard sizes for microfiches are 75 x 125 mm., 90 x 120 mm., 105 x 148 mm., 105 x 150 mm., and 228 x 152 mm.[29] There is a current interest on the part of librarians in reducing the number of the sizes of all types of microreproductions.[30] The International Organization for Standardization and the American Standards Association have also indicated interest in this problem.

MICROCARDS. Microreduced text on paper the size of a catalog card is intended to reduce bulk, cut text cost, provide catalog information, and eliminate binding cost.[31] More and more titles are becoming available from the Microcard Foundation and from other publishers.[32] Many of the earlier titles available on microcards have been in the fields of social sciences and humanities, but recent additions have included the sciences and technology.[33] Rider has emphasized the fact that microcarding represents a form of publication.[34] Production costs are divided among a larger number of copies than in usual microfilming projects. Editions of microcards usually begin with 25 copies and often run to over 100 copies. It is also possible to order on microcards only a part of a larger title as needed, e.g., a volume of a set, an issue of a periodical, or a chapter or other portion of a book.

Two microcard projectors, each providing approximately 24-power magnification, are available. The standard machine has a screen of about 11" x 13" in size, while the smaller portable reader has a

9″ x 12″ screen. Microcards are being increasingly used for research in libraries.[35]

MICROPRINT. Erickson [36] refers to Microprint as achieving "by a printing press operation the same degree of reduction and sharpness achieved by microphotography." Albert Boni, president of the Readex Microprint Corporation which has developed microprinting, outlines the purposes of the medium as follows:

1. To make possible publication of research material in small editions at low cost.
2. To deliver a product that requires no apparatus or special care to protect it from deterioration.
3. To obtain a product that makes possible an easy and quick location of research references when using a reader. This is accomplished by standard arrangement on the card of the Microprints of individual pages of the original text.

Available materials on Microprint are not yet as abundant as microfilms or microcards. Certain bibliographies, such as those of Sabin and Church, have been republished on Microprint. Arrangements have been made to issue on Microprint, the British House of Commons *Sessional Papers,* 1801–1900,[37] the New York *Times,* the LC *Subject Catalog,* and publications of the United Nations. It is estimated that the average doctoral dissertation can be issued in this form for $25 to $50. On the basis of tests made by the Bureau of Standards, Readex Microprints should remain legible for at least fifty years.[38]

The Readex, the reader used to project Microprint, is manufactured in the standard model and in a newspaper model. The Readex is equipped to make it possible to locate easily through a dial system any one of the pages on a Microprint card which contains 100 pages, ten across and ten down.

MINIATURE FACSIMILE. In its present form as developed by Edwards Brothers, miniature facsimile involves a four-to-one reduction in size. Such material can be read with the naked eye, and in this respect it differs from microprinting. Periodicals especially have been issued in miniature facsimile. It is feasible to put material in stock as soon as twenty-five orders have been placed.

CATALOGING AND STORAGE

Librarians have made efforts to keep the cataloging of microfilm simple.[39] Classification in some libraries is on a broad subject basis, with the films added in numerical sequence. The handling of Microprint offers no special problems, since the materials are in sheet form and similar to books. The cataloging of microcards has also been considered recently.[40] Bacon has pointed out that it has been effective to use the cataloging information which appears on microcards for preparing a card for the general catalog. The microcard itself is then kept in a separate catalog for use by the patron.

A number of libraries have had to make special provisions for the control of temperature, humidity, and dust in places used for the storage of microfilms and other types of photographic materials.[41] This frequently has been the result of failure to provide for appropriate housing conditions for the care of books. As noted earlier, microfilms are frequently stored on reels (100 to 120 feet), although short runs of materials are sometimes cut into fixed lengths and kept in envelopes or small booklets or attached to index cards. Filmsort, Inc. (formerly Film 'n File, Inc.), has developed Filmsort cards in which one or more frames of microfilm are inserted in cards. The cards may be coded by punching the edges, thus facilitating sorting and filing operations.

FUTURE POSSIBILITIES

As libraries grow and more emphasis is placed on the storage of library materials, especially the less-used runs of periodicals, newspapers, and other bulky materials, the application of photographic techniques to library problems will increase. In the 1952 report[42] of the Midwest Inter-Library Center, listings of newspapers (foreign and domestic) are included. In six months, 31 reels of foreign newspapers were received. Microfilm copies of 16 U.S. newspapers are received regularly. Large collections of microfilms and other photographic copies of library materials have already been assembled in major libraries. Smaller libraries, especially those of a technical and scientific character, are enlarging their services to include microreproduction of articles for bibliographic and abstracting operations. Undoubtedly, the end has not been reached in the use of photography and microphotography for library purposes. While there has been some resistance on the part of library readers toward the use of film and projectors, even this objection has diminished. Librarians will need to consider just when it is proper to discard materials and replace them with film copies. This has been a problem in academic libraries particularly, since faculty members have been concerned about the loss of originals in a library's holdings.

COOPERATIVE PHOTOGRAPHY

The largest area for cooperative activity in library photography has been in microreproduction. A considerable number of projects have been carried out in collaboration with commercial firms, probably the most extensive of which have been the microfilming of doctoral dissertations and the microfilming of periodicals to be kept by the subscriber in lieu of the bound volume. Both of these projects have been undertaken by University Microfilms. Abstracts of the dissertations are available in the firm's publication *Dissertation Abstracts*.

Cooperation among libraries themselves until recently has been limited almost exclusively to the use of microfilm as a means of facilitating interlibrary loan, of reducing the storage space required for bulky materials such as newspapers, and of procuring rare or expensive materials which were unavailable by purchase or loan. Since the end of World War II these activities have been intensified and extended. Considerable emphasis is being placed on the microfilming of newspapers and other material on wood-pulp paper. Some programs are under way and others proposed for a comprehensive attempt to secure on microfilm a record of cultural source materials throughout the world.

More and more it is being pointed out that for reasons of economy and in consideration of the vast scope of certain contemplated and needed projects, wide-scale cooperation among libraries is essential. Born points out the need for careful planning and notes that "no research institution can arrive at a completely rational internal policy on acquisitions, or preservation, or exploitation through the medium of extensive microfilm operations unless there exists an acceptable national plan for acquisitions, preservation, exploitation through the medium of microfilm." [43] Impressed with this need, Born proposed it for the consideration of the International Federation for Documentation as an international program.[44]

In 1949, Lacy [45] suggested five basic considerations for cooperative microfilming and since then certain of the gaps he indicated have been filled in. The points he brought out and their current status are as follows:

(1) Commonly accepted technical standards. The Committee on Photographic Reproduction of Research Materials of the Association of Research Libraries, in collaboration with the Library of Congress, has published "A Proposed Standard for the Microphotographic Reproduction of Newspapers," [46] and the American Standards Association has proposed standards for microfilm and microfilm readers.

(2) A clearing house of information. A Microfilming Clearing House has been established at the Library of Congress, and its *Bulletin* is published irregularly as an appendix to the Library of Congress *Information Bulletin.* Libraries are thus kept informed of work completed and in progress, and suggestions for unfilled needs can be made.

(3) A planning committee. A Committee on Cooperative Microfilm Projects has been established as part of the ALA Board on Resources of American Libraries.

(4) Availability. This involves primarily the question of pricing, so that no library will be called upon to bear an undue burden of the cost. Pertinent also is the attempt to work out the problem so that

there will not be a vast number of positive reprints to the virtual exclusion of new negatives that might have been made with the same expenditure of money.

(5) Interlibrary loan of microfilm. As mentioned above, microfilm has been used for a number of years as a substitute for interlibrary loan, but it is only recently that loan from a collection of microfilm has been proposed. Loan of microfilm would be subject to procedures similar to those in effect at present for conventional material.

To Lacy's five points, Born [47] added a sixth, that of an international network of microfilming centers. The Library of Congress has suggested to the government of Italy that such a center be established there. With the experience which may be gained from this pilot project as a guide, other centers might be set up elsewhere. The International Federation for Documentation,[48] under the sponsorship of UNESCO, has recently completed a directory of world microfilm facilities, and this will form a basis for further work in the field. UNESCO [49] is also responsible for a recent survey of microfilm use, which includes a directory of microfilm equipment and manufacturers.

Cooperative activities such as the Philadelphia Bibliographical Center's *Union List of Microfilms* should not be overlooked. Organizations outside the library field, working in cooperation with libraries, are conducting projects such as that of the American Historical Association to microfilm cultural documents throughout the world. There has been cooperation between the Library of Congress and state historical groups. The Southeastern Library Association, in cooperation with the TVA, has microfilmed scientific journals needed in the region.[50]

Cooperation in use of microcards is as yet less advanced, and virtually all of the activity in promoting use of the medium has been that of commercial enterprises. However, in 1954, the Association of College and Reference Libraries began to issue its *ACRL Microcard Series.*

XXII. Machines, Operations, and Modern Libraries

THOUGH librarianship has enjoyed no sweeping changes in its techniques or concepts such as have occurred in industry, nearly every library of any size has employed mechanical devices or simplified operations to ease the burden on its employees or to increase the services which it can render with the funds available. Some of these devices and operations have been described in earlier chapters. From the Gaylord charging machine to the experimental photographic composing machines now being developed, devices of great diversity are beginning to affect library operations. Librarians as a group, however, have not ordinarily grasped the significance of the changes which might be wrought through adaptation of techniques developed in business and industry—or at least have not always translated these into new and improved methods of operation.

COSTS

The average librarian has not paid much attention to costs except as he knows the total amount of his budget, the amount he may spend for books and periodicals or personnel, and except as he has been forced from time to time to present budgets to his appropriating authority. Reference has already been made to studies of cataloging costs. Businesses and industries, however, have been forced to make constant and detailed studies of their costs of operation *per unit of production*, so that they may arrive at selling prices which will yield profits and still be in line with competitors. In particular, the work of Rautenstrauch,[1] one of the first industrial engineers, has yielded principles which may profitably be studied in any effort to give increased library services to more people.

The two major classifications of costs are the constant and the variable. Both may be expressed in terms of the *total* cost of operation and the *per unit* cost of operation. Constant costs, for the most part, are those which arise from possession of physical facilities—buildings, book stocks, and machines of one kind or another. Insurance payments, mortgages (or the obligations arising out of bond issues), rent, depreciation, a certain portion of heating and power charges, and certain personnel costs are examples of constant costs. Even a library in a dormant state must become less valuable with age (depreciation) and it must be protected—heated in cold weather and watched over in some way. But it is assumed that there is activity—work—in libraries. If all work done in a library were to be tallied in terms of work units,[2] the burden of the *total* constant cost could be allotted, and a *per unit* constant cost established. This per unit cost would tend to vary, dropping as production mounted (i.e., if few units of work were accomplished, it would tend to be higher than if a great many units of work were accomplished), even though constant costs as a sum tend not to vary, provided that there is a relatively stable organization and a relatively complete physical plant.

There are actually two categories within the term *constant* costs. *Fixed* costs are those which cannot be reduced, barring complete disintegration of the organization and disposition of physical property. *Regulated* costs are those which are subject to some administrative control (salaries of executives, for example), but which vary only slightly during any short period of time.

Variable costs arise out of the operation of an organization. Personnel and materials usually are the major variable charges, but heat, light, and power, above those minimum charges already mentioned, also are variable. The sum of these costs of production decreases as the number of work units accomplished increases, provided the *skill of the operators*, the *quality of materials*, and the *method employed* remain relatively constant.[3] It takes one book pocket, one bookplate, so much ink, paste, and other materials and a certain number of man-minutes to "process" the first book purchased. The processing of the one-hundredth book purchased takes approximately the same amount of materials and labor. Thus, though the *total* of variable costs mounts with work units performed, the *unit variable cost* remains about the same.[4]

It is important to remember that unit costs can be altered, and it is frequently through the introduction of machines and/or improved methods of operation that they are affected.

Morris [5] describes some of the techniques which were used to guide thinking in connection with revisions at the New York Public Library, in serial record forms and equipment, purchase order forms, and gift request and follow-up letters. Librarians have worked closely with representatives of business record specialists in developing systems of correlated order forms for the purchase of books. The procedure involves a consideration of what has to be done, what is now being done, and what is the best way of performing the required operations.

SCIENTIFIC MANAGEMENT

The complaint has been made that mechanical devices or "management studies" are too expensive for the library. The implication, though this would generally be denied, is that staff time is not expensive. If a staff member dips a brush into a jar of paste, spreads the paste on a label, and places the label in a book, money has been expended, for the staff member is paid for his time. If the brush goes from jar to label enough times, the cost of a label-pasting machine has been expended. Granting that some libraries (perhaps far too many) are too small and too poorly supported to make any capital expenditures (money spent for enlargement or improvement of physical facilities, including introduction of machines), there still is room for the improvement of existing practices.

It is always necessary to know in detail the facts of any proposal for changes in methods, since most appropriating bodies must be convinced that capital expenditure can reduce unit costs before they will approve the necessary funds. It will be apparent to anyone who reads thoroughly the literature of librarianship that careful studies of operations based on factual data are the exception. This fact will not excuse forever the lack of such studies.

Scientific management (or management analysis) is an attitude of critical, objective evaluation of achievement. At the operating level, it is aimed at the collection of data through controlled experiment and the analysis of those data with a view to reduction of cost and/or expansion of services. In addition, it may be said to be nontraditional and creative. It is nontraditional in that it seeks, where old methods or concepts seem not to solve current problems, to evolve new methods and concepts on many levels without reference to past procedures. It is creative in that it seeks to study the questions of what has not been done as well as the questions of how best to continue vital activities. It differs from the term *library administration* in its stress on controlled experiment and the study of the details of operation wherever possible. It also is novel in that it stresses the contribution to management which can be made by each individual, no matter what his status. Management analysis may be summed up in the industrial engineers' motto that "there is always a better way." The implication is that there is no one best method of doing anything—even when the method has been arrived at through objective study.

There is considerable danger of confusing the techniques of scientific management with the critical attitude itself, and the intensive specialization of labor resulting, in part, from the use of these techniques has had some widely felt and unfortunate consequences. Principally, depriving the worker of his sense of accomplishment, formerly derived from seeing the product of his labor in use, may have contributed to widening the rift between librarian and staff. The necessary repetition of a single task hour after hour and day after day constitutes a prodigal waste of talent, or, at least, of mental energy.

The term *work simplification* denotes a comprehensive use of specific techniques. It has as its key the words *eliminate, simplify, com-*

bine, and *rearrange.* Its thesis is that any piece of work being done involves some operations which can be dropped completely, that of those remaining some can be simplified, and that it may be possible to combine into a single operation or a better sequence some of the remaining simplified ones. Work simplification, as used in industrial (or management) engineering involves *motion and time study, process analysis, work-place layout, methods study,* and some other techniques for studying work being done. Where work simplification is applied to office management, it becomes concerned with the assignment of responsibilities to departments or individuals, the design and distribution of forms, and other techniques somewhat less well defined than those first mentioned. A consciousness of good personnel practice is implicit in today's practice of work study.

Motion and time study and the related *micromotion study* [6] rely upon the use of timers and motion photography in recording the hand and body movements of an individual at work. A motion picture of a worker, taken so as to include a mechanism for timing, is studied first to determine the cycle of work and to arrive at an average time for the cycle. Further study is directed toward improvement of the method, the place of work, and the tools or equipment used, with particular attention to reducing the number and complexity of motions.

Process analysis charts the operations, transportations, delays, inspections, and storages involved in the production of an article. Once the charting has been set down on a standard form, it is studied to discover unnecessary steps. Timing of each step is sometimes carried out so that this technique may result in a rearrangement of the entire process, or even an altered design for the finished product.

While continuing attention is always given in work simplification to the use of mechanical devices and to the arrangement of work in a convenient manner, the specific study of *work-place layout* concentrates on these points. It has been discovered that certain types of hand and arm motions are more tiring than others, that simultaneous motions (right hand to right side of body and left hand to left side of body) are less fatiguing than single motions, and that there are "best" areas of motion and "maximum" areas of motion. Utilizing these concepts, the place of work may be laid out so as to enable the worker to produce at maximum capacity but with lessened effort.

Methods study, sometimes used as a general term to cover motion and time study and other related techniques, attempts to compare methods employed by several workers doing the same type of work, so as to determine the most efficient.

This list of techniques is by no means complete, and is intended to serve only as an introduction to this field. These methods have been developed for use in industry but few have been adapted for specific use in libraries. They are not substitutes for thought and imagination, but only means of expressing problems. Some librarians —perhaps especially those who are most concerned with new solutions to old problems—have tended to confuse part of an operation with the whole operation. As Shaw [7] has pointed out, using microfilm as an example,

> The cost of supplying a page of text to a user in microfilm is lower than the cost of supplying a single copy in some other forms. But the cost of reading machines, the time spent in the special handling and indexing required, and in similar operations, *all of which are part of the cost of the end product*, must be computed as part of the total cost of supplying and using microfilm, if comparisons are to be valid.

PERSONNEL. Personnel policy is of great importance to any program of management analysis and improvement. The objectives of a library, no matter how desirable and well stated, cannot be achieved unless staff members can be found who are capable of doing the necessary work, and unless they can be kept on the staff. Of great importance is the development of a favorable scientific management attitude within the total staff.[8] This will be more easily accomplished among a group of people who are satisfied that they are being fairly treated under a well-defined policy and a smoothly running personnel program than in a situation where such matters are left in doubt.

Two specific matters related to personnel should be made clear in the initial stages of a management improvement program. First, all members of the staff should be assured that greater efficiency in methods will not result in dismissal of personnel, but that the changes resulting from normal turnover of personnel will be taken advantage of to make necessary adjustments. Thus, it should be apparent to the staff that it will not be "working itself out of a job." The objective of the program should clearly be to free staff time so that they may assume truly professional responsibilities. Second, in the process of studying staff assignments, it may seem desirable to reassign duties in such a manner as to reduce the number of professional positions and increase the number of subprofessional or clerical positions. In some instances, such changes will require budgetary approval, and arguments in defense of the changes will have to be presented. The plan for the collection of data should include, therefore, the progression of ideas on each operation or department studied. Throughout, the greatest possible degree of staff participation should be encouraged by all possible means and through full explanation of the goals sought.

EXAMPLES OF APPLICATION

Relatively few examples of applications of scientific management in libraries are available, since the field has not been explored to any great extent. However, an outstanding example of a detailed explanation which is generally available is Hardkopf's study in the processing division of the Circulation Department of the New York Public Library.[9] In a sense, this example is unfortunate in that very few libraries are faced with the quantity of work that must flow through the New York Public Library. The benefits realized will be dismissed by some as attainable only in the very large library, though this is not the case. The savings in money and the added service to the public resulting from time savings are remarkable. Hardkopf, in her original study, estimated that the improved methods of that time would result in savings of approximately $5,090.90 per year to the library.[10] Subsequent improvements have made it possible to prepare a book for the shelves in about three and one half minutes at an approximate cost of twenty-five cents. The method employed was to chart the progress of a book through the preparation procedure using process (or flow) analysis charts. The charts were studied to spot unnecessary or unduly laborious operations, and, finally, a new flow chart was devised which rearranged the operations, eliminated some, and made use of certain mechanical devices.

An example of methods study may be found in Shaw's report of an experiment in alphabetizing cards to be used in preparing a bibliography. Using only manual methods, 10,000 cards could be put into order in about 56 hours. When International Business Machines were used, the same operation took about 106 hours, but the data accumulated from the experiment were detailed enough to show that the greatest amount of time was consumed in machine sorting after the sixth column of the coding had been reached. Using the machines to sort the first five columns and manual methods to complete the job, the cards could be arranged in about 23 hours.[11]

Motion and time study (and micromotion study) have had relatively little place in the application of management analysis in libraries. These techniques are designed to shave seconds from operations in industrial situations where exactly the same materials are used in exactly the same manner time after time. In only a few cases do comparable situations exist in the library. The library staff performs many repetitive tasks, but rarely are the materials exactly the same at all times. It may be feasible to use time and motion study, more or less undiluted, after an initial survey of operations by other techniques and the cream of potential savings has been skimmed off. Too, it may be that the principles of motion and time study may be adapted to the library situation, but we have not yet reached either stage in most libraries.

In the Newark Public Library a new book-processing line has recently been put into operation. As an example of workplace layout, it represents a radical departure from previous methods used at Newark, and at the same time benefits from the experience of the New York Public Library. Books are placed on wooden trays so that they may be pushed from station to station on roller tracks without being lifted and carried or transferred to and from book trucks. The information on catalog cards, shelf-list cards, book cards, and book pockets has been standardized so that all can be produced from a single Addressograph stencil. Where book numbers were formerly lettered by hand, a lettering device using heated type has been installed.

As noted in earlier chapters, various circulation systems using photographic, punched card, or audio devices have been installed. Most such systems are based upon identifying the circulation of a book (book identification and borrower identification) with a serial or transaction number, rather than through sorting files of charge cards. The systems represent savings in that they do away with the filing of charge cards and the slipping of books.

The development of photo-offset processes such as those used in the production of the *Bibliography of Agriculture* and the *Current List of Medical Literature* has brought some distinct and welcome changes in the area of bibliographical control. Further improvements in the services which libraries can offer—on a large or small scale—await only the imaginative use of scientific management and the development of new machines and methods to implement new solutions to old problems.

The array of equipment used in business and industry which also has been applied to library operations is wide. Punched cards (either machine sorted or marginal punched) have been used in circulation, serials records, acquisitions, borrower registration, and some other departments. Visible files (Kardex, Cardineer, etc.) have found similar wide application where formerly the standard 3″ x 5″ catalog card was used. Catalog cards and other records have been reproduced by Mimeograph, Multilith, Multigraph, Photostat, and a wide variety of other "near-print" processes.[12] Information concerning these and other equipment and products is included regularly in several sources.[13]

DOCUMENTATION AND MECHANICAL APPLICATIONS

In the field of activity known as documentation considerable attention is being given to the application of streamlined methods and mechanical apparatus. Documentation has been variously defined, sometimes not too clearly, but one of the most recent attempts at explanation is by Taube. He writes:

> Documentation as the designation of the total complex of activities involved in the communication of specialized information includes the activities which constitute special librarianship plus the prior activities of preparing and reproducing materials and the subsequent activity of distribution.[14]

Taube further explains the relationship of publishing to documentation as follows: "To the extent that responsibility for preparing primary materials is corporate rather than individual, to the extent that the initial preparation is guided and determined by the ultimate purpose of distribution to a special audience, preparation of the document is a part of documentation." [15] Some may disagree with the effort to include publishing under documentation, but this is not the essential point in the program of documentation. A clear statement of the program of the American Documentation Institute, which has as its object "to advance the principles and techniques of recorded information," is provided by Evans.[16] The four emphases of the program are (1) technical developments (printing, and other forms of reproduction, selecting and sorting devices), (2) publication of research materials—both the raw materials and the product, (3) bibliographic improvement in all disciplines, so that there may be more unity among them, and (4) the study of copyright.

Documentation is an international problem, rather than a local or national one, and international conferences on scientific and bibliographic services have been endeavoring to sift out problems and establish programs for clarifying the field.[17] Among the topics considered by international conferences are (1) International Committee on Bibliography, (2) Bibliography in certain geographical regions, (3) National bibliographical planning bodies, (4) Scientific information conferences, (5) National libraries and information centers, (6) Depositories for papers unsuitable for publication, (7) Directories of information sources, (8) Lists of publications and national bibliographies, (9) International exchange of scientific literature, (10) Translations, (11) Scientific periodicals, (12) Preparation of manuscripts, (13) Terminology, (14) Copyright, (15) Reprints, (16) Committees on abstracting, (17) Lists of abstracting services and of periodicals covered by them, (18) Gaps in abstracting coverage, (19) Cooperation among abstracting services, (20) Preparation and format of abstracts, (21) Support by international organizations for abstracting activities, (22) Reviews and annual reports, (23) Compendia and data tables, (24) Classification and coding, (25) Chemical notation, (26) Mechanical selection, (27) Research on uses of information, (28) Cooperative cataloging, (29) Reproduction of materials, (30) Training and status of information specialists, and (31) Training of scientists in use of information services. The Royal Society (London) and UNESCO have played the leading role in supporting these programs, with the Library of Congress actively involved with various personnel and projects. American librarians might well give attention to current developments which are discussed in *American Documentation*, the English quarterly *Journal of Documentation*, and the *UNESCO Bulletin for Libraries*.

Notes

CHAPTER I. INTRODUCTION

1. L. R. Wilson, "Introduction," in *The Acquisition and Cataloging of Books,* ed. by W. M. Randall (Chicago, University of Chicago Press, 1940), pp. v–vii. R. D. Leigh, "Operations," Chapter 9 in *The Public Library in the United States* (New York, Columbia University Press, 1950).

2. A. M. McAnally, "Recent Developments in Cooperation," *College and Research Libraries,* 12:123–132, April, 1951.

3. J. L. Wheeler, "Streamlining 'Technical Processes' in Small Libraries," *Wilson Library Bulletin,* 28:422–424, January, 1954. Clyde L. Pettus, "Cataloging in Small Public Libraries: A Survey," *Journal of Cataloging and Classification,* 9:83–107, June, 1953.

CHAPTER II. THE TECHNICAL SERVICES IN THE LIBRARY PROGRAM

1. L. R. Wilson, R. B. Downs, and M. F. Tauber, *Report of a Survey of the Libraries of Cornell University for the Library Board of Cornell University, October 1947–February 1948* (Ithaca, Cornell University, 1948), Chapter VI.

2. L. R. Wilson and M. F. Tauber, *The University Library* (Chicago, University of Chicago Press, 1945), p. 142.

3. J. L. Cohen, "The Technical Services Division in Libraries: A Symposium. A General Consideration of the Technical Services Division in Libraries," *College and Research Libraries,* 10:46–49, January, 1949.

4. C. B. Joeckel and Leon Carnovsky, *A Metropolitan Library in Action: A Survey of the Chicago Public Library* (Chicago, University of Chicago Press, 1940), p. 155.

5. R. C. Swank, "The Catalog Department in the Library Organization," *Library Quarterly,* 18:24–32, January, 1948. See also J. J. Lund, "The Cataloging Process in the University Library: A Proposal for Reorganization," *College and Research Libraries,* 3:212–218, June, 1942.

6. K. D. Metcalf, "The Essentials of an Acquisition Program," in *The Acquisition and Cataloging of Books*, ed. by W. M. Randall (Chicago, University of Chicago Press, 1940), pp. 85–86.

7. "The Technical Services Division in Libraries: A Symposium," *College and Research Libraries*, 10:46–68, January, 1949. See also Esther J. Piercy, "Report on Technical Processes Department, Presented to Board of Directors, Worcester Free Public Library, 11 September 1945" (Worcester, Mass., 1945).

8. J. L. Cohen, *op. cit.*

9. M. F. Tauber and L. Q. Mumford, *Report of a Survey of the Technical Services of the Columbia University Libraries, December 28, 1943–January 8, 1944*, Revised draft, 1944 (New York, Columbia University Libraries, 1947), pp. 56–57. In an article by C. M. White, "Assistant Directors in the Columbia University Libraries," *College and Research Libraries*, 8:360–367, July, 1947, the general and specific functions of the three assistant directors at Columbia are discussed. Changes were made in 1948 which eliminated the position of "assistant director: general administration," but which retained the "assistant director: technical services." In 1953, a further change eliminated the position of associate director, and the (general) assistant director was given a new grouping of responsibilities. At present, the head cataloger (catalog librarian) reports directly to the director of libraries, and the head of acquisitions is also supervisor of the binding and photography departments. See R. H. Logsdon, "Changes in Organization at Columbia," *College and Research Libraries*, 15:158–160, April, 1954.

10. Donald Coney, "The Administration of the Technical Processes," in *Current Issues in Library Administration*, ed. by C. B. Joeckel (Chicago, University of Chicago Press, 1939), pp. 177–178.

11. Alex Ladenson, "The Acquisition and Cataloging Departments," *Library Quarterly*, 18:200–205, July, 1948.

12. *Ibid.*, p. 203.

13. B. A. Custer, "The Technical Services Division in Libraries: A Symposium. The Large Public Library," *College and Research Libraries*, 10:49–53, January, 1949.

14. E. B. Colburn, "The Value to the Modern Library of a Technical Services Department," *College and Research Libraries*, 11:47–53, January, 1950.

15. Margaret C. Brown, "The Technical Services Division in Libraries: A Symposium. The Small Public Library," *College and Research Libraries*, 10:53–57, January, 1949. See also J. A. Humphrey, "Pratt Reshapes Its Processing," *Library Journal*, 73:1345–1350, October 1, 1948.

16. C. I. Barnard, *The Functions of the Executive* (Cambridge, Harvard University Press, 1946), p. 60. A useful volume which discusses the fundamentals of administration and organization is M. T. Copeland's *The Executive at Work* (Cambridge, Harvard University Press, 1951).

17. W. E. Wright, "Some Aspects of Technical Processes," *Library Trends*, 1:73, July, 1952. See also A. H. Trotier, "Organization and Administration of Cataloging Processes," *Library Trends*, 2:264–278, October, 1953. Trotier calls attention to the organization of cataloging in relation to other services.

CHAPTER III. ACQUISITIONS: FUNCTIONS AND ORGANIZATION

1. R. B. Downs, "Problems in the Acquisition of Research Materials," in *The Acquisition and Cataloging of Books*, ed. by W. M. Randall (Chicago, University of Chicago Press, 1940), p. 75.

2. D. C. Mearns, *The Story Up to Now, The Library of Congress, 1800–1946* (Washington, D.C., 1947), pp. 211–212. This book contains a statement of the objectives of the Library of Congress in regard to collecting.

3. L. R. Wilson and R. C. Swank, *Report of a Survey of the Library of Stanford University for Stanford University, Nov. 1946–March 1947* (Chicago, American Library Association, 1947), pp. 75–76.

4. K. D. Metcalf, "The Essentials of an Acquisition Program," in *The Acquisition and Cataloging of Books*, ed. by W. M. Randall (Chicago, University of Chicago Press, 1940), pp. 76–94. K. D. Metcalf, "Problems of Acquisition Policy in a University Library," *Harvard Library Bulletin*, 4:293–303, Autumn, 1950. See also papers by A. E. Bestor, Jr., W. G. Rice, Stanley Pargellis, Louis Gottschalk, H. H. Fussler, L. S. Thompson, in the *Library Quarterly*, Vol. 23, No. 3, July, 1953. While the discussion in the present text considers acquisition work on the basis of current practice, these authors discuss changes in scholarship which have affected research libraries. The student will recognize in these discussions concern for the future on fundamental questions involving the extent of knowledge of libraries and the library profession, library cooperation, finance, personnel, and mechanical and technological changes. The October, 1953, issue of *College and Research Libraries* also contains a series of papers which are helpful in orienting the student in problems of acquisition policies. These papers by H. H. Fussler, Robert Vosper, and Eileen Thornton are concerned with academic library acquisition policy.

5. American Library Association, *Post-War Standards for Public Libraries* (Chicago, 1943), pp. 67–70. This work is being revised by the

Public Libraries Division of the American Library Association. A useful body of information on standards is contained in "California Public Library Standards," a special issue of the *News Notes of California Libraries,* 48:357–431, July, 1953.

6. This is made evident by an examination of the published policies of libraries. *The Policy on Scope and Coverage* (1951) of the Armed Forces Medical Library (formerly Army Medical Library), and the *Acquisition Policy* (1953) of the John Crerar Library are two examples of policy statements. They contain definitions of various types of collections, e.g., "skeletal collection," "reference collection," "research collection," "exhaustive collection." Readers will also be interested in the type of specific acquisitions by a cooperative center (see R. T. Esterquest, "Midwest Inter-Library Center: Acquisition Policy and Program, 1950–1953," *College and Research Libraries,* 15:47–49, January, 1954). Helpful publications on acquisitional policy and procedure in the field of public libraries are *Book Selection Policies and Procedures,* ed. by Marion E. Hawes and Dorothy Sinclair, and *Selection Policies for Children's Books,* by Elizabeth H. Gross (both published by the Enoch Pratt Free Library, Baltimore, in 1950); and *Book Selection Procedures Manual* (Preliminary ed., February 1, 1954, issued for internal use by the New York Public Library Circulation Department).

7. J. P. Boyd, "A Landmark in the History of Library Cooperation in the United States," *College and Research Libraries,* 8:101–109, April, 1947. R. Peiss, "Report on Europe," *ibid.,* pp. 113–119.

8. E. E. Williams, *Farmington Plan Handbook* (Bloomington, Ind., Association of Research Libraries, 1953).

9. R. B. Downs, *op. cit.*

10. A. C. Potter, *The Library of Harvard University,* 4th ed. (Cambridge, Harvard University, 1934).

11. R. B. Downs, *Resources of Southern Libraries* (Chicago, American Library Association, 1938).

12. R. E. Ellsworth and N. L. Kilpatrick, "Midwest Reaches for the Stars," *College and Research Libraries,* 9:136–144, April, 1948. R. S. Frodin, "The Midwest Inter-Library Corporation," *ALA Bulletin,* 43:170–172, May, 1949. See also R. T. Esterquest, *op. cit.,* note 6 above.

13. Fremont Rider, *The Scholar and the Future of the Research Library* (New York, Hadham Press, 1944), pp. 81–82.

14. T. R. Barcus, "Buying Books for 92 Junior Colleges," *College and Research Libraries,* 1:78–83, December, 1939. R. M. Lester, "Carnegie Corporation Aid to College Libraries," *ibid.,* pp. 72–77, 83.

15. T. R. Barcus, *op. cit.,* p. 80.

16. J. P. Boyd, *op. cit.*

17. D. P. Lockwood, "Cooperative Acquisitions in the United States *versus* a World Library," *College and Research Libraries,* 8:110–112, April, 1947.

18. E. E. Williams, *op. cit.,* p. 3.

19. K. D. Metcalf, "The Farmington Plan after Three Years," *Harvard Library Bulletin,* 5:122–125, Winter, 1951.

20. E. E. Williams, *op. cit.,* p. 64.

21. C. W. David and R. Hirsch, "Importations of Foreign Monographs under the Influence of the Farmington Plan," *College and Research Libraries,* 11:101–105, July, 1950.

22. *Ibid.,* p. 105.

23. "Documents Expediting Project." Report (July, 1950) from Homer Halvorson to cooperating libraries.

24. For an explanation of one library's solution to this problem, see Leta E. Adams, "Organization of Internal Processes in Book Selection for Public Libraries," in *The Practice of Book Selection,* ed. by L. R. Wilson (Chicago, University of Chicago Press, 1940), pp. 190–208.

25. W. O'D. Pierce, *Work Measurement in Public Libraries* (New York, Social Science Research Council, 1949), p. 28.

26. J. P. Danton, "The Selection of Books for College Libraries: An Examination of Certain Factors Which Affect Excellence of Selection," *Library Quarterly,* 5:419–436, October, 1935. Douglas Waples and H. D. Lasswell, *National Libraries and Foreign Scholarship* (Chicago, University of Chicago Press, 1936), pp. 199–202. H. H. Fussler, "The Bibliographer Working in a Broad Area of Knowledge," *College and Research Libraries,* 10:199–202, July, 1949. E. M. Grieder, "The Foundations of Acquisition Policy in the Small University Library," *College and Research Libraries,* 10:208–214, July, 1949.

27. K. D. Metcalf. See note 4.

28. S. A. McCarthy, *Report of a Survey of the Library of the University of New Hampshire, January–February,* 1949 (Ithaca, N.Y., 1949), pp. 39–40.

29. R. W. Orr, *The Library at Iowa State,* 3: [20], October 21, 1949.

30. L. R. Wilson, R. B. Downs, and M. F. Tauber, *op. cit.,* pp. 66–70.

31. R. W. Christ, "Acquisition Work in College Libraries," *College and Research Libraries,* 10:17–23, January, 1949.

32. T. P. Fleming and J. H. Moriarty, "Essentials in the Organization of Acquisition Work in University Libraries," *College and Research Libraries,* 1:229–234, June, 1940.

33. *Ibid.*, p. 232.

34. R. W. Christ, *op. cit.*

35. U.S. Library of Congress, *Annual Report of the Librarian of Congress for the Fiscal Year Ending June 30, 1952* (Washington, D.C., 1953), chart facing p. 88. *Annual Report of the Librarian of Congress for the Fiscal Year Ending June 30, 1953* (Washington, D.C., 1954), chart facing p. 94.

CHAPTER IV. TYPES OF MATERIALS AND THEIR SOURCES: PURCHASES

1. U.S. Office of Education, *Statistics of Public Libraries in Cities with Populations of 100,000 or More: 1952*, Circular No. 372, April, 1953 (Washington, D.C., 1953).

2. *College and Research Libraries*, 15:68–69, January, 1954.

3. K. D. Metcalf and E. E. Williams, "The Finances of the Harvard University Library," *Harvard Library Bulletin*, 7:339, Autumn, 1953.

4. Columbia University Libraries, *Report of the Director of Libraries for the Academic Year Ending June 30, 1947* (New York, 1948), pp. 16–17.

5. R. B. Downs, "Uniform Statistics for Library Holdings," *Library Quarterly*, 16:63–69, January, 1946. G. R. Lyle, "Counting Library Holdings," *College and Research Libraries*, 11:69–72, January, 1950.

6. Public libraries such as those of Baltimore, Boston, Brooklyn, Chicago, Cincinnati, Cleveland, Detroit, Los Angeles, Milwaukee, New York, Philadelphia, Pittsburgh, and St. Louis; academic libraries such as those of California, Chicago, Columbia, Cornell, Duke, Harvard, Illinois, Michigan, Minnesota, Ohio State, Pennsylvania, Princeton, Stanford, Texas, and Yale.

7. L. C. Merritt, "The Administrative, Fiscal and Quantitative Aspects of the Regional Union Catalog" in R. B. Downs, *Union Catalogs in the United States* (Chicago, American Library Association, 1942), p. 62. Examples of specific gaps are suggested by U.S. Library of Congress, *Select List of Unlocated Research Books*. Washington, No. 1—, 1937—.

8. *Directory of U.S. Dealers in Old and Rare Books*, 1949 ed. (Marietta, Ga., Continental Book Co., 1949), p. [iii].

9. Nathan Van Patten, "The University Library and the Book Collector," *PNLA Quarterly*, 14:70, January, 1950.

10. "The Out-of-Print Department," *Stechert-Hafner Book News*, 4:18, October, 1949. "Stechert-Hafner—Serving the Library World," *Stechert-Hafner Book News*, 8:28–30, November, 1953. See also J. C. Borden, "Tapping the O.P. Market," *Arkansas Libraries*, 5:9–13, October, 1948.

11. Nathan Van Patten, "Buying Policies of College and University Libraries," *College and Research Libraries*, 1:64–70, December, 1939. See also discussion by T. P. Fleming, *ibid*., pp. 70–71.

12. Fleming Bennett, "Prompt Payment of Bookdealers' Invoices," *College and Research Libraries*, 15:387–395+, October, 1953.

13. "Methods of Tapping the Second Hand and Out-of-Print Market" (Ms., 1950). Dealers' catalogs will continue to be a primary source for older books. The admonitions of J. G. E. Hopkins and the editor of the *Antiquarian Bookman* should, if taken seriously, help to make them more effective tools (see J. G. E. Hopkins, "An Editor Looks at Dealers' Catalogs," *Antiquarian Bookman*, 12:783–785, September 19, 1953; "Book Trade Catalogs." *ibid*., 12:782). Hopkins offers suggestions in simplifying bibliographical style and typography, while the editor provides a detailed listing of factors on physical layout, style, and contents. Librarians interested in issuing a catalog for the purposes of sale, exchange, purchases, or exhibits might well examine these factors. A recent source of price information on older books is J. N. Heard, *Bookman's Guide to Americana* (Washington, D.C., Scarecrow Press, 1953).

14. S. A. McCarthy, *Report of a Survey of the Library of the University of New Hampshire, January–February, 1949* (Ithaca, N.Y., 1949), p. 28.

15. L. R. Wilson, R. B. Downs, M. F. Tauber, *Report of a Survey of the Libraries of Cornell University for the Library Board of Cornell University, October 1947–February 1948* (Ithaca, Cornell University, 1948), pp. 66–67.

16. University of California Libraries, *Annual Report, 1948–49. Part IV, Los Angeles Campus* (Los Angeles [1949]), p. 4.

17. John Fall, "Problems of American Libraries in Acquiring Foreign Publications," *Library Quarterly*, 24:101–113, April, 1954.

18. C. F. Gosnell, "Values and Dangers of Standard Book and Periodical Lists for College Libraries," *College and Research Libraries*, 2:216–220, June, 1941.

The Gosnell study relates the experience of Queens College Library in selecting its original stock of books. The procedure was to take apart the Shaw lists (1931 and 1940 Supplement) and the Mohrhardt list for general books and Mudge for reference books, and then distribute the titles among the faculty for approval and additional selection or suggestions. The order cards were clips cut from the lists and pasted on cards. Periodicals were selected from the above lists and from lists compiled by Lyle, Walter, and Hilton. "The lists were fundamental, and suggestive stimulants as well; but in no sense were they regarded as restrictive.

They were always subject to reinterpretation in the light of the curriculum." (p. 217)

In analyzing the lists (year of publication against number of books) Gosnell found a distinct curve indicating that the compilers of the lists had selected relatively recent books for the most part. Gosnell then concludes that any list compiled will include principally books published within the fifty years immediately preceding the compilation and will include more books for each year as it draws closer to the time of compilation. On this basis, Gosnell projects a "standard curve" for the live collection. He assumes that there is an optimum size for a college collection which will be maintained by accessioning and discarding each year at a standard rate. A sample of the collection might then provide a basis for evaluating the collection to see whether it is being kept up at the proper rate.

The most obvious and immediate conclusion to be drawn from this study is that the librarian who attempts to use one of the standard lists today runs an excellent chance of (1) not being able to buy the books he selects because of their age, and (2) the books he may be able to buy are likely to be relatively obsolete.

19. L. R. Wilson and M. F. Tauber, *The University Library* (Chicago, University of Chicago Press, 1945), pp. 324–326.

20. A recent effort to set down factors in periodical acquisition policies was made by Kenneth B. Shaw in "Periodical Aquisition Policies," *ASLIB Proceedings*, 5:81–86, May, 1953. Shaw presents two useful tables in his discussion. Table 1 is concerned with characteristics or qualities in periodicals which are subject to change, such as title, frequency, price, format, etc. Table 2 is a tentative list of factors which may need consideration before secondhand periodicals are acquired, such as the nature of the acquiring library, relationship to other libraries, the periodical itself, and the run offered. Each of these is broken down into more specific points or questions which should be raised. Acquisition problems of periodicals and serials are also discussed in David Grenfell's *Periodicals and Serials* (London, Aslib, 1953).

21. C. H. Brown, "Librarianship and the Sciences," in *Challenges to Librarianship*, ed. by Louis Shores (Tallahassee, Florida State University, 1953), pp. 74–76. Brown makes a strong case for the retention of old files of scientific periodicals and for the need of filling gaps in missing issues or volumes in research library collections. The H. W. Wilson Company, in New York, and other dealers maintain large stocks of back files of periodicals which are sold to libraries.

22. R. B. Downs, "Problems of German Periodicals," *College and Re-*

search Libraries, 8:303–309, July, 1947. Reuben Peiss, "Problems in the Acquisition of Foreign Scientific Publications," *Department of State Bulletin,* 22:151–155, January, 1950.

23. Anne M. Boyd and Rae Elizabeth Rips, *United States Government Publications,* 3d ed. (New York, H. W. Wilson, 1952). L. R. Wilson and M. F. Tauber, *The University Library* (Chicago, University of Chicago Press, 1945), pp. 329–342. Ellen P. Jackson, *The Administration of the Government Documents Collection, ACRL Monograph,* No. 5, January, 1953.

24. E. B. Jackson, "Acquisitions: Sources and Techniques," *American Documentation,* 3:94–100, April, 1952; and "How to Obtain Research and Development Reports from the Government," *Special Libraries,* 44:101–108, March, 1953. A recent study by Bernard M. Fry, *Library Organization and Management of Technical Reports Literature* (Washington, D.C., The Catholic University of America Press, 1953), includes a detailed analysis of the conditions and techniques of acquisition of technical reports. Various papers given at the "Workshop on Production and Use of Technical Reports," held at Catholic University, April 13–19, 1953, are of direct use to acquisitions personnel in their search for unpublished reports. It is planned to publish these papers.

25. R. W. Orr and W. H. Carlson, *Report of a Survey of the Library of Texas A. and M. College, October,* 1949 *to February,* 1950 (College Station, Texas, Texas A. and M. College, 1950), p. 39. See also R. H. Muller, "The Selection of Newspapers for the College Library," *College and Research Libraries,* 10:27–31, July, 1949.

26. L. R. Wilson and R. C. Swank, *Report of a Survey of the Library of Stanford University for Stanford University, November 1946–March* 1947 (Chicago, American Library Association, 1947).

27. See appendixes to LC *Information Bulletin,* "Microfilm Clearing House;" see also Philadelphia Bibliographical Center and Union Library Catalogue, *Union List of Microfilms,* ed. by Eleanor E. Campion (Ann Arbor, Edwards Bros., 1951). The Library of Congress Union Catalog Division has recently issued a *Selected List of United States Newspapers Recommended for Preservation by the A.L.A. Committee on Cooperative Microfilm Projects* (Washington, D.C., 1953). A useful bibliography is *Microfilms and Microcards: Their Use in Research, a Selected List of References,* compiled by Blanche P. McCrum (Washington, D.C., Library of Congress, 1950).

28. E. B. Espenshade, "No One Source for Acquiring Maps," *Library Journal,* 75:431–432, March 15, 1950.

29. *Ibid.,* p. 431.

30. Ena L. Yonge, "Map Procurement in the Special Library," *Special Libraries*, 44:173–174, May–June, 1953.

31. E. DeWald, "Map Procurement in Government Agencies," *Special Libraries*, 44:175–177, May–June, 1953.

32. L. R. Wilson and R. C. Swank, *op. cit.*, p. 159. See also Irving Lieberman, ed., *Proceedings, Audio-Visual Workshop, Prior to the 1953 Conference of the American Library Association* (Berkeley, Cal., 1953).

33. G. R. Lyle, *The Administration of the College Library*, 2d ed., rev. (New York, H. W. Wilson, 1949), p. 407.

CHAPTER V. OPERATIONS IN ORDER WORK

1. U.S. Library of Congress, Descriptive Cataloging Division, *Cooperative Cataloging Manual* (Washington, D.C., U.S. Government Printing Office, 1944), pp. 61–100.

2. Columbia University Libraries, "Routines Involved in the Use of Correlated Order Forms." Its *Director's Memorandum* 46–3 [New York, 1946]. The text as printed here includes modifications of the original to conform to certain changes in procedure made since these forms were first introduced.

3. Fleming Bennett, "Prompt Payment of Bookdealers' Invoices: An Approach to Standards," *College and Research Libraries*, 14:387–392+, October, 1953.

4. G. N. Hartje, "Centralized Serial Records in University Libraries," *Serial Slants*, 1:15–19, January, 1951. See also P. L. Berry, "Library of Congress Serial Record Techniques," *Serial Slants*, 3:14–18, July, 1952. J. E. Skipper, "Organizing Serial Records at the Ohio State University Libraries," *College and Research Libraries*, 14:39–45, January, 1953.

5. See Bella Shachtman, "Simplification of Serials Records Work," *Serial Slants*, 3:6–13, July, 1952; and "Current Serial Records—an Experiment," *College and Research Libraries*, 14:240–242+, July, 1953.

6. Alexander Moffit, "Punched Cards Records in Serials Acquisitions," *College and Research Libraries*, 7:10–13, January, 1946.

7. Lena Biancardo, "Desiderata Files in College and University Libraries," (M.S. essay, School of Library Service, Columbia University, 1950). See also G. W. Bergquist, *Report of the Out-of-Print Survey* (Chicago, American Library Association, 1952).

8. R. W. Christ, "Aquisition Work in Ten College Libraries" (M.S. essay, Columbia University, 1948), pp. 30–31.

9. Dorothy E. Chamberlain, "In-Process Records," *College and Research Libraries*, 7:335–338, October, 1946.

10. Harry Dewey, "Pre-Cataloging—A Must for the Modern Library," *College and Research Libraries,* 10:224, July, 1949.

11. Margaret L. Johnson, "The Yale Collection of Dealers' Catalogs," *College and Research Libraries,* 7:67–73, January, 1946.

12. W. O'D. Pierce, *Work Measurement in Public Libraries* (New York, Social Science Research Council, 1949).

13. R. W. Christ, "Acquisition Work in College Libraries," *College and Research Libraries,* 10:17–23, January, 1949. This paper is based on the author's Master's essay, note 8.

14. T. D. Morris, "Techniques of Appraising the Administrative Strength of an Organization," *College and Research Libraries,* 13:111–116, April, 1952. See also Cresap, McCormick, and Paget, *The New York Public Library. Survey of Acquisitions* (New York, 1951). This report is available only on loan. It contains many useful suggestions for the very large research library.

15. A. P. Sweet, "Forms in Acquisition Work," *College and Research Libraries,* 14:396–404+, October, 1953.

16. R. R. Shaw, *The Use of Photography for Clerical Routines: A Report to the American Council of Learned Societies* (Washington, D.C., American Council of Learned Societies, 1953); and "Photoclerical Routines at USDA," *Library Journal,* 78:2064–2070, December 1, 1953.

17. Acquisitions work for special types of libraries presents problems which differ somewhat from those met by the usual public or academic library. Various sources are available to the student. Among them are M. O. Price, *Order Work in a Law Library* (New York, School of Library Service, Columbia University, 1941). William Roalfe, *The Libraries of the Legal Profession* (St. Paul, Minn., West, 1953). *A Handbook of Medical Library Practice,* ed. by Janet Doe (Chicago, American Library Association, 1943; now being revised). *Technical Libraries: Their Organization and Management,* ed. by Lucille Jackson (New York, Special Libraries Association [1951]).

18. For a detailed listing of works in each of these groups, see Constance M. Winchell, *Guide to Reference Works,* 7th ed. (Chicago, American Library Association, 1951). This is a reworking of the original *Guide* by Isadore G. Mudge; a *Supplement* was issued in 1954.

CHAPTER VI. GIFTS AND DEPOSITS

1. Lester Condit, *A Pamphlet about Pamphlets* (Chicago, University of Chicago Press, 1939), p. 74.

2. U.S. Library of Congress, *Annual Report of the Librarian of Con-*

gress for the Fiscal Year Ending June 30, 1953 (Washington, D.C., U.S. Government Printing Office, 1954), p. 20.

3. For example, see Nathan Van Patten, "The University Library and the Book Collector," *PNLA Quarterly*, 14:69–71, January, 1950. L. C. Powell, "From Private Collection to Public Institution, The William Andrews Clark Memorial Library," *Library Quarterly*, 20:101–108, April, 1950.

4. Yale University Library, *Report of the Librarian, 1948–1949*, Bulletin of Yale University (New Haven, Yale University Press, 1949), p. 14.

5. *Ibid.*, 1952–1953, pp. 15 and 17.

6. E. Eberstadt, "The William Robertson Coe Collection of Western Americana," *Yale University Library Gazette*, 23:41–42, 1949.

7. "Funds Recently Established and Gifts," *Yale University Library Gazette*, 23:196, 1949.

8. L. S. Thompson, "Of Bibliological Mendicancy," *College and Research Libraries*, 14:373–378, October, 1953.

9. Nathan Van Patten, *op. cit.*, p. 72.

10. W. S. Lewis, "Yale Library Associates," *Yale University Library Gazette*, 6:1, 1931.

11. ALA College and University Postwar Planning Committee and the Association of College and Reference Libraries, *College and University Libraries and Librarianship* (Chicago, American Library Association, 1946), pp. 64–65.

12. L. R. Wilson and R. W. Orr, *Report of a Survey of the Libraries of the Alabama Polytechnic Institute, November 1948–March 1949* (Auburn, Ala., Alabama Polytechnic Institute, 1949), pp. 64–65.

13. The authors are grateful to Alfred H. Lane for assistance with this section. Mr. Lane is the compiler of *Staff Manual of the Gift and Exchange Division* (New York, Columbia University Libraries, 1949).

14. J. L. McCamy, *Government Publications for the Citizen* (New York, Columbia University Press, 1949), p. 29. See also U.S. Superintendent of Documents, *Monthly Catalog of United States Government Publications*, September, 1953, pp. 157–168.

15. R. B. Eastin, "Let's Use Public Documents," *Library Journal*, 73:1554–1558, November, 1948. See also "Problems of Document Bibliography and Distribution," *College and Research Libraries*, 15:33–46, January, 1954.

16. A discussion of current problems of acquiring and organizing documents appears in Violet A. Cabeen and C. D. Cook, "Organization of Serials and Documents," *Library Trends*, 2:199–216, October, 1953.

CHAPTER VII. DUPLICATES AND EXCHANGES

1. A. Passier, *Les Échanges Internationaux Littéraires et Scientifiques* (Paris, Picard, 1880). An excellent résumé of early exchanges appears in *Conference on International Cultural, Educational, and Scientific Exchanges Princeton University–November 25–26, 1946; Preliminary Memoranda,* by E. E. Williams [and] Ruth V. Noble . . . (Chicago, American Library Association, 1947), pp. 83–99. (In these notes it will be referred to under the names of E. E. Williams and Ruth V. Noble.)

2. Elizabeth M. Richards, "Alexander Vattemare and His System of International Exchanges" (M.S. essay, Columbia University, 1934).

3. J. B. Childs, "Experience of the Library of Congress under the International Exchange Act," *Public Documents,* 1935 (Chicago, American Library Association, 1936), pp. 64–67. E. E. Williams and Ruth V. Noble, *op. cit.,* pp. 73, 84–85. U. S. Library of Congress, Processing Dept., *The Role of the Library of Congress in the International Exchange of Official Publications,* by Robert D. Stevens (Washington, D.C., 1953).

4. Kathleen M. Ruckman, "Gifts and Exchanges in the University Library" (M.A. essay, University of Illinois, 1936). I. MacIver, "The Exchange of Publications as a Medium for the Development of the Book Collection," *Library Quarterly,* 8:491–502, October, 1938. Juanita Terry, "Exchanges as a Source of Acquisition—with Special Emphasis on College and University Publications" (M.S. essay, Columbia University, 1939).

5. E. E. Williams and Ruth V. Noble, *op. cit.,* p. 88.

6. United States Book Exchange, *Newsletter,* Vol. 1, 1949—. See also *The United States Book Exchange* (Washington, 1952).

7. United States Book Exchange, *Newsletter,* Vol. 2, No. 2, March–April, 1950, p. 1.

8. U.S. Library of Congress, *Annual Report of the Librarian of Congress for the Fiscal Year Ending June* 30, 1953 (Washington, 1954), p. 25.

9. United States Book Exchange, *Newsletter,* Vol. 5, No. 3, June, 1953.

10. See E. E. Williams and Ruth V. Noble, *op. cit.,* p. 85. An extensive study by L. J. Kipp, *The International Exchange of Publications* (Wakefield, Mass., The Murray Print Co., 1950), contains materials on the development of exchange, bases of exchange programs, exchange with Latin America, operational machinery and problems, and developments of potential importance to exchange.

11. A. H. Lane, "Exchange Work in College and University Libraries" (M.S. essay, Columbia University, 1950), pp. 16–17.

12. Mildred V. Naylor, "The Exchange," *Bulletin of the Medical Library Association*, 34:167–175, July, 1946. See the "Report of the Exchange Committee" in the annual proceedings of the Medical Library Association, e.g., *Bulletin of the Medical Library Association*, 42:65–67, January, 1954.

13. Mary Irwin, ed., *American Universities and Colleges*, 6th ed. (Washington, American Council on Education, 1952), pp. 59–60.

14. *Dissertation Abstracts*, Vol. 1 to date, Ann Arbor, Mich., University Microfilms, 1938 to date (Vols. 1–11, 1938–1951, issued with the title *Microfilm Abstracts*).

15. M. F. Tauber and W. H. Jesse, *Report of a Survey of the Libraries of the Virginia Polytechnic Institute* (Blacksburg, Virginia Polytechnic Institute, 1949), p. 46.

16. *Ibid.*

17. A. H. Lane, *op. cit.*, pp. 6–7.

18. R. W. Orr and W. H. Carlson, *Report of a Survey of the Library of the Texas A and M College, October, 1949 to February, 1950* (College Station, Texas, Texas A. and M. College, 1950), pp. 103–104.

19. *Ibid.*, p. 102.

20. Report from A. H. Lane, December 22, 1953.

21. U.S. Library of Congress, *Annual Report of the Librarian of Congress for the Fiscal Year Ending June 30, 1949* (Washington, U.S. Government Printing Office, 1950), p. 11.

22. *Ibid.*, 1952, p. 57.

23. *Ibid.*, chart facing p. 96.

24. *Ibid.*

25. T. Kleberg, "Report of the Sub-Committee on the Exchange of University Publications," International Federation of Library Associations, *Publications*, 12:121–123, 1947.

26. *Ibid.*

27. A. H. Lane, *op. cit.*, p. 45.

28. *Ibid.*, p. 16.

29. L. R. Wilson and M. F. Tauber, *Report of a Survey of the University of South Carolina for the University of South Carolina, February–May, 1946* (Columbia, S.C., University of South Carolina, 1946). The following statement appears on p. 43: "No system of exchanges now exists for the University Library as a whole. The Law Library has been engaged in an exchange program since 1937, when an enabling act was passed by the General Assembly requiring copies of certain pub-

lications to be delivered to the Law Library of the University of South Carolina for the purpose of exchange. The materials included 25 copies of the Acts of the General Assembly, 7 copies of the Acts and Joint Resolutions of the General Assembly, 25 copies of any Constitutional Convention of the State of South Carolina, 25 copies of the Code of Laws of South Carolina, and 49 copies of the Reports of the Supreme Court of South Carolina. As a result of this exchange act, the Law Library now receives currently the reports of 32 states, the acts of 20 states, and the codes of 4 states."

30. E. E. Williams and Ruth V. Noble, *op. cit.*, p. 82.

31. *Ibid.*, Chapter VII.

32. See note 12.

33. The service of the American Association of Law Libraries Exchange includes some service to nonparticipating libraries.

34. Due to the difficulty of having slips accurately filed by student assistants, it was decided to enter slips for certain types of materials directly on a check list (e.g., H. B. Merican, "A Check List of State Judicial Council Reports from Their Beginning Through 1947," *Law Library Journal*, 41:135–144, May, 1948.)

35. Exchanges between libraries are usually made on open exchange (no particular effort made to evaluate each piece of material).

36. Where a notice is sent in lieu of the slip, it consists of a double postcard. It is assumed that a library receiving same will return the second portion of the postcard with a notation as to whether the exchange was effected. Upon receipt of the latter, the listings are corrected.

37. "Recommendations of the Special Committee on the Law Library Exchange," *Law Library Journal*, 45:477, November, 1952. Listings are not held for more than two years. Listings contain now only texts, monographs, treatises, legal periodicals (including law review and bar association publications, other than proceedings), and United States government documents. "Report of the Committee on Exchange Files," *Law Library Journal*, 46:304, August, 1953.

38. Evah Ostrander, "Report of the Committee on Periodical Exchange," in American Theological Library Association, *Summary of Proceedings*, Second Annual Conference, Dayton, Ohio, June 14–15, 1948, [n.p., n.d.], pp. 21–22.

39. J. S. Judah, "A System of Duplicate Periodical Exchange," *ibid.*, pp. 22–23.

40. American Theological Library Association, *Summary of Proceedings*, Seventh Annual Conference, June 11–12, 1953. [n.p., n.d.], p. 65.

41. A. H. Lane, *op. cit*, p. 30.

42. A. H. Lane, "The Economics of Exchange," *Serial Slants*, 3:19–22, July, 1952. See also W. Cantelmo, "The Disposal of Duplicates," *College and Research Libraries*, 2:333–336, September, 1941.

43. C. C. Mish, "Duplicate Exchange Service," in *The Union Library Catalogue of the Philadelphia Metropolitan Area, 1936–1946: a Tenth Anniversary Report* (Philadelphia, 1946), pp. 22–27.

44. Janice W. Sherwood and Eleanor E. Campion, "Union Library Catalogue: Services, 1950. Quo Vadis?" *College and Research Libraries*, 13:104, April, 1952. This article contains considerable data on union catalogs as of 1950.

45. R. T. Esterquest, "The Pacific Northwest Bibliographic Center," *College and Research Libraries*, 1:56–57, January, 1947.

CHAPTER VIII. CATALOGS AND CATALOGING: DEVELOPMENT AND FUNCTIONS

1. Beverley Ruffin, "Some Developments Towards Modern Cataloging Practice In University Libraries as Exemplified in the Printed Book Catalogs of Harvard and Yale before the year 1876" (M.S. essay, Columbia University, 1935).

2. Ruth Schley, "Cataloging in the Libraries of Princeton, Columbia, and the University of Pennsylvania before 1876" (M.S. essay, Columbia University, 1946).

3. *Ibid.*, pp. 38–43.

4. Beverley Ruffin, *op. cit.*

5. Sarah R. Corcoran, "A Study of Cataloging Practice through 1830 as shown in the Printed Book Catalogs of Six Libraries of City of New York" (M.S. essay, Columbia University, 1936). Discusses the New York Society Library, New York Hospital Library, New York Historical Society Library, The Apprentices' Library, The Mercantile Library, and the Lyceum of Natural History Library.

6. Ruth Schley, *op. cit.*

7. Theodore Besterman, "The Library of Congress and the Future of Its Catalogue," *Journal of Documentation*, 1:194–205, March, 1946. "Symposium on 'The Library of Congress and the Future of Its Catalogue' by Theodore Besterman," *Journal of Documentation*, 2:245–254, March, 1947.

8. Fremont Rider, *The Scholar and the Future of the Research Library* (New York, Hadham Press, 1944), p. 12.

9. U.S. Library of Congress, *Annual Report of the Librarian of Congress for the Fiscal Year Ending June 30, 1953* (Washington, D.C., U.S. Government Printing Office, 1954), pp. 35–36.

10. The figures were obtained by correspondence or through annual reports of the institutions.

11. U.S. Library of Congress, *Annual Report of the Librarian of Congress for the Fiscal Year Ending June 30, 1953* (Washington, U.S. Government Printing Office, 1954), p. 135.

12. Janice W. Sherwood and Eleanor E. Campion, "Union Library Catalogue: Services, 1950. Quo Vadis?" *College and Research Libraries*, 13:106, April, 1952.

13. A. B. Berthold, "The Future of the Catalog in Research Libraries," *College and Research Libraries*, 8:20–22, 53, January, 1947.

14. A. D. Osborn and Susan M. Haskins, "Catalog Maintenance," *Library Trends*, 2:279–289, October, 1953.

15. Fremont Rider, "Alternatives for the Present Dictionary Card Catalog," in *The Acquisition and Cataloging of Books*, ed. by W. M. Randall (Chicago, University of Chicago Press, 1940), pp. 153–154.

16. W. I. Fletcher, *Library Journal*, 30:141–144, March, 1905.

17. Fremont Rider, *op. cit.*

18. A. B. Berthold, *op. cit.*

19. H. L. Leupp, "Probable Trends in University Libraries," *College and Research Libraries*, 1:60, December, 1939.

20. Pierce Butler, "The Research Worker's Approach to Books—The Humanist," in *The Acquisition and Cataloging of Books*, ed. by W. M. Randall (Chicago, University of Chicago Press, 1940), p. 282.

21. R. R. Shaw, "The Research Worker's Approach to Books—The Scientist," in *The Acquisition and Cataloging of Books*, ed. by W. M. Randall (Chicago, University of Chicago Press, 1940), p. 299.

22. K. L. Taylor, "Subject Catalogs *vs.* Classified Catalog," in *The Subject Analysis of Library Materials*, ed. by M. F. Tauber (New York, School of Library Service, Columbia University, 1953), pp. 100–113.

23. Harry Dewey, "Some Special Aspects of the Classified Catalog," in *The Subject Analysis of Library Materials*, ed. by M. F. Tauber (New York, School of Library Service, Columbia University, 1953), pp. 114–129.

24. Mary D. Herrick, "The Development of a Classified Catalog for a University Library," *College and Research Libraries*, 14:418–424, October, 1953.

25. I. W. Thom, "The Divided Catalog in College and University Libraries," *College and Research Libraries*, 10:236–241, July, 1949.

26. Amy W. Nyholm, "California Examines Its Divided Catalog," *College and Research Libraries*, 9:195–201, July, 1948.

27. Anne E. Markley, "The University of California Subject Catalog

Inquiry: A Study of the Subject Catalog Based on Interviews with Users," *Journal of Cataloging and Classification*, 6:88–95, Fall, 1950.

28. C. J. Frarey, "Studies in the Use of the Subject Catalog: Summary and Evaluation," in *The Subject Analysis of Library Materials*, ed. by M. F. Tauber (New York, School of Library Service, Columbia University, 1953), pp. 147–166.

29. C. S. Spalding, "The Use of Catalog Entries at the Library of Congress," *Journal of Cataloging and Classification*, 6:95–100, Fall, 1950.

30. W. H. Brett, III, "The Use of the Subject Catalog by the General Reference Service of a University Library," *Journal of Cataloging and Classification*, 7:17–18, Winter, 1951.

31. L. N. Ridenour, R. R. Shaw, and A. G. Hill, *Bibliography in an Age of Science* (Urbana, University of Illinois Press, 1951).

32. C. D. Gull, "Substitutes for the Card Catalog," *Library Trends*, 2:318–329, October, 1953.

33. C. S. Spalding, "Library of Congress Catalogs: Proposed Expansion into Current Author and Subject Catalogs of American Library Resources," *College and Research Libraries*, 15:15–20, January, 1954.

34. C. W. David. "The Reproduction of the National Union Catalog," *College and Research Libraries*, 15:20–26, January, 1954.

35. R. B. Downs, "Report and Supplementary Report on the National Union Catalog and Related Matters." Appendix to the LC *Information Bulletin*, August 9–15, 1949, pp. 1–3.

36. C. D. Gull, *op. cit.*, p. 327.

37. M. F. Tauber, "Subject Cataloging and Classification Approaching the Crossroads," *College and Research Libraries*, 3:149–155, March, 1942.

38. Andrew Osborn, *Library Journal*, 74:1012–1013, July, 1949.

39. Mortimer Taube, "The Cataloging of Publications of Corporate Authors," *Library Quarterly*, 20:1–20, January, 1950.

40. Seymour Lubetzky, "The Cataloging of Publications of Corporate Authors: A Rejoinder," *Library Quarterly*, 21:1–12, January, 1951. See also Mortimer Taube, "To the Editor of the *Library Quarterly*," *Library Quarterly*, 21:155–156, April, 1951. The Library of Congress issued Lubetzky's *Cataloging Rules and Principles* in 1953.

41. H. B. Van Hoesen, "Perspective in Cataloging, with Some Applications," *Library Quarterly*, 14:102–103, April, 1944.

42. W. C. Simonton, "Duplication of Entries in the Subject Catalog of a University Library and Subject Bibliographies in English Literature" (M.S. essay, Columbia University, 1948).

43. C. J. Frarey, "Subject Heading Revision by the Library of Congress" (M.S. essay, Columbia University, 1951).

44. "Subject Cataloging Clearing House," *Library Journal*, 72:713–714, May 1, 1947.

45. In 1953, the Harvard University Press issued *Catalogue of the Lamont Library*, prepared by Philip J. McNiff and members of the library staff. The volume is a classified arrangement of the titles in the Lamont Library.

46. R. C. Swank, "Subject Catalogs, Classifications, or Bibliographies? A Review of Critical Discussions, 1876–1942," *Library Quarterly*, 14:316, July, 1944.

47. R. E. Ellsworth, "The Administrative Implications for University Libraries of the New Cataloging Code," *College and Research Libraries*, 3:137, March, 1942.

48. The term "cooperative cataloging" is generally distinguished from "centralized cataloging" in that the latter refers to a single agency which catalogs for a wider group of libraries. This may be within a library system with branch or departmental libraries, or by a central agency such as the H. W. Wilson Company. The Library of Congress, in a sense, is involved in both cooperative and centralized cataloging. It is a centralized office for producing cards.

49. U.S. Library of Congress, Descriptive Cataloging Division, *Cooperative Cataloging Manual for the Use of Contributing Libraries* (Washington, D.C., U.S. Government Printing Office, 1944).

50. Lucile M. Morsch, "Cooperation and Centralization," *Library Trends*, 2:353, October, 1953. This is an excellent summary of cooperation and centralization, and considers activities in foreign countries as well as in the United States.

51. Velva J. Osborn, "A History of Cooperative Cataloging in the United States" (Unpublished M.A. paper, Graduate Library School, University of Chicago, 1944).

52. U.S. Library of Congress, *Annual Report of the Librarian of Congress for the Fiscal Year Ending June 30, 1942* (Washington, D.C., U.S. Government Printing Office, 1943), p. 45.

53. Berthold Altmann, "Centralized Cataloging: Its Principles and Organization in the United States and in Germany" (Unpublished M.A. paper, Graduate Library School, University of Chicago, 1944).

54. F. B. Rogers, "Cataloging and Classification at the Army Medical Library," *Bulletin of the Medical Library Association*, 39:28–33, January, 1951.

55. T. P. Fleming, "Cooperative Cataloging," *Bulletin of the Medical Library Association,* 39:38–39, January, 1951.

56. Sigmund von Frauendorfer, "International Unification of Cataloging?" *College and Research Libraries,* 12:245–252, July, 1951.

57. M. F. Tauber, ed., *The Subject Analysis of Library Materials* (New York, School of Library Service, Columbia University, 1953).

58. Mortimer Taube, "Possibilities for Cooperative Work in Subject Controls," *American Documentation,* 3:21–28, January, 1952.

59. International Organization for Standardization, *Lay-out of Periodicals* (Its ISO/TC46 [Secretariat-80] 148, 9 August 1951).

60. International Organization for Standardization, *International System for the Transliteration of Cyrillic Characters* (Its ISO/TC46 [Secretariat-45] 93, 28 February 1951). See also Frits Donker Duyvis, "Standardization as a Tool of Scientific Management," *Library Trends,* 2:410–427, January, 1954.

61. International Organization for Standardization, "Bibliographical References." Its *Draft ISO Recommendation,* No. 24 (ISO/TC46 [Secretariat-137] 231 E, July, 1953).

62. For a thorough discussion of union catalogs and bibliographical centers, see Robert B. Downs, ed., *Union Catalogs in the United States* (Chicago, American Library Association, 1942). See also Janice W. Sherwood and Eleanor E. Campion, "Union Library Catalog: Services, 1950. Quo Vadis?" *College and Research Libraries,* 13:101–106+, April, 1952.

63. J. H. P. Pafford, *Library Co-operation in Europe* (London, Library Association, 1935), pp. 85–120.

64. A union catalog lists by author in one alphabet, the books, pamphlets, periodicals, and other materials owned by cooperating libraries within a particular region or country, and tells where copies are located. Occasionally union catalogs appear in other forms.

65. W. W. Bishop, "Union Catalogs," *Library Quarterly,* 7:36–49, January, 1937. M. F. Tauber, "Other Aspects of Union Catalogs," *Library Quarterly,* 9:411–431, October, 1939. J. E. Van Male, "Union Catalogs and the Point of Diminishing Returns," *Catalogers' and Classifiers' Yearbook,* 8:29–30, 1939.

66. D. C. Weber, "The Fate of Foreigners in the Widener Catalogues," *Harvard Library Bulletin,* 7:349–356, Autumn, 1953.

67. F. X. Doherty, "New England Deposit Library, Organization and Administration," *Library Quarterly,* 19:1–18, January, 1949.

68. R. S. Frodin, "The Midwest Inter-Library Corporation," *ALA Bulletin*, 43:170–172, May, 1949.

69. *Ibid.*

70. For further information concerning this highly interesting project and its development, see the *Annual Report* and the monthly *Newsletter* of the Midwest Inter-Library Center; R. T. Esterquest, "Progress Report on the Midwest Inter-Library Center," *College and Research Libraries*, 12:67–70, January, 1951, and "The Midwest Inter-Library Center," *Journal of Higher Education*, 24:1–44, January, 1953. For some of the problems involved, see R. E. Ellsworth, "Tasks of the Immediate Future," *Library Quarterly*, 22:18–20, January, 1952.

71. F. B. Ludington, "Hampshire Inter-Library Center," *ALA Bulletin*, 46:10–12, January, 1952.

72. C. M. White, "New Mechanism in the Organization of Library Service in the Northeast," *College and Research Libraries*, 11:228–237, July, 1950. K. D. Metcalf, "Proposal for a Northeastern Regional Library," *College and Research Libraries*, 11:238–244, July, 1950.

CHAPTER IX. CATALOG ENTRIES AND DESCRIPTION

1. Beverley Ruffin, "Toward a Sound National Program in Cataloging," *College and Research Libraries*, 10:227–232+, July, 1949.

2. Julia Pettee, "The Development of Authorship Entry and the Formulation of Authorship Rules as Found in the Anglo-American Code," *Library Quarterly*, 6:270–299, July, 1936.

3. H. A. Sharp, *Cataloguing; a Textbook for Use in Libraries*, 4th ed. (London, Grafton, 1948), p. 321.

4. C. C. Jewett, *On the Construction of Catalogues of Libraries, and of a General Catalogue; and Their Publication by Means of Separate Stereotyped Titles. With Rules and Examples* (Washington, D.C., Smithsonian Institution, 1852).

5. H. A. Sharp, *op. cit.*, p. 322.

6. *Library Journal*, 8:251–254, September–October, 1883.

7. H. A. Sharp, *op. cit.*, p. 323.

8. A. L. Walter, "Fifty Years Young: Library of Congress Cards," *College and Research Libraries*, 13:305–308, October, 1952.

9. U.S. Library of Congress, Descriptive Cataloging Division, *Rules for Descriptive Cataloging in the Library of Congress* (Washington, D.C., U.S. Government Printing Office, 1949), p. 2.

10. American Library Association, *Catalog Rules: Author and Title Entries* (Chicago, 1908), p. vii.

11. New York Regional Catalog Group, "Summary of Discussion of Need for Revision of Catalog Code," in *Catalogers' and Classifiers' Yearbook*, 3:20–29, 1932.

12. J. C. M. Hanson, "Revision of A.L.A. Catalog Rules," in *Catalogers' and Classifiers' Yearbook*, 3:1–19, 1932.

13. Vatican, Biblioteca Apostolica Vaticana, *Rules for the Catalog of Printed Books*, tr. from the 2d Italian ed. by The Very Rev. Thomas J. Shanahan and others, ed. by W. E. Wright (Chicago, American Library Association, 1948).

14. American Library Association, Division of Cataloging and Classification, A.L.A. *Cataloging Rules for Author and Title Entries*, 2d ed. (Chicago, 1949), p. ix.

15. Lucile M. Morsch, "A Study on the Establishing of Personal Names for the Catalog," U.S. Library of Congress, Processing Department, *Cataloging Service:* Bulletin, 17:6 and 8, May, 1948.

16. *Ibid.*, p. 7.

17. U.S. Library of Congress, Processing Department, *Cataloging Service:* Bulletin, 20:2, June, 1949.

18. *Ibid.*, 17:6, May, 1948.

19. Columbia University, School of Library Service, *Sample Catalog Cards*, 2d ed. (New York, 1950).

20. See C. F. Gosnell, *Spanish Personal Names: Principles Governing Their Formation and Use* (New York, H. W. Wilson, 1928). See also Maria Luisa Monteiro, *Nomes Brasilieros: um Problema na Catalogação* (São Paulo, Escola de Biblioteconomia, 1948).

21. ALA *Cataloging Rules*, pp. 52–54.

22. *Ibid.* pp. 137–142.

23. *Ibid.*, p. 148.

24. A. D. Osborn, "Cataloging Developments in the United States 1940–1947," International Federation of Library Associations *Publications*, 12:71, 1947.

25. J. C. M. Hanson, "Corporate Entry *versus* Title Entry," *Library Quarterly*, 5:457–466, October, 1935.

26. Mortimer Taube, "The Cataloging of Publications of Corporate Authors," *Library Quarterly*, 20:1–20, January, 1950.

27. Seymour Lubetzky, "The Cataloging of Publications of Corporate Authors: A Rejoinder," *Library Quarterly*, 21:1–12, January, 1951. In a letter to the editor of the *Library Quarterly*, 21:155–156, April, 1951, Taube suggests the points of agreement.

28. Seymour Lubetzky, *Cataloging Rules and Principles; a Critique of the A.L.A. Rules for Entry and a Proposed Design for Their Revision.*

Prepared for the Board on Cataloging Policy and Research of the A.L.A. Division of Cataloging and Classification (Washington, D.C., Processing Department, U.S. Library of Congress, 1953).

29. "ALA Rules for Entry: the Proposed Revolution; Papers Presented at a Conference on the Lubetzky Report, June 22, 1953," by M. F. Tauber, Susan M. Haskins, R. E. Ellsworth, Florence M. Gifford, Hazel Dean, and Seymour Lubetzky, *Journal of Cataloging and Classification*, 9:123–142, September, 1953.

30. John Ansteinsson, "Unification of Cataloging Rules," International Federation of Library Associations *Publications*, 13:72, 1949.

31. J. L. Dewton, "International Cataloging Rules," U. S. Library of Congress *Information Bulletin*, September 6–12, 1949, pp. 8–10. See also Sigmund von Frauendorfer, "International Unification of Cataloging?" *College and Research Libraries*, 12:245–252, July, 1951.

32. W. B. Ellinger, "Remarks [on Form Headings, etc.] by Werner B. Ellinger," in the "Proceedings of Forty-Third Annual Meeting of the American Association of Law Libraries held at Seattle, Washington, July 24 to July 27, 1950," *Law Library Journal*, 43:279–289, November, 1950; and "Non-Author Headings," *Journal of Cataloging and Classification*, 10:61–73, April, 1954.

33. ALA *Cataloging Rules*, pp. 62, 63.

34. *Ibid.*, Glossary, p. 230.

35. *Ibid.*, p. 8.

36. *Ibid.*, p. 7.

37. Margaret Mann, *Introduction to Cataloging and the Classification of Books*, 2d ed. (Chicago, American Library Association, 1943).

38. Columbia University, School of Library Service, *Sample Catalog Cards*, Example no. 10.

39. U.S. Library of Congress, Processing Department, *Cataloging Service:* Bulletin, 20:2–4, June, 1949.

40. U.S. Library of Congress, Descriptive Cataloging Division, *Rules for Descriptive Cataloging in the Library of Congress* (Adopted by the American Library Association) (Washington, D.C., 1949). *Supplement 1949–51* (Washington, D.C., 1952). *Phonorecords*, preliminary ed. (Washington, D.C., 1952). *Motion Pictures and Filmstrips*, 2d preliminary ed. (Washington, D.C., 1953). *Books in Raised Characters*, preliminary ed. (Washington, D.C. 1953).

41. U.S. Library of Congress, Descriptive Cataloging Division, *Rules for Descriptive Cataloging*, p. 7.

42. Jennie D. Pritchard, "The Practices of Simplified Cataloging in

Large University and Research Libraries" (M.S. essay, Columbia University, 1951).

43. U.S. Library of Congress, Descriptive Cataloging Division, *Rules for Descriptive Cataloging*, pp. v–vi. See also W. E. Wright, "How Little Cataloging Can Be Effective?" *College and Research Libraries*, 15:167–170+, April, 1954.

44. B. M. Fry, *Library Organization and Management of Technical Reports Literature* (Washington, D.C., The Catholic University of America Press, 1953), Chapter 4. F. E. Croxton, "Cataloging Information in the U.S. Atomic Energy Commission" (M.S. essay, Columbia University, 1953; also issued in mimeographed form). J. C. Morris, *Corporate Entry Guide for Report Literature at Oak Ridge National Laboratory Library*, preliminary ed. [Oak Ridge, Tenn.], 1953.

45. Sarita Robinson and Dorothy Charles, "Problems in the Production of Subject Indexes," in *The Subject Analysis of Library Materials*, ed. by M. F. Tauber (New York, School of Library Service, Columbia University, 1953), pp. 204–217.

46. Cf. R. L. Collison, *Indexes and Indexing* (New York, John de Graff, 1953). This volume contains a useful section on "Further Reading."

CHAPTER X. SUBJECT HEADINGS

1. An interesting and informative account of the evolution and development of the varieties of subject catalogs described here briefly will be found in Julia Pettee, *Subject Headings* (New York, H. W. Wilson, 1947), Chapter II.

2. Mary D. Herrick, "The Development of a Classified Catalog for a University Library," *College and Research Libraries*, 14:418–424, October, 1953.

3. For a comprehensive discussion of the divided catalog, its frequency and problems, see I. W. Thom, "The Divided Catalog in College and University Libraries" (M.S. essay, Columbia University, 1948). A summary article based on the complete essay will be found in *College and Research Libraries*, 10:236–241, July, 1949, Part I.

4. Julia Pettee, *op. cit.*, pp. 25–28.

5. Helen G. Field, "Subject Headings in Scientific Libraries," *Journal of Cataloging and Classification*, 8:140–144, December, 1952.

6. D. J. Haykin, *Subject Headings; a Practical Guide* (Washington, D.C., U.S. Government Printing Office, 1951), pp. 21–25.

7. C. J. Frarey, "Subject Heading Revision by the Library of Con-

gress, 1941–1950" (M.S. essay, School of Library Service, Columbia University, 1951), p. 26.

8. D. J. Haykin, *op. cit.*, pp. 27–36.

9. C. A. Cutter, *Rules for a Dictionary Catalog*, 4th ed. (Washington, D.C., U.S. Government Printing Office, 1904), pp. 66–80.

10. Minnie E. Sears, "Practical Suggestions for the Beginner in Subject Heading Work," in *Sears List of Subject Headings*, 7th ed., revised by Bertha M. Frick (New York, H. W. Wilson, 1954), pp. [xi]–xxvi.

11. Vatican, Biblioteca Apostolica Vaticana, *Rules for the Catalog of Printed Books*, tr. from the 2d Italian ed. (Chicago, American Library Association, 1948), Part III: Subject Entry, pp. 294–316.

12. D. J. Haykin, *op. cit.*

13. Julia Pettee, *op. cit.*

14. Margaret Mann, *Introduction to Cataloging and the Classification of Books*, 2d ed. (Chicago, American Library Association, 1943), pp. 136–170.

15. A discussion of the organization of subject heading work appears in L. R. Wilson and R. W. Orr, *Report of a Survey of the Libraries of Alabama Polytechnic Institute, November 1948–March 1949* (Auburn, Alabama Polytechnic Institute, 1949), pp. 73–75. Iowa State College Library has separated descriptive from subject cataloging and classification for many years.

16. H. E. Bliss, *The Organization of Knowledge in Libraries*, 2d ed., rev. (New York, H. W. Wilson, 1939), pp. 154–177.

17. S. R. Ranganathan, *Theory of the Library Catalogue* (Madras, Madras Library Association, 1938), p. 161.

18. See, for example, papers by Kanardy Taylor and Harry Dewey in *The Subject Analysis of Library Materials*, ed. by M. F. Tauber (New York, Columbia University, School of Library Service, 1953), pp. 100–129.

19. D. J. Haykin, *op. cit.*, pp. 90–91.

20. M. Ruth MacDonald. Remarks made during discussion period at Institute on Subject Analysis of Library Materials, Columbia University, June 24–29, 1952. See her "Cataloging at the Armed Forces Medical Library, 1945–1952," *Journal of Cataloging and Classification*, 9:58–78, June, 1953.

21. American Library Association, *List of Subject Headings for Use in Dictionary Catalogs* (Boston, Library Bureau, 1895).

22. U.S. Library of Congress, *Literature Subject Headings . . . and Language Subject Headings*, 5th ed. (Washington, D.C., U.S. Government Printing Office, 1926); *Subject Subdivisions*, 6th ed. (Washing-

ton, D.C., U.S. Government Printing Office, 1924, reprinted 1936); *Subject Headings with Local Subdivisions*, 5th ed. (Washington, D.C., U.S. Government Printing Office, 1935). U.S. Library of Congress, Subject Cataloging Division, *Period Subdivisions Under Names of Places Used in the Dictionary Catalogs of the Library of Congress*, comp. and ed. by Marguerite V. Quattlebaum (Washington, D.C., U.S. Government Printing Office, 1950).

23. U.S. Library of Congress, Subject Cataloging Division, *Subject Headings Used in the Dictionary Catalogs of the Library of Congress*, 5th ed., ed. by Nella Jane Martin (Washington, D.C., U.S. Government Printing Office, 1948). The sixth edition is in preparation.

24. For some indication of the extent and nature of this revision program, see the study by C. J. Frarey, *op. cit.*

25. Minnie E. Sears, *Sears List of Subject Headings*, 7th ed., revised by Bertha M. Frick (New York, H. W. Wilson, 1954).

26. For some provocative comments on the need for a list like Sears in smaller library collections, see Marie L. Prevost, "Selection and Standards of Subject Headings for Use in Public Libraries," *Journal of Cataloging and Classification*, 8:135–136, December, 1952.

27. W. E. Wright, "Subject Headings in the Reference Department of the New York Public Library," in *Bookman's Holiday* (New York, The New York Public Library, 1943), pp. 431–436.

28. Julia Pettee, *List of Theological Subject Headings and Corporate Church Names*, 2d ed. (Chicago, American Library Association, 1947).

29. Clyde E. Pettus, *Subject Headings in Education* (New York, H. W. Wilson, 1938).

30. M. J. Voigt, *Subject Headings in Physics* (Chicago, American Library Association, 1944).

31. Special Libraries Association, *Classification Schemes and Subject Headings Lists Loan Collection of Special Libraries Association*, comp. by Isabel L. Towner, rev. ed. (New York, 1951).

32. The Welch Medical Library of Johns Hopkins University has been working on such a study of medical lists for several years. Massachusetts Institute of Technology is sponsoring a similar project for scientific and technological subject headings. Margaret E. Egan at the Graduate Library School of the University of Chicago is directing similar studies and comparisons of subject headings in the social sciences. See her "Subject Heading in Specialized Fields," in *The Subject Analysis of Library Materials*, ed. by M. F. Tauber (New York, School of Library Service, Columbia University, 1953), pp. 83–99.

33. Described in F. B. Rogers, "Army Medical Library Catalog, 1951," *Journal of Cataloging and Classification*, 8:150–152, December, 1952.

34. Cf. Margaret Mann, *op. cit.*, pp. 155–170.

35. D. J. Haykin, *op. cit.*, pp. 92–96.

36. Harriet D. MacPherson, "Building a List of Subject Headings," *Special Libraries*, 24:44–46, March, 1933.

37. Bertha E. Buelow, "Revision of Subject Headings and Their Transfer to an Authority File," *Wisconsin Library Bulletin*, 30:96–97, May, 1934.

38. C. J. Frarey, "The Control and Revision of Subject Headings" (Unpublished term paper, L.S. 377, School of Library Service, Columbia University, 1949).

39. D. J. Haykin, *op. cit.*, p. 89.

40. Patricia B. Knapp, "The Subject Catalog in the College Library, an Investigation of Terminology" (M.A. essay, University of Chicago, 1943).

41. C. J. Frarey, "Subject Heading Revision by the Library of Congress, 1941–1950," (M.S. essay, 1951), pp. 28–30.

42. Marie L. Prevost, "Approach to Theory and Method in General Subject Heading," *Library Quarterly*, 16:140–151, April, 1946.

43. F. B. Rogers, *op. cit.*

44. Patricia B. Knapp, *op. cit.*

45. Mary Eloise Rue, "Preferences of Elementary School Children for Subject Heading Form" (M.A. essay, University of Chicago, 1946).

46. D. J. Haykin, *op. cit.*

47. C. J. Frarey, "Subject Heading Revision by the Library of Congress, 1941–1950," (M.S. essay, 1951), pp. 34–43.

48. "Cataloger's Choice," U.S. Library of Congress, Processing Department, *Cataloging Service:* Bulletin, 22:3, June, 1950.

49. C. J. Frarey, "Subject Heading Revision by the Library of Congress, 1941–1950," (M.S. essay, 1951), p. 61.

50. Hazel Benjamin, "Selection and Standards of Subject Headings for Use in an Industrial Relations Library," *Journal of Cataloging and Classification*, 8:137–140, December, 1952.

51. Alex Ladenson, "Some Random Observations on Subject Cataloging," *Library Journal*, 69:584–586, July, 1944.

52. Harriet D. MacPherson, *op. cit.*

53. F. B. Rogers, *op. cit.*

54. C. J. Frarey, "Studies of Use of the Subject Catalog: Summary and Evaluation," in *The Subject Analysis of Library Materials*, ed. by M. F.

Tauber (New York, Columbia University, School of Library Service, 1953), pp. 147–166. See also C. J. Frarey, "Practical Problems in Subject Heading Work: A Summary," *ibid.*, pp. 218–224, and "Developments in Subject Cataloging," *Library Trends*, 2:217–235, October, 1953.

55. L. C. Merritt, *Use of the Subject Catalog in the University of California Library* (Berkeley, Calif., University of California Press, 1951; University of California Publications in Librarianship, Vol. 1, No. 1).

56. See, for example, J. C. Morris, "The Duality Concept in Subject Analysis" [Oak Ridge, Tenn., 1953]. This study contains a discussion of coordinate indexing developed by Mortimer Taube and his associates.

CHAPTER XI. CLASSIFICATION

1. L. E. LaMontagne, "Historical Background of Classification," in *The Subject Analysis of Library Materials*, ed. by M. F. Tauber (New York, School of Library Service of Columbia University, 1953), pp. 11–28; and J. H. Shera, "Classification: Current Functions and Applications to the Subject Analysis of Library Materials," in *The Subject Analysis of Library Materials, op. cit.*, pp. 29–42. See also B. I. Palmer, "Classification," *Library Trends*, 2:236–248, October, 1953.

2. Margaret Mann, *Introduction to Cataloging and the Classification of Books*, 2d ed. (Chicago, American Library Association, 1944), p. 33.

3. W. C. B. Sayers, A *Manual of Classification for Librarians and Bibliographers*, 2d ed., rev. (London, Grafton, 1944), p. 79.

4. *Ibid.*, p. 13.

5. H. E. Bliss, *The Organization of Knowledge and the System of the Sciences* (New York, H. W. Wilson, 1929), p. 143.

6. E. C. Richardson, *Classification: Theoretical and Practical* (New York, Scribner, 1912), p. 1.

7. Grace O. Kelley, *The Classification of Books* (New York, H. W. Wilson, 1937), p. 15. Leo LaMontagne, of the Library of Congress, is at present developing a history of classification.

8. Margaret M. Herdman, *Classification: an Introductory Manual*, 2d ed. (Chicago, American Library Association, 1947), p. 3.

9. E. C. Richardson, *op. cit.*, p. 66.

10. Margaret M. Herdman, *op. cit.*, p. 3.

11. See note 9.

12. W. C. B. Sayers, *op. cit.*, p. 34.

13. E. C. Richardson, *op. cit.*, p. 11.

14. Ruth Rutzen, "Shelving for Readers," *Library Journal*, 77:478–482,

March 15, 1952. Detroit Public Library, Home Reading Services, *The Reader Interest Classification in the Detroit Public Library* (Detroit, 1952).

15. Margaret M. Herdman, *op. cit.*, p. 4.

16. H. E. Bliss, *The Organization of Knowledge in Libraries and the Subject-Approach to Books* (New York, H. W. Wilson, 1939), p. 13.

17. Grace O. Kelley, *op. cit.*, p. 59.

18. Margaret Mann, *op. cit.*, p. 44.

19. W. C. B. Sayers, *op. cit.*, p. 41.

20. Margaret Mann, *op. cit.*, p. 48.

21. *Ibid.*, p. 50.

22. W. C. B. Sayers, *op. cit.*, p. 56.

23. *Ibid.*, p. 75.

24. Grace O. Kelley, *op. cit.*, p. 66–82.

25. Melvil Dewey, *Decimal Classification and Relativ Index*, 14th ed. (Lake Placid, N.Y., Forest Press, 1942), p. 8.

26. Melvil Dewey, *Decimal Classification*, Standard (15th) ed. (Lake Placid, N.Y., Forest Press, 1951), p. xi.

27. International Federation for Documentation, *Classification décimale universelle*, 5. éd. internationale (Bruxelles, Editiones Mundaneum, 1951 to date); *Universal Decimal Classification*, complete English ed., 4th international ed. (Brussels, Keerberghen, 1936 to date). Another edition in English is in process of publication by the British Standards Institution.

28. Institut International de Bibliographie, *Classification décimale universelle*, ed. complète (Bruxelles, 1933), t. 4, p. 1534. The International Federation for Documentation decided in 1952 to discontinue the use of the symbol +.

29. Elizabeth D. Marsh, "Army Medical Library Classification; Preliminary Edition, 1948," *Bulletin of the Medical Library Association*, 41:335, October, 1953.

30. Catherine W. Grout, *An Explanation of the Tables Used in the Schedules of the Library of Congress Classification* (New York, School of Library Service, Columbia University, 1940).

31. "Libraries Using the Library of Congress Classification as a Whole or in Part," in U.S. Library of Congress, *Report of the Librarian of Congress, 1937* (Washington, D.C., U.S. Government Printing Office, 1937), pp. 241–44.

32. H. E. Bliss, *A Bibliographic Classification, Extended by Systematic Auxiliary Schedules for Composite Specification and Notation*, 2d ed. (New York, H. W. Wilson, 1952–53). 4 vols. in 3.

33. Mortimer Taube, "Bibliographic Classification," *College and Research Libraries*, 14:453–455, October, 1953.

34. S. R. Ranganathan, *Colon Classification*, 4th ed. (Madras, India, Madras Library Association, 1952).

35. *Ibid.*, p. 2.3.

36. B. I. Palmer, "Classification," *Library Trends*, 2:241–242, October, 1953.

37. Harvard College Library, Lamont Library, *Classification Scheme of the Lamont Library* (Cambridge, Mass., 1950), p. v.

38. R. O. Pautzsch, "The Classification Scheme for the Lamont Library," *Harvard Library Bulletin*, 4:126–127, Winter, 1950.

39. *Ibid.*

40. See note 37.

41. R. O. Pautzsch, *op. cit.*

42. New York, Union Theological Seminary Library, *Classification* (New York, 1939). A detailed account of the theoretical basis of this scheme will be found in Julia Pettee's article, "A Classification for a Theological Library," *Library Journal*, 36:611–624, December, 1911.

43. *Ibid.*, p. iii.

44. *Ibid.*, p. iv.

45. *Ibid.*, p. vii.

46. *Ibid.*, p. v.

47. Sophia H. Glidden, *A Library Classification for Public Administration Materials* (Chicago, Public Administration Service and the American Library Association, 1942), p. vii.

48. *Ibid.*, p. x.

49. *Ibid.*, p. 2.

50. *Ibid.*, p. 4.

51. Special Libraries Association, *Classification Schemes and Subject Headings Lists Loan Collection*, comp. by Isabel L. Towner, rev. ed. (New York, 1951).

CHAPTER XII. PRE-CATALOGING AND POST-CATALOGING OPERATIONS

1. Zelda L. Osborne in "Can Student Aides Do the Processing?" *Library Journal*, 74:1409+, October 1, 1949, recounts the experience of the University of Houston in assigning students to most of these activities because of staff shortages. Though students cannot maintain the same high level of efficient operation obtainable with a regular staff, their level of performance suggests strongly that it is a serious misuse of professional personnel to assign them to the tasks discussed in this chapter.

2. Jewel C. Hardkopf, "An Application of Methods and Motions Techniques in Preparing Books in the New York Public Library" (M.S. essay, Columbia University, 1949).

3. William Stern, "New York Public Library Centralizes Its Processing," *Library Journal*, 75:1213–1215, July, 1950.

4. B. A. Custer, "Detroit Public Library Expedites Processing Activities," *Library Journal*, 73:32+, January 1, 1948.

5. See, for example, F. K. W. Drury, *Order Work for Libraries* (Chicago, American Library Association, 1930), pp. 162–182. For a classic statement, see Melvil Dewey, "A Model Accession Catalogue," *Library Journal*, 1:315–320, May, 1877.

6. For example, 52–1007, which means that the item carrying this number is the one thousand seventh to be added to the library collection during 1952. F. K. W. Drury, *op. cit.*, discusses some of the variant practices noted in this chapter.

7. Dorothy E. Chamberlain, "In-Process Records," *College and Research Libraries*, 7:335–338, October, 1946.

8. Dorothy F. Livingston, "Controlled Cataloging: an Experiment at Yale," *College and Research Libraries*, 8:11–16, January, 1947.

9. Harry Dewey, "Precataloging—a Must for the Modern Library," *College and Research Libraries*, 10:221–226, July, 1949, Part I.

10. Dorothy M. Cooper, "Circulates Books before They Are Processed," *Library Journal*, 73:1255, September 15, 1949.

11. T. F. Currier, "Preliminary Cataloging," *College and Research Libraries*, 1:235–240, June, 1940.

12. Harry Dewey, *op. cit.*

13. Dorothy F. Livingston, *op. cit.*

14. Dorothy E. Chamberlain, *op. cit.* It should be observed here that Chamberlain reports a situation which no longer exists at NYPL. Within the last several years, careful study of processing and preparation routines, together with the development of new management techniques, have resulted in shorter time lags in all phases of preparations work.

15. Detailed information on the availability of cards and procedures for ordering them may be obtained directly from the Card Division, Library of Congress, and from the H. W. Wilson Company.

16. For some provocative comments and observations on the relative efficiency of these different types of serial record equipment, see Bella Shachtman, "Simplification of Serial Records Work," *Serial Slants*, 3:6–13, July, 1952.

17. In the traveling card system an extra card is used. Holdings are added to the official record and to the extra card, and the extra card is

then inserted in the public record in place of the entry to which the latest information on holdings has not been added. The card removed from the public catalog then becomes the traveling card to be retained by the serials assistant until holdings have to be changed to record another volume added, at which time the process described in outline here is repeated. To maintain an extra entry card for each serial title adds to the expense of serial processing operations, but the saving in time for changing public records of holdings is presumed to offset this added cost.

For a discussion of the scope of processing operations for serial publications, Gable's *Manual of Serials Work* (Chicago, American Library Association, 1937) is useful, but somewhat out of date. David Grenfell's *Periodicals and Serials: Their Treatment in Special Libraries* (London, Aslib, 1953) contains detailed discussion on acquisition, organization, and servicing of serials.

18. Techniques for constructing the various kinds of book numbers commonly used in libraries are described in Bertha Barden, *Book Numbers* (Chicago, American Library Association, 1937), and by Anna C. Laws in U.S. Library of Congress, Classification Division, *Author Notation in the Library of Congress* (Washington, D.C., U.S. Government Printing Office, 1920).

19. R. G. Adams, "Librarians as Enemies of Books," *Library Quarterly*, 7:317–331, July, 1937.

20. A. D. Osborn and Susan M. Haskins, "Catalog Maintenance," *Library Trends*, 2:279–289, October, 1953.

21. A. L. Walter, "Fifty Years Young: Library of Congress Cards," *College and Research Libraries*, 13:305–308, October, 1952.

22. Bernard Karpel, "Photography Plays Part in Catalog-Card Making," *Library Journal*, 75:345–347, February 15, 1950.

23. Marjorie E. Bowers, "Cataloging with Stencils," *Library Journal*, 65:462–463, June 1, 1940.

24. R. H. Logsdon, "Veterans Administration Speeds Cataloging Procedures," *Library Journal*, 73:166–168, February 1, 1948.

25. J. M. Dawson, "Xerography in Card Reproduction," *College and Research Libraries*, 15:57–60, January, 1954. C. D. Gull, "Instrumentation," *Library Trends*, 2:103–126, July, 1953.

26. American Library Association, *Rules for Filing Catalog Cards* (Chicago, American Library Association, 1942).

27. For a discussion of major reclassification and recataloging projects, see Chapter XIII.

28. A. D. Osborn, "'Arrearages'—Ugly Word," *Library Journal*, 76:1866–1867, November 15, 1951.

29. U.S. Library of Congress, *Departmental and Divisional Manual No. 4: Catalog Maintenance Division* (Washington, 1950), p. 14.

30. This set of code numbers was devised originally by John H. Moriarty; it has been modified and supplemented by Altha E. Terry.

31. Altha E. Terry, "Techniques for Expanding the Card Catalog of a Large Library," *College and Research Libraries,* 13:242–245, July, 1952.

32. Gertrude Merritt and C. J. Frarey, "Costs of Expanding the Card Catalog of a Large Library," *College and Research Libraries,* 15:87–89, January, 1954.

33. Frarey has estimated that approximately one quarter of all subject headings used by the Library of Congress were revised in some way between 1941 and 1950, not including new subject headings added which increased the total list by about 50 percent. The largest number of changes involved the addition or cancellation of *see also* references, and other changes in the order of their frequency were: (1) outright cancellation of subject headings, (2) changes in practice for subdivision by place under existing headings, (3) definition or redefinition of headings, (4) changes of headings to *see* references, and (5) changes of *see* references to headings. Cf. C. J. Frarey, "Subject Heading Revision by the Library of Congress, 1941–1950" (M.S. essay, Columbia University, 1951), pp. 20, 24, 50.

34. "Subject Cataloging Clearing House," *Library Journal,* 72:1176–1177, September 1, 1947.

35. Helen K. Starr, "Subject Headings in a Changing World," *Library Journal,* 59:205, March 1, 1934.

36. Estelle Brodman, "Practical or Service Aspects of Medical Subject Headings," *Bulletin of the Medical Library Association,* 36:102–107, April, 1948.

37. C. J. Frarey, *op. cit.*, p. 21.

38. U.S. Library of Congress, *op. cit.*, pp. 3–5.

39. Jennette E. Hitchcock and F. Bernice Field, "Yale Meets Its Catalog," *College and Research Libraries,* 12:220–229, July, 1951.

40. At Duke University, the insurance report rendered annually lists all books lost during the year covered, together with their value. The total claim is then adjusted to include an equitable charge for processing costs, and a gross claim is obtained. The net claim paid by the insurance company represents the gross less the value of any books reported lost in previous insurance reports and recovered during the insurance year. See also C. W. Mixer, "Insurance Evaluation of a University Library's Collections," *College and Research Libraries,* 13:18–23, January, 1952, and R. D. Rogers, "Appraising a Research Collection," *College and Research Libraries,* 13:24–29, January, 1952.

CHAPTER XIII. RECLASSIFICATION AND RECATALOGING

1. M. F. Tauber, "Reclassification and Recataloging in College and University Libraries" (Unpublished Ph.D. dissertation, University of Chicago, 1941).

2. D. M. Bentz and Thera P. Cavender, "Reclassification and Recataloging," *Library Trends*, 2:249–278, October, 1953. This paper reviews many of the developments in reclassification and recataloging since the Tauber report in 1941. Bentz and Cavender also have additional data on costs, as well as information on operations and techniques.

3. Richard Shoemaker, "Reclassifying the John Cotton Dana Library of the Newark Colleges of Rutgers University" *Journal of Cataloging and Classification*, 5:19–23, Winter, 1949.

4. The Washington, D.C., Public Library reclassified its collections from the Cutter Expansive Classification to Dewey because reorganized service arrangements in the subject divisions suggested a need for some reorganization of the collections. See D. M. Pearson, "Library Reclassifies Books," *Library Journal*, 74:919–923, June 15, 1949.

In addition to the reasons recorded, there are several others which a number of librarians regarded as "trivial." The fundamental consideration in this respect is that while a reason may be trivial from the point of view of theory, actually it may be a deciding factor in the mind of the librarian. Three of these reasons, for example, were as follows: (1) Reclassification was instituted primarily because a member of the staff, usually the librarian or head cataloger, came from a library which had used the LC system; (2) reclassification seemed wise because other libraries were adopting the LC schedules; and (3) reclassification was introduced because discussions in journals and conferences praised the LC system as a means of arranging scholarly book collections.

5. M. F. Tauber, *op. cit.*

6. Few librarians believe that any classification system can be so perfect or so perfectly applied that future adjustments will not be required.

7. Richard Shoemaker, *op. cit.*

8. Rosamund H. Danielson, "Reclassification, Recataloging and Revision of Stock," *Library Journal*, 69:1033–1035, December 1, 1944.

9. H. L. Boisen, "A Venture in Reclassification," *College and Research Libraries*, 6:67–72, December, 1944.

10. A. C. Gerould and R. W. Noyes, "Shortcuts in Reclassifying Literature," *Journal of Cataloging and Classification*, 7:41–42, Spring, 1951.

11. D. M. Pearson, *op. cit.*

12. M. F. Tauber, "Reorganizing a Library Book Collection—Part II," *College and Research Libraries,* 6:341–345, September, 1945.

13. See L. R. Wilson, R. B. Downs, and M. F. Tauber, *Report of a Survey of the Libraries of Cornell University* (Ithaca, Cornell University, 1948).

CHAPTER XIV. THE CATALOGING DEPARTMENT: ADMINISTRATIVE PROBLEMS

1. L. R. Wilson and M. F. Tauber, *The University Library* (Chicago, University of Chicago Press, 1945), Chapter IV. See also A. H. Trotier, "Organization and Administration of Cataloging Processes," *Library Trends,* 2:264–278, October, 1953.

2. L. R. Wilson and R. C. Swank, *Report of a Survey of the Library of Stanford University, for Stanford University, November 1946–March 1947* (Chicago, American Library Association, 1947), pp. 92–93.

3. Hazel Dean, "Size of Cataloging Staffs in Academic Libraries," *College and Research Libraries,* 7:52–57, January, 1947.

4. Jerrold Orne, "We Have Cut Our Cataloging Costs," *Library Journal,* 73:1475–1478, October 15, 1948.

5. Margaret Mann, *Introduction to Cataloging and the Classification of Books,* 2d ed. (Chicago, American Library Association, 1943), pp. 264–267. A complete study of staff size and costs has recently been made by F. Reichmann in "Costs of Cataloging," *Library Trends,* 2:290–317, October, 1953. Reichmann considers many of the difficulties of measuring costs of cataloging, and tried to work out a formula to measure production on the basis of personnel. Lucile M. Morsch, "Scientific Management in Cataloging," *Library Trends,* 2:470–483, January, 1954, also considers the problem of measurement. Morsch includes a useful summary of the steps which are usually taken in the analysis of problems.

6. Pauline A. Seely, "Personnel in Catalog Departments in Public Libraries: A Survey," *Journal of Cataloging and Classification,* 8:39–69, June, 1952.

7. Mary D. Herrick, "Status of Worker Morale Among College Catalogers," *College and Research Libraries,* 11:33–39, January, 1950. See also Franz Grasberger, "On the Psychology of Librarianship," *Library Quarterly,* 24:43, January, 1954.

8. R. A. Miller, "The Technical and Administrative Functions of the Library," in *Library Buildings for Library Service,* ed. by H. H. Fussler (Chicago, American Library Association, 1947), pp. 37 ff.

9. J. L. Wheeler and A. M. Githens, *The American Public Library Building* (New York, C. Scribner's Sons, 1941), Chapter 17.

10. J. O. Kraehenbuehl, "Lighting the Library," *College and Research Libraries,* 2:231–236, June, 1941; see also "Library Table Lighting," *ibid.,* 2:306–317, September, 1941.

11. Enoch Pratt Free Library, Baltimore, *Catalog Department Manual,* prepared by Lucile M. Morsch (Baltimore, Enoch Pratt Free Library, 1940). A number of college and university libraries have also developed staff manuals for catalog departments.

12. R. E. Kingery, "A Management Engineering Look at Cataloging," *College and Research Libraries,* 14:52–56, January, 1953.

13. Olive J. Fresch, "Cataloging for Branch Libraries" (M.S. essay, Columbia University, 1940). Janet Dickson, "Centralized Cataloging in College and University Libraries" (M.S. essay, Columbia University, 1946), summarized in *College and Research Libraries,* 8:225–231, July, 1947.

14. Cf. W. O'D. Pierce, *Work Measurment in Public Libraries* (New York, Social Science Research Council, 1949). See also note 5, above.

15. See papers in *Journal of Cataloging and Classification,* 7:89–109, Fall, 1951: R. Engelbarts, "Cataloging of Accumulated Material at UCLA and at Yale"; Elizabeth C. Borden, "Cataloging of Arrearages at the University of Pennsylvania"; Lela de Otte Surrey, "Arrearages in Cataloging at the Brooklyn Public Library"; Lucile M. Morsch, "Cataloging Arrearages in the Library of Congress"; M. F. Tauber, "Summary of Solutions to Arrearage Problem"; and Altha E. Terry, "Statement on Uncataloged Arrears in the Columbia University Libraries." See also Andrew D. Osborn, " 'Arrearages'—Ugly Word," *Library Journal,* 76:1863–1867, November 15, 1951.

16. For example, see Columbia University Libraries, "Annual Report of the Catalog Librarian." This has been mimeographed for the past few years.

17. Donald Coney, "Management in College and University Libraries," *Library Trends,* 1:83–94, July, 1952.

18. M. F. Tauber, "Training of Catalogers and Classifiers," *Library Trends,* 2:330–341, October, 1953.

CHAPTER XV. CONSERVATION OF LIBRARY MATERIALS: GENERAL ORGANIZATION AND ADMINISTRATION

1. R. G. Adams, "Librarians as Enemies of Books," *Library Quarterly,* 7:317–331, July, 1937. See also "Rare Books in the University Library," *College and Research Libraries,* 10:[289]–308, July, 1949.

2. See, for example, L. R. Wilson and M. F. Tauber, *Report of a Survey*

of the University of South Carolina Library for the University of South Carolina, February–May, 1946 (Columbia, S.C., University of South Carolina, 1946), pp. 49–51.

3. Pelham Barr, "Book Conservation and the University Library," *College and Research Libraries*, 7:214–219, July, 1946.

4. L. R. Wilson, R. B. Downs, and M. F. Tauber, *Report of a Survey of the Libraries of Cornell University for the Library Board of Cornell University, October 1947–February 1948* (Ithaca, N.Y., Cornell University, 1948), pp. 83–84.

5. Pelham Barr, *op. cit.*, p. 215.

6. U.S. Library of Congress, *Representative Positions in the Library of Congress* (Washington, U.S. Government Printing Office, 1948), pp. 157–158.

7. L. C. Powell, "Rare Book Code," *College and Research Libraries*, 10:307–308, July, 1949.

8. Margaret Hutchins, *Introduction to Reference Work* (Chicago, American Library Association, 1944), p. 141.

9. W. R. Thurman, "Conservation of Periodical and Reference Volumes," *Library Journal*, 67:804, October 1, 1941.

10. Margaret Hutchins, *op. cit.*, pp. 136–137.

11. Margaret H. Hughes, "Periodical Binding Schedules for Improved Service in University and College Libraries" (M.S. essay, Columbia University, 1949); also in summary, *College and Research Libraries*, 13:223–226+, July, 1952.

12. Columbia University Libraries, "Binding Practices," in its *Technical Services Memorandum*, No. 27, February 27, 1947.

13. Pelham Barr, *op. cit.*, pp. 217–218.

14. Dorothy H. Litchfield, "Departmental and Divisional Libraries," *College and Research Libraries*, 2:237–240, June, 1941.

15. Pelham Barr, *op. cit.*, p. 218.

16. *Ibid.*

17. *Ibid.*

18. *Ibid.*

CHAPTER XVI. CONSERVATION OF LIBRARY MATERIALS: FINANCE, PERSONNEL, AND OTHER ASPECTS

1. "College and University Library Statistics 1952–53," *College and Research Libraries*, 15:69, January, 1954.

2. W. P. Kellam, "College Binding Has Its Problems," *Library Journal*, 64:522–524, April 1, 1949.

3. Blanche P. McCrum, *An Estimate of Standards for the College Library,* 2d ed., revised (Lexington, Va., Washington and Lee University, 1937).

4. Columbia University Libraries, *Report of the Director of Libraries for the Academic Year Ending June, 1948* (New York, 1949), p. 16.

5. L. R. Wilson and R. W. Orr, *Report of a Survey of the Libraries of the Alabama Polytechnic Institute, November 1948–March 1949* (Auburn, Ala., The Institute, 1949), p. 67.

6. E. W. Browning, "More Training Needed in Bookbinding and Book Conservation," *Library Journal,* 75:190–191, February 1, 1950.

7. *Ibid.*

8. Louis Shores, "Do Librarians and Binders Play Fair?" *Library Journal,* 74:704–707, May 1, 1949.

9. U.S. Library of Congress, *Representative Positions in the Library of Congress* (Washington, D.C., U.S. Government Printing Office, 1948), p. 159.

10. Louis Shores, *op. cit.,* p. 705.

11. Chicago, American Library Association, 1948, pp. 67–68.

12. U.S. Library of Congress, *op. cit.,* pp. 159–161.

13. H. M. Lydenberg and John Archer, *The Care and Repair of Books,* 3d ed. (New York, R. R. Bowker, 1945), p. 4–5. This is an excellent manual that all librarians should have in their working collections.

14. *Ibid.,* p. 12.

15. Fremont Rider, *Compact Book Storage* (New York, Hadham Press, 1949).

16. H. M. Lydenberg and John Archer, *op. cit.,* p. 14.

17. *Ibid.*

18. On May 23, 1952, a consent judgment terminating antitrust restraints in furnishing library binding services was rendered against the Library Binding Institute. U.S. *vs.* Library Binding Institute, Civil No. 66–278, U.S. District Court for the Southern District of New York, (CCH 1952 Trade Cases, ¶67,289).

19. Cf. A. H. Trotier, "Some Persistent Problems of Serials in Technical Processes," *Serial Slants,* 1:10–12, January, 1951. Charles H. Brown, "Proposal for Study of Increased Costs of Serials and Binding," *College and Research Libraries,* 12:303, July, 1951. John B. Stratton, "Library Binding Practices in College and University Libraries" (M.S. essay, Columbia University, 1952). Flora B. Ludington, "Book Preservation," *ALA Bulletin,* 47:425–426, October, 1953.

20. The Committee is "to act in an advisory capacity to librarians on any matters pertaining to binding, care, and repair of library collections;

to facilitate discussion and solution of problems of common interest to binders and libraries; to study the specifications for library binding adopted by the A.L.A. Council; to encourage their widespread use by librarians and binders; to suggest revisions thereof to the Council; and to receive recommendations on binding from any source whatsoever." *ALA Bulletin*, 45:381, December, 1951.

21. American Library Association, Committee on Binding, *Binding for Small Libraries* (Chicago, American Library Association Publishing Board, 1909), Library Handbook, No. 5.

22. Pelham Barr, "What is the Co-operative Program on Binding?" *Library Journal*, 66:316, April 15, 1941.

23. "Free Services," *Book Life*, 1:12, December, 1939.

24. L. N. Feipel and E. W. Browning, *Library Binding Manual*. Prepared under the direction of the Joint Committee of the ALA and LBI (Chicago, American Library Association, 1951).

25. Emma G. Wright and E. B. Barnes, "Binding at the University of Oregon," *Serial Slants*, 2:1–5, January, 1952.

CHAPTER XVII. CONSERVATION OF LIBRARY MATERIALS: THE BINDERY WITHIN THE LIBRARY AND THE HANDLING OF SPECIAL MATERIALS

1. J. T. Gerould, *The College Library Building* (New York, Scribner, 1932), pp. 87–88.

2. M. F. Tauber, *A Report on the Technical Services in the Dartmouth College Library, March–May*, 1952 (Hanover, N.H., 1952), pp. 23–27 and 42–50.

3. Statistics furnished by Printing Office, New York Public Library.

4. University of Minnesota Library, *Annual Report*, 1951–52 (Minneapolis, Minn., 1953), p. 27. In the *University of Minnesota Library News* for May 28, 1951, attention was called to the fact that bindery costs have been increasing to such extent that the question was raised as to the wisdom of continuing the bindery within the library. It was specifically noted that "Because larger binderies use mass production methods, and do less 'custom' or specialized work at standard rates, library binding generally can be done more cheaply by competitive bidders than we can do it ourselves." See also Fremont Rider, "Does Our Bindery Pay?" Wesleyan University Library, *About Books*, 18:4–5, March–June, 1948.

5. Columbia University Libraries, Binding Department, Report, 1952–53 (typewritten), chart I.

6. See Fremont Rider, *Compact Book Storage* (New York, Hadham Press, 1950), for an explanation of this experiment.

7. Statistics furnished by Fremont Rider, Librarian of Wesleyan University.

8. Indiana State Library, Extension Division, *Do's and Don't's of Book Repairing* (Indianapolis, 1949), p. 1.

9. *Ibid.*

10. Hellmut Lehmann-Haupt, ed., *Bookbinding in America: Three Essays* (Portland, Me., Southworth-Anthoensen Press, 1941), pp. 190–191.

11. Columbia University Libraries, "Binding Procedure," *Serials Manual, 1946* (New York, 1946). Columbia University Libraries, Bindery, "Binding Practices and Procedures," Revised October, 1952. (New York, 1952).

12. Neal Harlow, "Conservation of Newspaper Resources," *California Library Bulletin,* 9:19, September, 1948.

13. C. S. Paine, "Microfilm in the Small College Library," *College and Research Libraries,* 3:224–229, June, 1942.

14. *Ibid.*, pp. 227–228.

15. See, for example, Philadelphia Bibliographical Center and Union Library Catalogue. *Union List of Microfilms,* ed. by Eleanor E. Campion, revised, enlarged, and cumulated edition (Ann Arbor, J. W. Edwards, 1951). "Microfilm Clearing House," in Library of Congress *Information Bulletin* (various issues). "Newspaper Microfilming Project; Catalogue No. 2," *Canadian Library Association Bulletin,* 5:201–212, May, 1949 (also later compilations).

16. Melvin Oathout and Evelyn Oathout, "A Pamphlet Method for Research Libraries," *College and Research Libraries,* 8:414–421, October, 1947.

17. Lester Condit, *A Pamphlet about Pamphlets* (Chicago, University of Chicago Press, [1939]), p. 76.

18. Norma O. Ireland, *The Pamphlet File in School, College, and Public Libraries,* Useful Reference Series, No. 84 (Boston, The F. W. Faxon Company. Revised and enlarged ed., 1954).

19. R. W. Desmond, *Newspaper Reference Methods* (Minneapolis, University of Minnesota Press, 1933). A useful English publication is J. Lewis, *Newspaper Libraries* (London, Library Association, 1952).

20. R. W. Desmond, *op. cit.*, pp. 109–113.

21. L. A. Brown, *Notes on the Care and Cataloging of Old Maps* (Windham, Conn., Hawthorn House, 1941).

22. Clara Egli Le Gear, *Maps; Their Care, Repair and Preservation in Libraries* (Washington, D.C., Library of Congress, 1949).

23. H. M. Lydenberg and John Archer, *The Care and Repair of Books*, 3d ed. (New York, R. R. Bowker, 1945), pp. 83–92.

24. John Archer, "A Ten-Year Test of Bindings," *New York Public Library Bulletin*, 40:97–99, February, 1936.

25. *Ibid.*, p. 99.

26. H. M. Lydenberg and John Archer, *op. cit.*, pp. 83–84.

27. Adelaide E. Minogue, *The Repair and Preservation of Records* (Washington, National Archives, 1943), Bulletin of the National Archives, No. 5.

28. D. L. Evans, "The Lamination Process; a British View," *American Archivist*, 9:320–322, October, 1946. See also A. W. Kremer, "The Preservation of Wood Pulp Publications," *College and Research Libraries*, 15:205–209, April, 1954. Kremer considers, in addition to lamination, the techniques of sizing, silking, tissuing, transparent coating, and print transfer. Many authorities dispute the findings of Evans.

29. W. J. Barrow, "The Barrow Method of Laminating Documents," *Journal of Documentary Reproduction*, 2:147–151, June, 1939.

30. H. M. Lydenberg and John Archer, *op. cit.*, p. 24.

31. D. C. Hetherington, "Mold Preventive for Bookbindings," *College and Research Libraries*, 7:261, July, 1946.

32. H. B. Weiss and R. H. Carruthers, *Insect Enemies of Books* (New York, New York Public Library, 1937), p. 5. An annotated and indexed bibliography on pp. 21–47 of this work is most useful; it includes references from ancient to modern times.

33. Thomas H. Iiams and T. D. Beckwith, "Notes on the Causes and Prevention of Foxing in Books," *Library Quarterly*, 5:407–418, October, 1935. See also T. H. Iiams, "Foxing and the Deterioration of Books" (M. A. thesis, University of Chicago, 1939).

34. H. M. Lydenberg and John Archer, *op. cit.*, p. 65.

CHAPTER XVIII. CIRCULATION OPERATIONS: REGISTRATION

1. L. R. Wilson, *The Geography of Reading* (Chicago, University of Chicago Press, 1938), p. 96.

2. American Library Association, *A National Plan for Public Library Service* (Chicago, American Library Association, 1948), p. 17.

3. Bernard Berelson, *The Library's Public* (New York, Columbia University Press, 1949), p. 102.

4. H. J. Carr, "Registration of Book Borrowers," *Library Journal*, 12:340, September–October, 1877.

5. New York Public Library, *Rules and Instructions for the Staff of the Circulation Desk*, 3d ed. (New York, 1941), p. 22.

6. Pittsburgh, Carnegie Library, *Routine Book* (Pittsburgh [1949]), p. 11.

7. St. Louis, Public Library, *Customs of Administration and Procedure as Observed by the Staff of the St. Louis Public Library*, rev. ed. ([St. Louis, Mo.], 1938).

8. Pittsburgh, Carnegie Library, *Routine Book*, p. 12.

9. Rochester, Public Library, *Staff Instruction Book* (Rochester, N.Y., 1940), paragraphs 265–269.

10. Letter from the Head of Reference & Circulation Departments, Oberlin College [cited by] Guy R. Lyle, in *The Administration of the College Library* (New York, H. W. Wilson, 1949), p. 149.

11. University of Illinois Library, *Staff Manual* (Urbana, Ill., 1947), p. 57.

12. Antioch College Library, *Staff Manual* (Yellow Springs, Ohio, 1940), p. 19.

13. Wesleyan University Library, *Staff Manual* (Middletown, Conn., 1949), paragraph 604.

14. University of Texas Library, *General Staff Manual* (Austin, Texas, 1949), p. 24.

15. M. A. Miller, "Loan Clientele of State University and Land-Grant College Libraries," *College and Research Libraries*, 6:39–40, December, 1944.

16. Milwaukee Public Library, *Procedure Manual for the Staff* (Milwaukee, Wis., 1947), paragraph 244.

17. New York Public Library, Memorandum . . . effective July 1, 1952, Item 4, p. 3.

18. Pittsburgh, Carnegie Library, *Routine Book*, p. 22.

19. Mildred W. Sandoe, *County Library Primer* (New York, H. W. Wilson, 1942), p. 96.

20. Gretchen K. Schenk, *County and Regional Library Service* (Chicago, American Library Association, 1954), p. 218.

21. "Registration—Your Library's Charge Account Record," *Library News Bulletin*, 10:8–9, November, 1942.

CHAPTER XIX. CIRCULATION OPERATIONS: LOANS

1. Bernard Berelson, *The Library's Public* (New York, Columbia University Press, 1949), p. 51.

2. E. V. Baldwin and W. E. Marcus, *Library Costs and Budgets* (New York, R. R. Bowker, 1941), p. 83. See also W. O'D. Pierce, *Work*

Measurement in Public Libraries (New York, Social Science Research Council, 1949), p. 34. Although Pierce reports on the time used in charging by several systems, he notes that the data are not very reliable "due to lack of definition."

3. Melvil Dewey, "Principles Underlying Charging Systems," *Library Journal*, 3:217, August, 1878.

4. E. V. Baldwin and W. E. Marcus, *op. cit.*, p. 82.

5. H. F. McGaw, "Self Charging System," *Wilson Library Bulletin*, 16:658–660, April, 1942.

6. "Mr. Smith Goes to the Library," *Library Journal*, 63:304–305, April, 1942.

7. Evelyn G. Baker, "Self Charging," *Wilson Library Bulletin*, 15:508, February, 1941.

8. P. J. McNiff, "The Charging System of the Lamont Library," *Harvard Library Bulletin*, 3:438–440, Autumn, 1949.

9. A. T. Hamlin and W. W. Wright, "Goodbye to the Book Card," *Library Journal*, 73:1716–1720, December, 1948.

10. Sister Helen, "Simplified Circulation Records for a College Library," *Library Journal*, 66:201–203, March 1, 1941.

11. Dorothy M. Cooper, "University of Washington Adopts Michigan Tabbing System," *Library Journal*, 75:1424–1426, September 1, 1950.

12. L. C. Lynn, "We Do It This Way," *Catholic Library World*, 12:190–191, March, 1941.

13. R. R. Shaw, "Reducing the Cost of the Lending Process," *ALA Bulletin*, 35:504–510, October, 1941.

14. S. W. Smith, "—and a Few Machines," *Library Journal*, 74:1044–1047, July, 1949.

15. Tera Bailey, "Charlotte Experiments with Audio Charging," *Library Journal*, 75:1065–1069, June 15, 1950.

16. H. S. Hacker, "Erie County Bookmobile Carries First Photocharger," *Library Journal*, 74:869–870, June, 1949.

17. S. W. Smith, *op. cit.*, p. 1047.

18. Margery Quigley, "Library Facts from International Business Machine Cards," *Library Journal*, 66:1065–1067, December, 1941.

19. International Business Machines Corporation, *IBM Accounting: Circulation Control for Public Libraries* (New York, 1947).

20. G. G. Young, "Borrower Merely Signs His Name," *Library Journal*, 74:12–16, January, 1949.

21. R. U. Blasingame, Jr., "The Applications of International Business Machines in Libraries" (M.S. essay, Columbia University, 1950),

p. 15. A recent discussion of IBM circulation work is by Margaret Klausner, in "IBM Circulation Control," *Library Journal*, 77:2165–2166, December 15, 1952. It describes the installation and the results in the Stockton and San Joaquin County Library system. See also R. S. Casey and J. W. Perry, *Punched Cards: Their Application in Science and Industry* (New York, Reinhold, 1951), and R. W. Parker, *Library Applications of Punched Cards: A Description of Mechanical Systems* (Chicago, American Library Association, 1952).

22. W. H. Kaiser, "No Machines Used in This Charging System," *Library Journal*, 75:512–513, March 15, 1950; and *The Wayne County Charging System: A Manual of Installation, Operation, and Evaluation* (Detroit, 1950).

23. P. J. McNiff, *op. cit.*, p. 439.

24. F. G. Kilgour, "A New Punched Card for Circulation Records," *Library Journal*, 64:131–133, February 15, 1939.

25. H. F. McGaw, *Marginal Punched Cards in College and Research Libraries* (Washington, D.C., Scarecrow Press, 1952).

CHAPTER XX. CIRCULATION: OTHER OPERATIONS AND RECORDS

1. C. D. Kent, "The 28-Day Loan," *Ontario Library Review*, 33:109–110, May, 1949.

2. Margaret R. Post, "Gary's Staff of Skeptics Find Borrowers Limit Unwarranted," *Library Journal*, 72:1022, July, 1947.

3. A. E. Bostwick, *The American Public Library*, 3d ed. (New York, Appleton, 1923), p. 56.

4. Enid F. Tanner, "Rental Service," *Library Journal*, 60:674–675, September, 1935.

5. Rice Estes, "The Lending Service Library," *College and Research Libraries*, 7:256–259, July, 1946.

6. Katharine D. Patterson and Katherine H. Berthold, "Fines—an Overdue Problem," *Library Journal*, 63:181–183, March 1, 1938.

7. Wilhelm Munthe, *American Librarianship from a European Angle* (Chicago, American Library Association, 1939), p. 105.

8. W. R. Lansberg, "Current Trends in the College Reserve Room," *College and Research Libraries*, 11:120–124, April, 1950.

9. Margie M. Helm, "Duplicate Copies of Collateral References for College Libraries," *Library Quarterly*, 4:420–435, July, 1934.

10. "General Interlibrary Loan Code 1952," *College and Research Libraries*, 13:350-358, October, 1952.

11. *Annual Report of the Librarian of Congress for the Fiscal Year*

Ending June 30, 1952 (Washington, D.C., U.S. Government Printing Office, 1953), p. 9.

12. "General Interlibrary Loan Code 1952," p. 351.

13. James G. Hodgson and Robert W. Kidder, "Errors and Incomplete Entries in Interlibrary Loan Requests," *College and Research Libraries*, 13:336–341, October, 1952.

14. C. M. Winchell, *Locating Books for Interlibrary Loan* (New York, H. W. Wilson, 1930).

15. *Union List of Serials in Libraries of the United States and Canada* (New York, H. W. Wilson, 1943). Supplements have been issued. See A. D. Osborn, "The Future of the *Union List of Serials*," *College and Research Libraries*, 14:26–28, January, 1954.

16. Special Libraries Association, *Special Library Resources* (New York, 1941–1947), 4 vols.

17. "General Interlibrary Loan Code 1952," p. 350.

18. *Ibid.*, p. 351.

19. Margaret D. Uridge, "Labor Saving Form Aids Interlibrary Loan," *Library Journal*, 76:1010–1011, June 15, 1951.

20. W. W. Wright, "Interlibrary Loan—Smothered in Tradition," *College and Research Libraries*, 13:332–336, October, 1952.

21. Mary Lou Lucy, "Interlibrary Loans in a University Library," *College and Research Libraries*, 13:344–349, October, 1952.

22. J. G. Hodgson, "A Preliminary Report on Interlibrary Loan Costs," *College and Research Libraries*, 13:327–331, October, 1952.

23. Some research libraries have recently introduced fees for library use by "outsiders." See articles by Wylie Sypher, K. D. Metcalf, C. M. White, and L. R. Wilson, in *College and Research Libraries*, 13:295–300, October, 1952.

24. W. H. Jesse, *Shelf Work in Libraries* (Chicago, American Library Association, 1952). Contains bibliographical footnotes.

25. Dean Battles, Howard Davis and William Harms, "A Motion and Time Study of a Library Routine," *Library Quarterly*, 13:241–244, July, 1943.

26. F. H. Forrest, "An Experiment in Charging in the Circulation Department, Columbia University Library" (M.S. essay, Columbia University, 1952). See also Louise Stubblefield and F. H. Forrest, "Columbia's New Charging System," *College and Research Libraries*, 14:381–386, October, 1953.

27. H. H. Henkle, "John Crerar Develops New Shelf Number System," *Library Journal*, 75:849–850, May, 1950.

CHAPTER XXI. PHOTOGRAPHIC SERVICE IN LIBRARIES

1. H. H. Fussler, *Photographic Reproduction for Libraries* (Chicago, University of Chicago Press, 1942).

2. G. Miles Conrad, "New Methods of Reproduction, Publication, and the Design of Technical Reports," *American Documentation*, 3:168–75, August, 1952. See also V. D. Tate, "An Appraisal of Microfilm," *American Documentation*, 1:91–99, April, 1950.

3. R. R. Shaw, "Photo-Clerical Experiment," *College and Research Libraries*, 13:303–304, October, 1952; and *The Use of Photography for Clerical Routines* (Washington, American Council of Learned Societies, 1953).

4. Information from Hubbard Ballou, in charge of the Photographic Services, Columbia University Libraries. Many institutions have their own photographic departments. The *Directory of Microfilm Services in the United States and Canada*, issued in a revised edition in 1946 by the Special Libraries Association, contains information on the availability and type of photographic services provided in specific institutions. Such agencies as the Armed Forces Medical Library, the United States Department of Agriculture Library, and the Library of Congress are equipped for prompt and extensive photographic service to libraries and researchers. The American Chemical Society has also set up a service for its members so that through the use of coupons purchased from the Society Photostatic or microfilm copies may be procured.

5. "Correlation of Forms of Microtext for Library Use," *College and Research Libraries*, 14:298–301, July, 1953.

6. Philadelphia Union Catalogue and Bibliographical Center, *Union List of Microfilms*, ed. by Eleanor E. Campion (Philadelphia, 1951). See also "Microfilm Clearing House" in various issues of the Library of Congress *Information Bulletin*.

7. H. H. Fussler, *op. cit.* R. C. Binkley, *Manual on Methods of Reproducing Research Materials* (Ann Arbor, Edwards Bros., 1936). A publication (in two parts, loose-leaf for supplementary material) which discusses international problems and new developments in the reproduction of research materials is the *Manual on Document Reproduction and Selection*, published by the International Federation for Documentation, and printed with the financial assistance of UNESCO (F.I.D. Publication No. 264, The Hague, 1953). It includes a general introduction by Ralph R. Shaw. It contains illustrations and equipment specifications. Part II is to be issued later.

8. R. C. Binkley, *op. cit.*, pp. 71–72. H. H. Fussler, *op. cit.*, pp. 191–192.

9. R. R. Shaw, "Should Scientists Use Microfilm?" *Library Quarterly*, 14:229–233, July, 1944.

10. A. B. Berthold, "The Union Catalog Idea," in *The Cataloging and Acquisition of Books*, ed. by W. M. Randall (Chicago, University of Chicago Press, 1940), p. 246. The Photostat has also been used for this purpose.

11. Anna M. Monrad, "The Use of the Dexigraph in Making an Official Catalog," *Library Journal*, 57:213–222, March 1, 1932.

12. R. C. Binkley, *op. cit.*, p. 73.

13. H. H. Fussler, *op. cit.*, pp. 193–194.

14. *American Documentation*, 1:53, January, 1950.

15. G. Miles Conrad, *op. cit.*

16. J. G. Hodgson, *The Use of Xerography in Libraries* (Fort Collins, Colorado A. and M. College Library, 1952). A bibliography of 25 items is included. See also J. M. Dawson, "Xerography in Card Reproduction," *College and Research Libraries*, 15:57–60, January, 1954.

17. "Electronic Composing Machine," *Medical Library Association Bulletin*, 38:215–216, April, 1950.

18. H. M. Silver, "Near Print Draws Nearer," *Journal of Documentation*, 5:55–68, September, 1949; and "New Methods of Printing and Reproducing Scholarly Materials," *American Documentation*, 2:54–58, January, 1951. Walter Clark, "Document Reproduction by Photography in the United States," *Photographic Science and Technique*, Series II, Vol. 1:31–37, May, 1954.

19. H. M. Silver, *op. cit.*

20. See also Violet A. Cabeen and C. D. Cook, "Organization of Serials and Documents," *Library Trends*, 2:199–216, October, 1953, especially pp. 208–212 on Microreproduction of Serials and Documents.

21. H. H. Fussler, *op. cit.*

22. M. F. Tauber, "Use of Microphotography in University Libraries," *Journal of Documentary Reproduction*, 4:150–157, September, 1941.

23. M. F. Tauber, "Problems in the Use of Microfilms, Microprint, and Microcards in Research Libraries," *Industrial and Engineering Chemistry*, 42:1467–1468, August, 1950.

24. United Nations Educational, Scientific and Cultural Organization, *Enquête de l'Unesco sur l'emploi du microfilm, 1951: Unesco Survey of Microfilm Use, 1951*. Reprint from *UNESCO Bulletin for Libraries*, Vol. 6, Nos. 2/3, February/March, 1952, and Nos. 5/6, May/June, 1952 (Paris, 1952).

25. L. K. Born, "A National Plan for Extensive Microfilm Operations," *American Documentation,* 1:66–75, April, 1950.

26. A. J. Eaton, "Toward a State-Wide Newspaper Microfilming Program," *College and Research Libraries,* 14:22–30, January, 1953.

27. E. B. Power, "Microfilm as a Substitute for Binding," *American Documentation,* 2:33–39, January, 1951.

28. Fremont Rider, "Microcards *vs.* the Cost of Book Storage," *American Documentation,* 2:39–44, January, 1951.

29. United Nations Educational, Scientific and Cultural Organization, *op. cit.,* pp. 12–13.

30. *Ibid.* See also note 5.

31. Fremont Rider, *The Scholar and the Future of the Research Library* (New York, Hadham Press, 1944).

32. *The Microcard Bulletin,* No. 1—, June, 1948— (Middletown, Conn., Microcard Foundation, 1948—).

33. *Ibid.,* see especially No. 6, December, 1950.

34. Fremont Rider, "Microcards, a New Form of Publication," *Industrial and Chemical Engineering,* 42:1462–1463, August, 1950.

35. D. E. Gray, "Practical Experience in Microfacsimile Publication," *American Documentation,* 3:58–61, January, 1952. Consideration is given to the Navy Research Section's experience with microcards.

36. E. L. Erickson, "Microprint: A Revolution in Printing," *Journal of Documentation,* 7:184–187, September, 1951.

37. E. L. Erickson, "The Sessional Papers," *Library Journal,* 78:13–17, January 1, 1953.

38. H. H. Fussler, *op. cit.,* p. 196.

39. H. H. Fussler, *op. cit.,* pp. 81–90. See also M. F. Tauber, "Cataloging and Classifying Microfilm," *Journal of Documentary Reproduction,* 3:10–25, March, 1940. U.S. Library of Congress, *Rules for Descriptive Cataloging in the Library of Congress* (Washington, 1949), pp. 97–100.

40. Grace W. Bacon, "Handling Microcards in Libraries," *College and Research Libraries,* 11:372–373, October, 1950.

41. H. H. Fussler, *op. cit.,* pp. 93–100.

42. Midwest Inter-library Center, Chicago, *Third Annual Report of the Midwest Inter-library Corporation and the Midwest Inter-library Center, from July 1, 1951 to June 30, 1952* (Chicago, 1952), p. 12.

43. L. K. Born, *op. cit.*

44. L. K. Born, "Planning for Microfilm Operations," *American Documentation,* 2:1–5, January, 1951.

45. Dan Lacy, "Microfilming as a Major Acquisitions Tool: Policies, Plans and Problems," *Library of Congress Quarterly Journal of Acquisitions*, 6:8–17, May, 1949.

46. *American Documentation*, 1:46–50, January, 1950.

47. L. K. Born, "Microfilming Abroad," *College and Research Libraries*, 11:250–258, July, 1950.

48. International Federation for Documentation, *Directory of Microfilm and Photocopying Services*, prelim. ed. (The Hague, 1950), Bulletin, No. 244.

49. United Nations Educational, Scientific and Cultural Organization, *op. cit.*

50. Louis Shores, "Library Co-operation in the Southeast," *Library Quarterly*, 22:340, October, 1952.

CHAPTER XXII. MACHINES, OPERATIONS, AND MODERN LIBRARIES

1. Walter Rautenstrauch, *Principles of Modern Industrial Organization* (New York, Pitman, 1943), *Economics of Industrial Management* (New York, Funk and Wagnalls, 1949).

2. See, for one method, E. E. Wight, "A Study of Weighted Work Units in the Newark Public Library," *Library Quarterly*, 18:45–51, January, 1948.

3. T. D. Morris, "Techniques of Appraising the Administrative Strength of an Organization," *College and Research Libraries*, 13:111–116, April, 1952. Robert E. Kingery, "A Management Engineering Look at Cataloging," *College and Research Libraries*, 14:52–56, January, 1953.

4. Some savings may be effected through quantity purchase of materials, thus reducing the unit variable cost. This factor has not been considered intentionally, since its effect varies greatly from place to place and from operation to operation.

5. T. D. Morris, *op. cit.*, pp. 114–115.

6. A comprehensive and widely used text in this field is R. M. Barnes, *Motion and Time Study Applications* (New York, Wiley, 1942).

7. R. R. Shaw, "Management, Machines and the Bibliographic Problems of the Twentieth Century," in *Bibliographic Organization*, ed. by J. H. Shera and Margaret E. Egan (Chicago, University of Chicago Press, 1951), p. 210.

8. The January, 1954, issue of *Library Trends* is devoted to "Scientific Management in Libraries," edited by R. R. Shaw. It considers many of the problems of finance, personnel, equipment, facilities, and operations involved in the effective management of libraries. See also "Man-

agement Improvements in Libraries," *College and Research Libraries*, 15:188–204, April, 1954; papers by M. F. Tauber, T. D. Morris, and R. E. Kingery.

9. Jewel C. Hardkopf, "An Application of Methods and Motion Techniques in Preparing Books in the New York Public Library" (M.S. essay, Columbia University, 1949).

10. *Ibid.*, p. 36.

11. R. R. Shaw, "Management, Machines, and the Bibliographical Problems of the Twentieth Century," *op. cit.*, pp. 215–216.

12. R. R. Shaw, *The Use of Photography for Clerical Routines: A Report to the American Council of Learned Societies* (Washington, D.C., American Council of Learned Societies, 1953).

13. See, for example, *PNLA Quarterly*, 18:92–98, January, 1954 (and January issues of preceding years), for the report of the Committee on Library Supplies and Equipment of PNLA. See also "Library Buying Guide 1954," *Library Journal*, 79:515–538, March 15, 1954 (and in January issues in 1952 and 1953). "Guide to Library Equipment and Supplies," *ALA Bulletin*, 47:304–324, July–August, 1953 (supplemented by "Goods and Gadgets" section in later issues); *Technical Libraries: Their Organization and Management*, ed. by Lucille Jackson, (New York, Special Libraries Association, 1951), Chapter IV, contains listings of equipment and dealers. The catalogs of various companies, such as Bro-Dart Industries, Demco Library Supplies, Gaylord Brothers, Globe-Wernicke Co., Library Bureau (Remington Rand), and Library Efficiency Corporation, contain descriptions of library supplies and equipment.

14. Mortimer Taube, "Special Librarianship and Documentation," *Special Libraries*, 43:206, July–August, 1952. See also Mortimer Taube and Associates, *Studies in Coordinate Indexing* (Washington, D.C., Documentation, Inc., 1953).

15. *Ibid.*, p. 206.

16. L. H. Evans, "ADI's Tasks," *American Documentation*, 1:127–130, August, 1950.

17. Helen M. Brownson, comp., "Recommendations and Results of International Conferences on Scientific and Bibliographic Services," *American Documentation*, 3:29–55, January, 1952. A good summary of problems of documentation is found in S. C. Bradford, *Documentation*, with an Introduction by Dr. Jesse H. Shera and Margaret E. Egan. 2d ed. (London, Crosby Lockwood, 1953). The discussion by Shera and Egan considers some of the questions which have developed since the first edition of Bradford's monograph.

Index